SECOND EDITION

W9-AZU-238

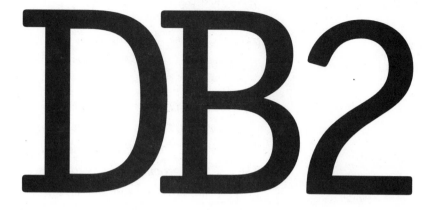

DB2

for the

PART 1 **COBOL**

Programmer

Curtis Garvin

Steve Eckols

MIKE MURACH & ASSOCIATES

2560 West Shaw Lane, Suite 101 • Fresno, CA 93711-2765

Authors:	Curtis Garvin
	Steve Eckols
Editor:	Mike Murach
Cover design:	Zylka Design
Design and production:	Tom Murach

Related Murach books:	*DB2 for the COBOL Programmer, Part 2*
	CICS for the COBOL Programmer, Part 1
	CICS for the COBOL Programmer, Part 2
	The CICS Programmer's Desk Reference
	IMS for the COBOL Programmer, Part 1
	IMS for the COBOL Programmer, Part 2
	MVS TSO, Part 1
	MVS TSO, Part 2
	MVS JCL
	VS COBOL II

Printed in the United States of America.
10 9 8 7 6 5 4 3 2 1

ISBN: 1-890774-02-2

Library of Congress Cataloging-in-Publication Data
Garvin, Curtis, 1961-
   DB2 for the COBOL programmer : version 4.1/Curtis Garvin, Steve
Eckols. -- 2nd ed.
     p. cm.
   ISBN 1-890774-02-2 (pbk.: v. 1)
   1. Database management. 2. IBM Database. 3. COBOL (Computer
program language) 4. SQL (Computer program language)   I. Eckols,
Steve. II Title.
QA76.9.D3G385   1998
005.75'65--dc21

                                     98-40935
                                         CIP

Contents

Introduction

DB2 is the primary database management system (DBMS) for IBM mainframe computers that run under the MVS operating system. Although you can use several different methods to work with DB2 databases, most DB2 work on a mainframe is done through COBOL programs. The intent of this book is to show you how to develop those COBOL programs.

4 ways this book differs from other DB2 books

- This is the only DB2 book that's designed just for COBOL application programmers. In contrast, most other DB2 books focus on database administration or ad hoc processing to the exclusion of many of the DB2 essentials for COBOL programming.

- When you complete section 1 of this book...just 142 pages...you'll be a confident, competent, beginning DB2 programmer. You'll be developing COBOL programs that access, add, delete, or update the data in one or more DB2 tables. Just as important, you'll understand how DB2 works...and you'll find that lets you add to your skills more quickly than you'd be able to otherwise.

- To help you learn more easily, this book presents 12 complete COBOL programs run under the MVS operating system using DB2 version 4.1. These programs let you see clearly how the DB2 code you're learning fits in with your COBOL code. And once you've used these programs for training, they become time-saving models for the programs you develop on the job.

- After you use this book to learn DB2 programming, it becomes the best reference guide you've ever used. Why? Because all the content is logically organized by function under headings that clearly identify the information chunks, so it's easy and fast to find what you're looking for. And all of the essential information for each function is summarized in the illustrations, so you read less to get the information you need.

What's new in this edition

The first edition of this book was based on DB2 version 2. With the release of DB2 version 4, though, some significant enhancements became available. As a result, the primary purpose of this second edition is to present the new language and features that became available with versions 3 and 4. That means every chapter has been thoroughly revised and updated to reflect these versions.

However, as we updated each chapter, we also realized that three of the chapters in *Part 2* of this series actually belong in this book. That way, this book presents all the DB2 features that every COBOL programmer needs to know for just about every program. These new chapters cover (1) the data manipulation features, (2) the error handling features, and (3) the locking features.

What this book teaches

This book assumes that you already have COBOL experience or at least have taken a first course in COBOL. With that as background, this book shows you how to use Structured Query Language (SQL) within a COBOL program to retrieve and update DB2 databases.

To get you started right, the four chapters in section 1 present the basic skills for working with a DB2 database from a COBOL program. In chapters 1 and 2, you'll learn how to retrieve data from a single DB2 table. In chapter 3, you'll learn how to add rows to, delete rows from, and update rows in a single table. And in chapter 4, you'll learn how to retrieve data from two or more related tables at the same time by using unions and joins. When you complete this section, you'll be writing production COBOL programs for everyday DB2 processing.

In section 2, each of the seven chapters lets you expand your basic skills so you can process DB2 data with more expertise. In chapter 6, for example, you'll learn how to use the column functions to summarize or average the data in one column of a table. In chapter 8, you'll learn how to work with variable-length columns and nulls. And in chapter 11, you'll learn how to maximize locking efficiency so your programs don't tie up the system. To make this section as easy to use as possible, each chapter is written as an independent unit; that means you can read the chapters in any sequence you prefer. When you complete this section, you'll be able to process DB2 data efficiently in a wide range of situations.

In section 3, you'll learn the skills you need for binding, precompiling, compiling, link editing, and testing your COBOL programs. In chapter 12, you'll learn to use DB2I (short for DB2 Interactive), which is a DB2 development tool for preparing a COBOL program online. In chapter 13, you'll learn how to do these programming tasks in batch, without using DB2I. In chapter 14, you'll learn how to use SPUFI, a DB2I facility, for testing SQL statements and creating test tables. And in chapter 15, you'll learn how to use the Query Management Facility (QMF) to add data to the test tables you create with SPUFI. Because you may want to test a program early in your training, you can read the chapters in this section any time after you complete chapter 1.

What about *Part 2*?

When you complete *DB2 for the COBOL Programmer, Part 1*, you'll have the DB2 skills that every application programmer needs. Then, to raise your skills to the next professional level, you'll want to get *DB2 for the COBOL Programmer, Part 2*. When you complete that book, you'll have the skills of a senior programmer or programmer/analyst. That includes skills like: using dynamic SQL; working with distributed DB2 data; using stored procedures; handling DB2 data in CICS programs; using the database administration features that let you set up a quality assurance environment for testing DB2 programs; and using QMF for functions like preparing ad hoc reports for users who need information in a hurry.

How to download the 12 example programs and other files from our web site

As we mentioned earlier, the 12 programs in this book not only teach you DB2 processing, they're also time-saving models for your own programs. That's why we make them available to you on our web site, along with some other useful files that you can use for program development tasks (there are JCL job streams, for example). By downloading these files to your system, you'll save hours of entry time.

To download the files, go to the Downloads portion of our web site (*www.murach.com/downloads*). From there, you can download the zip file for this book to a default folder on your system. Then, from your Windows Explorer, double-click on the name of the downloaded file to expand it into its component files in this folder: C:\Murach\DB2\Part1. Since all of the files are in ASCII (text) format, you can then open them with a word processor or a text editor.

Please let us know how this book works for you

If you have any comments about this book, we would enjoy hearing from you. That's why there's a postage-paid comment form at the back of this book. And if this book helps you learn what you wanted to know, we'd be especially delighted to hear about it. That's what makes it all worthwhile.

Curtis Garvin
Author

Mike Murach
Editor

Section 1

The basics of DB2 programming in COBOL

The goal of this section is to get you started with DB2 programming in CO-BOL as quickly and easily as possible. As a result, chapter 1 introduces you to DB2, the Structured Query Language, and the essential skills for developing COBOL programs that use embedded SQL to access data from DB2 databases. When you complete this chapter, you'll be able to code simple programs of your own.

After this introduction, chapter 2 shows you how to write programs that get data from one database table. Chapter 3 shows how to write programs that modify one database table by adding, deleting, or updating rows. And chapter 4 shows how to use unions and joins to get data from two or more tables. When you complete this section, you'll have the basic skills that you need for developing any program that retrieves or modifies DB2 data.

1

Introduction to DB2 and embedded SQL

In this chapter, you'll be introduced to DB2 and to the SQL language that you use for working with the data in a DB2 database. Then, you'll see how embedded SQL can be used in a COBOL program. By the time you complete this chapter, you'll know how to code simple COBOL programs that get data from DB2 databases on IBM mainframe computers.

DB2 and the relational database model

In 1970, Dr. E. F. Codd developed a model for a new type of database called a *relational database*. This type of database eliminated some of the problems that were associated with flat files and hierarchical databases like IMS. By using the relational model, you can reduce data redundancy, which saves disk storage and leads to efficient data retrieval. You can also access and modify the data in a way that is both intuitive and efficient.

DB2, or *Database 2*, is a *relational database management system* (*RDBMS)* that runs on IBM mainframe computers. Because DB2 also runs on AS/400 mid-range computers and on PCs, DB2 can be used throughout an organization. In this book, you'll learn how to use DB2 through COBOL programs on an IBM mainframe.

How a relational database table is organized

The model for a relational database states that data is stored in one or more *tables*. It also states that each table can be viewed as a two-dimensional array consisting of horizontal *rows* and vertical *columns*. This is illustrated by the relational database table in figure 1-1. In this table, each row contains information about a single customer.

At the intersection of each column and row is a *value*. In this figure, for example, the highlighted value is DENVILLE, which is the city for customer number 400002. The term *value* can be misleading, though, since it can be an alphanumeric (or *string*) value, a numeric value, or nothing (a *null* value).

In practice, the rows and columns of a relational database table are often referred to by the terms *records* and *fields*. This makes sense because each row is comparable to a record in a traditional file, and each column is comparable to a field. As a result, these terms can be used interchangeably.

If a table contains one or more columns that uniquely identify each row in the table, you can define these columns as the *primary key* of the table. For instance, the primary key of the customer table in this figure is the customer number, which has been given the name CUSTNO.

Indexes provide an efficient way to access the rows in a table based on the values in one or more columns. Because applications typically access table rows by referring to their key values, each table requires a *unique index* for its primary key. But you can define indexes for other columns as well. Like a key, an index can include one or more columns.

A customer table

		Columns		Value		

Primary Key

CUSTNO	FNAME	LNAME	ADDR	CITY	STATE	ZIPCODE
400001	KEITH	JONES	4501 W MOCKINGBIRD	DALLAS	TX	75209
400002	KAREN	ANNELLI	40 FORD RD	DENVILLE	NJ	07834
400003	SUSAN	HOWARD	1107 SECOND AVE	REDWOOD CITY	CA	94063
400004	CAROL ANN	EVANS	74 SUTTON CT	GREAT LAKES	IL	60088
400005	ELAINE	ROBERTS	12914 BRACKNELL	CERRITOS	CA	90701

Rows

Concepts

- A relational database uses tables to store and manipulate data. Each table consists of one or more *rows*, or *records*, that contain the data for a single entity. Each row contains one or more *columns*, or *fields*, with each column representing a single item of data.

- The data in a specific column of a specific row can be referred to as a *value*.

- Most tables contain a *primary key* that uniquely identifies each row in the table. The primary key often consists of a single field, but it can also consist of two or more fields. In the table above, the customer number (CUSTNO) is the primary key.

- An *index* can be applied to any column in a table to improve performance when rows are accessed based on the values in that column. At the least, each table requires a *unique index* for its primary key.

Figure 1-1   How a relational database table is organized

How the tables in a relational database are related

The tables in a relational database can be related to other tables by values in specific columns. This is where the term *relational* comes from. The two tables shown in figure 1-2 illustrate this concept. Here, each row in the customer table is related to one or more rows in the invoice table. This is called a *one-to-many relationship*.

Typically, relationships exist between the primary key in one table and a *foreign key* in another table. The foreign key is one or more columns in a table that refer to the primary key in another table.

Although one-to-many relationships are the most common, two tables can also have a one-to-one or many-to-many relationship. If a table has a *one-to-one relationship* with another table, the data in the two tables could be stored in a single table. Because of that, one-to-one relationships are used infrequently.

In contrast, a *many-to-many relationship* is usually implemented by using an intermediate table that has a one-to-many relationship with the two tables in the many-to-many relationship. In other words, a many-to-many relationship can usually be broken down into two one-to-many relationships.

The relationship between a customer table and an invoice table

CUSTNO	FNAME	LNAME	STREET	CITY	STATE	ZIPCODE
400001	KEITH	JONES	4501 W MOCKINGBIRD	DALLAS	TX	75209
400002	KAREN	ANNELLI	40 FORD RD	DENVILLE	NJ	07834
400003	SUSAN	HOWARD	1107 SECOND AVE	REDWOOD CITY	CA	94063
400004	CAROL ANN	EVANS	74 SUTTON CT	GREAT LAKES	IL	60088
400005	ELAINE	ROBERTS	12914 BRACKNELL	CERRITOS	CA	90701

Primary key   Foreign key

INVNO	INVCUST	INVDATE	INVTOTAL	PAYTOTAL	CRTOTAL
003584	400004	1998-04-28	51.75		
003585	400005	1998-04-28	292.83		
003586	400002	1998-04-28	68.87	68.87	
003587	400001	1998-04-28	22.09		
003588	400003	1998-04-28	57.63		
003589	400005	1998-04-28	711.05		150.00
003590	400001	1998-04-28	110.49	110.49	

Concepts

- The tables in a relational database are related to each other through their key fields. In the tables above, the customer number is used to relate the customer and invoice tables.

- In the customer table, the customer number field is the *primary key*. In the invoice table, the invoice number field is the primary key.

- In the invoice table, the customer field is called a *foreign key* because it identifies a related row in the customer table.

- Three types of relationships can exist between tables. The most common type is *a one-to-many relationship* as illustrated above. A table can also have a *one-to-one relationship* or a *many-to-many relationship* with another table.

Figure 1-2   How the tables in a relational database are related

How to use SQL to work with a DB2 database

To work with the data in a relational database, you use *Structured Query Language*, or *SQL*. Although SQL is a standard language, each database management system is likely to have its own extensions and variations, commonly called a *dialect*. So when you use SQL, you need to make sure that you're using the dialect that's supported by your RDBMS. In this book, of course, you'll learn the dialect for DB2.

Figure 1-3 summarizes some of the common SQL statements for DB2. As you see, these statements can be divided into two categories. The statements that you use for defining and managing a database are called the *data definition language*, or *DDL*, *statements*. These statements are normally used by *database administrators*, or *DBAs*, as they do jobs like defining tables, modifying and deleting tables, and managing the disk space used for the tables.

In contrast, the statements that you use to work with the data in a database are called the *data manipulation language*, or *DML*, *statements*. These include the SELECT, INSERT, UPDATE, and DELETE statements, and these are the statements that the application programmer uses. Although the execution of any one of these statements can be referred to as a *query*, the term *query* is commonly used to refer to just the execution of SELECT statements, while the term *action query* is used to refer to the other DML statements.

Three DML statements specific to the DB2 dialect are the OPEN, FETCH, and CLOSE statements. You use these statements after you use a SELECT statement that returns more than one row to the program. These statements then use a cursor to move from one row to another.

Incidentally, SQL is pronounced either S-Q-L or *sequel* in conversation. Throughout this book, we use the first pronunciation so we refer to "an SQL statement," not "a SQL statement."

SQL statements for data definition

Statement	Description
CREATE/ALTER/DROP DATABASE	Creates, alters or drops a database.
CREATE/ALTER/DROP STOGROUP	Creates, alters or drops a storage group.
CREATE/ALTER/DROP TABLESPACE	Creates, alters or drops a table space in the specified database.
CREATE/ALTER/DROP TABLE	Creates, alters or drops a table in the specified database.
CREATE/ALTER/DROP INDEX	Creates, alters or drops an index for the specified table.
CREATE/DROP VIEW	Creates or drops a view of the specified database.
CREATE/DROP ALIAS	Creates or drops an alias of a table or a view that may or may not be on the current server.
CREATE/DROP SYNONYM	Creates or drops a synonym of a table or a view that must be on the current server.

SQL statements for data manipulation

Statement	Description
SELECT	Retrieves data from one or more tables.
INSERT	Inserts one or more new rows into a table.
UPDATE	Updates one or more rows in a table.
DELETE	Deletes one or more rows from a table.
OPEN	Opens a cursor.
FETCH	Positions a cursor on the next row of its result table and assigns the values of that row to host variables.
CLOSE	Closes a cursor.

Concepts

- SQL statements can be divided into two categories: the *data definition language* (*DDL*) that lets you define the *objects* in a database, and the *data manipulation language* (*DML*) that lets you work with the data in a database.

- Application programmers typically work with the DML statements, while *database administrators (DBAs)* use the DDL statements.

- The execution of a SELECT statement is commonly referred to as a *query*. In contrast, the execution of an INSERT, UPDATE, or DELETE statement can be referred to as an *action query*.

- Although SQL is a standard language, each vendor has its own *SQL dialect*, which may include extensions to the standards like the OPEN, FETCH, and CLOSE statements above.

Figure 1-3   An introduction to the Structured Query Language

How to query a single database table

Figure 1-4 shows how to use a SELECT statement to get data from a single database table. Although the syntax of the SELECT statement presented in this figure has been simplified, it illustrates its basic function, which is to retrieve selected columns and rows from a database.

The syntax summary at the top of this figure uses conventions that are similar to those in COBOL manuals. Capitalized words are keywords; lower-case words indicate the variables that you must supply; brackets [ ] indicate that a phrase is optional; and the elipsis (…) indicates that you can code a series of like items. To separate the items in an SQL statement, you can use one or more spaces, and you can continue an SQL statement on the next line with just one restriction that you'll learn about later in this chapter.

If you study the SELECT statement below the syntax summary, you can see how the two are related. Here, the SELECT statement retrieves columns from a table named MM01.INVOICE. It selects a row from this invoice table only if it has a balance owed that's greater than zero. And it sorts the returned rows by the balance due in descending sequence.

Please note in this SELECT statement that the last column in the query (BALANCE) is calculated by subtracting the payment total (PAYTOTAL) and the credit total (CRTOTAL) from the invoice total (INVTOTAL). In other words, the column named BALANCE doesn't actually exist in the database. This type of column is called a *calculated value*, and it exists only in the results of the query.

Although it's not indicated in the figure, you can select all of the columns in a table by coding an asterisk (*) in place of the column names. For example, this statement will select all of the columns from the invoice table:

```
SELECT * FROM MM01.INVOICE
```

For efficiency, though, you should only select the columns that you need from a table.

Figure 1-4 also shows the *result table* that is returned by the SELECT statement. A result table is a logical table that's created temporarily within the database. When you use a SELECT statement in an application program to return a DB2 result table that consists of more than one row, you must code the SELECT statement within a DECLARE CURSOR statement. Then, you can use the *cursor* to move from one row to another as explained in the next chapter.

As you might guess, queries can have a significant effect on the performance of a program. In general, the more columns and rows that are requested by a query, the longer it takes to return the result table. When you design a query, then, you should try to keep the number of columns and rows to a minimum.

The syntax of a SELECT statement that retrieves data from one table

```
SELECT column-list
    FROM table-name
       [WHERE selection-condition]
    [ORDER BY sort-column [DESC][, sort-column [DESC]…]
```

A SELECT statement that retrieves and sorts selected columns and rows from an INVOICE table

```
SELECT INVNO, INVDATE, INVTOTAL,
       INVTOTAL - PAYTOTAL - CRTOTAL AS BALANCE
    FROM MM01.INVOICE
    WHERE INVTOTAL - PAYTOTAL - CRTOTAL > 0
    ORDER BY BALANCE DESC
```

The INVOICE table

INVNO	INVCUST	INVDATE	INVTOTAL	PAYTOTAL	CRTOTAL
003584	400004	1998-04-28	51.75		
003585	400005	1998-04-28	292.83		
003586	400002	1998-04-28	68.87	68.87	
003587	400001	1998-04-28	22.09		
003588	400003	1998-04-28	57.63		
003589	400005	1998-04-28	711.05		150.00
003590	400001	1998-04-28	110.49	110.49	

The result table

INVNO	INVDATE	INVTOTAL	BALANCE
003589	1998-04-28	711.05	561.05
003585	1998-04-28	292.83	292.83
003588	1998-04-28	57.63	57.63
003584	1998-04-28	51.75	51.75
003587	1998-04-28	22.09	22.09

Concepts

- The result of a SELECT query is a *result table* like the one above. It consists of all of the columns and rows requested by the SELECT statement.

- Values in the result table that are calculated from values in the base table are called *calculated values*.

- When a result table contains more than one row, a *cursor* is used to identify the individual rows in the table and to scroll through those rows. When you use DB2 from a COBOL program, this means that the SELECT statement is coded within a DECLARE CURSOR statement. This is explained in chapter 2.

Figure 1-4   How to query a single database table

How to modify the data in a table

Figure 1-5 presents the basic syntax of the SQL INSERT, UPDATE, and DELETE statements. You use the INSERT statement to insert one or more rows into a table. As you can see, the syntax of this statement is different depending on whether you're adding a single row or selected rows.

To add a single row to a table, you specify the name of the table you want to add the row to, the names of the columns you're supplying data for, and the values for those columns. The example in this figure adds a row to a customer table and supplies the values for each of the columns in the table. Here, the names that are preceded by a colon represent fields in the COBOL program called *host variables*. These variables must be coded in the same sequence as the columns in the column list.

To add more than one row to a table, you include a SELECT statement within the INSERT statement. Then, the SELECT statement retrieves rows from one or more tables based on the conditions you specify, and the INSERT statement adds those rows to another table. In the example in this figure, the SELECT statement selects all the columns from the rows in the customer table with customer numbers less than 300000 and inserts them into an old customer table named MM01.OLDCUST.

To change the values of one or more columns in a table, you use the UPDATE statement. On this statement, you specify the name of the table you want to update, expressions that indicate the columns you want to change and how you want to change them, and a condition that indicates the row or rows you want to change. In the example in this figure, the row with a customer number equal to the value in the host variable named :CUSTNO is updated, and the updated values for six columns are supplied by six other host variables.

To delete rows from a table, you use the DELETE statement. In this statement, you specify the table you want to delete one or more rows from and a condition that indicates the rows you want to delete. The DELETE statement in this figure deletes the row from the customer table with customer number equal to the value in the host variable named :CUSTNO.

How DB2 handles referential integrity and locking

In chapter 3, you'll learn how to write COBOL programs that use INSERT, UPDATE, and DELETE statements to modify a database table. There, you'll also learn how DB2 enforces *referential integrity*. This means, for example, that DB2 doesn't let you add a row to an invoice table unless it has a matching row in the customer table. This also means that DB2 doesn't let you delete a row from the customer table if it has matching rows in the invoice table.

Another feature that's provided automatically by DB2 is *locking*. This means that a row is locked when one user is updating it so another user can't overwrite the first user's update. This feature is explained in chapter 11.

The syntax of an INSERT statement that adds a single row

```
INSERT INTO table-name
    [(column-list)]
    VALUES (value-list)
```

A statement that adds a single row to a table

```
INSERT INTO MM01.CUST1
        ( CUSTNO,   FNAME,    LNAME,     ADDR,
          CITY,     STATE,    ZIPCODE
VALUES (:CUSTNO,  :FNAME,  :LNAME,   :ADDR,
        :CITY,    :STATE,  :ZIPCODE)
```

The syntax of an INSERT statement that adds selected rows

```
INSERT INTO table-1
    SELECT-statement
```

A statement that adds selected rows from one table to another table

```
INSERT INTO MM01.OLDCUST
    SELECT *
        FROM MM01.CUST1
        WHERE CUSTNO < '300000'
```

The syntax of an UPDATE statement

```
UPDATE table-name
    SET expression-list
    WHERE selection-condition
```

A statement that changes the values of the columns in a row

```
UPDATE MM01.CUST1
    SET FNAME   = :FNAME,
        LNAME   = :LNAME,
        ADDR    = :ADDR,
        CITY    = :CITY,
        STATE   = :STATE,
        ZIPCODE = :ZIPCODE,
    WHERE CUSTNO = :CUSTNO
```

The syntax of a DELETE statement

```
DELETE FROM table-1
    WHERE condition
```

A statement that deletes one customer row

```
DELETE FROM MM01.CUST1
    WHERE CUSTNO = :CUSTNO
```

Figure 1-5   How to modify the data in a table

How to join data from two or more tables

Figure 1-6 presents the *explicit syntax* for a SELECT statement that retrieves data from two or more tables. This syntax became available with version 4 of DB2, but the earlier syntax is still supported by this version. Within this syntax you can see two more of the conventions used in this book. Braces { } indicate a choice between items, and the pipe (|) separates those options. For instance, you can code INNER, LEFT OUTER, RIGHT OUTER, or FULL OUTER before the keyword JOIN.

When you retrieve data from two or more tables, it is called a *join* because the data is joined together into a single result table. For example, the SELECT statement in this figure joins data from the invoice and customer tables into a single result table.

An *inner join*, or *equi-join*, is the most common type of join. When you use an inner join, rows from the two tables in the join are included in the result table if their related columns match. These matching columns are specified in the SELECT statement. In the example in this figure, rows from the invoice and customer tables are included only if the value of the CUSTNO column in the customer table matches the value of the INVCUST column in one or more rows in the invoice table. If there aren't any invoices for a particular customer, that customer isn't included in the result table.

The second type of join is an *outer join*. These types of joins are distinguished by which unmatched rows they keep. In a *left outer join*, all of the rows in the first table are included in the result table. In a *right outer join*, all of the rows in the second table are included. And in *a full outer join*, the unmatched rows of both tables are included. If, for example, I had used a left outer join in this figure, all of the rows in the customer table would have been included in the result table, even if no matching rows were found in the invoice table.

Although this figure shows only how to join data from two tables, you should know that you can extend this syntax to join data from additional tables. If, for example, you also want to include line item data from a table named MM01.LINEITEM and the name of the invoice number column in that table is LIINV, you can code the FROM clause of the SELECT statement like this:

```
FROM MM01.CUSTOMER
    INNER JOIN MM01.INVOICE
        ON CUSTNO = INVCUST
    INNER JOIN MM01.LINEITEM
        ON INVNO = LIINV
```

Then, you can include any of the columns in the LINEITEM table in the column list of the SELECT statement.

In chapter 4, you'll learn how to develop programs that use joins. You'll also learn how to develop programs that get data from two or more tables by using *unions*.

The syntax of a SELECT statement that joins two tables

```
SELECT column-list
    FROM table-name
        {INNER |{LEFT | RIGHT | FULL} [OUTER]} JOIN table-name
            ON join-condition
        [WHERE selection-condition]
    [ORDER BY sort-column [DESC][, sort-column [DESC]]...
```

A SELECT statement that joins data from a customer and an invoice table

```
SELECT LNAME, INVNO, INVDATE, INVTOTAL
    FROM MM01.CUST1
        INNER JOIN MM01.INV1
        ON CUSTNO = INVCUST
    WHERE STATE = 'CA'
    ORDER BY LNAME, INVTOTAL DESC
```

The result table defined by the SELECT statement

LNAME	INVNO	INVDATE	INVTOTAL
HOWARD	003588	1998-04-28	57.63
ROBERTS	003589	1998-04-28	711.05
ROBERTS	003585	1998-04-28	292.83

Concepts

- A *join* lets you combine data from two or more tables into a single result table. The type of join you choose determines how the data is combined.

- An *inner join*, also called an *equi-join*, returns rows from both tables only if their related columns match.

- *Outer joins* are distinguished by which unmatched rows they keep. A *left outer join* keeps all of the rows from the first table named; a *right outer join* keeps all of the rows from the second table; and a *full outer join* keeps all of the rows from both tables.

- Here again, when a result table contains more than one row, a cursor is used to identify the individual rows in the table and to scroll through those rows. When you use DB2 from a COBOL program, this means that the SELECT statement is coded within a DECLARE CURSOR statement as explained in detail in chapter 2.

Figure 1-6   How to join data from two or more tables

How to create and use a view

A view is a definition of a set of rows and columns that's stored with the database. The view is normally created by the database administrator, then used by COBOL programs.

One use of views is to restrict the data that users have access to. If, for example, you want to restrict the access to payroll information, you can create a view that doesn't include sensitive salary information. Another use of views is to present the data in a database in a consistent format. Then, even if the structure of the database changes, the view can remain the same.

To create a view, you use the CREATE VIEW statement as summarized in figure 1-7. This just stores the SELECT statement for the view with the database. This statement can get data from a single table as shown in figure 1-4 or it can join two or more tables as shown in the previous figure. Note, however, that you can't update, delete, or insert data when you use a view that joins tables.

To use a view, you issue a SELECT statement that refers to the view. When that statement is executed, the view is created. Then, the SELECT statement extracts data from the view.

The example in this figure shows how to create a view that selects data from an employee table where the department number starts with a B. Since different column names aren't listed after the view name, the column names of the view are the same as those of the table. However, you can also create a view that has different column names than those in the underlying tables with code like this:

```
CREATE VIEW V1 EMP_NO, DEPT_NO, LAST, FIRST, EXT AS
    SELECT EMPNO, DEPTNO, LNAME, FNAME, EXT
        FROM MM01.EMPLOYEE
            WHERE DEPTNO LIKE 'B%'
```

Then, the column names of the view are the ones you've listed.

Notice that the WITH CHECK OPTION clause is not used in the CREATE VIEW statement in these examples. Without this clause, though, no check is made to see that inserts or updates conform to the definition of the view, and this creates some curious possibilities. For instance, a user with the proper privileges can insert a new row with a value of E21 for DEPTNO, then not be able to select the row just inserted because it isn't within the view.

The syntax of the CREATE VIEW statement

```
CREATE VIEW view-name AS
    SELECT-statement
    [WITH CHECK OPTION]
```

An employee table

EMPNO	DEPTNO	LNAME	FNAME	EXT
3001	B12	VASQUEZ	DEBBIE	23
3002	B12	HOWARTH	JOHN	44
3003	D44	SMITH	HENRY	24
3008	B22	JONES	EILEEN	12
3010	D45	WILLIAMS	TIM	56
3022	D45	THOMPSON	BARRY	14
3050	D47	JOHNSON	SHIELA	33

A CREATE VIEW statement that creates a view of the employee table

```
CREATE VIEW V1 AS
    SELECT  EMPNO,  DEPTNO,  LNAME,  FNAME,  EXT
        FROM MM01.EMPLOYEE
            WHERE DEPTNO LIKE 'B%'
```

A SELECT statement that retrieves data from the V1 view

```
SELECT  *
    FROM MM01.V1
    ORDER BY DEPTNO, LNAME
```

The result table

EMPNO	DEPTNO	LNAME	FNAME	EXT
3002	B12	HOWARTH	JOHN	44
3001	B12	VASQUEZ	DEBBIE	23
3008	B22	JONES	EILEEN	12

Concepts

- A *view* is a stored definition of a set of rows and columns. A view can present any or all of the data in one or more tables, and, in most cases, is interchangeable with a table.

- A view doesn't exist until a SELECT statement that refers to it is executed. Then, the SELECT statement selects rows from the view.

- When you modify the data in a view that is created from one table, the modifications are done to the underlying table. In contrast, you can't update, delete, or insert data in a view that joins two or more tables.

Figure 1-7   How to create and use a view

A COBOL program that uses embedded SQL

When you write a COBOL program that accesses or modifies the data in a DB2 database, you code SQL statements within the COBOL program. These statements can be referred to as *embedded SQL statements*, or *embedded SQL*. To help you understand how this works, this chapter is now going to present a short but complete program that uses embedded SQL. It is a simple inquiry program that gets customer information from a DB2 database and displays the customer information on a user's screen.

The interactive screen

Figure 1-8 presents the opening screen for the program. It just asks the user to enter a customer number so the program can get the data for that customer or 999999 so the program can end.

The second screen in this figure shows the data that has been displayed by the program after the user has entered two customer numbers. First, the data for customer 400001 is displayed. Then, a message is displayed for customer number 400017 indicating that there is no customer row for that number. To end the program, the user has entered 999999 in the last line of the screen.

The screens in this figure and throughout this book show the mainframe output as it appears in a PC window when using a program called EXTRA! This program lets you attach your PC to an IBM mainframe via a direct, remote, or LAN connection. You can then use that window of your PC as a mainframe terminal. In this case, the top two lines of the window are the title bar and menu bar of EXTRA! The remaining lines are the terminal display.

The opening screen for the customer inquiry program

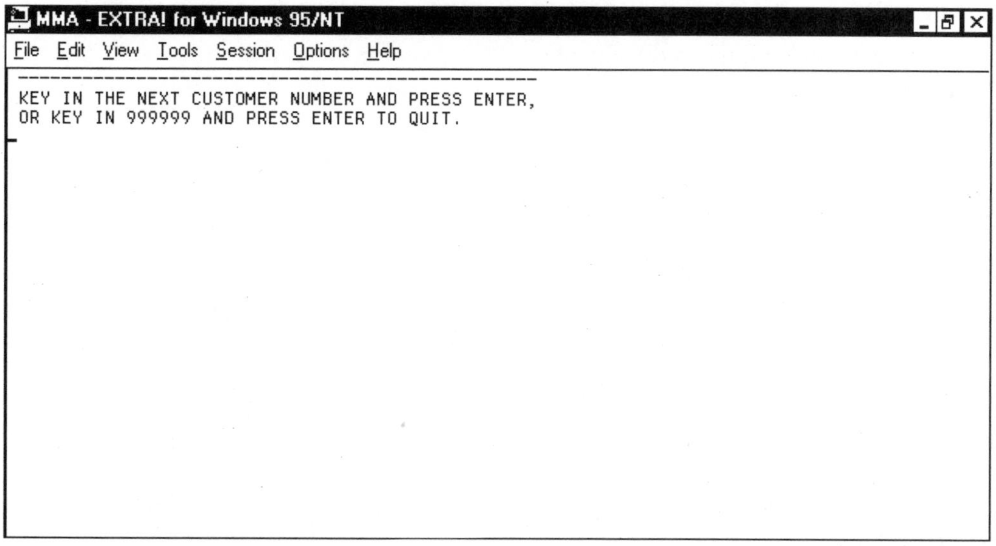

```
MMA - EXTRA! for Windows 95/NT                                    _ ⊡ ✕
File  Edit  View  Tools  Session  Options  Help
---------------------------------------------------------
KEY IN THE NEXT CUSTOMER NUMBER AND PRESS ENTER,
OR KEY IN 999999 AND PRESS ENTER TO QUIT.
_
```

The interactive screen after the user has entered two customer numbers

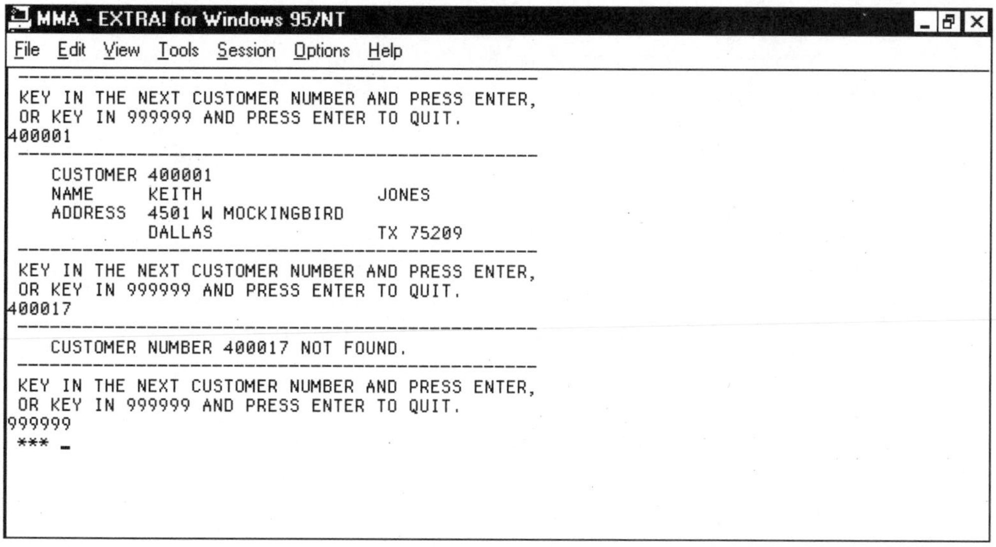

```
MMA - EXTRA! for Windows 95/NT                                    _ ⊡ ✕
File  Edit  View  Tools  Session  Options  Help
---------------------------------------------------------
KEY IN THE NEXT CUSTOMER NUMBER AND PRESS ENTER,
OR KEY IN 999999 AND PRESS ENTER TO QUIT.
400001
---------------------------------------------------------
    CUSTOMER 400001
    NAME      KEITH                  JONES
    ADDRESS   4501 W MOCKINGBIRD
              DALLAS                 TX 75209
---------------------------------------------------------
KEY IN THE NEXT CUSTOMER NUMBER AND PRESS ENTER,
OR KEY IN 999999 AND PRESS ENTER TO QUIT.
400017
---------------------------------------------------------
    CUSTOMER NUMBER 400017 NOT FOUND.
---------------------------------------------------------
KEY IN THE NEXT CUSTOMER NUMBER AND PRESS ENTER,
OR KEY IN 999999 AND PRESS ENTER TO QUIT.
999999
*** _
```

Figure 1-8   The interactive screen for the customer inquiry program

The DCLGEN output

The customer data that's displayed on the screen for this program is retrieved from a customer table that's in a DB2 database. This table has the form and data shown in figure 1-1.

When you develop a COBOL program that gets data from a DB2 table, you include a description of the rows in the table called a *host structure*. Although you can code a host structure by yourself, it's easier to let DB2 develop it for you from the data definitions for the database. This is done by a utility that comes with DB2 called DCLGEN, which stands for *Declarations Generator*. You'll be introduced to this utility later in this chapter.

In figure 1-9, you can see the DCLGEN output for the customer table. The first shaded block is an SQL DECLARE TABLE statement that names the table and defines each of its columns. This can be referred to as a *table declaration*, and it is taken right out of the DB2 catalog for the table.

The second shaded block in this figure is the host structure. It contains the COBOL definitions of the *host variables* you can use for a table. These are the fields that receive the data that's returned for a row when an SQL statement is executed. These fields can also hold the data that's used to update a row or to add a row to a table. As you've already seen, you precede the name of a host variable with a colon when you use it in an SQL statement.

In the host variable declarations in this example, all of the fields contain character data. However, DB2 also supports the ten other data types that are summarized in this figure. In most cases, it is obvious how the DB2 declarations relate to the COBOL pictures and usages. For a complete explanation, though, please refer to chapter 7.

When you use DCLGEN to create the COBOL definitions for the host variables, you can be sure that the COBOL definitions correspond correctly to the DB2 data types. In addition, you supply the level-1 COBOL name for this host structure. In this example, I supplied the COBOL name CUSTOMER-ROW when I generated the declarations.

Normally, DCLGEN output is stored as a member of a partitioned data set so it can be included in the working-storage section of a COBOL program. This is comparable to copying the COPY member for the record description of a VSAM file into a COBOL program. You'll see how this works in a moment.

The DCLGEN output for the customer table

```
******************************************************************
* DCLGEN TABLE(MM01.CUSTOMER)                                    *
*        LIBRARY(MM01.DB2.DCLGENS(CUSTOMER))                     *
*        ACTION(REPLACE)                                         *
*        LANGUAGE(COBOL)                                         *
*        STRUCTURE(CUSTOMER-ROW)                                 *
*        QUOTE                                                   *
* ... IS THE DCLGEN COMMAND THAT MADE THE FOLLOWING STATEMENTS   *
******************************************************************
      EXEC SQL DECLARE MM01.CUSTOMER TABLE
      ( CUSTNO                      CHAR(6) NOT NULL,
        FNAME                       CHAR(20) NOT NULL,
        LNAME                       CHAR(30) NOT NULL,
        ADDR                        CHAR(30) NOT NULL,
        CITY                        CHAR(20) NOT NULL,
        STATE                       CHAR(2) NOT NULL,
        ZIPCODE                     CHAR(10) NOT NULL
      ) END-EXEC.
******************************************************************
* COBOL DECLARATION FOR TABLE MM01.CUSTOMER                      *
******************************************************************
01   CUSTOMER-ROW.
     10 CUSTNO              PIC X(6).
     10 FNAME               PIC X(20).
     10 LNAME               PIC X(30).
     10 ADDR                PIC X(30).
     10 CITY                PIC X(20).
     10 STATE               PIC X(2).
     10 ZIPCODE             PIC X(10).
******************************************************************
* THE NUMBER OF COLUMNS DESCRIBED BY THIS DECLARATION IS 7       *
******************************************************************
```

The DB2 data types

Data Type	COBOL Picture	COBOL Usage	Description
CHAR	PIC X(n)	DISPLAY	Fixed-length character (EBCDIC) data
VARCHAR	PIC X(n)	DISPLAY	Variable-length character data
SMALLINT	PIC S9(4)	COMP or COMP-4	Halfword integer data
INTEGER	PIC S9(9)	COMP or COMP-4	Fullword integer data
DECIMAL	PIC S9(n)V9(n)	COMP-3	Packed-decimal data
DATE	PIC X(10)	DISPLAY	Date data (yyyy-mm-dd)
TIME	PIC X(8)	DISPLAY	Time data (hh.mm.ss)
TIMESTAMP	PIC X(26)	DISPLAY	Date and time data with microseconds (yyyy-mm-dd-hh.mm.ss.mmmmmm)
GRAPHIC	PIC G(n)	DISPLAY-1	Double-byte character set (DBCS) data
VARGRAPHIC	PIC G(n)	DISPLAY-1	Variable-length DBCS data
FLOAT	None	COMP-1 or COMP-2	Floating-point data in single- or double-precision format

Figure 1-9   The DCLGEN output for the customer inquiry program

The structure chart

Figure 1-10 presents a *structure chart* for this program. This is the design document that we recommend for developing structured COBOL programs, so we're going to include a structure chart for each COBOL program that's presented in this book. When you design a program with a structure chart, the process can be referred to as *structured design*, or *top-down design*.

The top module (000) in the structure chart in this figure represents the entire program. This module performs module 100 to display the information for each customer row until the user ends the program. Module 100 in turn performs module 110 to accept the next customer number from the screen, and then performs module 120 to get the customer row that corresponds to that customer number. If module 120 gets the customer row, module 100 performs module 130 to display that data on the screen. But if the customer row can't be found, module 100 performs module 140 to display an error message.

After you design the structure chart for a program, it becomes a guide to the COBOL code for the program. For each module in the chart, there is one COBOL paragraph in the Procedure Division and the name of that paragraph is the combination of the number and name used in the structure chart. For instance, the name of the COBOL paragraph that corresponds to module 100 is 100-DISPLAY-CUSTOMER-ROW. Once you get used to structure charts, you'll see that they can help you understand the logic of the related COBOL code.

The structure chart

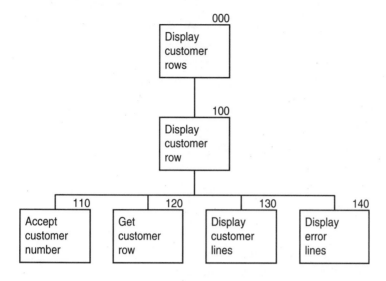

Description

- Each box on the chart represents one module of the program, and each module represents a single function.

- The chart is designed from the top down by dividing each module into its component functions.

- The design process continues until each of the modules represents an independent function that can be coded in a single COBOL paragraph…without the use of in-line PERFORM statements.

- The name for each COBOL paragraph is derived from the module number and module name as in 000-DISPLAY-CUSTOMER-ROWS.

- This design process provides an easy method for dividing a large program into manageable components.

Figure 1-10   The structure chart for the customer inquiry program

The COBOL listing

Figure 1-11 presents the COBOL code for this program. Although you normally use CICS to develop an interactive program like this, this program uses DISPLAY statements that execute under TSO to keep the interactive programming simple. That way, you can focus on the code that relates to DB2 without being distracted by the complexities of CICS.

If you study the code for this program, you'll notice that you don't have to code anything for the database table in the Input-Output Section of the Environment Division or in the File Section of the Data Division. Instead, you just name the table you want to access when you code the SQL SELECT statement. Then, DB2 gets the information it needs for that table from its DB2 catalogs.

In contrast, for each VSAM file that you use in a COBOL program, you have to code a COBOL SELECT statement in the Input-Output Section. You also have to code a file description (FD) and record description in the File Section.

In the Working-Storage Section of this program, you can see the definitions for two *switches*. In our shop, a switch can have either a Yes (Y) or No (N) value, and the switch name always ends with SW or SWITCH. In this case, the end-of-inquiries switch is given a starting value of No, while the customer-found switch isn't given a starting value.

After the switch definitions are two SQL INCLUDE statements. The first statement includes the DCLGEN output that's shown in figure 1-9, which defines the host variables for the rows in the customer table. Then, you can refer to any of those variables in the Procedure Division of the program. The second statement includes the definition of the SQL communication area, which you'll learn more about in a moment.

If you have much COBOL experience, you should be able to follow the code in the Procedure Division with little or no explanation. But to help you get used to our coding style, I'll explain the code in this first program.

The first paragraph in the Procedure Division consists of a single PERFORM statement that performs module 100 until the end-of-inquiries switch has been set to Yes. Then, the second paragraph (module 100) controls the processing for each customer number that the user enters at the terminal.

The code for module 100 starts by performing module 110, which gets a customer number from the user's screen and sets the end-of-inquiries switch to Yes if the number is 999999. Module 100 then tests this switch. If the switch value is Yes, no other processing is done by module 100, control returns to module 000, and the program ends. But if the value is No, module 100 continues by setting the value of the customer-found switch to Yes and performing module 120 to get the customer row that corresponds to the customer number. Then, if the customer row is found, module 100 performs module 130 to display the customer lines; otherwise, it performs module 140 to display an error message.

The customer inquiry program   **Page 1**

```
IDENTIFICATION DIVISION.
*
PROGRAM-ID.      CUSTINQ.
*
ENVIRONMENT DIVISION.
*
INPUT-OUTPUT SECTION.
*
FILE-CONTROL.
*
DATA DIVISION.
*
FILE SECTION.
*
WORKING-STORAGE SECTION.
*
01  SWITCHES.
*
    05   END-OF-INQUIRIES-SW      PIC X    VALUE 'N'.
         88   END-OF-INQUIRIES             VALUE 'Y'.
    05   CUSTOMER-FOUND-SW        PIC X.
         88   CUSTOMER-FOUND               VALUE 'Y'.
*
    EXEC SQL
        INCLUDE CUSTOMER
    END-EXEC.
*
    EXEC SQL
        INCLUDE SQLCA
    END-EXEC.
*
PROCEDURE DIVISION.
*
000-DISPLAY-CUSTOMER-ROWS.
*
    PERFORM 100-DISPLAY-CUSTOMER-ROW
        UNTIL END-OF-INQUIRIES.
    STOP RUN.
*
100-DISPLAY-CUSTOMER-ROW.
*
    PERFORM 110-ACCEPT-CUSTOMER-NUMBER.
    IF NOT END-OF-INQUIRIES
        MOVE 'Y' TO CUSTOMER-FOUND-SW
        PERFORM 120-GET-CUSTOMER-ROW
        IF CUSTOMER-FOUND
            PERFORM 130-DISPLAY-CUSTOMER-LINES
        ELSE
            PERFORM 140-DISPLAY-ERROR-LINES.
*
```

Figure 1-11   The COBOL listing for the customer inquiry program (part 1 of 2)

Now, if you look at the code for the last four modules of the program, you can see how they work. First, module 110 uses DISPLAY statements to display the starting lines on the screen. Then, it issues an ACCEPT statement to accept the customer number that the user enters into the host variable named CUSTNO. Last, it uses an IF statement to set the end-of-inquiries switch to Yes if this customer number is 999999.

The next paragraph is for module 120, and this is the paragraph that uses an embedded SQL statement. The FROM clause in this SELECT statement says that the data should be retrieved from that table named MM01.CUSTOMER, and the WHERE clause says that the data should be retrieved from the customer row with the CUSTNO key that's equal to the value of the variable named :CUSTNO. The colon that precedes this variable name indicates that it's a host variable, not a database column. The rest of the SELECT statement says that the seven columns named should be retrieved from the customer row and stored in the host variables named in the INTO clause. Then, DB2 moves the value for the first column that's named in the SELECT clause into the first host variable that's named in the INTO clause; the second column into the second host variable; and so on.

The IF statement that follows this embedded SQL statement determines whether DB2 was able to find a customer row with a key that matched the value in the host variable. To determine that, the IF statement tests the value of a variable named SQLCODE. This is one of the fields in the SQL communication area that has been included in the Working-Storage Section, and this field gets set to a value of zero if DB2 finds a matching row. If this value isn't zero, this field gets set to another value and this IF statement changes the value of the customer-found switch from Yes to No. This switch, of course, is used by module 100 to determine what happens next.

If a matching customer row has been found, module 130 is performed. Otherwise, module 140 is performed. As you can see, module 130 uses DISPLAY statements to display the host variables that contain the customer information on the user's terminal, while module 140 uses DISPLAY statements to display an error message.

With few exceptions, when you write a COBOL program in the structured style that's illustrated by this program, you should be able to read the paragraphs in the Procedure Division from the top down. Yes, you'll occasionally want to look ahead to make sure a switch has been set right by a lower-level paragraph, but that's about all. You should also be able to code the paragraphs in the Procedure Division from the top down. Those are two of the benefits that you get from the methods of structured design and structured coding that are illustrated in this book.

The customer inquiry program

```
110-ACCEPT-CUSTOMER-NUMBER.
*
    DISPLAY '----------------------------------------------------'.
    DISPLAY 'KEY IN THE NEXT CUSTOMER NUMBER AND PRESS ENTER,'.
    DISPLAY 'OR KEY IN 999999 AND PRESS ENTER TO QUIT.'.
    ACCEPT CUSTNO.
    IF CUSTNO = '999999'
        MOVE 'Y' TO END-OF-INQUIRIES-SW.
*
120-GET-CUSTOMER-ROW.
*
    EXEC SQL
        SELECT CUSTNO,         FNAME,         LNAME,
               ADDR,           CITY,          STATE,
               ZIPCODE
        INTO   :CUSTNO,        :FNAME,        :LNAME,
               :ADDR,          :CITY,         :STATE,
               :ZIPCODE
        FROM   MM01.CUSTOMER
            WHERE  CUSTNO = :CUSTNO
    END-EXEC.
*
    IF SQLCODE NOT = 0
        MOVE 'N' TO CUSTOMER-FOUND-SW.
*
130-DISPLAY-CUSTOMER-LINES.
*
    DISPLAY '----------------------------------------------------'.
    DISPLAY '    CUSTOMER ' CUSTNO.
    DISPLAY '    NAME     ' FNAME ' ' LNAME.
    DISPLAY '    ADDRESS  ' ADDR.
    DISPLAY '             ' CITY ' ' STATE ' ' ZIPCODE.
*
140-DISPLAY-ERROR-LINES.
*
    DISPLAY '----------------------------------------------------'.
    DISPLAY '    CUSTOMER NUMBER ' CUSTNO ' NOT FOUND.'.
*
```

Figure 1-11   The COBOL listing for the customer inquiry program (part 2 of 2)

Three skills for using embedded SQL

If you review the code in figure 1-11, you can see that relatively few lines are related to the use of DB2. In addition, these lines are relatively easy to code. As a result, you only need to learn a few new skills to code a simple DB2 COBOL program like the one in this chapter.

How to code embedded SQL statements

Figure 1-12 summarizes the rules that you need to follow when you code embedded SQL statements. First, each statement must start with EXEC SQL and end with END-EXEC. (Notice that there's a hyphen between END and EXEC but none between EXEC and SQL). Second, you must code embedded SQL statements in columns 12 through 72, whether they are in the Data Division or the Procedure Division. Third, when you continue a string constant from one line to another, you must start the continued line with a quotation mark, but whether you use a single mark (') or a double mark (") depends on the options you use for the DB2 precompiler. Fourth, you can't code an SQL statement in a COPY member because the precompiler does its processing before the COPY members are copied into the program by the compiler.

The last rule in this figure says that you must code a period after an SQL statement's END-EXEC whenever it is followed by another SQL statement. (If you're a CICS programmer, this may surprise you because CICS doesn't require a period in the same situation.) This can cause a problem when two consecutive SQL statements are coded within an IF statement so the period after the END-EXEC statement ends the IF statement. In this case, you have to code around this requirement.

The recommendation that we make in this figure is that you use spacing and indentation to make your SQL statements easier to read. This is illustrated by the first coding example after the recommendation. The second example gives some idea of what an SQL statement can look like when you ignore this recommendation. This recommendation, of course, also applies to COBOL coding, and it is illustrated throughout the programs in this book.

Rules

- Start each SQL statement with EXEC SQL, and end each statement with END-EXEC.
- Code the lines of the SQL statement in columns 12 through 72.
- To continue a string constant from one line to another, the first non-blank character in the continued line must be a quotation mark.
- Don't code an SQL statement in a COBOL COPY member.
- When one SQL statement immediately follows another, always code a period after the END-EXEC for the first statement.

Recommendation

- Use spacing and alignment to make each statement more readable.

How the use of spacing and alignment can improve readability

```
EXEC SQL
    SELECT CUSTNO,    FNAME,    LNAME,    ADDR,
           CITY,      STATE,    ZIPCODE
    INTO   :CUSTNO,   :FNAME,   :LNAME,   :ADDR,
           :CITY,     :STATE,   :ZIPCODE
    FROM   MM01.CUSTOMER
    WHERE  CUSTNO = :CUSTNO
END-EXEC.
```

A SQL statement that's more difficult to read

```
EXEC SQL
    SELECT CUSTNO,FNAME,LNAME,ADDR,CITY,
    STATE,ZIPCODE
    INTO :CUSTNO,:FNAME,:LNAME,
    :ADDR,:CITY,:STATE,:ZIPCODE
    FROM MM01.CUSTOMER
    WHERE CUSTNO = :CUSTNO
END-EXEC.
```

Figure 1-12   How to code embedded SQL statements

How to use INCLUDE statements

Figure 1-13 shows the syntax of the INCLUDE statement that's used to include DCLGEN output or the SQL communication area in the Working-Storage Section of a program. To include DCLGEN output, you supply the member name for the output as illustrated by the first example of an IN-CLUDE statement. To include the SQL communication area, you code SQLCA as illustrated by the second example. In both cases, the statements must be preceded by EXEC SQL and followed by END-EXEC.

How to use the SQL communication area

Figure 1-13 also shows the complete definitions for the fields in the SQL communication area that is included in a program. Of these, the SQLCODE field is the one that DB2 puts a return value in after each SQL statement is executed. This value indicates whether or not the SQL operation was successful. As a result, you need to check the value of the SQLCODE field after almost every SQL statement.

Below the COBOL code for the fields in this area, you can see a summary of the codes that DB2 returns to the SQLCODE field. If the code is zero, the operation was successful. And if the code is a positive value, the statement was successful but with some exceptional condition. Within this category, the value of plus 100 means that the row couldn't be found or that you've reached the end of a cursor-controlled result table.

In contrast, when DB2 returns a negative value to the SQLCODE field, it indicates that the statement failed. What your program does then depends on the application. In some cases, you can ignore the error and continue. In others, you need to report the error and end the program. And in the worst case, you need to reverse the work the program has already done before you end the program.

As you progress through this book, you'll see coding examples that deal with a variety of SQLCODE values. You'll also be introduced to cases in which you need to check the contents of some of the other fields in the SQL communication area. To get a complete list of the values that DB2 returns in the SQLCODE field, you can refer to appendix B.

The syntax of the INCLUDE statement

```
EXEC SQL
    INCLUDE {member-name|SQLCA}
END-EXEC.
```

An INCLUDE statement for DCLGEN output

```
EXEC SQL
    INCLUDE CUSTOMER
END-EXEC.
```

An INCLUDE statement for the SQL communication area

```
EXEC SQL
    INCLUDE SQLCA
END-EXEC.
```

The SQL communication area (SQLCA) fields

```
01   SQLCA.
     05 SQLCAID    PIC X(8).
     05 SQLCABC    PIC S9(9) COMP-4.
     05 SQLCODE    PIC S9(9) COMP-4.
     05 SQLERRM.
        49 SQLERRML PIC S9(4) COMP-4.
        49 SQLERRMC PIC X(70).
     05 SQLERRP    PIC X(8).
     05 SQLERRD    OCCURS 6 TIMES
                   PIC S9(9) COMP-4.
     05 SQLWARN.
        10 SQLWARN0 PIC X.
        10 SQLWARN1 PIC X.
        10 SQLWARN2 PIC X.
        10 SQLWARN3 PIC X.
        10 SQLWARN4 PIC X.
        10 SQLWARN5 PIC X.
        10 SQLWARN6 PIC X.
        10 SQLWARN7 PIC X.
     05 SQLEXT.
        10 SQLWARN8 PIC X.
        10 SQLWARN9 PIC X.
        10 SQLWARNA PIC X.
        10 SQLSTATE PIC X(5).
```

SQLCODE meanings

SQLCODE Value	Meaning
Zero	Statement successful
Positive	Statement successful, but with some exceptional condition
+100	Row not found or end of data
Negative	Serious error detected

Figure 1-13   How to use INCLUDE statements and the SQL communication area

How DB2 works with MVS systems

When you write COBOL programs for IBM mainframes, the programs run under the MVS operating system. That's true whether MVS is the primary operating system for a single mainframe or whether MVS is running under OS/390, which is running multiple copies of MVS on a S/390 Parallel Sysplex system. To understand how DB2 and some of the MVS programs and facilities work together, you should know how DB2 and VSAM work together and you should know what other programs you need to use as you develop your COBOL programs.

How DB2 and VSAM work together

Figure 1-14 shows how an application program gets data when it uses standard files and how it gets data when it uses DB2. When a program uses standard files, it gets the data through the MVS *access methods*. Although several different access methods are available with MVS, most applications today use the *Virtual Storage Access Method*, or *VSAM*.

When a program uses VSAM files, VSAM keeps track of many of the hardware details like the disk location for each record, the physical block size, and so on. However, the program still needs to keep track of details like the structure of the data in each record. As a result, if the structure of the data is changed, each program that uses it also needs to be changed.

In contrast, when a program uses a DB2 database, the database management system (DB2) keeps track of the data structures. This makes the application programs that use the database *data independent*. Then, if the structure of the data in a table is changed, only the programs that are affected by the changes need to be changed, not all the programs that use data in that table.

Standard file processing

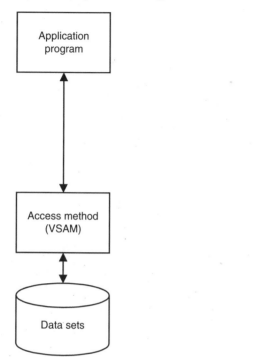

DB2 processing

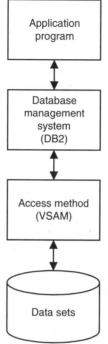

Description

- When a COBOL program works with standard files, it uses the access methods provided by MVS. Today, the Virtual Storage Access Method (VSAM) is the most widely-used method for processing files.

- The access method keeps track of physical details like the disk address for each record and the block size. This lets the COBOL programmer focus on other file handling details like record descriptions and retrieval logic.

- When a COBOL program works with a DB2 database, DB2 takes on more of the file handling details so the COBOL program becomes *data independent*. Then, the database administrator can make changes to the database with a minimal affect on the programs that use the database.

- DB2 uses VSAM as its access method. In other words, DB2 does the database processing that's requested by a COBOL program, but the actual disk operations are done by VSAM.

Figure 1-14   How DB2 and VSAM work together

How to develop a COBOL program that accesses DB2 data

When you develop a COBOL program that uses VSAM files, the *source program* needs to be *compiled* and *link edited* before it can be tested. When you develop a COBOL program that uses a DB2 database, though, there are some extra steps. The complete process is illustrated in figure 1-15.

After you've entered the source program into the system, the first step is to run the *DB2 precompiler* on the source program. This produces two output files. The first is a *modified source program* in which each of the SQL statements has been translated into the COBOL statements that invoke the appropriate DB2 interface functions. Although the precompiler leaves the original SQL statement in the source program, it converts them to comments so they will be ignored by the COBOL compiler. If you want to see what this looks like, appendix A presents the listing of the modified source program for the inquiry program in this chapter.

The second file produced by the precompiler is a *database request module*, or *DBRM*. It contains information about how your program will use DB2 and will be used as input in a later step of this development process.

After the precompiler is finished, the COBOL compiler compiles the modified source program into an *object module*. Then, the *linkage editor* links the object module with other required modules including DB2 interface modules. This produces a *load module*.

Before the load module can be executed, though, DB2 must *bind* the program. This bind procedure uses the DBRM that was created by the precompiler to check all the DB2 functions used in the program to make sure they are valid and that you are authorized to perform them. In addition, this procedure selects the most efficient way for DB2 to implement the functions your program requests.

In this book, you'll learn how to bind a program into a *package*, which is a single DBRM with optimized access paths. You'll also learn how to bind a *plan* so it consists of all of the packages that are grouped in one or more *collections*. As you will see in chapter 12, this is the most efficient binding strategy, even though many shops still bind programs directly into plans.

The output of this procedure is an *application plan* that contains information about how DB2 will complete each database request made by your program. As you can see in this figure, the load module, DB2 catalog, and DB2 directory (which contains the application plan) are required when a program is executed.

The steps required to prepare a DB2 COBOL program

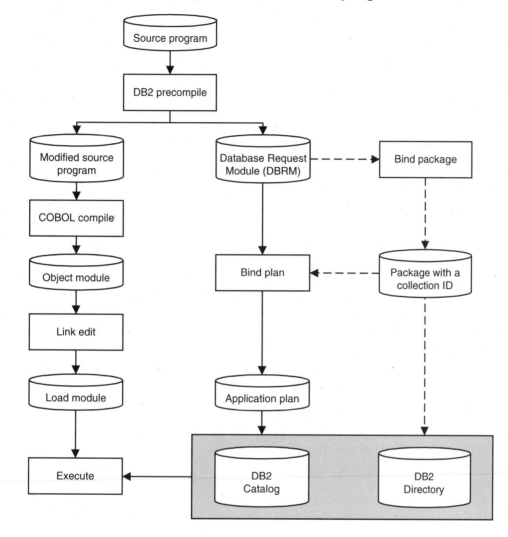

Notes

- The DB2 catalog stores information about the plan and package.
- The DB2 directory stores the actual plan and package.
- The load module, DB2 catalog, and DB2 directory must all be available when you execute a program.
- You can bind a program to a package or directly to a plan. However, you can't run a program that is bound to a package until that package is bound to a plan. For efficiency, a program should be bound to a package that is bound to a plan.

Figure 1-15   How to develop a COBOL program that accesses DB2 data

How to use DB2I as you develop a COBOL program

The easiest way to do most of the program development tasks when you work with DB2 data is to use a DB2 program that's commonly referred to as *DB2I*, which stands for *DB2 Interactive*. To start this program, you access DB2I through TSO/ISPF. This displays the DB2I Primary Option Menu shown in figure 1-16.

To perform the steps that are summarized in figure 1-15, you choose the Program Preparation option. Once you set up the preparation panels so DB2I knows where your program libraries are and what options you want to use, you just have to type in the member name of the source program to prepare and run your program. In chapter 12, you can learn how to set these panels up.

Besides program preparation, DB2I also provides other useful functions for DB2 programmers. Of these, the two most important ones are the SPUFI and DCLGEN options.

SPUFI, called *spoofy* in conversation, stands for *SQL Processor Using File Input*. This facility lets you compose SQL statements interactively, submit them for execution, and get the results at your terminal. As a result, you can use this facility to test the SQL statements you're going to use in a COBOL program before you actually code the program. You can also use this facility to create a table or display the contents of a table after a test run. In chapter 14, you can get the details for using this program.

DCLGEN, on the other hand, is the option you use for creating the SQL table declaration and host structure for each table that you use in a program. Normally, the output for each table is stored as a member of a partitioned data set. Then, you can use the SQL INCLUDE statement to include this output in each COBOL program that uses the table. In chapter 12, you can learn how to use this option.

The DB2I Primary Option Menu

```
MMA - EXTRA! for Windows 95/NT                                    _ 🗗 ×
File  Edit  View  Tools  Session  Options  Help
                        DB2I PRIMARY OPTION MENU           SSID: DSN
COMMAND ===> _

Select one of the following DB2 functions and press ENTER.

  1   SPUFI                   (Process SQL statements)
  2   DCLGEN                  (Generate SQL and source language declarations)
  3   PROGRAM PREPARATION     (Prepare a DB2 application program to run)
  4   PRECOMPILE              (Invoke DB2 precompiler)
  5   BIND/REBIND/FREE        (BIND, REBIND, or FREE plans or packages)
  6   RUN                     (RUN an SQL program)
  7   DB2 COMMANDS            (Issue DB2 commands)
  8   UTILITIES               (Invoke DB2 utilities)
  D   DB2I DEFAULTS           (Set global parameters)
  X   EXIT                    (Leave DB2I)




    F1=HELP      F2=SPLIT     F3=END      F4=RETURN    F5=RFIND     F6=RCHANGE
    F7=UP        F8=DOWN      F9=SWAP     F10=LEFT     F11=RIGHT    F12=RETRIEVE
```

The three most useful options

Option	Description
SPUFI	Process SQL statements and display the returned data in table format.
DCLGEN	Prepare the DCLGEN output for a table so it can be included in a COBOL program.
PROGRAM PREPARATION	Precompile, compile, link edit, bind, and run a program.

Figure 1-16   How to use DB2I as you develop a COBOL program

How to use the Query Management Facility

Ad hoc processing refers to getting the data for a one-time inquiry like a sales manager's request for a listing of all the customers in Philadelphia whose invoices total $10,000 or more in the last six months. Obviously, then, it doesn't make sense to develop a COBOL program for ad hoc processing. Instead, you can use a software package that's designed for this type of processing. One of the most popular of these is IBM's *Query Management Facility*, or *QMF*.

In figure 1-17, you can see the SQL Query and Report panels for QMF. In the SQL Query panel, you can enter a complete SQL statement. Then, when you select the Run option, QMF gets the data from the database and returns the data in the form of a report that's displayed in the Report panel. Besides those basic capabilities, QMF also provides features that help you build an SQL statement and format the returned report the way you want it.

Although QMF can be used by end users who want to get information from a database, it requires more technical knowledge than most end users have. As a result, QMF is used more frequently by programmers than end users. Like SPUFI, QMF can help a programmer test SQL statements before they are used in a program. Unlike SPUFI, though, QMF is easier to use and provides more flexibility for formatting the results. In chapter 15, you can learn how to use QMF for adding data to the tables that you create with SPUFI, and in *Part 2* of this series you can learn how to master this valuable development tool.

The QMF SQL Query panel

```
 MMA - EXTRA! for Windows 95/NT                                    _  X
 File  Edit  View  Tools  Session  Options  Help
 SQL QUERY                                      MODIFIED  LINE    1

 SELECT INVNO, INVDATE, INVTOTAL, CUSTNO, FNAME, LNAME, CITY, STATE
    FROM MM01.INV1
       INNER JOIN MM01.CUST1
          ON INVCUST = CUSTNO
    ORDER BY INVNO;








 *** END ***


 1=Help        2=Run        3=End        4=Print     5=Chart      6=Draw
 7=Backward    8=Forward    9=Form      10=Insert   11=Delete    12=Report
 OK, QUERY is displayed.
 COMMAND ===> _                                      SCROLL ===> PAGE

```

The Report panel for the above query

```
 MMA - EXTRA! for Windows 95/NT                                    _  X
 File  Edit  View  Tools  Session  Options  Help
 REPORT                                 LINE 1      POS 1      79


   INVNO    INVDATE        INVTOTAL  CUSTNO  FNAME             LNAME
   -------  ----------     --------  ------  ----------------  -----------------
   003584   1998-04-28        51.75  400004  CAROL             EVANS
   003585   1998-04-28       292.83  400005  ELAINE            ROBERTS
   003586   1998-04-28        68.87  400002  KAREN             ANNELLI
   003587   1998-04-28        22.09  400001  KEITH             JONES
   003588   1998-04-28        57.63  400003  SUSAN             HOWARD
   003589   1998-04-28       711.05  400005  ELAINE            ROBERTS
   003590   1998-04-28       110.49  400001  KEITH             JONES


 *** END ***



 1=Help        2=           3=End        4=Print     5=Chart      6=Query
 7=Backward    8=Forward    9=Form      10=Left     11=Right     12=
 OK, this is the REPORT from your RUN command.
 COMMAND ===> _                                      SCROLL ===> PAGE

```

Figure 1-17   How to use the Query Management Facility

Perspective

The goal of this chapter has been to get you started with DB2 as quickly as possible. If this chapter has succeeded, you should now be able to code a simple COBOL program that gets data from one row of a DB2 table at a time. Of course, there's a lot more to DB2 programming than that.

With that as background, though, you're ready for the other chapters in section 1 of this book. In chapter 2, you'll learn how to use a cursor to process a multi-row result table. In chapter 3, you'll learn how to use the INSERT, UPDATE, and DELETE statements to modify a table. And in chapter 4, you'll learn how to join the data from two or more tables into a single result table. When you complete this section, you'll have a solid set of DB2 skills.

Whenever you're ready to develop and test your first DB2 program, though, you can skip from section 1 to chapter 12 in section 3. There, you can learn how to use DB2I to prepare and test a program that you've coded. Once you've learned that, you can return to section 1 to learn more about DB2 programming.

2

How to retrieve DB2 data from a single table

In the last chapter, you learned how to use an SQL SELECT statement to build a result table that contains a single row. Now, in this chapter, you'll learn more about the coding of a SELECT statement. You'll also learn how to code this statement so it builds a result table that contains more than one row and how to use a cursor to process the rows in a multi-row result table.

The syntax of the SELECT statement

Figure 2-1 presents the complete syntax of the SELECT statement. When you code it with an INTO clause, the statement can only build a result table that contains a single row. In this case, you code the statement within EXEC SQL and END-EXEC statements in the Procedure Division of a COBOL program as illustrated by the program in chapter 1.

In contrast, when you want to build a result table that contains more than one row, you code the SELECT statement within a DECLARE CURSOR statement and without the INTO clause. Then, you use a cursor to process the rows in the multi-row result table. This is explained in figures 2-5, 2-6, and 2-7, and this is illustrated by the COBOL program that's presented in this chapter.

If you study the syntax in figure 2-1, you can see that you've already been introduced to the first four clauses in chapter 1. Now, this chapter will present them in more detail. In contrast, the WITH clause isn't presented in detail until chapter 11; it is included in this syntax summary only for completeness.

Syntax

```
SELECT column-specification [AS result-column]
    [, column-specification [AS result-column]]…
    [INTO {:host-var [, :host-var]… | :host-structure}]
    FROM {table-name | view-name}
        [WHERE selection-condition]
    [WITH isolation-level]
```

Explanation

column-specification	Describes what the SELECT statement should put in the corresponding column of the result table (see figure 2-2).
result-column	The name to be used for the associated column-specification in the result table. Typically used to give a name to a column that's derived from a function or expression.
host-var	The COBOL name of the host variable into which DB2 will place the data for the corresponding column-specification in the SELECT clause. You must precede each COBOL host variable name with a colon.
host-structure	The COBOL name of the group item into which DB2 will place the data it retrieves from the table.
table-name	The name of the table from which you want to retrieve data.
view-name	The name of the view from which you want to retrieve data.
selection-condition	A test that SQL will apply to each row in the base table to determine whether to include it in the result table (see figure 2-4).
isolation-level	Specifies the isolation level at which the statement is executed (see chapter 11).

Description

- You can only code the INTO clause in a SELECT statement in the Procedure Division. This type of statement, which can be referred to as a SELECT INTO statement, can only generate a result table that contains a single row.

- If the result table of a SELECT INTO statement is empty, DB2 assigns a value of +100 to the SQLCODE field in the SQL communication area. In this case, no values are placed in the host variables.

- If the result table of a SELECT INTO statement contains more than one row, DB2 assigns a value of -811 to the SQLCODE field.

- If you want to generate a multi-row result table, you code a SELECT statement without an INTO clause in a DECLARE CURSOR statement. Then, you use a cursor to move from one row to another (see figures 2-5, 2-6, and 2-7).

Figure 2-1   The syntax of the SELECT statement

How to code the SELECT clause

When you code a SELECT statement, you code column specifications right after the word SELECT. These specifications are for the columns that you want in the result table. Although most of the data in these columns normally comes directly from the tables in a database (the *base tables*), you can also code column specifications that get data from the COBOL program or from calculated values. These alternatives are summarized in figure 2-2.

The first two examples of column specifications in this figure get values from a table in a database. When you code an asterisk, all of the columns in the base table are put into the result table. When you code a list of column names, just those columns are put into the result table.

The third and fourth examples in this figure include column specifications that get data from the COBOL program. The third specification in the third example gets data from a host variable in the working-storage section of the COBOL program. The third specification in the fourth example is a literal.

The fifth, sixth, and seventh examples in this figure show how to use calculated values as column specifications. The second column specification in the fifth example is an arithmetic expression that adds the data in three columns of the base table to create a calculated value named INVOICETOTAL. To code an expression like this, you use *arithmetic operators* to combine host variables, column values, and literals the same way you code an expression within a COBOL COMPUTE statement.

The sixth example illustrates how to combine, or *concatenate*, character data using the I I operator. Here, the FNAME and LNAME columns are concatenated with a literal that contains a single space. This creates a column in the result table that's named FULLNAME. The length of a column like this in the result table is the sum of the lengths of the elements that make it up.

This last example shows how to use one of DB2's built-in functions to create a calculated value. Here, the SUM function adds an employee's SALARY and BONUS and stores the result as INCOME. In chapters 6 and 7, you can learn more about using the built-in functions.

After each column specification, you can code an AS clause. This clause specifies the name you want to use for that column in the result table. Typically, this clause is used to give a name to a column that's derived from a function or an expression, but you can also use it to give a column in the result table a different name than the one used in the base table.

Six ways to code column specifications

Source	Option	Syntax	Examples
Base table value	All columns	*	`SELECT *`
	Column name	column-name	`SELECT FNAME, LNAME, STATE`
Program value	Host variable name	:host-var	`SELECT FNAME, LNAME, :STATE`
	Constant value	literal	`SELECT FNAME, LNAME,` `   'IS A CALIFORNIA RESIDENT'`
Calculated value	Result of a calculation	Arithmetic expression	`SELECT INVNO, INVSUBT + INVSHIP` `   + INVTAX AS INVOICETOTAL`
	Result of a concatenation	Character expression	`SELECT FNAME || ' ' || LNAME` `   AS FULLNAME`
	Result of a function	Function	`SELECT SUM(SALARY+BONUS)` `   AS INCOME`

Arithmetic operators in order of precedence

Minus sign before a value (negation)

Multiplication or division (* or /)

Addition or subtraction (+ or -)

Description

- Use SELECT * only when you need to retrieve all of the columns from a table.
- Literals in DB2 are treated the same as they are in COBOL. For a text string, you code the literal between quotation marks; for a numeric value, you omit the quotation marks.
- You can use parentheses in an arithmetic expression whenever there's any doubt about the sequence in which the operations will be performed. Then, the operations in the inner parentheses are done first, followed by the operations in the outer sets of parentheses.

Note

- The maximum number of column specifications is 750.

Figure 2-2   How to code the SELECT clause

How to code the INTO clause

Figure 2-3 illustrates the use of the INTO clause of the SELECT statement. This clause names the COBOL host variables that are used to store the result table values that DB2 returns to the program. You saw how this worked in chapter 1. (Remember that a SELECT statement that uses an INTO clause can only return a one-row result table.)

As these examples show, you can code a host variable for each column in the result table or you can code a host structure. If you code host variables, you must be sure that you code them in the same sequence as the column specifications in the SELECT clause. If you code a host structure, its elementary items must define the columns specified in the SELECT clause. For instance, the host structure named CUSTOMER-ROW in the second example must define all of the columns in the customer table since all of the columns are retrieved by the SELECT clause (*).

When you define the host variables, you need to be sure that their data types are compatible with the data types of the corresponding result table columns. You also need to be sure that the host variables are long enough to contain the information DB2 tries to store in them. If you use the DCLGEN host variable definitions, of course, errors are less likely to occur.

Even if you use DCLGEN output, you still need to code host variables for those column specifications that get data from calculated values or from the COBOL program. This is illustrated by the third and fourth examples in this figure. In the third example, INVOICE-TOTAL is a host variable that is used to store the calculated value in the second column specification. In the fourth example, LITERAL-MESSAGE is a host variable that's used to store the literal in the third column specification.

How to code the FROM clause

The FROM clause in a SELECT statement identifies the table that contains the data you want to retrieve. A typical table name has two parts, separated by a period. The first part identifies the person who created the table. The second part identifies the table. In the SELECT statements in figure 2-3, for example, the table names are MM01.CUSTOMER and MM01.INVOICE, where MM01 identifies the creator and CUSTOMER and INVOICE identify the tables.

You can also specify a view name in the FROM clause of a SELECT statement. Then, as you learned in the last chapter, the result table is derived from a view of a base table, instead of from the base table itself. Although a table and a view are different entities in terms of the database, they usually work the same in terms of COBOL programming.

An INTO clause that uses host variables

```
SELECT     FNAME,  LNAME,   STATE
    INTO :FNAME,  :LNAME,  :STATE
    FROM MM01.CUSTOMER
        WHERE CUSTNO = :CUSTNO
```

An INTO clause that uses a host structure

```
SELECT     *
    INTO   CUSTOMER-ROW
    FROM MM01.CUSTOMER
        WHERE CUSTNO = :CUSTNO
```

An INTO clause that provides a host variable for a calculated value

```
SELECT    INVNO,  INVSUBT + INVSHIP + INVTAX AS INVOICETOTAL
    INTO :INVNO, :INVOICE-TOTAL
    FROM MM01.INVOICE
        WHERE INVCUST = :INVCUST
```

An INTO clause that provides a host variable for a literal

```
SELECT    FNAME,  LNAME, ' IS A CALIFORNIA RESIDENT'
    INTO :FNAME,  :LNAME, :LITERAL-MESSAGE
    FROM MM01.CUSTOMER
        WHERE CUSTNO = :CUSTNO AND STATE = 'CA'
```

Description

- The host variables in the INTO clause must be coded in the same sequence as the corresponding column specifications.

- The data type of a host variable must be compatible with the value assigned to it.

- A host variable doesn't have to be part of the DCLGEN output. A host variable can be coded anywhere in working-storage.

Figure 2-3   How to code the INTO clause

How to code the WHERE clause

Figure 2-4 summarizes the use of a simple WHERE clause. This clause is used to specify a *selection condition* that identifies what rows DB2 should retrieve. Although this clause is optional, every row in a table is retrieved if this clause is omitted.

In a simple WHERE clause, the condition consists of an expression, a *comparison operator*, and another expression. This is illustrated by the examples in this figure. As you will learn in chapter 5, though, DB2 also provides keywords and logical operators that let you code more elaborate selection conditions.

The first example in this figure selects a row for the result table if the value in its CUSTNO column is the same as the value of the CUSTNO host variable. In order for this statement to work, the customer number must be moved to the host variable before the COBOL program issues this SELECT statement. Since the CUSTOMER table was designed so the CUSTNO value in each row is unique, this WHERE clause can return no more than one row.

The second example in this figure specifies a literal value for the second expression in the WHERE clause. As a result, this statement selects a row for the result table only if the CUSTNO column contains the specified value. Although you usually won't code an expression that uses a literal in a SELECT statement within a COBOL program, you will use literals when you use SPUFI or QMF to do ad hoc processing. Incidentally, the literal in this example is enclosed in quotes even though it consists entirely of numbers because the CUSTNO column is defined as a CHAR data type.

The third example in this figure selects a row for the result table if the STATE column contains the value stored in the STATE host variable. Since the values in the STATE column are not unique, this SELECT statement can return more than one row. As a result, you shouldn't code the INTO clause with this type of statement, and you shouldn't code it in the Procedure Division. Instead, you should code it within a DECLARE CURSOR statement, which you'll learn about next. The same is true if you use the other comparison operators shown in this figure, since they typically return more than one row.

The syntax of the WHERE clause

```
[WHERE expression operator expression]
```

Comparison operators

=		Is equal to		
>		Is greater than		
<		Is less than		
¬ = or <>		Is not equal to	or	Is less than or greater than
¬ > or <=		Is not greater than	or	Is less than or equal to
¬ < or >=		Is not less than	or	Is greater than or equal to

A WHERE clause that retrieves a row when the customer number equals the value of a host variable

```
SELECT     FNAME,  LNAME
    INTO :FNAME, :LNAME
    FROM  MM01.CUSTOMER
        WHERE CUSTNO = :CUSTNO
```

A WHERE clause that retrieves a row when the customer number equals the value of a literal

```
SELECT     FNAME,  LNAME
    INTO :FNAME, :LNAME
    FROM  MM01.CUSTOMER
        WHERE CUSTNO = '555455'
```

A WHERE clause that can retrieve multiple rows

```
SELECT     FNAME,  LNAME
    FROM  MM01.CUSTOMER
        WHERE STATE = :STATE
```

Description

- The first expression in a WHERE clause is usually the name of a column, and the second expression is usually a host variable or a literal value. Since both expressions must contain like data, you can't compare numeric data to character data, even if the character data contains nothing but numbers.

- If you want to create a result table with a single row, you usually use the equals (=) operator to identify a column with a unique value. If you identify a column whose value is not unique or if you use one of the other operators, multiple rows may be retrieved.

- A column name that you include in a WHERE clause does not have to be one of the columns specified in the SELECT clause.

Figure 2-4   How to code the WHERE clause

How to use cursors to process multiple rows

To process a result table that contains more than one row in a COBOL program, you have to use a cursor. A *cursor* is a pointer that identifies the *current row* in a result table. When you use a cursor, you work through a result table one row at a time, much as you read through a standard sequential file.

Figure 2-5 describes the four SQL statements that are used for cursor processing and lists their COBOL equivalents. Only one, the DECLARE CURSOR statement, doesn't have a direct parallel in standard COBOL. This statement is used to define the result table and the cursor that's used to process it.

The first example in this figure is a DECLARE CURSOR statement that defines a cursor named ACCTCURS. As you can see, five columns are selected from an employee table where the department number equals the value placed in a host variable named DEPTNO. Here, the INTO clause isn't coded because this statement returns a result table with more than one row. Later, the FETCH statement, which has an INTO clause, is used to move the data into the host variables, one row at a time.

The second example in this figure is an OPEN statement that opens the ACCTCURS cursor. When this statement is executed, DB2 first executes the SELECT statement within the DECLARE CURSOR statement, which creates a cursor-controlled result table. Then, DB2 positions the cursor just before the first row in the result table.

The third example in this figure is a FETCH statement that fetches the next row of the cursor-controlled result table into host variables. When DB2 processes a FETCH statement, it moves the cursor to the next row, thus making it the current row. Then, DB2 moves the contents of the current row into the host variables or host structure that's specified in the INTO clause. Within a COBOL program, you can repeatedly execute FETCH statements until all the rows in the result table have been processed.

The fourth example in this figure is a CLOSE statement that closes the ACCTCURS cursor. After you close a cursor, you can issue the OPEN statement to open it again and do further processing. For instance, you could place a new value in the DEPTNO variable before opening the cursor so the result table will have different data. If you don't need to use the cursor again, though, DB2 will automatically close the cursor when your program terminates.

The SQL statements for cursor processing

SQL statement	Description	COBOL equivalent
DECLARE CURSOR	Defines a result table and names a cursor for it.	None
OPEN cursor-name	Creates the result table and positions the cursor before the first row in the table.	OPEN file-name
FETCH cursor-name	Fetches the next row from the result table.	READ file-name
CLOSE cursor-name	Closes the result table.	CLOSE file-name

A DECLARE CURSOR statement that defines a cursor named ACCTCURS

```
EXEC SQL
    DECLARE ACCTCURS CURSOR FOR
        SELECT EMPNO, DEPTNO, FNAME, LNAME, EXT
        FROM MM01.EMP
            WHERE DEPTNO = :DEPTNO
END-EXEC.
```

An OPEN statement that creates the result table defined by the ACCTCURS cursor

```
EXEC SQL
    OPEN ACCTCURS
END-EXEC.
```

A FETCH statement that fetches the next row in the ACCTCURS result table

```
EXEC SQL
    FETCH ACCTCURS
        INTO :EMPNO, :DEPTNO, :FNAME, :LNAME, :EXT
END-EXEC.
```

A CLOSE statement that closes the ACCTCURS cursor

```
EXEC SQL
    CLOSE ACCTCURS
END-EXEC.
```

Figure 2-5   SQL statements for cursor processing

How to declare a cursor

Figure 2-6 presents the syntax of the DECLARE CURSOR statement. In the next chapter, you'll learn how to use the FOR UPDATE OF and WITH HOLD clauses, so you can concentrate on the other aspects of this statement right now.

In the SELECT statement that's coded within a DECLARE CURSOR statement, you can use the full range of options that you learned about earlier in this chapter. You can also code the DISTINCT keyword to exclude duplicate rows (rows that are identical) from the result table. And you can code the ORDER BY clause to sort the rows in the result table, which you'll learn more about in a moment.

In the example in this figure, the DECLARE CURSOR statement defines a result table with a cursor named CUSTCURS. This table will contain the FNAME and LNAME columns from the rows in the MM01.CUSTOMER table where the state column contains the value CA. As you can see, the SELECT statement doesn't include an INTO clause, because it is invalid within a DECLARE CURSOR statement.

The syntax of the DECLARE CURSOR statement

```
EXEC SQL
    DECLARE cursor-name CURSOR [WITH HOLD] FOR
        SELECT [DISTINCT] column-specification [AS result-column]
                        [, column-specification [AS result-column]]…
            FROM table-name
                [WHERE selection-condition]
        {[FOR UPDATE OF update-column [, update-column]…] |
         [ORDER BY sort-column [DESC] [, sort-column [DESC]]…]}
    END-EXEC.
```

Explanation

cursor-name	The name to be used for the new cursor.
WITH HOLD	Prevents the cursor from being closed as a result of a commit operation (see chapters 3 and 11).
DISTINCT	Specifies that duplicate (identical) rows should not be included in the result table.
update-column	The name of a column for which you want to enable updates.
sort-column	The name or number of the column in the result table by which DB2 sorts the result table. The first sort-column you specify is the primary sort column; the second is the secondary sort column; and so on.
DESC	Specifies that the values in the associated sort-column should be presented in descending sequence. If you omit DESC, the values will be presented in ascending sequence.

A DECLARE CURSOR statement that defines a cursor named CUSTCURS

```
EXEC SQL
    DECLARE CUSTCURS CURSOR FOR
        SELECT FNAME, LNAME
        FROM MM01.CUSTOMER
            WHERE STATE = 'CA'
    END-EXEC.
```

Note

- You can code the DECLARE CURSOR statement in the Working-Storage Section or in the Procedure Division, as long as it appears before any other statements that refer to the cursor. Since it is a declarative statement and not an action statement, it is typically coded in the Working-Storage Section.

Figure 2-6   The SQL DECLARE CURSOR statement

How to open a cursor

As you've already learned, the SQL OPEN statement generates the result table specified by a DECLARE CURSOR statement and positions the cursor before the first row. As you can see in figure 2-7, all you code on the OPEN statement is the cursor name you supplied in the DECLARE CURSOR statement.

How to retrieve a row from a cursor-controlled result table

Figure 2-7 also presents the syntax of the SQL FETCH statement. Here, the INTO clause specifies either a list of host variables or a host structure where the data from a row in the result table will be stored in the COBOL program. You code this clause just as you code an INTO clause in a SELECT statement that produces a one-row result table.

When a FETCH statement is executed, DB2 advances the cursor one row in the result table. Then, it moves the column data from the current row into the COBOL host variables or host structure. In this example, the FNAME and LNAME columns that were specified in the SELECT statement of the CUSTCURS cursor are stored in the host variables named :FNAME and :LNAME.

A typical COBOL program will fetch one row after another and process the data in that row until there are no more rows in the result set. This directly parallels the way you use a READ statement to work through the records in a sequential file. When there are no more rows in the result table and a FETCH statement is executed, DB2 places a value of +100 in the SQLCODE field so the program can test for this condition. This is illustrated by the COBOL program that's presented in this chapter.

How to close a cursor

When you finish using a cursor-controlled result table, you should issue the SQL CLOSE statement shown in figure 2-7. As with the OPEN statement, all you code on the CLOSE statement is the name of the cursor that was specified in the DECLARE CURSOR statement.

Since DB2 automatically closes all cursor-controlled result tables when a program ends, the only time you must close a cursor is when you plan to open it again before the program ends. However, if your program does any processing after you've finished with a cursor-controlled result table, you should close it to allow DB2 to release the resources that it requires.

The SQL OPEN statement

```
EXEC SQL
    OPEN cursor-name
END-EXEC.
```

An OPEN statement that creates a result table and cursor

```
EXEC SQL
    OPEN CUSTCURS
END-EXEC.
```

The SQL FETCH statement

```
EXEC SQL
    FETCH cursor-name
        INTO {:host-var [, :host-var]… | :host-structure}
END-EXEC.
```

A FETCH statement that fetches the next row from the result table

```
EXEC SQL
    FETCH CUSTCURS
        INTO :FNAME, :LNAME
END-EXEC.
```

The SQL CLOSE statement

```
EXEC SQL
    CLOSE cursor-name
END-EXEC.
```

A CLOSE statement that closes the result table and cursor

```
EXEC SQL
    CLOSE CUSTCURS
END-EXEC.
```

Note

- A cursor-controlled result table is not generated until an OPEN statement is executed.
- When a FETCH statement is executed and there are no more rows in the result table, DB2 returns a value of +100 to the SQLCODE field.

Figure 2-7   The SQL OPEN, FETCH, and CLOSE statements

How to sort the rows in a result table

To sort the rows in a result table before you process them, you code the ORDER BY clause in the SELECT statement within the DECLARE CURSOR statement as illustrated by the examples in figure 2-8. Here, the first example sorts the records in the result table by last name. Since DESC isn't specified, the records are sorted in ascending sequence. In contrast, the second example sorts the records in the result table in descending sequence by invoice total.

The third example in this figure specifies two sort columns. In this case, the result table is first sorted by customer number (INVCUST) in ascending sequence. Then, within each customer number, the rows are sorted by invoice total in descending sequence. Notice that the WHERE clause has been omitted from this statement so all the records in the invoice table will be included in the result table.

The fourth example in this figure shows that you can identify a sort column by specifying the number of the column in the result table instead of its name. As a result, this statement produces the same result table as the statement in the first example. To make this clause easier to understand, though, you should code the column name whenever possible.

The last example in this figure shows how to sort a result table by a column that consists of a calculated value. Here, the AS clause is used on the SELECT statement to name the calculated value TOTAL. Then, this name is used in the ORDER BY clause.

When you sort the rows in a cursor-controlled result table, the table is *read-only*. This means that you can't insert, update, or delete rows in this table. You'll understand the implications of this after you read chapter 3.

DECLARE CURSOR statements that sort the result tables

Rows are sorted by last name in ascending sequence

```
EXEC SQL
    DECLARE CUSTCURS CURSOR FOR
        SELECT FNAME, LNAME
            FROM MM01.CUSTOMER
                WHERE STATE = 'CA'
        ORDER BY LNAME
END-EXEC.
```

Rows are sorted by invoice total in descending sequence

```
EXEC SQL
    DECLARE INVCURS CURSOR FOR
        SELECT INVCUST, INVNO, INVDATE, INVTOTAL
            FROM MM01.INVOICE
                WHERE INVCUST = :CUSTNO
        ORDER BY INVTOTAL DESC
END-EXEC.
```

Rows are sorted by invoice total in descending sequence within customer number in ascending sequence

```
EXEC SQL
    DECLARE INVCURS CURSOR FOR
        SELECT INVCUST, INVNO, INVDATE, INVTOTAL
            FROM MM01.INVOICE
        ORDER BY INVCUST, INVTOTAL DESC
END-EXEC.
```

Rows are sorted by the second column in the result table

```
EXEC SQL
    DECLARE CUSTCURS CURSOR FOR
        SELECT FNAME, LNAME
            FROM MM01.CUSTOMER
                WHERE STATE = 'CA'
        ORDER BY 2
END-EXEC.
```

Rows are sorted by a calculated value

```
EXEC SQL
    DECLARE INVCURS CURSOR FOR
        SELECT INVNO, INVDATE, INVTOTAL + INVTAX AS TOTAL
            FROM MM01.INVOICE
        ORDER BY TOTAL
END-EXEC.
```

Note

- A cursor-controlled result table that is sorted by the ORDER BY clause is read-only.

Figure 2-8   How to sort the rows in a result table

A COBOL program that processes a result table with more than one row

Now, so you can see how cursor processing works in a COBOL program, this chapter presents an expanded version of the program presented in chapter 1. This is a sales inquiry program that gets data from one row of a customer table at a time by using a SELECT INTO statement. It also gets data from a multi-row invoice table by using cursor processing.

The interactive screen

Like the program in chapter 1, the sales inquiry program in this chapter runs at a TSO terminal and accepts a series of customer numbers from the user. For each customer number, the program gets customer information from a customer table. It also gets the related invoice information for that customer from an invoice table. Because the invoice result table may contain more than one row for a customer, the sales inquiry program must use a cursor to process it.

To show how the database information is displayed, figure 2-9 presents the screen output for two user sessions with the sales inquiry program. In the first screen, you can see an inquiry for a customer who has made three purchases. The first line for this customer shows the data that's retrieved from the customer table; the next three lines show the data that's retrieved from the invoice table; and the last two lines show the summary data that's developed by the COBOL program. To end this session, the user has entered 999999.

In the second screen in this figure, you can see two more customer inquiries. The first inquiry shows customer and total data for a customer that didn't have any related rows in the invoice table. The second one shows the error message that's displayed when the user enters a customer number that can't be found in the customer table. This session also ends when the user enters 999999.

Example 1

During the first inquiry session, the program displays information from three invoice rows for the customer number the user enters.

```
MMA - EXTRA! for Windows 95/NT                                    _ |日| X

File  Edit  View  Tools  Session  Options  Help

------------------------------------------------
KEY IN THE NEXT CUSTOMER NUMBER AND PRESS ENTER,
OR KEY IN 999999 AND PRESS ENTER TO QUIT.
400015
------------------------------------------------
   CUSTOMER 400015 -- VIVIAN              GEORGE

   INVOICE 062319 1998-03-17     181.42
   INVOICE 062320 1998-03-17    3405.00
   INVOICE 062333 1998-05-17     178.23
                               ------------
   TOTAL BILLED                 3764.65
   INVOICES ISSUED                    3

------------------------------------------------
KEY IN THE NEXT CUSTOMER NUMBER AND PRESS ENTER,
OR KEY IN 999999 AND PRESS ENTER TO QUIT.
999999
*** _
```

Example 2

During the second inquiry session, the user requests sales information for two customers. The first customer has no sales on file. The second customer's number wasn't found.

```
MMA - EXTRA! for Windows 95/NT                                    _ |日| X

File  Edit  View  Tools  Session  Options  Help

------------------------------------------------
KEY IN THE NEXT CUSTOMER NUMBER AND PRESS ENTER,
OR KEY IN 999999 AND PRESS ENTER TO QUIT.
400008
------------------------------------------------
   CUSTOMER 400008 -- TIM                 JOHNSON

   TOTAL BILLED                  0.00
   INVOICES ISSUED                  0

------------------------------------------------
KEY IN THE NEXT CUSTOMER NUMBER AND PRESS ENTER,
OR KEY IN 999999 AND PRESS ENTER TO QUIT.
400020
------------------------------------------------
   CUSTOMER NUMBER 400020 NOT FOUND.
------------------------------------------------
KEY IN THE NEXT CUSTOMER NUMBER AND PRESS ENTER,
OR KEY IN 999999 AND PRESS ENTER TO QUIT.
999999
*** _
```

Figure 2-9   The interactive screen for the sales inquiry program

The DCLGEN output

Since this program uses the same customer table as the program in chapter 1, the DCLGEN output for this table isn't presented in this chapter. If you want to review this output, though, you can refer back to figure 1-9. In addition, this program uses the DCLGEN output for the invoice table that's presented in figure 2-10.

The first column in the invoice table, INVCUST, contains the customer number that relates a row in this table to the customer table. In other words, INVCUST is a foreign key. Because a single customer can have more than one invoice, more than one invoice row can contain the same value in the INVCUST column. In contrast, the invoice number column, INVNO, is the primary key for the invoice table, and the value in this column uniquely identifies each row in the table.

In the SQL declarations for this table, you can see that two new data types are used. The DATE data type describes a 10-character date that can be displayed in that format on the interactive screen. In some programs, though, you will want to modify this date format by using one of the functions that are presented in chapter 7. After the date column, you can see four columns that are declared with the DECIMAL data type.

Although the program in this chapter uses DCLGEN output to describe the host variables that are used, you should remember that you don't have to use this output in your program. Instead, you can define the host variables anywhere in working-storage using your own COBOL descriptions. Then, you only have to define host variables for the columns that your program uses, not all the columns in each base table. When you define your own host variables, though, you must be sure that each COBOL description is compatible with the data type of the column that will be stored in the variable.

DCLGEN output for the invoice table

```
********************************************************************
* DCLGEN TABLE(MM01.INVOICE)                                      *
*         LIBRARY(MM01.DB2.DCLGENS(INVOICE))                      *
*         ACTION(REPLACE)                                         *
*         LANGUAGE(COBOL)                                         *
*         STRUCTURE(INVOICE-ROW)                                  *
*         QUOTE                                                   *
* ... IS THE DCLGEN COMMAND THAT MADE THE FOLLOWING STATEMENTS    *
********************************************************************
        EXEC SQL DECLARE MM01.INVOICE TABLE
        ( INVCUST                      CHAR(6) NOT NULL,
          INVNO                        CHAR(6) NOT NULL,
          INVDATE                      DATE NOT NULL,
          INVSUBT                      DECIMAL(9,2) NOT NULL,
          INVSHIP                      DECIMAL(7,2) NOT NULL,
          INVTAX                       DECIMAL(7,2) NOT NULL,
          INVTOTAL                     DECIMAL(9,2) NOT NULL,
          INVPROM                      CHAR(10) NOT NULL
        ) END-EXEC.
********************************************************************
* COBOL DECLARATION FOR TABLE MM01.INVOICE                        *
********************************************************************
 01  INVOICE-ROW.
     10  INVCUST           PIC X(6).
     10  INVNO             PIC X(6).
     10  INVDATE           PIC X(10).
     10  INVSUBT           PIC S(7)V9(2) USAGE COMP-3.
     10  INVSHIP           PIC S(5)V9(2) USAGE COMP-3.
     10  INVTAX            PIC S(5)V9(2) USAGE COMP-3.
     10  INVTOTAL          PIC S(7)V9(2) USAGE COMP-3.
     10  INVPROM           PIC X(10).
********************************************************************
* THE NUMBER OF COLUMNS DESCRIBED BY THIS DECLARATION IS 8        *
********************************************************************
```

Description

- This DCLGEN output illustrates the use of two more data types. If you refer back to figure 1-9, you can see that the DATE data type provides for a ten-character date (yyyy-mm-dd). You can also see that the DECIMAL format provides for packed-decimal data with a specific number of digits before and after the decimal point.

- In the second portion of this DCLGEN output, you can see that the COBOL declarations for the host variables are compatible with the data types in the table declaration.

- When you include DCLGEN output in a COBOL program, you can be sure that the COBOL declarations are compatible with the data types. However, you don't have to use DCLGEN output. Instead, you can code your own COBOL declarations for the host variables.

- When you code your own COBOL declarations, you only need to code declarations for the columns you're going to retrieve; you don't have to code one declaration for each column in the table.

Figure 2-10   The DCLGEN output for the invoice table

The structure chart

Figure 2-11 presents the structure chart for the sales inquiry program. At the higher levels of control, this program works much like the program in chapter 1. Module 000 performs module 100 until the user signals the end of the program by entering 999999 as a customer number. Then, each time module 100 is performed, it performs module 110 to accept a customer number from the user, module 120 to get the related information from a row in the customer table, and module 130 to display that information.

The structure of this program differs from the program in chapter 1 where it deals with the invoice table. In particular, module 140 manages the functions that are needed to retrieve all the rows for the current customer from the invoice result table. To open the cursor-controlled result table, module 140 performs module 150. To get the invoice information from the rows for the current customer, module 140 performs module 160 until there are no more rows. And to close the result table when there are no more rows, module 140 performs module 190.

After the cursor-controlled table is closed, the program goes back to module 100, which performs module 200 to display the total lines for a customer. Then, the program goes back to module 000, which performs module 100 again unless the user has entered 999999 as the customer number in module 110. If you have any trouble following how all this is going to work, it should become clear as soon as you start reviewing the COBOL listing.

The structure chart

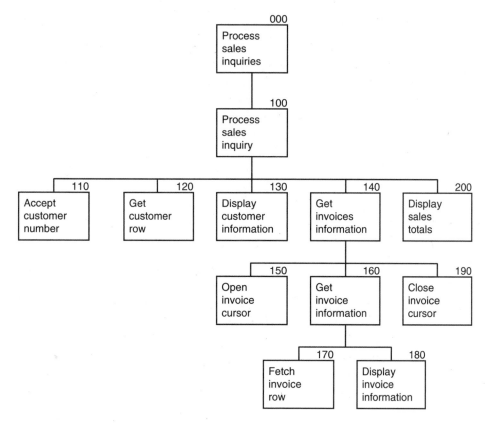

Description

- Module 000 in this structure chart performs module 100 once for each customer number that the user enters until the user ends the program by entering 999999 as the customer number.

- Module 100 performs module 110 to accept a customer number from the user; performs module 120 to get the row for that customer; and performs module 130 to display the information in that row. Then, module 100 performs module 140 once for each row in the invoice table that is related to the customer. When there are no more invoice rows for that customer, module 100 performs module 200 to display the invoice totals for that customer.

- Each time module 140 is performed, it performs module 150 to open a cursor for an invoice result table that includes all the invoice rows for the customer that's being processed. Then, module 140 performs module 160 once for each invoice row. When all the invoices have been processed, module 140 performs module 190 to close the invoice cursor.

- Each time module 160 is performed, it performs module 170 to fetch the next invoice row in the cursor-controlled result table that has been opened. Then, module 160 performs module 180 to display the invoice information for that row.

Figure 2-11   The structure chart for the sales inquiry program

The COBOL listing

Figure 2-12 presents the source code for the sales inquiry program. If you review the switches in working-storage, you can see that two new ones have been added to the code for the chapter 1 program. These switches indicate (1) whether a valid cursor-controlled table has been created by the OPEN statement in module 150, and (2) whether the end of the invoice result table has been reached by the FETCH statement in module 170.

This program also includes two sets of fields for the totals the program accumulates as it processes the invoice rows for a customer. One group contains the INVOICES-COUNT and INVOICES-TOTAL fields that the program increments for each invoice row it processes. The other group contains the EDITED-COUNT and EDITED-TOTAL fields that are the edited versions of the total data that the program displays.

After these fields, you'll find four SQL statements. The first two statements direct the precompiler to include the library members that contain the DCLGEN output for the customer and invoice tables. The third statement includes the SQL communication area fields. And the fourth statement is the DECLARE CURSOR statement for the cursor-controlled result table.

Within this DECLARE CURSOR statement, the SELECT statement specifies that the result table will contain three columns. When the OPEN statement generates this result table, DB2 compares the current value of the host variable CUSTNO with the contents of the INVCUST column in the invoice table to determine which rows to include in the result table.

The sales inquiry program   **Page 1**

```
IDENTIFICATION DIVISION.
*
PROGRAM-ID.     SALESINQ.
*
ENVIRONMENT DIVISION.
*
INPUT-OUTPUT SECTION.
*
FILE-CONTROL.
*
DATA DIVISION.
*
FILE SECTION.
*
WORKING-STORAGE SECTION.
*
 01  SWITCHES.
*
     05  END-OF-INQUIRIES-SW     PIC X    VALUE 'N'.
         88  END-OF-INQUIRIES             VALUE 'Y'.
     05  CUSTOMER-FOUND-SW       PIC X    VALUE 'Y'.
         88  CUSTOMER-FOUND              VALUE 'Y'.
     05  VALID-CURSOR-SW         PIC X    VALUE 'Y'.
         88  VALID-CURSOR                VALUE 'Y'.
     05  END-OF-INVOICES-SW      PIC X    VALUE 'N'.
         88  END-OF-INVOICES             VALUE 'Y'.
*
 01  INVOICE-TOTAL-FIELDS    COMP-3.
*
     05  INVOICES-COUNT     PIC S9(5)    VALUE ZERO.
     05  INVOICES-TOTAL     PIC S9(7)V99 VALUE ZERO.
*
 01  EDITED-TOTAL-FIELDS.
*
     05  EDITED-COUNT       PIC Z(4)9.
     05  EDITED-TOTAL       PIC Z(6)9.99.
*
     EXEC SQL
         INCLUDE CUSTOMER
     END-EXEC.
*
     EXEC SQL
         INCLUDE INVOICE
     END-EXEC.
*
     EXEC SQL
         INCLUDE SQLCA
     END-EXEC.
*
     EXEC SQL
       DECLARE INVCURS CURSOR FOR
           SELECT   INVNO, INVDATE, INVTOTAL
               FROM MM01.INVOICE
               WHERE INVCUST = :CUSTNO
     END-EXEC.
*
```

Figure 2-12   The COBOL listing for the sales inquiry program (part 1 of 3)

If you have much COBOL experience, you should now be able to follow the code in the Procedure Division with little difficulty. Nevertheless, the text that follows describes some highlights.

To start, module 000 performs module 100 until the end-of-inquiries switch is turned on. Then, module 100 performs module 110 to get the next customer number, after which it performs some combination of modules 120, 130, 140, and 150 based on the settings of the end-of-inquiries and customer-found switches. In particular, when the user enters a valid customer number, module 100 performs module 120 to get the related customer row and module 130 to display the customer information. Then, it performs module 160 to get and display the information in each invoice row for that customer. When there are no more rows, module 100 performs module 200 to display the totals for that customer.

Once you understand that logic, you just need to make sure that the switches are turned on and off at the right times. In module 120, for example, if the SELECT statement can't find a customer row for the customer number that the user has entered into the CUSTNO field, DB2 returns a non-zero value in the SQLCODE field. Then, the program turns the customer-found switch off, so module 130 displays a not-found message and module 100 doesn't perform any other modules.

In module 140, if module 150 opens a valid result table, the total fields are reset to zero. Next, module 140 performs module 160 until there are no more invoice rows. Then, module 140 performs module 190 to close the result table.

The sales inquiry program   **Page 2**

```
PROCEDURE DIVISION.
*
 000-PROCESS-SALES-INQUIRIES.
*
     PERFORM 100-PROCESS-SALES-INQUIRY
         UNTIL END-OF-INQUIRIES.
     STOP RUN.
*
 100-PROCESS-SALES-INQUIRY.
*
     MOVE 'Y' TO CUSTOMER-FOUND-SW.
     PERFORM 110-ACCEPT-CUSTOMER-NUMBER.
     IF NOT END-OF-INQUIRIES
         PERFORM 120-GET-CUSTOMER-ROW
         PERFORM 130-DISPLAY-CUSTOMER-INFO
         IF CUSTOMER-FOUND
             PERFORM 140-GET-INVOICES-INFORMATION
             PERFORM 200-DISPLAY-SALES-TOTALS.
*
 110-ACCEPT-CUSTOMER-NUMBER.
*
     DISPLAY '-------------------------------------------------'.
     DISPLAY 'KEY IN THE NEXT CUSTOMER NUMBER AND PRESS ENTER,'.
     DISPLAY 'OR KEY IN 999999 AND PRESS ENTER TO QUIT.'.
     ACCEPT CUSTNO.
     IF CUSTNO = '999999'
         MOVE 'Y' TO END-OF-INQUIRIES-SW.
*
 120-GET-CUSTOMER-ROW.
*
     EXEC SQL
         SELECT   FNAME,  LNAME
             INTO :FNAME, :LNAME
             FROM MM01.CUSTOMER
             WHERE CUSTNO = :CUSTNO
     END-EXEC.
     IF SQLCODE NOT = 0
         MOVE 'N' TO CUSTOMER-FOUND-SW.
*
 130-DISPLAY-CUSTOMER-INFO.
*
     DISPLAY '-------------------------------------------------'.
     IF CUSTOMER-FOUND
         DISPLAY '  CUSTOMER ' CUSTNO ' -- ' FNAME ' ' LNAME
         DISPLAY ' '
     ELSE
         DISPLAY '  CUSTOMER NUMBER ' CUSTNO ' NOT FOUND.'.
*
 140-GET-INVOICES-INFORMATION.
*
     MOVE 'Y' TO VALID-CURSOR-SW.
     PERFORM 150-OPEN-INVOICE-CURSOR.
     IF VALID-CURSOR
         MOVE 'N' TO END-OF-INVOICES-SW
         MOVE ZERO TO INVOICES-COUNT
         MOVE ZERO TO INVOICES-TOTAL
         PERFORM 160-GET-INVOICE-INFORMATION
             UNTIL END-OF-INVOICES
         PERFORM 190-CLOSE-INVOICE-CURSOR.
*
```

Figure 2-12   The COBOL listing for the sales inquiry program (part 2 of 3)

In module 150, you can see the OPEN statement that actually creates the cursor-controlled result table that contains the invoice rows for the current customer. If the SQLCODE value that's returned isn't zero, though, this module turns off the valid-cursor switch so module 140 doesn't do any more processing for that customer number.

Module 160 is the one that is performed by module 140 until there are no more rows in the result table for the current customer. This module performs module 170 to fetch the data from the next invoice row. Then, if module 170 gets the next row, module 160 increments the total fields and performs module 180 to display the invoice data for that row.

In module 170, you can see the code that fetches the next row in the result table. After this statement is executed, an IF statement turns on the end-of-invoices switch if the SQLCODE value is 100 and turns off the valid-cursor switch if the SQLCODE isn't either 0 or 100.

In module 190, you can see that the valid-cursor switch is also turned off if the CLOSE statement for the cursor-controlled table doesn't return an SQLCODE value of zero to indicate that the close was successful. In module 200, if the valid-cursor switch has been turned off because the OPEN, FETCH, or CLOSE statement for the invoice table was unsuccessful, the module prints an error message. Otherwise, it prints the invoice totals for the current customer.

Although this sales inquiry program uses only one cursor, you should realize that a program can use more than one cursor at the same time. If, for example, you want to display line item information for each invoice displayed by this program, you could use a second cursor to process a line item result table. To do that, you include a DECLARE CURSOR statement that defines the line item result table, and you code OPEN, FETCH, and CLOSE statements to process the rows in that table for each invoice that's displayed.

The sales inquiry program   **Page 3**

```
 150-OPEN-INVOICE-CURSOR.
*
     EXEC SQL
         OPEN INVCURS
     END-EXEC.
     IF SQLCODE NOT = 0
         MOVE 'N' TO VALID-CURSOR-SW.
*
 160-GET-INVOICE-INFORMATION.
*
     PERFORM 170-FETCH-INVOICE-ROW.
     IF NOT END-OF-INVOICES
         IF VALID-CURSOR
             ADD 1        TO INVOICES-COUNT
             ADD INVTOTAL TO INVOICES-TOTAL
             PERFORM 180-DISPLAY-INVOICE-INFO.
*
 170-FETCH-INVOICE-ROW.
*
     EXEC SQL
         FETCH INVCURS
             INTO :INVNO, :INVDATE, :INVTOTAL
     END-EXEC.
     IF SQLCODE = 100
         MOVE 'Y' TO END-OF-INVOICES-SW
     ELSE
         IF SQLCODE NOT = 0
             MOVE 'N' TO VALID-CURSOR-SW.
*
 180-DISPLAY-INVOICE-INFO.
*
     MOVE INVTOTAL TO EDITED-TOTAL.
     DISPLAY ' INVOICE ' INVNO ' ' INVDATE ' ' EDITED-TOTAL.
*
 190-CLOSE-INVOICE-CURSOR.
*
     EXEC SQL
         CLOSE INVCURS
     END-EXEC.
     IF SQLCODE NOT = 0
         MOVE 'N' TO VALID-CURSOR-SW.
*
 200-DISPLAY-SALES-TOTALS.
*
     IF VALID-CURSOR
         MOVE INVOICES-TOTAL            TO EDITED-TOTAL
         MOVE INVOICES-COUNT            TO EDITED-COUNT
         IF INVOICES-TOTAL > 0
             DISPLAY '                            ------------'
         END-IF
         DISPLAY ' TOTAL BILLED          '      EDITED-TOTAL
         DISPLAY ' INVOICES ISSUED          ' EDITED-COUNT
         DISPLAY ' '
     ELSE
         DISPLAY ' '
         DISPLAY '     *** INVOICE RETRIEVAL ERROR   ***'
         DISPLAY ' '.
*
```

Figure 2-12   The COBOL listing for the sales inquiry program (part 3 of 3)

Perspective

Now that you've completed this chapter, you should be able to design and code a COBOL program that gets data from a one-row result table using a SELECT INTO statement or from a multi-row result table using a DB2 cursor. If you can do that, you understand how DB2 works and you're ready to continue.

In the next chapter, you'll learn how to use the INSERT, UPDATE, and DELETE statements to modify the data in a table. And in chapter 4, you'll learn how to use unions and joins to combine data from two or more tables into a single result table. When you finish those chapters, you'll have a complete view of what you can do with DB2.

Remember, though, that you can skip to section 3 whenever you need more information about developing and testing a DB2 program. In particular, you can skip to chapter 12 to learn how to use DB2I to prepare and test a program that you've coded. When you're done, you can return to section 1 to learn more about DB2 programming.

3

How to modify DB2 tables

In this chapter, you'll learn how to modify the data in a DB2 table. You'll also learn how to maintain the referential integrity of the tables in a database and how to recover from errors that take place during database processing. To help you learn these skills, this chapter presents two more complete COBOL programs.

How to use the UPDATE, DELETE, and INSERT statements

To modify the data in a DB2 table, you use three SQL statements. The UPDATE statement lets you modify the data in one or more rows. The DELETE statement lets you delete one or more rows. And the INSERT statement lets you add one or more rows.

How to use the UPDATE statement

Figure 3-1 presents the syntax for the UPDATE statement. Here, the WITH clause is included for completeness, even though it isn't presented in detail until chapter 11.

When you code an UPDATE statement, you use the SET clause to list the columns to be updated. After each of these column names, you code an equals sign followed by a host variable, a literal, an expression, or the keyword NULL to specify what the value in that column should be changed to.

The WHERE clause in the UPDATE statement identifies the row or rows to be updated. If more than one row is updated, all of the rows get updated with the data specified by the SET clause. This type of update can be referred to as a *searched update*, and all of the examples in this figure are searched updates.

In contrast, if you're updating a cursor-controlled result table, you can use the CURRENT OF phrase in the WHERE clause to update the current row in that table. This can be referred to as a *positioned update*, and this is illustrated in figure 3-3.

In the first example in figure 3-1, six columns in one row are updated by the data in the host variables for those columns. The WHERE clause in this example says that the updated row is the one with a customer number (CUSTNO) equal to the customer number in the corresponding host variable. Like the other examples in this figure, this is a searched update.

In the second example, all of the records with the zip code column equal to nine spaces have their zip codes changed to the literal 00000-0000. Because this is an alphanumeric literal, it is enclosed in quotation marks.

In the third example, the SET clause sets two fields to the values in expressions. The first expression adds the value in the host variable named INVTOTAL to the SALESTOT column in the row. The second expression adds the literal value 1 to the SALESCNT column in the row. Here again, the row that's updated is the one with customer number equal to the value in the corresponding host variable.

Not shown in these examples is the use of the NULL keyword, which puts a null value in a column. Note, however, that this can't be used for a column that has been defined as NOT NULL. If it is, the DB2 precompiler reports the error and ends with a return code of 4. If you ignore that and try to bind the program, the bind fails.

The syntax of the UPDATE statement

```
EXEC SQL
    UPDATE {table-name | view-name}
    SET column-name = {:host-var | literal | expression | NULL}
    [, column-name = {:host-var | literal | expression | NULL}]...
        [WHERE {search-condition [WITH isolation-level] |
                CURRENT OF cursor-name}]
END-EXEC.
```

A statement that changes six columns in one row of a table

```
EXEC SQL
    UPDATE  MM01.CUSTOMER
        SET FNAME  = :FNAME, LNAME  = :LNAME, ADDR   = :ADDR,
            CITY   = :CITY,  STATE  = :STATE, ZIPCODE = :ZIPCODE
        WHERE CUSTNO = :CUSTNO
END-EXEC.
```

A statement that changes one column in a set of rows to a literal value

```
EXEC SQL
    UPDATE   MM01.CUSTOMER
        SET    ZIPCODE = '00000-0000'
        WHERE ZIPCODE = '           '
END-EXEC.
```

A statement that changes two columns in one row to expression values

```
EXEC SQL
    UPDATE   MM01.CUSTHIST
        SET    SALESTOT = SALESTOT + :INVTOTAL,
               SALESCNT = SALESCNT + 1
        WHERE CUSTNO   = :CUSTNO
END-EXEC.
```

Description

- If more than one row is identified by the WHERE clause, they all get the changes in the SET clause. If the WHERE clause is omitted, all of the rows are updated. Although all the arithmetic operators are allowed in a SET clause expression, concatenation isn't allowed.

- The keyword NULL puts a null value in a column, but this can't be used for a column that's defined as NOT NULL.

- If a *check constraint* has been defined for a column, the value that the column is set to must satisfy the constraint.

- If the value in the SQLCODE field isn't zero, it means that the update failed so no changes were made to the table. When an update is successful, DB2 puts the number of records that were updated in the SQLERRD(3) field.

- The CURRENT OF phrase is used to update the current row in a cursor-controlled table.

Figure 3-1   How to use the UPDATE statement

Similarly, if a column has been defined with a *check constraint*, the value that it is set to must satisfy the constraint. If, for example, the check constraint for a customer number column says that the number must be between 400000 and 590000, a value of 700000 will cause the statement to fail.

When the UPDATE statement is successful, DB2 returns a value of zero in the SQLCODE field of the SQL communication area. Any other value means that the statement failed and no changes were made to the table. If the operation is successful, DB2 also puts a value that represents the number of records updated in the third member of the SQLERRD array in the communication area, which can be coded as SQLERRD(3).

How to use the DELETE statement

Figure 3-2 shows the syntax of the DELETE statement along with three examples. Here again, the WITH clause is included for completeness, even though it isn't presented in detail until chapter 11.

As you can see, the DELETE statement can delete one or more rows depending on the search condition in the WHERE clause. This can be referred to as a *searched delete*, and all of the examples in this figure are searched deletes.

In contrast, to delete the current row in a cursor-controlled result table, you code the CURRENT OF phrase in the WHERE clause. This can be referred to as a *positioned delete*, and you can see an example of this in the next figure.

As it does for the UPDATE statement, DB2 returns an SQLCODE value of zero for a successful deletion. It also returns the number of rows deleted in the third member of the SQLERRD array in the SQL communication area.

The syntax of the DELETE statement

```
EXEC SQL
    DELETE FROM {table-name | view-name}
        [WHERE {search-condition [WITH isolation-level] |
                CURRENT OF cursor-name}]
END-EXEC.
```

A DELETE statement that removes one row from a table

```
EXEC SQL
    DELETE FROM MM01.CUSTOMER
        WHERE CUSTNO = :CUSTNO
END-EXEC.
```

A DELETE statement that removes a set of rows from a table

```
EXEC SQL
    DELETE FROM MM01.CUSTOMER
        WHERE CUSTNO < '300000'
END-EXEC.
```

A DELETE statement that removes every row from a table

```
EXEC SQL
    DELETE FROM MM01.CUSTOMER
END-EXEC.
```

Description

- If more than one row is identified by the WHERE clause, all of them are deleted. If the WHERE clause is omitted, all records in the table are deleted.

- If the value in the SQLCODE field in the SQL communication area isn't zero, it means that the deletion failed. When a deletion is successful, DB2 puts the number of records that were deleted in the SQLERRD(3) field in the communication area.

- The CURRENT OF phrase is used to delete a row in a cursor-controlled table (see figure 3-3).

Figure 3-2   How to use the DELETE statement

How to update and delete rows in a cursor-controlled result table

In most programs that update or delete rows in a table, you don't need to use a cursor-controlled result table. When you do need to use one, though, you use the DECLARE CURSOR and OPEN CURSOR statements to open a cursor-controlled table. Next, you use the FETCH statement to move through the rows in the table. Then, when you reach a row that you want to update or delete, you issue an UPDATE or DELETE statement to perform a positioned update or delete.

Figure 3-3 illustrates an UPDATE and a DELETE statement that work with a DECLARE CURSOR statement. In these statements, you just use the CURRENT OF phrase in the WHERE clause to update or delete the current row in the table. If there isn't a current row, however, the statement won't work. This can happen if the result table hasn't been opened, if a row hasn't been fetched, or if the end of the table has been reached.

To be able to use the UPDATE statement to change the values in a base table through a cursor-controlled result table, you may have to identify the columns that can be modified. To do that, you code the FOR UPDATE OF clause in the DECLARE CURSOR statement as shown in this figure. This clause identifies all of the columns in the base table that you may need to change. However, if DB2's NOFOR precompiler option is in effect, you can omit the FOR UPDATE OF clause. This option became available with version 2.2 of DB2.

The WITH HOLD phrase that's coded in the DECLARE CURSOR statement in this figure prevents the cursor from being closed when a commit operation takes place. This is explained later in this chapter.

In the last portion of this figure, you can see some of the restrictions that apply to cursor-controlled tables. In brief, if the SELECT statement in a DECLARE CURSOR statement uses certain keywords, features, or a view, its cursor-controlled table becomes *read-only*. That means that you can't update or delete any of its rows.

A DECLARE CURSOR statement for a customer table

```
EXEC SQL
    DECLARE CUSTCURS CURSOR WITH HOLD FOR
        SELECT  CUSTNO, FNAME, LNAME, ADDR, CITY, STATE, ZIPCODE
          FROM MM01.CUSTOMER
          WHERE INVCUST < '300000'
        FOR UPDATE OF  FNAME, LNAME, ADDR, CITY, STATE, ZIPCODE
END-EXEC.
```

An UPDATE statement that changes the row at the current cursor position

```
EXEC SQL
    UPDATE  MM01.CUSTOMER
        SET FNAME   = :FNAME,    LNAME   = :LNAME,
            ADDR    = :ADDR,     CITY    = :CITY,
            STATE   = :STATE,    ZIPCODE = :ZIPCODE
        WHERE CURRENT OF CUSTCURS
END-EXEC.
```

A DELETE statement that removes the row at the current cursor position

```
EXEC SQL
    DELETE FROM MM01.CUSTOMER
        WHERE CURRENT OF CUSTCURS
END-EXEC.
```

Restrictions on UPDATE and DELETE statements

- You can't update or delete a row in a *read-only* table.

- A cursor-controlled table is a read-only table when it uses those DB2 features that are incompatible with updating and deleting. If, for example, a SELECT statement within a DECLARE CURSOR statement uses the DISTINCT keyword, its result table is read-only.

- A cursor-controlled table is read-only when the SELECT statement in its DE-CLARE CURSOR statement uses a union, a join, some categories of subqueries, a column function, or any of these keywords: DISTINCT, ORDER BY, GROUP BY, and HAVING. You'll learn about these features in section 2 of this book.

- A view is read-only when its SELECT statement uses a join, some types of subqueries, a column function, or any of these keywords: ORDER BY, GROUP BY, and HAVING.

Figure 3-3   How to update and delete rows in a cursor-controlled result table

How to use the basic INSERT statement

Figure 3-4 shows the syntax for the basic INSERT statement. This statement inserts just one row, and its VALUES clause provides the values that are used for the columns in the row. When you code the INSERT statement, you need to provide a value for each field in the row that is defined as NOT NULL or doesn't have a default value specified for it.

If you include the column names in the INTO clause as in the first example in this figure, you can code them in whatever order you prefer. Then, you need to code the values in the VALUES clause in the same order. If you omit the column names in the INTO clause, however, you need to code the values in the order that they were defined when the DB2 table was created.

When an INSERT statement is executed, DB2 returns a zero value in the SQLCODE field when the operation is successful. Any other value means that the operation failed.

Of particular interest, though, is an SQLCODE value of -803. This value means that the row you're trying to add contains a duplicate value in a column that has been defined as unique. If, for example, you try to add a new record with a primary key that equals the primary key value in a row that's already in the table, the operation fails. Then, you can change the key value and try the operation again.

The syntax of the INSERT statement with a VALUES clause

```
EXEC SQL
    INSERT INTO {table-name | view-name}
        [(column-name [, column-name]…)]
        VALUES ({:host-var | literal | NULL}
            [,{:host-var | literal | NULL}]…)
END-EXEC.
```

An INSERT statement that inserts seven columns into a new row

```
EXEC SQL
    INSERT INTO MM01.CUSTOMER
            ( CUSTNO,     FNAME,      LNAME,      ADDR,
              CITY,       STATE,      ZIPCODE)
    VALUES (:CUSTNO,    :FNAME,     :LNAME,     :ADDR,
             :CITY,     :STATE,     :ZIPCODE)
END-EXEC.
```

An INSERT statement that doesn't use column names in its INTO clause

```
EXEC SQL
    INSERT INTO MM01.CUSTOMER
    VALUES (:CUSTNO,    :FNAME,     :LNAME,     :ADDR,
             :CITY,     :STATE,     :ZIPCODE)
END-EXEC.
```

Description

- The INSERT statement with the VALUES clause is used to insert a single row into a table or view using the values provided or referenced.

- You can code the column names in the INTO clause in any order you wish, as long as you code the corresponding items in the VALUES clause in the same sequence.

- When the column names are omitted from the INTO clause, DB2 assumes that the VALUES clause will supply values for each column in the target table in the order they were defined when the DB2 table was created.

- You don't need to provide a value for a column that has been defined with a default value or for a column that allows null values. If a column has been defined as NOT NULL and without a default value, though, you must supply a value for it.

- The keyword NULL puts a null value in a column, but this can't be used for a column that's defined as NOT NULL.

- If a check constraint has been defined for a column, the value that's supplied for the column must satisfy the constraint.

- An SQLCODE value of -803 means that the statement failed because the row to be inserted contained a duplicate value in a column that is defined as unique.

Figure 3-4   How to use the basic INSERT statement

How to use an INSERT statement with a subquery

Figure 3-5 shows how to use a SELECT statement within an INSERT statement. In this case, the INSERT statement doesn't include a VALUES column, and the SELECT statement can be referred to as a *subquery*. When the INSERT statement is executed, one or more rows from the table named in the subquery are added to the table named in the INTO clause. This can be referred to as a *mass insert*.

In the first example in this figure, the subquery selects rows from a customer table (CUSTOMER) and inserts them into a customer history table (CUSTHIST). If you want to move the rows from the first table to the second table, you can code a DELETE statement right after the INSERT statement as shown in the second example.

When you use a subquery, the column names in the SELECT statement must create a result table that matches the table that's going to receive the inserted rows. That means the number of columns in both tables must be the same and the corresponding columns must have compatible data types and lengths. When the statement is successful, the SQLCODE value is zero and SQLERRD(3) receives a value equal to the number of rows that have been inserted. In chapter 9, you can learn more about the use of subqueries.

Incidentally, if you've worked with VSAM space management, the term "mass insert" may sound familiar. However, VSAM's MASSINSERT option has nothing to do with DB2's mass insert capability.

The syntax of the INSERT statement with a subquery

```
EXEC SQL
    INSERT INTO {table-name | view-name}
        [(column-name [, column-name]…)]
            SELECT-statement [WITH isolation-level]
END-EXEC.
```

An INSERT statement that uses a subquery

```
EXEC SQL
    INSERT INTO MM01.CUSTHIST
        SELECT *
            FROM MM01.CUSTOMER
            WHERE CUSTNO < '300000'
  END-EXEC.
```

INSERT and DELETE statements that move rows from one table to another

```
EXEC SQL
    INSERT INTO MM01.OLDHIST
        SELECT *
            FROM MM01.CUSTOMER
            WHERE CUSTNO < '300000'
END-EXEC.
EXEC SQL
    DELETE FROM MM01.CUSTOMER
        WHERE CUSTNO < '300000'
END-EXEC.
```

Description

- The INSERT statement with a *subquery* is used to insert one or more rows into a table or view using values from other tables or views. A subquery is a SELECT statement that's used within another SQL statement (see chapter 9).

- All of the rows selected by the subquery in an INSERT statement are added to the table named in the INTO clause. This can be referred to as a *mass insert*.

- The column names specified in the subquery must create a result table that matches the target table specified in the INTO clause.

- To move rows from one table to another, you can code an INSERT statement with a subquery followed by a DELETE statement as shown by the second example above.

- When the INSERT statement is successful (SQLCODE equal zero), DB2 puts the number of records inserted in the SQLERRD(3) field in the SQL communication area.

Figure 3-5   How to use an INSERT statement with a subquery

A COBOL program that maintains a DB2 table

To illustrate the use of the UPDATE, DELETE, and INSERT statements, this chapter now presents a simple COBOL program that maintains the data in a customer table. This is a batch program, not an interactive program, that gets the maintenance data from a VSAM file of transaction records.

The transaction record and the customer table

Figure 3-6 presents the COBOL code that describes the transaction record as well as the DCLGEN output for the customer table that's going to be maintained. The first field in each transaction record is a transaction code that tells whether the record represents an addition, update, or deletion.

Then, the remaining characters in each transaction record provide the data that's required for the transaction. For a deletion, that data consists of just the customer number field. For an update or addition, that data consists of the customer number and the data for each field in the updated or inserted record. To keep this program simple, the data for all the fields except the customer number is treated as a single field (CTR-CUSTOMER-DETAILS). The assumption is that this is a group field that contains the data for all of the columns in a customer row.

The DCLGEN output in this figure is the same output that you've seen in the previous chapters. After the six-character CUSTNO column, the remaining six fields account for a total of 112 characters. And this of course corresponds to the transaction data in the transaction records.

The COBOL description of the transaction record

```
01   CUSTOMER-TRANSACTION-RECORD.
*
     05   CTR-TRANSACTION-CODE      PIC X.
     05   CTR-TRANSACTION-DATA.
          10   CTR-CUSTOMER-NUMBER    PIC X(6).
          10   CTR-CUSTOMER-DETAILS   PIC X(112).
```

The DCLGEN output for the customer table

```
******************************************************************
* DCLGEN TABLE(MM01.CUSTOMER)                                    *
*        LIBRARY(MM01.DB2.DCLGENS(CUSTOMER))                     *
*        ACTION(REPLACE)                                         *
*        LANGUAGE(COBOL)                                         *
*        STRUCTURE(CUSTOMER-ROW)                                 *
*        QUOTE                                                   *
* ... IS THE DCLGEN COMMAND THAT MADE THE FOLLOWING STATEMENTS   *
******************************************************************
     EXEC SQL DECLARE MM01.CUSTOMER TABLE
     ( CUSTNO                      CHAR(6)  NOT NULL,
       FNAME                       CHAR(20) NOT NULL,
       LNAME                       CHAR(30) NOT NULL,
       ADDR                        CHAR(30) NOT NULL,
       CITY                        CHAR(20) NOT NULL,
       STATE                       CHAR(2)  NOT NULL,
       ZIPCODE                     CHAR(10) NOT NULL
     ) END-EXEC.
******************************************************************
* COBOL DECLARATION FOR TABLE MM01.CUSTOMER                      *
******************************************************************
01   CUSTOMER-ROW.
     10 CUSTNO              PIC X(6).
     10 FNAME               PIC X(20).
     10 LNAME               PIC X(30).
     10 ADDR                PIC X(30).
     10 CITY                PIC X(20).
     10 STATE               PIC X(2).
     10 ZIPCODE             PIC X(10).
******************************************************************
* THE NUMBER OF COLUMNS DESCRIBED BY THIS DECLARATION IS 7       *
******************************************************************
```

Description

- For this program, the transaction records in a VSAM entry-sequenced data set are used to maintain the records in a DB2 customer table.

- The CTR-TRANSACTION-CODE field in each transaction record indicates whether the record represents an update, deletion, or addition to the customer table.

- The 118 characters in CTR-TRANSACTION-DATA in the transaction record description correspond to the 118 characters in each row of the CUSTOMER table.

Figure 3-6   The transaction record and the customer table

The structure chart

Figure 3-7 presents the structure chart for this program. Here, the top-level module (000) performs the module at the second level (100) one time for each transaction record. Then, module 100 performs whatever third-level modules are needed to do the processing for each transaction record.

To read each transaction record, module 100 performs module 110. Then, for an addition transaction, module 100 performs module 120; for an update, it performs module 130; and for a deletion, it performs module 140. If the transaction code is invalid or if the operation of module 120, 130, or 140 is unsuccessful, module 100 also performs module 150. This module writes the original transaction record to a new VSAM file of invalid (bad) transactions.

The structure chart

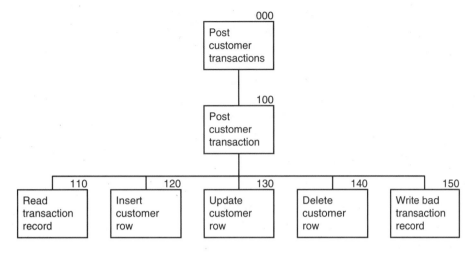

Description

- Module 000 in this structure chart performs module 100 until there are no more transaction records to be processed.

- Module 100 performs module 110 to read one transaction record. Then, based on the value in the transaction code, module 100 performs module 120, 130, or 140.

- Module 100 performs module 150 to write a transaction in the invalid transaction file (1) if the transaction code in the transaction record is invalid or (2) if module 120, 130, or 140 can't complete its operation on the customer table (SQLCODE not equal to zero).

Figure 3-7   The structure chart for the update program

The COBOL listing

Figure 3-8 presents the COBOL code for this program in three parts. If you have much COBOL experience, you should be able to follow it without any difficulty. But in case you're interested, here are some of the highlights.

In the File-Control paragraph of the Environment Division, you can see the COBOL SELECT statements for the two VSAM files: the customer transaction file (CUSTTRAN) and the invalid transaction file (BADTRAN). In the File Section of the Data Division, you can also see the file and record descriptions for the records in these files. As you would expect, both files are the same length (119 characters).

In the Working-Storage Section, you can see that this program uses two switches. The first is turned on when there are no more transaction records in the transaction file. The second is turned on whenever a transaction record is valid. After the switches, you can see two SQL INCLUDE statements. The first includes the DCLGEN output for the customer table. The second includes the SQL communication area.

The primary control module in this program is module 100. After it performs module 110 to read a transaction record, it uses an EVALUATE statement to evaluate the transaction code. It then performs module 120, 130, or 140 based on that evaluation. Or, it turns the valid transaction switch off when the transaction code isn't valid. The IF statement that follows this EVALUATE statement then performs module 150 if the valid transaction switch isn't on. As you can see in modules 120, 130, and 140, this switch also gets turned off when an SQL operation fails.

In module 120, the first statement moves the data from the transaction record to the customer row that represents the host structure that's described by the DCLGEN output. Then, an SQL statement inserts that data into a new row in the customer table. If the operation is successful, DB2 returns a value of zero to the SQLCODE field in the SQL communication area so the IF statement that follows doesn't do anything. But if the value isn't zero, the IF statement turns the valid transaction switch off, which means that module 100 performs module 150 to write the transaction to the invalid transaction file.

Similarly, module 130 starts by moving the transaction data to the customer row of the host structure. Next, an SQL statement performs the update operation. Then, an IF statement turns off the valid transaction switch if the operation fails.

In contrast to modules 120 and 130, module 140 deletes a record so it doesn't require all of the transaction data. As a result, its first statement moves just the customer number from the transaction record to the host variable. But otherwise, it works the same. After an SQL statement performs the deletion, an IF statement turns off the valid transaction switch if the operation fails.

The update program

```
IDENTIFICATION DIVISION.
*
PROGRAM-ID.      UPDTCUST.
*
ENVIRONMENT DIVISION.
*
INPUT-OUTPUT SECTION.
*
FILE-CONTROL.
*
    SELECT CUSTTRAN ASSIGN TO UT-S-CUSTTRAN.
    SELECT BADTRAN  ASSIGN TO UT-S-BADTRAN.
*
DATA DIVISION.
*
FILE SECTION.
*
FD  CUSTTRAN
    LABEL RECORDS ARE STANDARD
    RECORD CONTAINS 119 CHARACTERS.
*
01  CUSTOMER-TRANSACTION-RECORD.
*
    05  CTR-TRANSACTION-CODE        PIC X.
    05  CTR-TRANSACTION-DATA.
        10  CTR-CUSTOMER-NUMBER     PIC X(6).
        10  CTR-CUSTOMER-DETAILS    PIC X(112).
*
FD  BADTRAN
    LABEL RECORDS ARE STANDARD
    RECORD CONTAINS 119 CHARACTERS.
*
01  BAD-TRANSACTION-RECORD.
*
    05  BTR-TRANSACTION-CODE        PIC X.
    05  BTR-TRANSACTION-DATA        PIC X(118).
*
WORKING-STORAGE SECTION.
*
01  SWITCHES.
*
    05  END-OF-TRANSACTIONS-SW      PIC X    VALUE 'N'.
        88  END-OF-TRANSACTIONS              VALUE 'Y'.
    05  VALID-TRANSACTION-SW        PIC X    VALUE 'Y'.
        88  VALID-TRANSACTION               VALUE 'Y'.
*
    EXEC SQL
        INCLUDE CUSTOMER
    END-EXEC.
*
    EXEC SQL
        INCLUDE SQLCA
    END-EXEC.
*
```

Figure 3-8   The COBOL listing for the update program (part 1 of 3)

The update program

```
 PROCEDURE DIVISION.
*
 000-POST-CUST-TRANSACTIONS.
*
     OPEN INPUT  CUSTTRAN
         OUTPUT BADTRAN.
     PERFORM 100-POST-CUST-TRANSACTION
         UNTIL END-OF-TRANSACTIONS.
     CLOSE CUSTTRAN
         BADTRAN.
     STOP RUN.
*
 100-POST-CUST-TRANSACTION.
*
     MOVE 'Y' TO VALID-TRANSACTION-SW.
     PERFORM 110-READ-TRANSACTION-RECORD.
     IF NOT END-OF-TRANSACTIONS
         EVALUATE CTR-TRANSACTION-CODE
             WHEN 'A'   PERFORM 120-INSERT-CUSTOMER-ROW
             WHEN 'R'   PERFORM 130-UPDATE-CUSTOMER-ROW
             WHEN 'D'   PERFORM 140-DELETE-CUSTOMER-ROW
             WHEN OTHER MOVE 'N' TO VALID-TRANSACTION-SW
         END-EVALUATE
         IF NOT VALID-TRANSACTION
             PERFORM 150-WRITE-BAD-TRANS-RECORD.
*
 110-READ-TRANSACTION-RECORD.
*
     READ CUSTTRAN
         AT END
             MOVE 'Y' TO END-OF-TRANSACTIONS-SW.
*
 120-INSERT-CUSTOMER-ROW.
*
     MOVE CTR-TRANSACTION-DATA TO CUSTOMER-ROW.
     EXEC SQL
         INSERT INTO MM01.CUSTOMER
                 ( CUSTNO,    FNAME,     LNAME,     ADDR,
                 CITY,      STATE,     ZIPCODE)
             VALUES (:CUSTNO,  :FNAME,    :LNAME,    :ADDR,
                 :CITY,    :STATE,    :ZIPCODE)
     END-EXEC.
     IF SQLCODE NOT = 0
         MOVE 'N' TO VALID-TRANSACTION-SW.
*
```

Figure 3-8   The COBOL listing for the update program (part 2 of 3)

The update program   **Page 3**

```
130-UPDATE-CUSTOMER-ROW.
*
    MOVE CTR-TRANSACTION-DATA TO CUSTOMER-ROW.
    EXEC SQL
        UPDATE MM01.CUSTOMER
            SET FNAME   = :FNAME,
                LNAME   = :LNAME,
                ADDR    = :ADDR,
                CITY    = :CITY,
                STATE   = :STATE,
                ZIPCODE = :ZIPCODE
        WHERE   CUSTNO  = :CUSTNO
    END-EXEC.
    IF SQLCODE NOT = 0
        MOVE 'N' TO VALID-TRANSACTION-SW.
*
140-DELETE-CUSTOMER-ROW.
*
    MOVE CTR-CUSTOMER-NUMBER TO CUSTNO.
    EXEC SQL
        DELETE FROM MM01.CUSTOMER
            WHERE CUSTNO = :CUSTNO
    END-EXEC.
    IF SQLCODE NOT = 0
        MOVE 'N' TO VALID-TRANSACTION-SW.
*
150-WRITE-BAD-TRANS-RECORD.
*
    WRITE BAD-TRANSACTION-RECORD
        FROM CUSTOMER-TRANSACTION-RECORD.
*
```

Figure 3-8   The COBOL listing for the update program (part 3 of 3)

How DB2 provides for referential integrity and error recovery

When you write a program that issues INSERT, UPDATE, and DELETE statements, you need to be aware of DB2's referential integrity and error recovery features. The referential integrity feature helps you maintain the relationships between the rows in related tables. The error recovery feature lets you issue a COMMIT statement when a group of successful transactions is ready to be written to disk and a ROLLBACK statement when a group of transactions needs to be reversed.

How DB2 provides for referential integrity

Figure 3-9 presents the concepts and terms of the *referential integrity* feature. This feature can be used to enforce the integrity of the relationships between a *parent table* and a *dependent table*.

To enable this feature, the database administrator adds clauses to the CREATE TABLE statements that establish the *referential constraints* between the parent and the dependent table. In the examples in this figure, the PRIMARY KEY clause for the CUSTOMER table identifies the CUSTNO column as the *primary key*. Then, the FOREIGN KEY clause for the INVOICE table identifies the INVCUST column as the *foreign key* that refers to the CUSTNO column in the CUSTOMER table. The ON DELETE option for this foreign key is CASCADE, which means that any deletions of parent rows should be *cascaded* to the related rows in the invoice table.

Later, when an application program issues an INSERT, UPDATE, or DELETE statement that affects these tables, DB2 enforces the referential constraints that have been established by the CREATE TABLE statements. In particular, you can't add a row to a dependent table unless it has a foreign key that matches a value in the parent table. And you can't change the primary key of a row in a parent table that has matching foreign keys in a dependent table.

What happens when you try to delete a row in a parent table? That depends on the setting of the ON DELETE option. If the RESTRICT option is on, you can't delete a row in the parent table that has matching rows in a dependent table. If the CASCADE option is on, the row in the parent table is deleted along with all matching rows in the dependent table. And if the SET TO NULL option is on, the row in the parent table is deleted and the foreign keys in all related records in the dependent table are set to null values (if the foreign key isn't created as a NOT NULL column).

If you're an application programmer, that may be all you need to know about referential integrity because DB2 automatically enforces the referential constraints that have been established for related tables. Sometimes, though, you need to know how the ON DELETE option for a table is set. If it's set to RESTRICT and you need to delete a parent record and its related records, you need to delete the dependent records first, then the parent record.

CREATE TABLE statements for a parent and a dependent table

```
CREATE TABLE MM01.CUSTOMER
    (CUSTNO    CHAR(6)    NOT NULL,
     FNAME     CHAR(20)   NOT NULL,
     LNAME     CHAR(30)   NOT NULL,
     ADDR      CHAR(30)   NOT NULL,
     CITY      CHAR(20)   NOT NULL,
     STATE     CHAR(2)    NOT NULL,
     ZIPCODE   CHAR(10)   NOT NULL,
     PRIMARY KEY (CUSTNO))
 IN DATABASE MMADBV


CREATE TABLE MM01.INVOICE
    (INVCUST   CHAR(6)        NOT NULL,
     INVNO     CHAR(6)        NOT NULL,
     INVDATE   DATE           NOT NULL,
     INVSUBT   DECIMAL(9,2)   NOT NULL,
     INVSHIP   DECIMAL(7,2)   NOT NULL,
     INVTAX    DECIMAL(7,2)   NOT NULL,
     INVTOTAL  DECIMAL(9,2)   NOT NULL,
     INVPROM   CHAR(10)       NOT NULL,
     PRIMARY KEY (INVNO),
     FOREIGN KEY CUSTNO (INVCUST)
        REFERENCES MM01.CUSTOMER
        ON DELETE CASCADE)
 IN DATABASE MMADBV
```

The INVCUST column in each row in the INVOICE table must equal a CUSTNO column in one row of the CUSTOMER table.

The deletion of a row in the CUSTOMER table cascades to the related rows in the INVOICE table.

Description

- *Referential integrity* means that each row in a *dependent table* must have a *foreign key* that is equal to a *primary key* in the *parent table*.

- Starting with DB2 release 2.1, CREATE TABLE statements can be coded so DB2 enforces referential integrity. Before that, the programmer was responsible for maintaining this integrity.

- When an SQL statement fails because it violates the *referential constraints* that have been established by the CREATE TABLE statements, DB2 returns an SQLCODE value in the -500 range.

The referential constraints

- When you use the INSERT statement, each row in a parent table must have a unique primary key, and each row in a dependent table must have a foreign key that's equal to a primary key in the parent table.

- When you use the UPDATE statement, the primary key in a parent table can't be changed if any rows in dependent tables refer to it.

- When you use the DELETE statement to delete a row in a parent table, the constraint option determines how referential integrity is enforced. With the CASCADE option, all related rows in dependent tables are deleted too. With the RESTRICT option, a row in a parent table can't be deleted if it has related rows in a dependent table. With the SET TO NULL option, the foreign keys in related rows are set to null values.

Figure 3-9   How DB2 provides for referential integrity

How to use the COMMIT and ROLLBACK statements for error recovery

It may surprise you to learn that DB2 doesn't write each change to a table on disk right after each INSERT, UPDATE, or DELETE statement is issued by a program. Instead, DB2 keeps track of the changes in virtual storage until a *commit point* is reached. Then, all the changes since the last commit point are written to the disk. This is summarized in figure 3-10.

The transactions that are held between the commit points make up a *unit of recovery*, or a *unit of work*. Until a unit of recovery has been committed, all of its transactions can be *rolled back*, or reversed. This is useful when an error occurs while processing a related group of transactions. Then, if one of the transactions in the group fails, you can roll back all of the related transactions. This helps maintain the validity of the data in the database.

To illustrate, suppose you're writing an update program that adds rows to an invoice and an invoice line item table. In this case, you don't want to add any rows to the parent invoice table unless you also add the dependent invoice line item rows. Then, if an INSERT function for the line item table fails, you can use the ROLLBACK statement to roll back all of the related transactions. But if all the transactions in the group are processed without error, you can use the COMMIT statement to commit the transactions in that unit of recovery.

If you don't include any COMMIT statements in a program, all of the transactions are held in the unit of recovery until the program reaches normal termination. In general, though, you shouldn't code a program without COMMITs because the larger the unit of recovery is, the more system resources the program uses. In addition, portions of the table that are affected by the unit of recovery are locked, which means that other programs can't access those rows. In all programs, then, you should include COMMIT statements that keep the unit of recovery at an appropriate size.

What is an appropriate or optimum size for a unit of recovery? That depends on factors like how many other users are going to be using the affected tables at the same time and how large the affected tables are. For some programs, you may need to issue a COMMIT statement after each group of related transactions has been successfully processed. For other programs, you may need to issue a COMMIT statement after a specific number of unrelated transactions has been processed like 10, 100, or 1000 transactions. When in doubt, you can often get some useful advice from the database administrator.

When you use COMMIT with a cursor-controlled result table, you usually code the WITH HOLD phrase in the DECLARE CURSOR statement as shown in figure 3-3. Otherwise, the cursor is closed whenever the program issues a COMMIT statement. When you code the WITH HOLD phrase, though, you can issue a FETCH statement after a COMMIT statement to move the cursor to the next row that hasn't been processed and continue processing.

The syntax of the SQL COMMIT statement

```
EXEC SQL
    COMMIT [WORK]
END-EXEC.
```

The syntax of the SQL ROLLBACK statement

```
EXEC SQL
    ROLLBACK [WORK]
END-EXEC.
```

Description

*   When a program issues an INSERT, UPDATE, or DELETE statement, DB2 doesn't immediately write the table modification to disk. Instead, it logs the changes in a data set and keeps track of the changes in virtual storage buffers.

*   When DB2 reaches a *commit point*, it writes the logged changes to the disk. An *implicit commit point* occurs when a program terminates normally by reaching a STOP or GOBACK statement. An *explicit commit point* occurs when a program issues an SQL COMMIT statement.

*   A *unit of recovery* (or *unit of work*) consists of the transactions that are logged between commit points.

*   DB2 *rolls back* (or reverses) all of the transactions in a unit of recovery when a program terminates abnormally or when a program issues a ROLLBACK statement.

*   If a program doesn't include any COMMIT statements, none of the transactions are committed until the program terminates normally. This, however, can seriously degrade performance. As a result, a production program should issue a COMMIT statement whenever a unit of recovery reaches an appropriate size.

*   You don't use COMMIT statements in CICS or IMS/DC programs because both are their own transaction managers. Instead, you use the commit mechanisms that they provide (the SYNCPOINT command in CICS; the CHKP or SYNC call in IMS). These mechanisms, however, have the same effect on a DB2 unit of recovery.

Special considerations for using cursor-controlled tables

*   When you use the COMMIT statement with a cursor-controlled table, you usually code the WITH HOLD clause in the DECLARE CURSOR statement. Then, after each COMMIT statement, you code a FETCH statement to move the cursor to the row following the one the cursor was on before the commit operation. However, the WITH HOLD clause causes locks to be held across commits. This can increase the number of timeouts and affect availability. See chapter 11 for details.

*   If the DECLARE CURSOR statement doesn't include the WITH HOLD clause, the cursor-controlled table is closed each time a COMMIT statement is issued. To continue, the program must open the cursor.

Figure 3-10   How to use the COMMIT and ROLLBACK statements

An enhanced COBOL program

To illustrate the use of the COMMIT and ROLLBACK statements, the next two figures present the structure chart and COBOL listing for an enhanced version of the update program in figure 3-8. This program issues a COMMIT statement after ten transactions have been successfully processed. It also issues a ROLLBACK statement when an unrecoverable error occurs.

The structure chart

Figure 3-11 presents the structure chart for this program. It is like the structure chart for the earlier version of the update program, but with two additional modules. Module 160 commits a unit of recovery when it consists of ten valid transactions, while module 200 rolls back a unit of recovery when an unrecoverable error occurs.

The structure chart

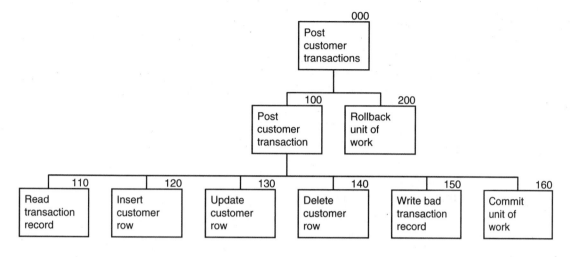

Description

- To provide for the rollback and commit functions, modules 200 and 160 have been added to the structure chart for the previous version of this update program.

- Module 160 is performed by module 100 whenever a unit of recovery consists of 10 valid transactions.

- Module 200 is performed by module 000 whenever an unrecoverable error occurs. After module 200 is performed, the program ends.

Figure 3-11   The structure chart for the enhanced update program

The COBOL listing

Figure 3-12 presents the COBOL listing for this enhanced update program. Here, the additions and changes to the earlier program are shaded so you can spot them easily.

In the Working-Storage Section, you can see that a third switch has been coded: ROLLBACK-REQUIRED-SW. This switch is turned on when the SQLCODE that's returned for a transaction indicates an unrecoverable error. Module 000 examines this switch to determine whether or not to perform module 200.

You can also see three new count fields in the Working-Storage Section. These keep counts of the valid transactions, the invalid transactions, and the number of transactions in the unit of work. Each time the unit-of-work count reaches ten, the program performs module 160 to commit the unit.

The enhanced update program   **Page 1**

```
IDENTIFICATION DIVISION.
*
PROGRAM-ID.    UPDTROLL.
*
ENVIRONMENT DIVISION.
*
INPUT-OUTPUT SECTION.
*
FILE-CONTROL.
*
    SELECT CUSTTRAN ASSIGN TO UT-S-CUSTTRAN.
    SELECT BADTRAN  ASSIGN TO UT-S-BADTRAN.
*
DATA DIVISION.
*
FILE SECTION.
*
FD  CUSTTRAN
    LABEL RECORDS ARE STANDARD
    RECORD CONTAINS 119 CHARACTERS.
*
01  CUSTOMER-TRANSACTION-RECORD.
*
    05  CTR-TRANSACTION-CODE        PIC X.
    05  CTR-TRANSACTION-DATA.
        10  CTR-CUSTOMER-NUMBER     PIC X(6).
        10  CTR-CUSTOMER-DETAILS    PIC X(112).
*
FD  BADTRAN
    LABEL RECORDS ARE STANDARD
    RECORD CONTAINS 119 CHARACTERS.
*
01  BAD-TRANSACTION-RECORD.
*
    05  BTR-TRANSACTION-CODE        PIC X.
    05  BTR-TRANSACTION-DATA        PIC X(118).
*
WORKING-STORAGE SECTION.
*
01  SWITCHES.
*
    05  END-OF-TRANSACTIONS-SW  PIC X    VALUE 'N'.
        88  END-OF-TRANSACTIONS          VALUE 'Y'.
    05  VALID-TRANSACTION-SW    PIC X    VALUE 'Y'.
        88  VALID-TRANSACTION            VALUE 'Y'.
    05  ROLLBACK-REQUIRED-SW    PIC X    VALUE 'N'.
        88  ROLLBACK-REQUIRED            VALUE 'Y'.
*
01  COUNT-FIELDS                COMP.
*
    05  VALID-TRANS-COUNT       PIC S9(9)    VALUE 0.
    05  INVALID-TRANS-COUNT     PIC S9(9)    VALUE 0.
    05  UNIT-OF-WORK-COUNT      PIC S9(9)    VALUE 0.
*
```

Figure 3-12   The COBOL listing for the enhanced update program (part 1 of 4)

In module 000, you can see the code for performing module 200 when an unrecoverable error occurs. You can also see the code for displaying the valid and invalid transaction counts when the program ends.

In module 100, you can see the code for performing module 160 when the unit of work reaches ten successful transactions. You can also see the code for incrementing the valid transaction, invalid transaction, and unit-of-work counts. After module 100 performs module 160, the unit-of-work count is reset to zero in preparation for the next unit of work.

In module 120, you can see the IF statement that sets the three switches used by this program. If the SQLCODE that's returned by DB2 is -803, which means that the program tried to add a row with a duplicate key, only the valid transaction switch is set to No. As a result, the program writes the transaction record to the bad transaction file and continues. However, if the SQLCODE is any other negative value, the end-of-transactions switch and the rollback-required switches are turned on too. This means that the program will end.

Similarly, in modules 130 and 140, you can see that the valid-transaction switch is turned off when the SQLCODE is +100, which means that the row to be updated or deleted doesn't exist. In this case, the program writes the transaction record to the bad transaction file and continues. But if the SQLCODE is any negative value, the other switches are turned on so the program will roll back the current unit of recovery and end.

Finally, in modules 160 and 200, you can see the use of the COMMIT and ROLLBACK statements. Although coding them is trivial, the difficulty in most programs is establishing the conditions for when they should be used. Notice that neither the COMMIT or ROLLBACK statement specifies a table or cursor so they commit or roll back the transactions for all the tables that the program is working with.

The enhanced update program   **Page 2**

```
    EXEC SQL
        INCLUDE CUSTOMER
    END-EXEC.
*
    EXEC SQL
        INCLUDE SQLCA
    END-EXEC.
*
 PROCEDURE DIVISION.
*
 000-POST-CUST-TRANSACTIONS.
*
    OPEN INPUT  CUSTTRAN
         OUTPUT BADTRAN.
    PERFORM 100-POST-CUST-TRANSACTION
        UNTIL END-OF-TRANSACTIONS.
    IF ROLLBACK-REQUIRED
        PERFORM 200-ROLLBACK-UNIT-OF-WORK
        DISPLAY '****** UPDATE NOT SUCCESSFUL ******'
        DISPLAY '          SQLCODE ' SQLCODE
        DISPLAY '******   ROLLBACK PERFORMED   ******'
        SUBTRACT UNIT-OF-WORK-COUNT FROM VALID-TRANS-COUNT
    ELSE
        DISPLAY '******    UPDATE SUCCESSFUL    ******'.
    CLOSE CUSTTRAN
          BADTRAN.
    DISPLAY VALID-TRANS-COUNT
            ' VALID TRANSACTION RECORDS PROCESSED.'.
    DISPLAY INVALID-TRANS-COUNT
            ' INVALID TRANSACTION RECORDS PROCESSED.'.
    STOP RUN.
*
 100-POST-CUST-TRANSACTION.
*
    MOVE 'Y' TO VALID-TRANSACTION-SW.
    PERFORM 110-READ-TRANSACTION-RECORD.
    IF NOT END-OF-TRANSACTIONS
        MOVE CTR-TRANSACTION-DATA TO CUSTOMER-ROW
        EVALUATE CTR-TRANSACTION-CODE
            WHEN 'A'   PERFORM 120-INSERT-CUSTOMER-ROW
            WHEN 'R'   PERFORM 130-UPDATE-CUSTOMER-ROW
            WHEN 'D'   PERFORM 140-DELETE-CUSTOMER-ROW
            WHEN OTHER MOVE 'N' TO VALID-TRANSACTION-SW
        END-EVALUATE
        IF NOT VALID-TRANSACTION
            ADD 1 TO INVALID-TRANS-COUNT
            PERFORM 150-WRITE-BAD-TRANS-RECORD
        ELSE
            ADD 1 TO VALID-TRANS-COUNT
            ADD 1 TO UNIT-OF-WORK-COUNT
            IF UNIT-OF-WORK-COUNT = 10
                PERFORM 160-COMMIT-UNIT-OF-WORK
                MOVE 0 TO UNIT-OF-WORK-COUNT.
*
```

Figure 3-12   The COBOL listing for the enhanced update program (part 2 of 4)

The enhanced update program

```
110-READ-TRANSACTION-RECORD.
*
    READ CUSTTRAN
        AT END
            MOVE 'Y' TO END-OF-TRANSACTIONS-SW.
*
120-INSERT-CUSTOMER-ROW.
*
    EXEC SQL
        INSERT INTO MM01.CUSTOMER
                   ( CUSTNO,    FNAME,      LNAME,      ADDR,
                     CITY,      STATE,      ZIPCODE)
            VALUES (:CUSTNO,   :FNAME,     :LNAME,     :ADDR,
                    :CITY,     :STATE,     :ZIPCODE)
    END-EXEC.
    IF SQLCODE = -803
        MOVE 'N' TO VALID-TRANSACTION-SW
    ELSE
        IF SQLCODE < 0
            MOVE 'N' TO VALID-TRANSACTION-SW
            MOVE 'Y' TO END-OF-TRANSACTIONS-SW
            MOVE 'Y' TO ROLLBACK-REQUIRED-SW.
*
130-UPDATE-CUSTOMER-ROW.
*
    EXEC SQL
        UPDATE MM01.CUSTOMER
            SET FNAME   = :FNAME,
                LNAME   = :LNAME,
                ADDR    = :ADDR,
                CITY    = :CITY,
                STATE   = :STATE,
                ZIPCODE = :ZIPCODE
            WHERE  CUSTNO  = :CUSTNO
    END-EXEC.
    IF SQLCODE = +100
        MOVE 'N' TO VALID-TRANSACTION-SW
    ELSE
        IF SQLCODE < 0
            MOVE 'N' TO VALID-TRANSACTION-SW
            MOVE 'Y' TO END-OF-TRANSACTIONS-SW
            MOVE 'Y' TO ROLLBACK-REQUIRED-SW.
*
```

Figure 3-12   The COBOL listing for the enhanced update program (part 3 of 4)

The enhanced update program   **Page 4**

```
140-DELETE-CUSTOMER-ROW.
*
    EXEC SQL
        DELETE FROM MM01.CUSTOMER
            WHERE CUSTNO = :CUSTNO
    END-EXEC.
    IF SQLCODE = +100
        MOVE 'N' TO VALID-TRANSACTION-SW
    ELSE
        IF SQLCODE < 0
            MOVE 'N' TO VALID-TRANSACTION-SW
            MOVE 'Y' TO END-OF-TRANSACTIONS-SW
            MOVE 'Y' TO ROLLBACK-REQUIRED-SW.
*
150-WRITE-BAD-TRANS-RECORD.
*
    WRITE BAD-TRANSACTION-RECORD
        FROM CUSTOMER-TRANSACTION-RECORD.
*
160-COMMIT-UNIT-OF-WORK.
*
    EXEC SQL
        COMMIT
    END-EXEC.
*
200-ROLLBACK-UNIT-OF-WORK.
*
    EXEC SQL
        ROLLBACK
    END-EXEC.
*
```

Figure 3-12   The COBOL listing for the enhanced update program (part 4 of 4)

Perspective

This chapter has presented the skills you need for adding, updating, and deleting rows in a table. As a result, you should now be able to maintain the tables in any database that you're working with. You should also be able to extract data from a single row of a table as shown in chapter 1 or from a cursor-controlled result table as shown in chapter 2.

To this point, though, you've been working with the data in one table at a time, even though one of the primary benefits of a relational database is working with the data in two or more related tables. In the next chapter, then, you'll learn how to extract a single result table from the data in two or more base tables. To do that, you use unions and joins and you start to experience the power of DB2.

4

How to use unions and joins

One of the strengths of a relational database management system like DB2 is its ability to combine data from two or more base tables into a single result table. You can do that using either a union or a join, and you'll learn how to use both in this chapter. Although unions are presented first, you'll soon see that joins are far more useful than unions.

How to use unions

DB2's *union* function lets you combine the contents of two or more interim result tables into one. These result tables can be drawn from two or more DB2 tables or from a single table.

The syntax of the union function

Figure 4-1 presents the syntax and rules for coding a union. As you can see, you just code two or more SELECT statements and connect them with the keyword UNION. Because this usually produces a multi-row result table, you code the SELECT statements within a DECLARE CURSOR statement in a COBOL program.

When DB2 processes the union, it creates one interim result table for each SELECT statement. Then, it combines the interim tables into a final result table. For this to work, all of the SELECT statements must lead to interim tables with the same number of columns and with compatible data types in each column.

To visualize how a union works, imagine that DB2 processes a union that consists of two SELECT statements. The first statement leads to an interim result table with 16 rows; the second one leads to an interim result table with 7 rows. Then, to complete the union, DB2 combines the 7 rows of the second table with the 16 rows of the first table.

If the names of the selected columns in each interim table are the same, those names are used in the final result table. When they're not the same, though, those columns use the names from the first SELECT statement. If this is misleading, you should use AS clauses to name those columns as shown in the second example in the next figure.

To make sure that the rows of the final result table are in a useful sequence, you can code the ORDER BY clause, which applies only to the final result table, not to the interim tables. This is illustrated by the example in this figure. Here, the rows in the final result table will be in last name (LNAME) sequence.

To include duplicate rows in the final result table, you code the keyword ALL after the word UNION. A *duplicate row* is one that has the same values as the corresponding columns in another row. To check for and eliminate duplicate rows, DB2 may have to sort the interim tables.

When you code a union and you're positive that duplicates cannot occur, you should code the ALL keyword. This eliminates the need for DB2 to go through the extra processing that checks for duplicates. In other words, as contradictory as it sounds, you should code the ALL keyword to allow duplicates when you're combining tables that you know won't produce any.

The syntax of the UNION function

```
SELECT-statement
    UNION [ALL]
        SELECT-statement
    [UNION [ALL]
        SELECT-statement]...
    [ORDER BY sort-column [DESC] [, sort-column [DESC]]...]
```

A union that combines the data for the customers in two different tables

```
    SELECT  CUSTNO,  FNAME,   LNAME
        FROM MM01.CUSTOMER
UNION ALL
    SELECT  CUSTNO,  FNAME,   LNAME
        FROM MM01.INACTCST
ORDER BY LNAME
```

Operation

- When you use a *union*, DB2 creates one interim result table for each SELECT statement used. Then, DB2 combines the interim result tables into a final result table.

Rules

- Because a union should return a result table of more than one row, it should be coded within a DECLARE CURSOR statement in a COBOL program.

- The interim result tables must have the same number of columns, and the data types of the columns in the first interim result table must be compatible with the corresponding columns in the other interim tables.

- If you use a union to combine columns with the same name, DB2 uses that name for the column in the final result table. If you use a union to combine columns with different names, DB2 uses the name in the first SELECT statement for the column in the final result table.

- Two rows are duplicates if each value in the first is equal to the corresponding value in the second. To make this determination, two null values are considered equal.

- To keep duplicates in the result table of a union, code the keyword ALL. For efficiency, you should also code ALL whenever you know that a union won't produce duplicates.

- If you use an ORDER BY clause, it must be placed after the last SELECT statement that is part of the union.

- A SELECT statement in a union can get data from a table or a view.

Figure 4-1   The syntax of the union function

How to combine data from two or more base tables

The common use of a union is to combine data that's taken from two or more base tables. In figure 4-2, for example, you can see how a union can be used to combine data from two different tables. Here, the ORDER BY clause is used to sort the final result table by PARTNO as the primary field and STATUS as the secondary field so the on hand row for each part number always comes before the ordered row.

The examples in this figure illustrate how a literal string can be used in the column specifications for each of the SELECT statements. Here, each row in the final result table that came from the PARTS_ON_HAND table has ON HAND in its first column, and each row that came from the ORDER_PARTS table has ORDERED in its first column. That makes it easy to tell which rows came from which tables.

The first example also shows that columns that don't have the same names in the interim tables use the first SELECT statement's column names in the final result table. Although this doesn't agree with the *DB2 V4 SQL Reference*, which states that columns that don't have the same names in the interim tables of UNION functions have unnamed columns in the final result table, the manual appears to be wrong. At the least, it is wrong based on my testing of the examples in this book and my experiences at other job sites.

Is this difference important? To judge for yourself, look at the name of the third column in the first result table in this figure. In this case, the column is named QTYOH, which is the third column name of the first SELECT statement. As a result, a user might think the second row of the third column represents 10 parts on hand. Actually, though, the numbers in this column can represent parts on hand or parts ordered.

The second example uses AS clauses to name the third column QUANTITY in both interim tables. This name is then used as the name of the third column in the final result table. This coding technique eliminates any possible confusion.

PARTS_ON_HAND table

PARTNO	COST	QTYOH
J025	5.25	100
J027	7.50	200
K011	10.00	500

ORDER_PARTS table

PARTNO	COST	QTYOR
J025	5.50	10
J027	8.00	100
K011	12.00	100

A union with different names in the third column

```
SELECT   'ON_HAND' AS STATUS, PARTNO, QTYOH,
         QTYOH * COST AS TOTAL_COST
    FROM MM01.PARTS_ON_HAND
UNION ALL
SELECT   'ORDERED' AS STATUS, PARTNO, QTYOR,
         QTYOR * COST AS TOTAL_COST
    FROM MM01.ORDER_PARTS
    ORDER BY PARTNO, STATUS
```

The result table

STATUS	PARTNO	QTYOH	TOTAL_COST
ON HAND	J025	100	525.00
ORDERED	J025	10	55.00
ON HAND	J027	200	1500.00
ORDERED	J027	100	800.00
ON HAND	K011	500	5000.00
ORDERED	K011	100	1200.00

A union that uses AS clauses so the third column names are the same

```
SELECT   'ON_HAND' AS STATUS, PARTNO, QTYOH AS QUANTITY,
         QTYOH * COST AS TOTAL_COST
    FROM MM01.PARTS_ON_HAND
UNION ALL
SELECT   'ORDERED' AS STATUS, PARTNO, QTYOR AS QUANTITY,
         QTYOR * COST AS TOTAL_COST
    FROM MM01.ORDER_PARTS
    ORDER BY PARTNO, STATUS
```

The result table

STATUS	PARTNO	QUANTITY	TOTAL_COST
ON HAND	J025	100	525.00
ORDERED	J025	10	55.00
ON HAND	J027	200	1500.00
ORDERED	J027	100	800.00
ON HAND	K011	500	5000.00
ORDERED	K011	100	1200.00

Figure 4-2   Unions that combine data from two different base tables

How to combine data selected from the same base table

Although you may never need to use this function, figure 4-3 shows how a union can be used to combine interim result tables that have been selected from the same base table. The first example prepares a result table without duplicates. The second example prepares a result table with duplicates.

In both examples, the first SELECT statement gets customer data when the state column contains the value of NJ, and the second SELECT statement gets the same customer data when the city column contains a value that starts with the letter D. With duplicates, a row that satisfies both conditions is included twice in the final result table.

Instead of using a union, though, you can code a compound WHERE condition in a SELECT statement like this:

```
SELECT  CUSTNO,  FNAME,  LNAME,  CITY,  STATE
    FROM MM01.CUST4
    WHERE STATE = 'NJ' OR CITY LIKE 'D%'
```

This produces the same result table as the union without duplicates in figure 4-3. In chapter 5, you can learn more about coding compound conditions like this one.

Why would you use a union for a selection that can be done by coding a compound condition? Because the union will execute more efficiently *under some circumstances*. If, for example, the rows in the customer table are indexed by the state and city columns, DB2 will use the indexes to make the selections for a union, but it won't use the indexes if you code a compound condition. In some cases, though, DB2 may have to sort the interim tables in a union like this to remove the duplicates, so it's not always clear which approach will lead to faster performance. When in doubt, you may need to test the alternatives or discuss them with your database administrator.

In general, you'll start by using a compound condition instead of a union to extract data from a single table. Then, if performance is a problem, you can consider using a union.

A customer table

CUSTNO	FNAME	LNAME	ADDR	CITY	STATE	ZIPCODE
400001	KEITH	JONES	4501 W MOCKINGBIRD	DALLAS	TX	75209
400002	ARREN	ANELLI	40 FORD RD	DENVILLE	NJ	07834
400003	SUSAN	HOWARD	1107 SECOND AVE	REDWOOD CITY	CA	94063
400004	CAROL	EVANS	74 SUTTON CT	GREAT LAKES	IL	60088
400005	ELANE	ROBERTS	12914 BRACKNELL	CERRITOS	CA	90701
400006	PAT	HONG	73 HIGH ST	SAN FRANCISCO	CA	94114
400007	PHIL	ROACH	25680 ORCHARD	DEARBORN HTS	MI	48125
400008	TIM	JOHNSON	145 W 27TH ST	SO CHICAGO HTS	IL	60411
400009	MARIANNE	BUSBEE	3920 BERWYN DR S	MOBILE	AL	36608
400010	ENRIQUE	OTHON	BOX 26729	RICHMOND	VA	23261

A union without duplicates

```
    SELECT    CUSTNO,    FNAME,    LNAME,    CITY,    STATE
        FROM MM01.CUST4
        WHERE STATE = 'NJ'
UNION
    SELECT    CUSTNO,    FNAME,    LNAME,    CITY,    STATE
        FROM MM01.CUST4
        WHERE CITY LIKE 'D%'
```

The result table

CUSTNO	FNAME	LNAME	ADDR	CITY	STATE	ZIPCODE
400001	KEITH	JONES	4501 W MOCKINGBIRD	DALLAS	TX	75209
400002	ARREN	ANELLI	40 FORD RD	DENVILLE	NJ	07834
400007	PHIL	ROACH	25680 ORCHARD	DEARBORN HTS	MI	48125

A union with duplicates

```
    SELECT    CUSTNO,    FNAME,    LNAME,    CITY,    STATE
        FROM MM01.CUST4
        WHERE STATE = 'NJ'
UNION ALL
    SELECT    CUSTNO,    FNAME,    LNAME,    CITY,    STATE
        FROM MM01.CUST4
        WHERE CITY LIKE 'D%'
```

The result table

CUSTNO	FNAME	LNAME	ADDR	CITY	STATE	ZIPCODE
400002	ARREN	ANELLI	40 FORD RD	DENVILLE	NJ	07834
400001	KEITH	JONES	4501 W MOCKINGBIRD	DALLAS	TX	75209
400002	ARREN	ANELLI	40 FORD RD	DENVILLE	NJ	07834
400007	PHIL	ROACH	25680 ORCHARD	DEARBORN HTS	MI	48125

Figure 4-3   Unions that combine data drawn from the same base table

How to use inner joins

DB2's *join* function lets you combine data from two or more base tables into a single result table. What, then, is the difference between a union and a join? In a union, DB2 combines *rows* from two or more interim result tables that have identical structures. But in a join, DB2 combines *columns* from two or more different base tables and creates a result table that has a different structure than any of the base tables.

The syntax of the inner join function

Figure 4-4 presents both the implicit and explicit syntax for coding an *inner join*. Before DB2 version 4.0, using the implicit syntax was the only way to code an inner join. With version 4.0, however, DB2 added the explicit syntax for the inner join and introduced the outer join function, which is covered later in this chapter. These SQL enhancements are consistent with the ANSI/ISO SQL entry-level standard of 1992.

When you code an inner join, the table specification can be either a table name or a view name. In fact, from the COBOL programmer's point of view, you can usually use a view anywhere you can use a table.

In the examples in this figure, the inner join is performed on the EMP and DEPT tables where E_EMPNO equals D_EMPNO and where the employee number is greater than 1000. In the statement that uses the implicit syntax, both of these conditions are coded in the WHERE clause. In contrast, in the statement that uses the explicit syntax, the join condition is coded in the ON clause while the selection condition is coded in the WHERE clause. This makes the explicit syntax somewhat easier to interpret

For that reason alone, we recommend that you use the explicit syntax when coding inner joins. In addition, the explicit syntax is the only syntax that you can use when coding outer joins so you may as well get used to it.

Now, if you look at the list of column specifications in the SELECT clauses in these examples, you'll realize that you can't tell which columns come from which table. This can make even a short statement difficult to interpret, but in a production environment it's not uncommon to work with statements that get forty or more columns from three or more joined tables. To get around this problem, you can self-document your statements by using qualified names and synonyms, which are presented next.

Incidentally, if you don't specify a join condition in the ON or WHERE clause, the result table is a combination of *every* row in the first table with *every* row in the second. This is called a *Cartesian product* or a *cross product*, and it is almost always useless.

The implicit syntax for the INNER JOIN function

```
SELECT column-specification [AS result-column]
    [, column-specification [AS result-column]]…
    FROM table-spec, table-spec [, table-spec]…
        [WHERE condition]
    [ORDER BY sort-column [DESC][, sort-column [DESC]]…]
```

The explicit syntax for the INNER JOIN function

```
SELECT column-specification [AS result-column]
    [, column-specification [AS result-column]]…
    FROM table-spec [, table-spec]…
        INNER JOIN table-spec
            [ON join-condition]
            [WHERE selection-condition]
        [INNER JOIN table-spec
            [ON join-condition]
            [WHERE selection-condition]]…
    [ORDER BY sort-column [DESC][, sort-column [DESC]]…]
```

An inner join that joins two tables on the employee number

Implicit syntax

```
SELECT  E_EMPNO,  DEPTNO,  LNAME,  FNAME
    FROM MM01.EMP, MM01.DEPT
    WHERE E_EMPNO = D_EMPNO
        AND E_EMPNO > '1000'
```

Explicit syntax

```
SELECT  E_EMPNO,  DEPTNO,  LNAME,  FNAME
    FROM MM01.EMP
        INNER JOIN MM01.DEPT
    ON E_EMPNO = D_EMPNO
        WHERE E_EMPNO > '1000'
```

Description

- DB2 processes a *join* by combining columns from two or more base tables and creates a result table with a new structure that is different than any of the base tables. *Inner joins* only include rows where the values in the joined columns match.

- Because an inner join should return a result table of more than one row, it should be coded within a DECLARE CURSOR statement in a COBOL program.

- A *table-spec* in the syntax above can be a table name or a view name.

- Both a view and a cursor are read-only if their SELECT statements include a join.

Figure 4-4   The syntax of the inner join function

When and how to use qualified names and synonyms

If you join data from two or more tables that have duplicate column names, you have to qualify those names when you refer to them in your SQL statements. For example, both tables in figure 4-5 have a product number column named PRODNO. As a result, you can't use the name PRODNO by itself because it would be ambiguous. Instead, it has to be qualified.

To form a *qualified name* for a column, you code the name of the table that the column is in, a period, and the column name. For instance,

```
MM01.PARTS.PRODNO
```

is the qualified name for the PRODNO column in the MM01.PARTS table.

The problem with using qualified names is that they can be hard to code and read. To give you some idea of this, the first example in this figure shows a join that uses all qualified names (even though some qualifications aren't necessary).

To get around this problem, DB2 lets you use *synonyms* to specify shorter names for the tables that you use in qualified names. To specify a synonym, you code a shorter name for a table after you name it in the FROM clause. This is illustrated by the second example in this figure. Here, the letter A is the synonym for the table named MM01.PARTS and the letter B is the synonym for the table named MM01.PRODUCTS. Then, in the SELECT clause, the synonyms A and B are used to qualify the column names. (In other contexts, synonyms may be called *aliases* or *correlation names*.)

When you use synonyms, they are in effect only within the statement in which you define them. Even within the same program, other statements can't use the synonyms unless they declare them in their own FROM clauses.

A good coding habit when using joins is to qualify all column names with synonyms even when none of the columns have the same name. That makes it easy to tell which columns are coming from which table, and that makes your code self-documenting. Without qualification, for example, you would have to look at the table documentation to tell which table the SUPPLIER column in this figure came from. With the qualified name A.SUPPLIER, though, you can tell that the column came from the A table, which is the PARTS table.

Please note in this example that the rows in the result table have the sequence of neither the PARTS table nor the SUPPLIER table. This illustrates that the sequence of the result table is unpredictable unless you include an ORDER BY clause. Without that clause, DB2 does the join in the most efficient way possible without regard for the resulting sequence.

PARTS table

PART	PRODNO	SUPPLIER
WIRE	10	AMCO
GLASS	35	BRADCO
PLASTIC	50	OK_CHEM
MAGNET	10	TURNER
BLADES	250	HOWARTH

PRODUCTS table

PRODNO	PRODUCT	PRICE
250	SAW	22.00
10	ALTERNATOR	55.50
45	PLIERS	75.75
50	RELAY	12.25

An inner join that uses qualified names

```
SELECT  MM01.PARTS.PART,   MM01.PARTS.SUPPLIER,
        MM01.PARTS.PRODNO, MM01.PRODUCTS.PRODUCT
    FROM MM01.PARTS
        INNER JOIN MM01.PRODUCTS
    ON MM01.PARTS.PRODNO = MM01.PRODUCTS.PRODNO
```

The same inner join with synonyms in the qualified names

```
SELECT  A.PART, A.SUPPLIER, A.PRODNO, B.PRODUCT
    FROM MM01.PARTS A
        INNER JOIN MM01.PRODUCTS B
    ON A.PRODNO = B.PRODNO
```

The result table

PART	SUPPLIER	PRODNO	PRODUCT
MAGNET	TURNER	10	ALTERNATOR
WIRE	AMCO	10	ALTERNATOR
PLASTIC	OK_CHEM	50	RELAY
BLADES	HOWARTH	250	SAW

Description

- A *qualified name* is made up of the table name, a period, and the column name.
- A *synonym* is an alternative name given to a table for use within one SELECT statement. The synonym can then be used in qualified names. By using a synonym that is shorter than the full name for a table, the qualified names can be shortened as shown above.
- If you don't code an ORDER BY clause in a join, the sequence of the rows in the result table is unpredictable.
- In the tables above, a part in the PARTS table, GLASS, isn't in the PRODUCTS table. And a product in the PRODUCTS table, PLIERS, isn't in the PARTS table. As a result, neither GLASS nor PLIERS appears in the result table.

Figure 4-5   Inner joins that use qualified names and synonyms

Inner joins that combine data from three or more tables

Figure 4-6 presents three simple inventory tables. These tables are part of an inventory data structure for a company that assembles and sells office furniture. The first table, ASSM, contains one row for each piece of office furniture assembled. The second table, PARTLIST, contains one row for each part required by each assembly. And the third table, CMPT, contains one row for each component required for the assemblies. Because they contain data that identify rows in other tables, ACODE and CCODE in the PARTLIST table are foreign keys.

To list the components that you need for each assembly, you need to get information from all three tables. The name of each assembly is in the ASSM table, the name of each component is in the CMPT table, and the relationship between the assemblies and the components are in the PARTLIST table. As a result, these tables provide a good basis for showing you how joins work.

The SELECT statements in this figure select five columns from the three tables, and they use qualified names with synonyms to make it easy to tell which columns are from which table. Since both the ASSM table and the CMPT table have a column named DESC, AS clauses are used to give them unique names in the result table. The names in other AS clauses are used in the ORDER BY clause to sort the result table in sequence by component code within assembly code.

The first SELECT statement in this figure uses the implicit syntax to join three of the tables. In contrast, the second statement uses the explicit syntax to join the tables. Here again, the explicit syntax is somewhat easier to interpret so we recommend that you use that syntax to join all of the tables.

When a join of three or more tables is executed, it is done in a series of steps and each step joins only two tables. In each step, the *composite table* (or *outer table*) is joined with the *new table* (or *inner table*). In the first step, the composite table is the first table named in the statement, but after that the composite table is the interim result table created in the previous step. For instance, the first step for the second example in this figure is to join the PARTLIST table with the ASSM table, thus creating an interim table. In the second step, the interim (composite) table is joined with the CMPT (new) table.

If you look at the first example in this figure, you can see that it's hard to tell which tables are joined in which sequence when you use the implicit syntax. Although you usually don't need to know that when you're doing an inner join, it sometimes matters when you're doing an outer join. That's another reason why you should use the explicit syntax whenever you code joins.

Assembly table (ASSM)

ACODE	DESC
A1	TABLE 24X36
A2	TABLE 30X60
A3	TABLE & RETURN

Parts list table (PARTLIST)

ACODE	CCODE	QTY
A1	C1	1
A1	C3	4
A2	C2	1
A2	C3	4
A3	C1	1
A3	C2	1
A3	C3	6
A3	C4	1

Component table (CMPT)

CCODE	DESC
C1	TABLE TOP 24X36
C2	TABLE TOP 30X60
C3	TABLE LEG
C4	RETURN CONNECTOR

An inner join that gets information from three inventory tables

```
SELECT  A.ACODE AS ASSM_CODE,  A.DESC AS ASSM_DESC,
        PL.CCODE AS CMPT_CODE, C.DESC AS CMPT_DESC,
        PL.QTY AS QUANTITY
    FROM MM01.PARTLIST PL, MM01.CMPT C, MM01.ASSM A
        WHERE A.ACODE = PL.ACODE
        AND   C.CCODE = PL.CCODE
    ORDER BY ASSM_CODE, CMPT_CODE
```

A better way to code this inner join

```
SELECT  A.ACODE AS ASSM_CODE,  A.DESC AS ASSM_DESC,
        PL.CCODE AS CMPT_CODE, C.DESC AS CMPT_DESC,
        PL.QTY AS QUANTITY
    FROM MM01.PARTLIST PL
        INNER JOIN MM01.ASSM A
            ON A.ACODE = PL.ACODE
        INNER JOIN MM01.CMPT C
            ON C.CCODE = PL.CCODE
    ORDER BY ASSM_CODE, CMPT_CODE
```

The result table

ASSM_CODE	ASSM_DESC	CMPT_CODE	CMPT_DESC	QUANTITY
A1	TABLE 24X36	C1	TABLE TOP 24X36	1
A1	TABLE 24X36	C3	TABLE LEG	4
A2	TABLE 30X60	C2	TABLE TOP 30X60	1
A2	TABLE 30X60	C3	TABLE LEG	4
A3	TABLE & RETURN	C1	TABLE TOP 24X36	1
A3	TABLE & RETURN	C2	TABLE TOP 30X60	1
A3	TABLE & RETURN	C3	TABLE LEG	6
A3	TABLE & RETURN	C4	RETURN CONNECTOR	1

Description

- Whenever a join is executed, it is done in a series of steps that join two tables at a time. In each step, the *composite* (or *outer*) *table* is joined to the *new* (or *inner*) *table*.

Figure 4-6   Inner joins that join information from three inventory tables

How to use outer joins

Version 4.0 of DB2 introduced outer joins as part of the SQL enhancements. These are consistent with the ANSI/ISO SQL entry level standards of 1992. An outer join differs from an inner join in that the outer join keeps rows from one table that do not match on the join condition with any row in the other table.

The syntax of the outer join function

Figure 4-7 presents the syntax and guidelines for coding an *outer join*. As you can see, this syntax is similar to the explicit syntax for inner joins shown in figure 4-4. Here, a table-specification can be a table name, a view name, or a subquery (which you'll learn more about in chapter 9). Since an outer join usually produces a multi-row result table, you code the SELECT statement within a DECLARE CURSOR statement in a COBOL program.

The outer join function supports left, right, and full outer joins. As this figure shows, the join types are distinguished by which unmatched rows they keep, and here again a join of two or more tables is done in a series of steps. In a *left outer join*, the result table keeps the unmatched rows from the first table accessed in the first step of a join or the composite table from the previous step. In a *right outer join*, the result table keeps unmatched rows from the new table that's added to the join. And in a *full outer join*, the result table keeps unmatched rows from both the composite table and the new table.

The first example in this figure presents a left outer join. This example is explained in the next figure. The second example presents a full outer join, and it is explained in figure 4-9.

Syntax

```
SELECT column-specification [AS result-column]
    [, column-specification [AS result-column]]…
    FROM table-spec [, table-spec]…
        {LEFT | RIGHT | FULL} [OUTER] JOIN table-spec
            [ON join-condition]
            [WHERE selection-condition]
        [ORDER BY sort-column [DESC][, sort-column [DESC]]…]
```

What outer joins do

Joins of this type	Keep unmatched rows from
Left outer join	The composite (outer) table
Right outer join	The new (inner) table
Full outer join	Both tables

A left outer join

```
SELECT  A.DEPTNO,  B.EMPNO
    FROM MM01.DEPT A
        LEFT JOIN MM01.EMP B
    ON A.DEPTNO = B.WORKDEPT
```

A full outer join

```
SELECT  A.DEPTNO,  B.EMPNO
    FROM MM01.DEPT A
        FULL JOIN MM01.EMP B
    ON A.DEPTNO = B.WORKDEPT
```

Description

- Because an *outer join* should return a result table of more than one row, it should be coded within a DECLARE CURSOR statement in a COBOL program.

- A *table-spec* in the syntax above can be a table name, a view name, or a subquery statement. Subquery statements, which are presented in chapter 9, are commonly used when three or more tables are joined.

- A *null row* is a row that has all of its columns filled with null values. In the first example above, each unmatched row of the DEPT table is joined with the null row of the EMP table. In the second example, each unmatched row of the DEPT table is joined with the null row of the EMP table, and each unmatched row of the EMP table is joined with the null row of the DEPT table.

- A full outer join can use only the equals (=) comparison operator, but left and right outer joins can use any of the comparison operators. Although you can use AND to combine join expressions when using the equal operator, OR and NOT aren't allowed.

- Both a view and a cursor are read-only if their SELECT statements include a join.

Figure 4-7   The syntax of the outer join function

How to use left outer joins

Figure 4-8 presents two tables, DEPT and EMP. Each row in the DEPT table consists of department number (DEPTNO) and department name (DEPTNAME), while each row in the EMP table consists of employee number (EMPNO) and the department the employee works in (WORKDEPT).

The left outer join in this example joins these two tables where the DEPTNO in the DEPT table equals the WORKDEPT in the EMP table. The composite (outer) table in this example is DEPT, because it is the first table accessed in the FROM clause. Since left outer joins keep unmatched rows from the composite (outer) table, any unmatched rows in the DEPT table are kept and any columns taken from the new (inner) table contain null values.

In this example, DEPTNO A02 and A05 in the DEPT table do not match any WORKDEPT rows in the EMP table. Therefore, the result table shows null values for the EMPNO column for both departments A02 and A05.

Why you don't need right outer joins

When an outer join is executed, DB2 converts a right outer join to a left outer join. Since this takes extra processing time, it makes sense to code all right outer joins as left outer joins.

To convert a right outer join to a left outer join, you just switch the places of the tables and change RIGHT to LEFT. For instance, when you convert this right outer join:

```
SELECT A.DEPTNO, B.EMPNO
    FROM MM01.DEPT A
        RIGHT JOIN MM01.EMP B
    ON A.DEPTNO = B.WORKDEPT
```

to a left outer join, it looks like this:

```
SELECT A.DEPTNO, B.EMPNO
    FROM MM01.EMP B
        LEFT JOIN MM01.DEPT A
    ON A.DEPTNO = B.WORKDEPT
```

Although both statements get the same result, the second one will be processed more efficiently.

Department table (DEPT)

DEPTNO	DEPTNAME
A01	ACCOUNTING
A02	PAYROLL
A03	OPERATIONS
A04	PERSONNEL
A05	MAINTENANCE

Employee table (EMP)

EMPNO	WORKDEPT
5001	A01
5002	A04
5003	A03
5004	A03
5005	A04
5006	A04
5007	A03
5008	A06

A left outer join

```
SELECT  A.DEPTNO,  A.DEPTNAME,  B.EMPNO
    FROM MM01.DEPT A
        LEFT JOIN MM01.EMP B
    ON A.DEPTNO = B.WORKDEPT
```

The result table

DEPTNO	DEPTNAME	EMPNO
A01	ACCOUNTING	5001
A02	PAYROLL	<null>
A03	OPERATIONS	5003
A03	OPERATIONS	5004
A03	OPERATIONS	5007
A04	PERSONNEL	5002
A04	PERSONNEL	5005
A04	PERSONNEL	5006
A05	MAINTENANCE	<null>

Description

- In this example, each unmatched row of the DEPT table is joined with the null row of the EMP table. As you can tell by the result table, there are no employees in the PAYROLL department or the MAINTENANCE department.

Figure 4-8   A left outer join that joins information from two tables

How to use full outer joins

Figure 4-9 presents a full outer join using the same tables as in the previous figure. By definition, a full outer join keeps the unmatched rows of both the composite (outer) table and the new (inner) table. In this example, the composite (outer) table is MM01.DEPT and the new (inner) table is MM01.EMP.

But if the unmatched rows of both tables are kept, does it matter which table is the composite table and which is the new table? The answer is No, if the full outer join function contains an ORDER BY clause. But the answer is Yes, if the ORDER BY clause isn't used. In that case, the order of the result table could be different depending on which table is coded first.

The full outer join in this example joins rows from the DEPT table with rows from the EMP table. Each unmatched row of the DEPT table is joined with the null row of the EMP table, and each unmatched row of the EMP table is joined with the null row of the DEPT table. As you can see, though, the result table doesn't contain any null values. That's because the null values have been replaced with literal values by the COALESCE function that's described next.

How to use the VALUE and COALESCE functions

DB2 has two functions that can substitute values for a null value. They are the VALUE and COALESCE functions. Although the function names are different, the functions work the same. Each returns the first argument in the expression list that isn't null.

In the example in this figure, departments A02 and A05 in the DEPTNO column in the DEPT table don't have a match in the WORKDEPT column in the EMP table. As a result, the join operation would normally put a null value in the result table for these employee number fields. In this case, though, the COALESCE function replaces any null value in the EMPNO column with the literal 'NO EMP' as shown in the result table.

Similarly, WORKDEPT A06 in the EMP table doesn't have a match in the DEPTNO column in the DEPT table. But this time, COALESCE functions are used to replace any null value in the DEPTNO column with the literal 'NO DEPT' and to replace any null value in the DEPTNAME column with the literal 'NO DEPT NAME.'

The syntax of the VALUE and COALESCE functions

```
VALUE(expression, expression,…)
COALESCE(expression, expression,…)
```

Department table (DEPT)

DEPTNO	DEPTNAME
A01	ACCOUNTING
A02	PAYROLL
A03	OPERATIONS
A04	PERSONNEL
A05	MAINTENANCE

Employee table (EMP)

EMPNO	WORKDEPT
5001	A01
5002	A04
5003	A03
5004	A03
5005	A04
5006	A04
5007	A03
5008	A06

A full outer join that uses the COALESCE function

```
SELECT   COALESCE(B.EMPNO, 'NO EMP') AS EMPNO,
         COALESCE(A.DEPTNO, 'NO DEPT') AS DEPTNO,
         COALESCE(A.DEPTNAME, 'NO DEPT NAME') AS DEPTNAME
    FROM MM01.DEPT A
         FULL JOIN MM01.EMP B
      ON A.DEPTNO = B.WORKDEPT
ORDER BY EMPNO
```

The result table

EMPNO	DEPTNO	DEPTNAME
NO EMP	A02	PAYROLL
NO EMP	A05	MAINTENANCE
5001	A01	ACCOUNTING
5002	A04	PERSONNEL
5003	A03	OPERATIONS
5004	A03	OPERATIONS
5005	A04	PERSONNEL
5006	A04	PERSONNEL
5007	A03	OPERATIONS
5008	NO DEPT	NO DEPT NAME

Description

- The VALUE and COALESCE functions return the first argument in the parameter list that isn't null.
- Although the *DB2 for MVS/ESA V4 SQL Reference* states that the VALUE and COALESCE functions can only be used with full outer joins, I find that these functions work with left and right outer joins as well.
- You can also use a VALUE or COALESCE function as an expression in the ON or WHERE condition of an outer join.

Figure 4-9 A full outer join that uses the COALESCE function

Outer joins that combine data from three or more tables

Figure 4-10 presents the DEPT and EMP tables used in the last two figures and adds a PROJ table. Each row in this table includes a project number, PROJNO, and an employee number, EMPNO, for an employee who is working on that project. For example, project P1011 has two employees working on it, employee numbers 5002 and 5006.

Within the SELECT statement in this figure, you can see a second SELECT statement in the FROM clause. This second SELECT, which is coded in parentheses, can be referred to as a *subquery*. In this example, the subquery does a full join of the DEPT and EMP tables on the department number column to create an interim table that's given the synonym C. The main SELECT statement then does a full join of the interim table and the PROJ table on the employee number column to create the final result table.

When you do outer joins of three or more tables, a subquery is commonly used to join two tables at a time. In the syntax in figure 4-7, remember that a table specification can be a table name, a view name, or a subquery. In chapter 9, you can learn more about the use of subqueries.

In the first COALESCE function in the example in figure 4-10, you can see that three expressions are coded: C.EMPNO, D.EMPNO, and 'NO EMP'. When this function is executed, it returns the first expression that isn't null. If you look at the last employee number in the final result table, you can see that it is 5010. But can you tell which table this number came from?

Since 5010 isn't in the EMPNO column of the interim table (C), C.EMPNO for employee number 5010 is null and the value didn't come from the interim table. But since 5010 is in the EMPNO column of the PROJ table (D), the employee number did come from this table. In contrast, the first two rows in the final result table have the value of the third expression 'NO EMP' in the EMP_NO column because neither department A02 nor A05 had a match in the WORKDEPT column of the EMP table.

In this example, AS clauses are used to name the result columns, and the ORDER BY clause sorts the result table by EMP_NO and DEPT_NO. If the AS clauses weren't used, the result table columns would be unnamed and the ORDER BY clause would have to specify column numbers like this:

```
ORDER BY 1, 2
```

If the ORDER BY clause weren't used, the result table wouldn't be in a meaningful sequence.

DEPT table

DEPTNO	DEPTNAME
A01	ACCOUNTING
A02	PAYROLL
A03	OPERATIONS
A04	PERSONNEL
A05	MAINTENANCE

EMP table

EMPNO	WORKDEPT
5001	A01
5002	A04
5003	A03
5004	A03
5005	A04
5006	A04
5007	A03
5008	A06

PROJ table

PROJNO	EMPNO
P1011	5002
P1011	5006
P1012	5001
P1013	5010
P1014	5003
P1014	5004
P1014	5005
P1015	5008

A full outer join that combines data from three tables

```
SELECT   COALESCE(C.EMPNO, D.EMPNO, 'NO EMP') AS EMP_NO,
         COALESCE(C.DEPTNO, C.WORKDEPT, 'NO DEPT') AS DEPT_NO,
         COALESCE(C.DEPTNAME, 'NO DEPT NAME') AS DEPT_NAME,
         COALESCE(D.PROJNO, 'NO PROJECT') AS PROJ_NO
    FROM
         (SELECT A.DEPTNO, A.DEPTNAME, B.EMPNO, B.WORKDEPT
             FROM MM01.DEPT A
                  FULL JOIN MM01.EMP B
             ON A.DEPTNO = B.WORKDEPT) C
         FULL JOIN MM01.PROJ D
             ON C.EMPNO = D.EMPNO
    ORDER BY EMP_NO, DEPT_NO
```

The interim table

DEPTNO	DEPTNAME	EMPNO	WORKDEPT
A01	ACCOUNTING	5001	A01
A04	PERSONNEL	5002	A04
A03	OPERATIONS	5003	A03
A03	OPERATIONS	5004	A03
A04	PERSONNEL	5005	A04
A04	PERSONNEL	5006	A04
A03	OPERATIONS	5007	A03
<null>	<null>	5008	A06
A02	PAYROLL	<null>	<null>
A05	MAINTENANCE	<null>	<null>

The result table

EMP_NO	DEPT_NO	DEPT_NAME	PROJ_NO
NO EMP	A02	PAYROLL	NO PROJECT
NO EMP	A05	MAINTENANCE	NO PROJECT
5001	A01	ACCOUNTING	P1012
5002	A04	PERSONNEL	P1011
5003	A03	OPERATIONS	P1014
5004	A03	OPERATIONS	P1014
5005	A04	PERSONNEL	P1014
5006	A04	PERSONNEL	P1011
5007	A03	OPERATIONS	NO PROJECT
5008	A06	NO DEPT NAME	P1015
5010	NO DEPT	NO DEPT NAME	P1013

Figure 4-10   A full outer join that joins information from three tables

A COBOL program that uses an inner join

Now that you've seen how joins work, this chapter is going to present a short but complete program that uses an inner join. This program produces a report, or register, that lists all the invoices in an invoice table, along with the name and number of the customer associated with each.

The customer and invoice tables

Figure 4-11 presents the two input tables for this program: the customer and the invoice table. These tables are related by the CUSTNO column in the customer table and the INVCUST column in the invoice table. In other words, INVCUST is a foreign key that refers to CUSTNO, which is a primary key. The primary key of the invoice table is INVNO.

The invoice table (INVOICE)

INVCUST	INVNO	INVDATE	INVSUBT	INVSHIP	INVTAX	INVTOTAL	INVPROM
400012	062308	1997-12-22	200.00	4.45	.00	204.45	PCQ3
400011	062309	1997-12-22	15.00	.00	.00	15.00	PCQ3
400011	062310	1998-02-22	140.00	7.50	.00	147.50	PCQ3
400014	062311	1998-02-22	178.23	3.19	.00	181.42	PCQ3
400002	062312	1998-02-22	162.00	11.07	.00	173.07	PCQ3
400011	062313	1998-03-14	22.00	.50	.00	22.50	RXTY
400003	062314	1998-03-14	140.00	.00	9.80	149.80	RXTY
400004	062315	1998-03-14	178.23	3.19	.00	181.42	RXTY
400010	062316	1998-03-14	140.00	7.50	.00	147.50	RXTY
400011	062317	1998-03-17	289.00	9.00	.00	298.00	RXTY
400012	062318	1998-03-17	199.99	.00	.00	199.99	PCQ3
400015	062319	1998-03-17	178.23	3.19	.00	181.42	RXTY
400015	062320	1998-03-17	3245.00	160.00	.00	3405.00	RXTY
400001	062321	1998-04-03	200.00	5.60	.00	205.60	PCQ4
400014	062322	1998-04-03	15.00	.00	.00	15.00	PCQ4
400011	062323	1998-04-11	925.00	24.00	.00	949.00	PCQ4
400014	062324	1998-04-14	178.23	3.19	.00	181.42	PCQ4
400002	062325	1998-04-17	140.00	7.50	.00	147.50	PCQ3
400011	062326	1998-04-20	178.23	3.19	.00	181.42	PCQ4
400003	062327	1998-04-23	200.00	7.50	14.00	221.50	PCQ4
400004	062328	1998-04-24	178.23	3.19	.00	181.42	PCQ4
400010	062329	1998-04-29	140.00	7.50	.00	147.50	PCQ4
400011	062330	1998-04-30	2295.00	14.00	.00	2309.00	PCQ4
400012	062331	1998-05-07	178.23	.00	.00	178.23	PCQ4
400013	062332	1998-05-09	178.23	.00	.00	178.23	PCQ4
400015	062333	1998-05-17	178.23	.00	.00	178.23	PCQ4

The customer table (CUSTOMER)

CUSTNO	FNAME	LNAME	ADDR	CITY	STATE	ZIPCODE
400001	KEITH	JONES	4501 W MOCKINGBIRD	DALLAS	TX	75209
400002	ARREN	ANELLI	40 FORD RD	DENVILLE	NJ	07834
400003	SUSAN	HOWARD	1107 SECOND AVE	REDWOOD CITY	CA	94063
400004	CAROL	EVANS	74 SUTTON CT	GREAT LAKES	IL	60088
400005	ELAINE	ROBERTS	12914 BRACKNELL	CERRITOS	CA	90701
400006	PAT	HONG	73 HIGH ST	SAN FRANCISCO	CA	94114
400007	PHIL	ROACH	25680 ORCHARD	DEARBORN HTS	MI	48125
400008	TIM	JOHNSON	145 W 27TH ST	SO CHICAGO HTS	IL	60411
400009	MARIANNE	BUSBEE	3920 BERWYN DR S	MOBILE	AL	36608
400010	ENRIQUE	OTHON	BOX 26729	RICHMOND	VA	23261
400011	WILLIAM C	FERGUSON	BOX 1283	MIAMI	FL	34002
400012	SD	HOEHN	PO BOX 27	RIDDLE	OR	97469
400013	DAVID R	KEITH	BOX 1266	MAGNOLIA	AR	71757
400014	R	BINDER	3425 WALDEN AVE	DEPEW	NY	14043
400015	VIVIAN	GEORGE	229 S 18TH ST	PHILADELPHIA	PA	19103
400016	J	NOETHLICH	11 KINGSTON CT	MERRIMACK	NH	03054

Figure 4-11   The contents of the customer and invoice tables

The invoice register

Figure 4-12 presents the printed invoice register that is prepared from the data in the customer and invoice tables. This register contains one line for each row in the invoice table that is matched by a row in the customer table. Here, the first five columns contain data from the invoice table, while the last three columns contain data from the customer table. Although the customer number column could come from either table, the program that follows gets it from the customer table.

The invoice register when using an inner join

```
INVOICE REGISTER - 08/05/98                                          PAGE: 001
  INVOICE       SUBTOTAL        TAX      SHIPPING        TOTAL   CUSTOMER

  062308         200.00        0.00          4.45       204.45   400012  SD             HOEHN
  062309          15.00        0.00          0.00        15.00   400005  ELANE          ROBERTS
  062310         140.00        0.00          7.50       147.50   400005  ELANE          ROBERTS
  062311         178.23        0.00          3.19       181.42   400014  R              BINDER
  062312         162.00        0.00         11.07       173.07   400002  ARREN          ANELLI
  062313          22.00        0.00          0.50        22.50   400011  WILLIAM C      FERGUSON
  062314         140.00        9.80          0.00       149.80   400003  SUSAN          HOWARD
  062315         178.23        0.00          3.19       181.42   400004  CAROL          EVANS
  062316         140.00        0.00          7.50       147.50   400010  ENRIQUE        OTHON
  062317         289.00        0.00          9.00       298.00   400011  WILLIAM C      FERGUSON
  062318         199.99        0.00          0.00       199.99   400012  SD             HOEHN
  062319         178.23        0.00          3.19       181.42   400015  VIVIAN         GEORGE
  062320        3245.00        0.00        160.00      3405.00   400015  VIVIAN         GEORGE
  062321         200.00        0.00          5.60       205.60   400001  KEITH          JONES
  062322          15.00        0.00          0.00        15.00   400014  R              BINDER
  062323         925.00        0.00         24.00       949.00   400011  WILLIAM C      FERGUSON
  062324         178.23        0.00          3.19       181.42   400014  R              BINDER
  062325         140.00        0.00          7.50       147.50   400002  ARREN          ANELLI
  062326         178.23        0.00          3.19       181.42   400011  WILLIAM C      FERGUSON
  062327         200.00       14.00          7.50       221.50   400003  SUSAN          HOWARD
  062328         178.23        0.00          3.19       181.42   400004  CAROL          EVANS
  062329         140.00        0.00          7.50       147.50   400010  ENRIQUE        OTHON
  062330        2295.00        0.00         14.00      2309.00   400011  WILLIAM C      FERGUSON
  062331         178.23        0.00          0.00       178.23   400012  SD             HOEHN
  062332         178.23        0.00          0.00       178.23   400013  DAVID R        KEITH
  062333         178.23        0.00          0.00       178.23   400015  VIVIAN         GEORGE

  TOTAL:       10072.06       23.80        285.26     10381.12           26 INVOICES ISSUED
```

Figure 4-12   The invoice register

The structure chart

Figure 4-13 presents the structure chart for this invoice register program. Here, module 000 has four subordinates. Module 100 issues the SQL statement that directs DB2 to create the cursor-controlled result table that this program uses. Then, if module 100 is successful, module 000 performs module 200 once for each row in the result table. Module 200 in turn performs module 210 to fetch the next row and module 220 to print the data that the row contains. This is the essential processing of the program.

When all the rows have been processed, module 000 performs module 300 to close the cursor. Then, it performs module 400 to print the total line of the register. You can see this total line at the bottom of the register in the previous figure.

In this structure chart, module 240 is used to write the first line on a new page of the register, and module 250 is used to write all of the other lines of the register. By isolating these WRITE statements in their own modules, a COBOL program that prints a report requires only two WRITE statements. This improves the efficiency of the program.

When a module is performed by more than one other module, it is called a *common module*. To identify a common module in a chart, we mark the upper right corner of its box with a triangle. In the structure chart in this figure, module 250 is a common module that's called by three other modules. When it's called by module 230, it's used to print the second heading line at the top of the register. When it's called by module 220, it's used to print an invoice line. And when it's called by module 400, it's used to print the total line.

The structure chart

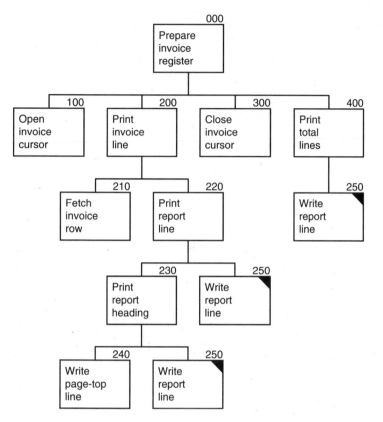

Description

- Module 000 in this structure chart performs module 100 to open the cursor-controlled result table for the joined customer and invoice tables. If the open statement is successful, module 000 performs module 200 once for each row in the result table until there are no more rows in the table. Then, module 000 performs module 300 to close the cursor and module 400 to print the total line for the invoice register.

- Module 200 performs module 210 to get the data from the next row in the result table. Then, it performs module 220 to print the next line on the invoice register.

- Module 220 performs module 230 if the next line should be printed on a new page of the invoice register. Whether or not module 220 performs module 230, it performs module 250 to write the next invoice line of the register.

- Module 230 performs module 240 to write the first heading line on a new page of a report and module 250 to write the other heading lines.

- Module 250 is a *common module*, which means that it is called by more than one module in the structure chart. The triangle in the upper right corner of a box in the structure chart indicates that it is a common module.

Figure 4-13   The structure chart for the invoice register program

The DCLGEN output and the COBOL listing

Figure 4-14 presents the DCLGEN output for the customer and invoice tables that the invoice register program uses, and figure 4-15 presents the COBOL listing for this program. Although this program is longer than the other programs you've seen so far, it isn't complicated. That's because most of the program is related to report-preparation tasks, not to DB2 operations.

On the first two pages of the COBOL listing, you can see the file description for the printer, the working-storage definitions for the switches and fields used by the program, and the definitions for the heading, report, and total lines printed by the program. If you have much COBOL experience, you shouldn't have any trouble interpreting this code.

```
*************************************************************************
* DCLGEN TABLE(MM01.CUSTOMER)                                          *
*        LIBRARY(MM01.DB2.DCLGENS(CUSTOMER))                           *
*        ACTION(REPLACE)                                               *
*        LANGUAGE(COBOL)                                               *
*        STRUCTURE(CUSTOMER-ROW)                                       *
*        QUOTE                                                         *
* ... IS THE DCLGEN COMMAND THAT MADE THE FOLLOWING STATEMENTS         *
*************************************************************************
     EXEC SQL DECLARE MM01.CUSTOMER TABLE
     ( CUSTNO                     CHAR(6) NOT NULL,
       FNAME                      CHAR(20) NOT NULL,
       LNAME                      CHAR(30) NOT NULL,
       ADDR                       CHAR(30) NOT NULL,
       CITY                       CHAR(20) NOT NULL,
       STATE                      CHAR(2) NOT NULL,
       ZIPCODE                    CHAR(10) NOT NULL,
     ) END-EXEC.
*************************************************************************
* COBOL DECLARATION FOR TABLE MM01.CUSTOMER                            *
*************************************************************************
 01  CUSTOMER-ROW.
     10  CUSTNO          PIC X(6).
     10  FNAME           PIC X(20).
     10  LNAME           PIC X(30).
     10  ADDR            PIC X(30).
     10  CITY            PIC X(20).
     10  STATE           PIC X(2).
     10  ZIPCODE         PIC X(10).
*************************************************************************
* THE NUMBER OF COLUMNS DESCRIBED BY THIS DECLARATION IS 7             *
*************************************************************************


*************************************************************************
* DCLGEN TABLE(MM01.INVOICE)                                           *
*        LIBRARY(MM01.DB2.DCLGENS(INVOICE))                            *
*        ACTION(REPLACE)                                               *
*        LANGUAGE(COBOL)                                               *
*        STRUCTURE(INVOICE-ROW)                                        *
*        QUOTE                                                         *
* ... IS THE DCLGEN COMMAND THAT MADE THE FOLLOWING STATEMENTS         *
*************************************************************************
     EXEC SQL DECLARE MM01.INVOICE TABLE
     ( INVCUST                    CHAR(6) NOT NULL,
       INVNO                      CHAR(6) NOT NULL,
       INVDATE                    DATE NOT NULL,
       INVSUBT                    DECIMAL(9, 2) NOT NULL,
       INVSHIP                    DECIMAL(7, 2) NOT NULL,
       INVTAX                     DECIMAL(7, 2) NOT NULL,
       INVTOTAL                   DECIMAL(9, 2) NOT NULL,
       INVPROM                    CHAR(10) NOT NULL,
     ) END-EXEC.
*************************************************************************
* COBOL DECLARATION FOR TABLE MM01.INVOICE                             *
*************************************************************************
 01  INVOICE-ROW.
     10  INVCUST         PIC X(6).
     10  INVNO           PIC X(60).
     10  INVDATE         PIC X(10).
     10  INVSUBT         PIC S(7)V(2) USAGE COMP-3.
     10  INVSHIP         PIC S(5)V(2) USAGE COMP-3.
     10  INVTAX          PIC S(5)V(2) USAGE COMP-3.
     10  INVTOTAL        PIC S(7)V(2) USAGE COMP-3.
     10  INVPROM         PIC X(10).
*************************************************************************
* THE NUMBER OF COLUMNS DESCRIBED BY THIS DECLARATION IS 8             *
*************************************************************************
```

Figure 4-14   The DCLGEN output for the customer and invoice tables

The invoice register program

```
     IDENTIFICATION DIVISION.
*
     PROGRAM-ID.      INVREG.
*
     ENVIRONMENT DIVISION.
*
     INPUT-OUTPUT SECTION.
*
     FILE-CONTROL.
*
         SELECT PRTOUT ASSIGN TO UT-S-PRTOUT.
*
     DATA DIVISION.
*
     FILE SECTION.
*
     FD   PRTOUT
          LABEL RECORDS ARE STANDARD
          BLOCK CONTAINS 0 RECORDS
          RECORD CONTAINS 132 CHARACTERS.
*
     01   PRTOUT-RECORD               PIC X(132).
*
     WORKING-STORAGE SECTION.
*
     01   SWITCHES.
          05   VALID-CURSOR-SW        PIC X    VALUE 'Y'.
               88   VALID-CURSOR               VALUE 'Y'.
               88   NOT-VALID-CURSOR           VALUE 'N'.
          05   END-OF-INVOICES-SW     PIC X    VALUE 'N'.
               88   END-OF-INVOICES            VALUE 'Y'.
*
     01   DATE-FIELDS.
          05   PRESENT-DATE           PIC 9(6).
          05   PRESENT-DATE-X         REDEFINES PRESENT-DATE.
               10   PRESENT-YEAR      PIC 99.
               10   PRESENT-MONTH     PIC 99.
               10   PRESENT-DAY       PIC 99.
*
     01   INVOICE-TOTAL-FIELDS        COMP-3.
          05   INVOICES-COUNT         PIC S9(9)       VALUE ZERO.
          05   INVOICES-SUBTOTAL      PIC S9(9)V99    VALUE ZERO.
          05   INVOICES-TAX           PIC S9(7)V99    VALUE ZERO.
          05   INVOICES-SHIPPING      PIC S9(7)V99    VALUE ZERO.
          05   INVOICES-TOTAL         PIC S9(9)V99    VALUE ZERO.
*
     01   PRINT-FIELDS                COMP-3.
          05   PAGE-COUNT             PIC S9(3)       VALUE ZERO.
          05   LINE-COUNT             PIC S9(3)       VALUE +999.
          05   LINES-ON-PAGE          PIC S9(3)       VALUE +50.
          05   SPACE-CONTROL          PIC S9(3)       VALUE +1.
*
```

Figure 4-15   The COBOL listing for the invoice register program (part 1 of 5)

The invoice register program   **Page 2**

```
01  HEADING-LINE-1.
    05  FILLER      PIC X(19)   VALUE 'INVOICE REGISTER - '.
    05  HLT-MONTH   PIC X(2).
    05  FILLER      PIC X       VALUE '/'.
    05  HLT-DAY     PIC X(2).
    05  FILLER      PIC X       VALUE '/'.
    05  HLT-YEAR    PIC X(2).
    05  FILLER      PIC X(63)   VALUE SPACES.
    05  FILLER      PIC X(6)    VALUE 'PAGE: '.
    05  HL1-PAGE    PIC X(5)    VALUE SPACES.
    05  FILLER      PIC X(31)   VALUE SPACES
*
01  HEADING-LINE-2.
    05  FILLER      PIC X(20)   VALUE 'INVOICE      SUBTOTAL'.
    05  FILLER      PIC X(20)   VALUE '          TAX    SHIP'.
    05  FILLER      PIC X(20)   VALUE 'PING         TOTAL  '.
    05  FILLER      PIC X(20)   VALUE 'CUSTOMER            '.
    05  FILLER      PIC X(20)   VALUE '                    '.
    05  FILLER      PIC X(20)   VALUE '                    '.
    05  FILLER      PIC X(12)   VALUE '            '.
*
01  REPORT-LINE.
    05  RL-INVNO    PIC X(6).
    05  FILLER      PIC X(2)    VALUE SPACES.
    05  RL-SUBTOTAL PIC Z(8)9.99.
    05  FILLER      PIC X(2)    VALUE SPACES.
    05  RL-TAX      PIC Z(6)9.99.
    05  FILLER      PIC X(2)    VALUE SPACES.
    05  RL-SHIPPING PIC Z(6)9.99.
    05  FILLER      PIC X(2)    VALUE SPACES.
    05  RL-TOTAL    PIC Z(8)9.99.
    05  FILLER      PIC X(2)    VALUE SPACES.
    05  RL-CUSTNO   PIC X(6).
    05  FILLER      PIC X(2)    VALUE SPACES.
    05  RL-FNAME    PIC X(20).
    05  FILLER      PIC X(2)    VALUE SPACES.
    05  RL-LNAME    PIC X(30).
    05  FILLER      PIC X(12)   VALUE SPACES.
*
01  TOTAL-LINE.
    05  FILLER      PIC X(8)    VALUE 'TOTAL: '.
    05  TL-SUBTOTAL PIC Z(8)9.99.
    05  FILLER      PIC X(2)    VALUE SPACES.
    05  TL-TAX      PIC Z(6)9.99.
    05  FILLER      PIC X(2)    VALUE SPACES.
    05  TL-SHIPPING PIC Z(6)9.99.
    05  FILLER      PIC X(2)    VALUE SPACES.
    05  TL-TOTAL    PIC Z(8)9.99.
    05  FILLER      PIC X(2)    VALUE SPACES.
    05  TL-COUNT    PIC Z(8)9.
    05  FILLER      PIC X(16)   VALUE ' INVOICES ISSUED'.
    05  FILLER      PIC X(47)   VALUE SPACES.
```

Figure 4-15   The COBOL listing for the invoice register program (part 2 of 5)

On the third page of the COBOL listing, you can see the four non-procedural SQL statements this program needs. The first two are INCLUDE statements for the DCLGEN output for the customer and invoice tables. The third is an INCLUDE statement for the SQL communication area. And the last is a DECLARE CURSOR statement that describes the result table that this program uses as it prepares the invoice register.

If you take a close look at the DECLARE CURSOR statement that's shaded here, you can see that its SELECT statement names eight columns, five from the invoice table and three from the customer table. Its ON clause says that the join should take place only when a customer number in the invoice table matches a customer number in the customer table. And its ORDER BY clause says the rows in the result table should be sorted by the invoice number column.

In the Procedure Division, module 000 opens the output file, prepares the date field for printing on the report, and then performs module 100 to open the cursor-controlled result table. When DB2 executes the OPEN statement in this module, it locates the DECLARE CURSOR statement, executes its SELECT statement, and generates the result table. If the cursor isn't opened successfully (SQLCODE NOT = 0), module 100 moves N to the valid cursor switch. Then, module 000 performs module 400 and ends the program.

On the other hand, if the cursor is opened successfully, module 000 performs module 200 until the end of the cursor-controlled result table is reached. Then, it performs module 300 to close the cursor and module 400 to print the total line on the register before it ends the program.

The invoice register program   **Page 3**

```
*
     EXEC SQL
         INCLUDE CUSTOMER
     END-EXEC.
*
     EXEC SQL
         INCLUDE INVOICE
     END-EXEC.
*
     EXEC SQL
         INCLUDE SQLCA
     END-EXEC.
*
     EXEC SQL
         DECLARE INVCURS CURSOR FOR
             SELECT A.INVNO,     A.INVSUBT,  A.INVTAX,   A.INVSHIP,
                    A.INVTOTAL,  B.CUSTNO,   B.FNAME,    B.LNAME
             FROM MM01.INVOICE A
                 INNER JOIN MM01.CUSTOMER B
             ON A.INVCUST = B.CUSTNO
         ORDER BY INVNO
     END-EXEC.
*
 PROCEDURE DIVISION.
*
 000-PREPARE-INVOICE-REGISTER.
*
     OPEN OUTPUT PRTOUT.
     ACCEPT PRESENT-DATE FROM DATE.
     MOVE PRESENT-MONTH TO HL1-MONTH.
     MOVE PRESENT-DAY    TO HL1-DAY.
     MOVE PRESENT-YEAR   TO HL1-YEAR.
     PERFORM 100-OPEN-INVOICE-CURSOR.
     IF VALID-CURSOR
         PERFORM 200-PRINT-INVOICE-LINE
             UNTIL END-OF-INVOICES
                 OR NOT-VALID-CURSOR
         PERFORM 300-CLOSE-INVOICE-CURSOR.
     PERFORM 400-PRINT-TOTAL-LINES.
     CLOSE PRTOUT.
     STOP RUN.
*
 100-OPEN-INVOICE-CURSOR.
*
     EXEC SQL
         OPEN INVCURS
     END-EXEC.
     IF SQLCODE NOT = 0
         MOVE 'N' TO VALID-CURSOR-SW.
*
```

Figure 4-15   The COBOL listing for the invoice register program (part 3 of 5)

On the fourth page of the COBOL listing, you can see module 200, which is performed over and over as the program works through the cursor-controlled result table. Each time it is performed, module 200 performs module 210 to retrieve the next invoice row. In this module, you can see that the FETCH statement uses the INTO clause to list the host variables in the DCLGEN output that are used for the values received from the invoice and customer tables.

If the FETCH statement retrieves a row successfully, module 200 increments the count and total fields, formats the report detail line, and performs module 220 to print the line. But if the FETCH statement encounters the end of the cursor-controlled result table (SQLCODE = 100), module 210 moves Y to END-OF-INVOICES-SW. And if any SQLCODE value other than 0 is encountered, module 210 moves N to VALID-CURSOR-SW. In either case, module 200 doesn't do any more processing and control goes back to module 000.

The invoice register program

```
200-PRINT-INVOICE-LINE.
*
    PERFORM 210-FETCH-INVOICE-ROW.
    IF NOT END-OF-INVOICES
        IF VALID-CURSOR
            ADD 1           TO INVOICES-COUNT
            ADD INVSUBT     TO INVOICES-SUBTOTAL
            ADD INVTAX      TO INVOICES-TAX
            ADD INVSHIP     TO INVOICES-SHIPPING
            ADD INVTOTAL    TO INVOICES-TOTAL
            MOVE INVNO      TO RL-INVNO
            MOVE INVSUBT    TO RL-SUBTOTAL
            MOVE INVTAX     TO RL-TAX
            MOVE INVSHIP    TO RL-SHIPPING
            MOVE INVTOTAL   TO RL-TOTAL
            MOVE CUSTNO     TO RL-CUSTNO
            MOVE FNAME      TO RL-FNAME
            MOVE LNAME      TO RL-LNAME
            PERFORM 220-PRINT-REPORT-LINE.
*
 210-FETCH-INVOICE-ROW.
*
    EXEC SQL
        FETCH INVCURS
            INTO :INVNO,    :INVSUBT,   :INVTAX,    :INVSHIP,
                 :INVTOTAL, :CUSTNO,    :FNAME,     :LNAME
    END-EXEC.
    IF SQLCODE = 100
        MOVE 'Y' TO END-OF-INVOICES-SW
    ELSE
        IF SQLCODE NOT = 0
            MOVE 'N' TO VALID-CURSOR-SW.
*
 220-PRINT-REPORT-LINE.
*
    IF LINE-COUNT > LINES-ON-PAGE
        PERFORM 230-PRINT-REPORT-HEADING
        MOVE 1 TO LINE-COUNT.
    MOVE REPORT-LINE TO PRTOUT-RECORD.
    PERFORM 250-WRITE-REPORT-LINE.
    ADD 1 TO LINE-COUNT.
    MOVE 1 TO SPACE-CONTROL.
*
 230-PRINT-REPORT-HEADING.
*
    ADD 1 TO PAGE-COUNT.
    MOVE PAGE-COUNT TO HL1-PAGE.
    MOVE HEADING-LINE-1 TO PRTOUT-RECORD.
    PERFORM 240-WRITE-PAGE-TOP-LINE.
    MOVE 2 TO SPACE-CONTROL.
    MOVE HEADING-LINE-2 TO PRTOUT-RECORD.
    PERFORM 250-WRITE-REPORT-LINE.
*
```

Figure 4-15   The COBOL listing for the invoice register program (part 4 of 5)

On the last page of the invoice register program, you can see that module 300 also turns on the valid-cursor switch if the cursor isn't closed successfully. Then, in module 400, you can see that this module prints the total line if the valid-cursor switch is still turned on. Otherwise, it prints an error message to alert the user that something went wrong.

Of course, this program is just a simple example of how you can use an inner join to solve an application problem. In a production environment, for example, you're not likely to write an invoice register program that lists all of the invoices a firm has issued. More likely, a program like this would include just the invoices for a specific day. To do that, though, all you have to add is an appropriate WHERE clause to the SELECT component of the DECLARE CURSOR statement.

But what if a user requested that this invoice report list all of the customers in the customer table, even those who aren't matched by rows in the invoice table? How could this program be modified to produce such a report? If you said to change the inner join to an outer join, you're right. And that's illustrated next.

The invoice register program

```
 240-WRITE-PAGE-TOP-LINE.
*
     WRITE PRTOUT-RECORD
         AFTER ADVANCING PAGE.
*
 250-WRITE-REPORT-LINE.
*
     WRITE PRTOUT-RECORD
         AFTER SPACE-CONTROL LINES.
*
 300-CLOSE-INVOICE-CURSOR.
*
     EXEC SQL
         CLOSE INVCURS
     END-EXEC.
     IF SQLCODE NOT = 0
         MOVE 'N' TO VALID-CURSOR-SW.
*
 400-PRINT-TOTAL-LINES.
*
     IF VALID-CURSOR
         MOVE INVOICES-SUBTOTAL  TO TL-SUBTOTAL
         MOVE INVOICES-TAX        TO TL-TAX
         MOVE INVOICES-SHIPPING   TO TL-SHIPPING
         MOVE INVOICES-TOTAL      TO TL-TOTAL
         MOVE INVOICES-COUNT      TO TL-COUNT
         MOVE TOTAL-LINE          TO PRTOUT-RECORD
     ELSE
         MOVE '****  DB2 ERROR -- INCOMPLETE REPORT  ****'
                                  TO PRTOUT-RECORD.
     MOVE 2 TO SPACE-CONTROL.
     PERFORM 250-WRITE-REPORT-LINE.
*
```

Figure 4-15   The COBOL listing for the invoice register program (part 5 of 5)

The program modifications for the use of an outer join

Figure 4-16 presents the invoice register for the previous program when it includes all of the customer rows. It also presents the DECLARE CURSOR statement that provides the outer join that's needed for preparing this register.

The invoice register

If you compare the register in figure 4-16 with the one in figure 4-12, you can see that the expanded register includes customers without invoice data. In this case, the INVOICE column contains the literal 'NONE' and all of the dollar columns contain zeros.

The coding changes

To provide for this expanded invoice register, you need only modify the DECLARE CURSOR statement in part 3 of figure 4-15 so it looks like the one in figure 4-16. As you can see, a FULL OUTER JOIN is used instead of the INNER JOIN, and VALUE functions are used to place literal values instead of null values in the five columns that are derived from the invoice table. In particular, these VALUE clauses put zeros in the four columns that are added to the totals for the register.

This program shows how easy it can be to modify the data that's extracted by a program when you're working with the tables in a DB2 database. In contrast, if the data for this program was extracted from indexed VSAM files, expanding the invoice register would require significant changes in the COBOL program.

The invoice register when using a full outer join

```
INVOICE REGISTER - 08/05/98                                              PAGE: 001
   INVOICE     SUBTOTAL        TAX    SHIPPING       TOTAL   CUSTOMER

   NONE            0.00       0.00        0.00        0.00   400005  ELANE         ROBERTS
   NONE            0.00       0.00        0.00        0.00   400006  PAT           HONG
   NONE            0.00       0.00        0.00        0.00   400007  PHIL          ROACH
   NONE            0.00       0.00        0.00        0.00   400008  TIM           JOHNSON
   NONE            0.00       0.00        0.00        0.00   400009  MARIANNE      BUSBEE
   NONE            0.00       0.00        0.00        0.00   400016  J             NOETHLICH
   062308        200.00       0.00        4.45      204.45   400012  SD            HOEHN
   062309         15.00       0.00        0.00       15.00   400011  WILLIAM C     FERGUSON
   062310        140.00       0.00        7.50      147.50   400011  WILLIAM C     FERGUSON
   062311        178.23       0.00        3.19      181.42   400014  R             BINDER
   062312        162.00       0.00       11.07      173.07   400002  ARREN         ANELLI
   062313         22.00       0.00        0.50       22.50   400011  WILLIAM C     FERGUSON
   062314        140.00       9.80        0.00      149.80   400003  SUSAN         HOWARD
   062315        178.23       0.00        3.19      181.42   400004  CAROL         EVANS
   062316        140.00       0.00        7.50      147.50   400010  ENRIQUE       OTHON
   062317        289.00       0.00        9.00      298.00   400011  WILLIAM C     FERGUSON
   062318        199.99       0.00        0.00      199.99   400012  SD            HOEHN
   062319        178.23       0.00        3.19      181.42   400015  VIVIAN        GEORGE
   062320       3245.00       0.00      160.00     3405.00   400015  VIVIAN        GEORGE
   062321        200.00       0.00        5.60      205.60   400001  KEITH         JONES
   062322         15.00       0.00        0.00       15.00   400014  R             BINDER
   062323        925.00       0.00       24.00      949.00   400011  WILLIAM C     FERGUSON
   062324        178.23       0.00        3.19      181.42   400014  R             BINDER
   062325        140.00       0.00        7.50      147.50   400002  ARREN         ANELLI
   062326        178.23       0.00        3.19      181.42   400011  WILLIAM C     FERGUSON
   062327        200.00      14.00        7.50      221.50   400003  SUSAN         HOWARD
   062328        178.23       0.00        3.19      181.42   400004  CAROL         EVANS
   062329        140.00       0.00        7.50      147.50   400010  ENRIQUE       OTHON
   062330       2295.00       0.00       14.00     2309.00   400011  WILLIAM C     FERGUSON
   062331        178.23       0.00        0.00      178.23   400012  SD            HOEHN
   062332        178.23       0.00        0.00      178.23   400013  DAVID R       KEITH
   062333        178.23       0.00        0.00      178.23   400015  VIVIAN        GEORGE

   TOTAL:      10072.06      23.80      285.26    10381.12           32 INVOICES ISSUED
```

The full outer join that replaces the inner join in the shaded portion of part 3 in figure 4-15

```
EXEC SQL
    DECLARE INVCURS CURSOR FOR
        SELECT  VALUE(A.INVNO, 'NONE') AS INVNO,
                VALUE(A.INVSUBT, 0) AS INVSUBT,
                VALUE(A.INVTAX, 0) AS INVTAX,
                VALUE(A.INVSHIP, 0) AS INVSHIP,
                VALUE(A.INVTOTAL, 0) AS INVTOTAL,
                B.CUSTNO AS CUSTNO, B.FNAME, B.LNAME
        FROM MM01.INVOICE A
            FULL JOIN MM01.CUSTOMER B
                ON A.INVCUST = B.CUSTNO
        ORDER BY INVNO, CUSTNO
END-EXEC.
```

Figure 4-16   The invoice register program when using a full outer join

Perspective

In practice, you'll find that most DB2 shops have used joins for many years. If you're a maintenance programmer working on older programs, though, you may only come across inner joins coded with the implicit format because that was all that was available prior to version 4. Today, however, version 4 is widely used in MVS shops and version 5 has been released for OS/390, so you'll find that most of the newer programs use explicit inner and outer joins.

Now that you've finished the last chapter in this first section of the book, you should have a solid understanding of what DB2 can do. You should know how to extract data from a single table as you work with one-row and multi-row result tables. You should know how to insert, update, and delete rows in a table. And you should know how to join the data from two or more rows into a single result table.

With that as background, you can now read the chapters in section 2 to expand on your coding skills. You can also read the chapters in section 3 to learn the skills you need for testing your programs. To a large extent, you can read the chapters in either section in whatever sequence you prefer, but be sure to read all of them because each one presents a useful set of skills.

Section 2

Other programming essentials

This section expands upon the introduction to DB2 programming in section 1 by presenting other skills that every DB2 programmer should have. When you complete this section, you should be able to design and code complete DB2 COBOL programs using the techniques of the best professional programmers.

To start, chapter 5 shows you how to use the IN, BETWEEN, and LIKE keywords of the WHERE clause and how to combine simple selection conditions with AND, OR, and NOT to create complex selection conditions. Then, chapter 6 shows you how to use column functions in a SELECT statement to do tasks like calculating averages and sums. Chapter 7 shows you how to use scalar functions to do tasks like converting data from one format to another, extracting substrings from larger strings, and determining the absolute age of a date item. And chapter 8 shows you how to work with variable length data and null values.

In chapter 9, you can learn how to use subquery statements, which are SELECT statements that are nested inside other SQL statements. In chapter 10, you can learn how to use the error-handling features of DB2 that go beyond checking the value of SQLCODE. And in chapter 11, you can learn how to optimize locking efficiency and concurrency as you modify the data in a table.

To make this section as easy to use as possible, each chapter is independent, which means you can read these chapters in whatever sequence you prefer. So, for example, if you want to learn more about error handling, you can skip to chapter 10 without reading the chapters that precede it. No matter what sequence you read these chapters in, though, make sure you read them all since each one presents useful DB2 skills.

5

How to use advanced selection conditions

In chapter 2, you learned how to code simple selection conditions in WHERE clauses that determine which rows will be retrieved into the result tables. Now, in this chapter, you can learn how to code advanced selection conditions. First, you'll learn how to use the IN, BETWEEN, and LIKE keywords in WHERE clauses. Then, you'll learn how to use the AND and OR operators in compound conditions. Last, you'll see a complete COBOL program that uses some of these features.

How to use the IN, BETWEEN, and LIKE keywords

IN, BETWEEN, and LIKE are DB2 keywords that have no equivalent in COBOL. When you use one of these keywords to start a phrase in a WHERE clause, the coding is usually simpler than the COBOL alternative.

How to use an IN phrase

Figure 5-1 presents the syntax for a WHERE clause that uses an IN phrase. When you use this phrase, the value of the item before the keyword IN is compared with the value of each of the items in the list that follows.

To illustrate, the first example in this figure selects those rows in a department table where the department number is equal to A01, B04, E02, or G07. When you use an IN phrase, commas must separate the items in the list and the entire list must be coded within parentheses, but the order of the items doesn't matter. As in COBOL, non-numeric literals must be enclosed in quotation marks, but numeric literals don't require quotation marks.

The second example uses two host variables to specify the state codes that should be used when the selection is done. When you use a statement like this, the program can get the values for the host variables interactively from the user.

The third example shows how the NOT keyword can be used in an IN phrase. Here, a row is selected from an employee table, but only for those employees who don't live in California or Washington. When you use the word NOT, though, you should be aware that DB2 doesn't use any indexes, which can degrade performance. That's one reason why it's usually best to avoid the use of the word NOT.

The syntax of a WHERE clause that uses an IN phrase

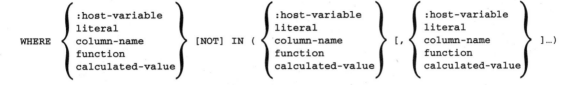

An IN phrase with a list of four alphanumeric literals

```
SELECT FNAME, LNAME, DEPTNO
    FROM MM01.DEPT
        WHERE DEPTNO IN ('A01', 'B04', 'E02', 'G07')
```

An IN phrase with a list of two host variables

```
SELECT FNAME, LNAME, EMPNO
    FROM MM01.EMP
        WHERE STATE IN (:STATE-CHOICE1, :STATE-CHOICE2)
```

An IN phrase that's preceded by NOT

```
SELECT FNAME, LNAME, EMPNO
    FROM MM01.EMP
        WHERE STATE NOT IN ('CA', 'WA')
```

Description

- Use an IN phrase to select each row that has a column value equal to one of those listed. Enclose the list in parentheses, and separate the items in the list by commas; the blanks are optional.

- Use the NOT keyword before an IN phrase to select each row that has a column value that doesn't equal one of the listed values. When you use NOT, however, DB2 doesn't use any indexes to do the selection, which can degrade performance.

- The order of the items in the list of values doesn't affect the order of the result.

- Using an IN phrase gives the same result as a set of conditions connected by OR.

- In all selection conditions, character comparisons are case sensitive. For example, two abbreviations for California that are often recognized as equivalent, CA and Ca, are not equivalent to DB2.

Figure 5-1   How to use an IN phrase in a WHERE clause

How to use a BETWEEN phrase

Figure 5-2 presents the syntax for a WHERE clause that uses a BETWEEN phrase. This is useful when you want to specify a range of values in the selection condition. The items that you code in this phrase give the values of the lower and upper limits of the range.

The first example in this figure selects the rows in a department table where the department number is between C00 and D31. Because the limits in a BETWEEN phrase are inclusive, this includes departments C00 and D31.

The second example uses the keyword NOT to select all the rows that don't have valid zip codes. Here again, though, DB2 doesn't use indexes when it processes the word NOT, so performance may suffer.

The third example uses numeric literals to set the lower and upper limits for a range of invoice totals. In this case, rows from the invoice table are selected where the invoice total is between $1,000 and $10,000. Notice that quotation marks aren't coded when you use numeric literals.

The last example in this figure shows how host variables can be used in a BETWEEN phrase. Here again, the program can get the values for the host variables from the terminal user. Some applications use this technique to let users browse the data when they don't know the exact search values.

The syntax of a WHERE clause that uses a BETWEEN phrase

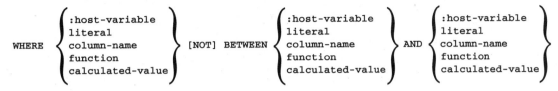

A BETWEEN phrase that uses two alphanumeric literals

```
SELECT FNAME, LNAME, DEPTNO
    FROM MM01.DEPT
        WHERE DEPTNO BETWEEN 'C00' AND 'D31'
```

A BETWEEN phrase that's preceded by NOT

```
SELECT FNAME, LNAME, EMPNO
    FROM MM01.EMP
        WHERE ZIPCODE NOT BETWEEN '00000-0000' AND '99999-9999'
```

A BETWEEN phrase that uses two numeric literals

```
SELECT INVNO, INVTOTAL
    FROM MM01.INVOICE
        WHERE INVTOTAL BETWEEN 1000 AND 10000
```

A BETWEEN phrase that uses two host variables

```
SELECT FNAME, LNAME, EMPNO
    FROM MM01.EMP
        WHERE LNAME BETWEEN :LOW-NAME-VALUE AND :HIGH-NAME-VALUE
```

Description

- Use a BETWEEN phrase to select rows in which a column has a value within two limits.

- Specify the lower limit of the BETWEEN phrase first, then the upper limit. These limits are *inclusive*.

- Use the NOT keyword before the BETWEEN phrase to select rows in which a column doesn't have a value within the two limits. Here again, though, DB2 doesn't use any indexes for the selection when you use NOT, which can degrade performance.

Figure 5-2   How to use a BETWEEN phrase in a WHERE clause

How to use a LIKE phrase

Figure 5-3 shows the syntax for a WHERE clause that uses a LIKE phrase. After the word WHERE, you code a column name that refers to a column that contains character data. Then, you code a literal or host variable that provides the *mask* that the selection will be based upon. This mask is a pattern of characters that DB2 uses to evaluate the contents of the column.

When you code the mask, you can use two special characters: the percent sign (%) and the underscore (_). The percent sign means that any number of characters, including zero characters, can stand in its position in the column value. And the underscore means that any single character can stand in its position in the column value.

The examples in this figure show how LIKE phrases can be used to select rows from a table that contains a CITY column. To retrieve rows where the values in the CITY column begin with LA, you code LA% as in the first example. In this case, the result table contains the four cities that meet this condition.

The second example directs DB2 to select rows where the value of the CITY column begins with the letter L and contains the letter S in any other position. In this case, the result table contains all of the cities in the base table except LE ROY.

If you want to find the city names that begin with LAS or LOS, you can code a mask like the one in the third example. Here, an underscore in the second position specifies not only that a matching string must begin with L, but that it must contain an S in position three. In this case, the result table contains LAS VEGAS and LOS ANGELES, but it also includes LAST CHANCE.

To limit this selection further, the mask in the last example specifies that the column value must start with L followed by any character, S, a space, and any other characters. This excludes LAST CHANCE from the result table.

Notice in all of these examples that each mask ends with a percent sign. That's to handle any extra spaces at the end of a column value. If, for example, you code

```
WHERE CITY LIKE 'LOS%S'
```

DB2 won't return any rows from the table because this mask specifies a value that contains LOS in the first three positions and S in the last position. However, since the CITY column is 20 character long, all of the values end with a space. That's why you need to code the WHERE clause like this:

```
WHERE CITY LIKE 'LOS%S%'
```

Then, DB2 will return a row for LOS ANGELES.

The syntax of a WHERE clause that uses a LIKE phrase

```
WHERE column-name [NOT] LIKE {literal | :host-variable}
```

CITY values, examples, and result tables

CITY values	SELECT statements	Result table values
LA ROSE	SELECT CITY	LA ROSE
LA SALLE	FROM MM01.CITIES	LA SALLE
LAS VEGAS	WHERE CITY LIKE 'LA%'	LAS VEGAS
LAST CHANCE		LAST CHANCE
LE ROY		
LEES CREEK	SELECT CITY	LA ROSE
LEESVILLE	FROM MM01.CITIES	LA SALLE
LOS ANGELES	WHERE CITY LIKE 'L%S%'	LAS VEGAS
		LAST CHANCE
		LEES CREEK
		LEESVILLE
		LOS ANGELES
	SELECT CITY	LAS VEGAS
	FROM MM01.CITIES	LAST CHANCE
	WHERE CITY LIKE 'L_S%'	LOS ANGELES
	SELECT CITY	LAS VEGAS
	FROM MM01.CITIES	LOS ANGELES
	WHERE CITY LIKE 'L_S %'	

Description

- Use a LIKE phrase to specify a character string that is similar to the column value of rows you want to select. However, you can only use a LIKE phrase with character or graphic data, not with numeric or datetime data.

- The literal or host variable after the word LIKE provides a *mask* that determines which values in the column satisfy the condition. Within the mask, you can use a percent sign (%) to indicate any string of zero or more characters and an underscore (_) to indicate any single character.

- Use the NOT keyword before a LIKE phrase to specify a character string that isn't similar to the column value of rows you want to select.

- DB2 may not be able to use an index (1) if you code the NOT keyword before a LIKE phrase or (2) if you code one of the special characters (% or _) at the beginning of the mask. So if performance is an issue, you should avoid these coding techniques.

Figure 5-3   How to use a LIKE phrase in a WHERE clause

How to use compound conditions

A *compound condition* combines two or more selection conditions (also called *predicates*) by connecting them with the AND or OR operators. When you code a compound condition, you can also use the NOT operator to specify the opposite of a predicate. In figure 5-5, you can see the syntax for a compound condition.

The ellipsis (…) at the end of the second search condition means that there's no limit to the number of predicates you can combine in a single compound condition.

How to use the AND and OR operators

To combine two predicates in a compound condition, you code either the AND or the OR operator between them. AND means a row must satisfy both predicates, while OR means a row must match at least one of the two.

When you combine three or more predicates with ANDs or ORs, DB2 first evaluates any NOT predicates. Then, it evaluates all of the AND relationships before it evaluates the ORs. To override this default sequence of evaluation, you can use parentheses as shown in the next figure.

The first example in figure 5-4 uses a compound condition to select customers who live in either Virginia or Maryland or California. This produces the same result table as the second example, which uses an IN phrase. In this case, there's no difference in performance, so you can use the coding that you prefer.

If you want to compare the contents of *different* columns, though, you can't use an IN phrase. If, for example, you want to select rows for employees who were hired before 1997 or who are making more than $40,000, you have to use two conditions connected with OR as in the third example.

Whenever you use the OR operator to connect predicates that refer to different columns, you should be aware that DB2 can't use any single-column indexes that are available. This, of course, can degrade the performance of the selection. DB2 can, however, use an index that spans both columns that are connected by the OR operator.

The last example in this figure uses the AND operator to connect two predicates that include host variables. In this case, the program can be coded so a terminal user can enter the first letters of a customer's last name and the customer's state code into the host variables. Then, the program can run the SELECT statement to get a result table that includes the matching customer rows. Here, both predicates must be satisfied in order for the row to be included in the result table.

The syntax for compound conditions

```
WHERE [NOT] search-condition-1 {AND | OR [NOT] search-condition-2}...
```

A compound condition that selects customers who live in Virginia or Maryland or California

```
SELECT FNAME, LNAME, CITY, STATE, ZIPCODE
    FROM MM01.CUSTOMER
        WHERE STATE = 'VA' OR STATE = 'MD' OR STATE = 'CA'
```

A statement that uses an IN phrase to select customers who live in Virginia or Maryland or California

```
SELECT FNAME, LNAME, CITY, STATE, ZIPCODE
    FROM MM01.CUSTOMER
        WHERE STATE IN ('VA', 'MD', 'CA')
```

A compound condition that uses the OR operator

```
SELECT EMPNO, HIREDATE, SALARY
    FROM MM01.EMPLOYEE
        WHERE HIREDATE < '1997-01-01' OR SALARY > 40000
```

A compound condition that uses the AND operator

```
SELECT FNAME, LNAME, CITY, STATE, ZIPCODE
    FROM MM01.CUSTOMER
        WHERE STATE = :STATE-STRING AND LNAME LIKE :NAME-STRING
```

Description

- Use AND to specify that the search must satisfy both of the conditions.
- Use OR to specify that the search must satisfy at least one of the conditions.
- When DB2 evaluates a compound condition, it evaluates the operators in this sequence: (1) NOTs, (2) ANDs, and (3) ORs.
- When you use OR to connect conditions, DB2 doesn't use any single-column indexes to do the selection, which can degrade performance. However, DB2 will use an index that spans both of the columns connected by the OR.

Figure 5-4   How to use the AND and OR operators

When and how to use parentheses in compound conditions

When DB2 interprets a compound condition, it follows a specific order. First, it evaluates the NOT operators that precede individual predicates. Next, it evaluates predicates that are connected by ANDs. Last, it evaluates predicates that are connected by ORs. If this isn't what you want, though, you can use parentheses to change this evaluation sequence. Then, DB2 first evaluates the conditions in the innermost sets of parentheses, followed by the conditions in the outer sets.

To illustrate the use of parentheses, figure 5-5 presents five examples of SELECT statements. To start, consider how you would code a SELECT statement that retrieves data for those customers whose last names begin with the letters GR and who live in either the state of New Jersey or in New York City. At first thought, you might code a WHERE clause like the first example in this figure.

Although this WHERE clause will produce a result table that contains information for the customers who live in New York City with the right last names, it will, unfortunately, include *all* New Jersey customers, regardless of their last names. That's because DB2 processes the conditions that are joined by AND before it deals with OR.

To override this evaluation sequence, you can enclose the two predicates connected by OR with parentheses, as shown in the second example. Here, DB2 checks the LNAME value not only for New York City customers, but also for New Jersey customers.

The placement of parentheses is also important when using NOT with AND and OR operators as illustrated by the third example in this figure. Can you tell which search condition the NOT affects? The first, the second, or both? In this case, the NOT keyword is part of the first predicate and has no affect on the second predicate. To negate both predicates, though, you can enclose the entire compound condition in parentheses and precede it with NOT, as shown in the fourth example.

But why use NOT logic in your programs when you can usually avoid it as illustrated by the fifth example in this figure? Here, the SELECT statement returns the same result table as the fourth example. It's also easier to understand and will probably perform faster. That's why it's usually worth taking the time to rephrase your WHERE clauses so they don't use NOT keywords. In the future, programmers who have to maintain your code will appreciate it.

A compound condition without parentheses

```
SELECT FNAME, LNAME, CITY, STATE, ZIPCODE
    FROM MM01.CUSTOMER
        WHERE STATE =      'NJ'
           OR CITY   LIKE 'NEW YORK%'
          AND LNAME LIKE 'GR%'
```

A compound condition with parentheses

```
SELECT FNAME, LNAME, CITY, STATE, ZIPCODE
    FROM MM01.CUSTOMER
        WHERE (STATE =      'NJ'
           OR  CITY   LIKE 'NEW YORK%')
          AND   LNAME LIKE 'GR%'
```

A compound condition with a NOT operator that negates one predicate

```
SELECT EMPNO, HIREDATE, SALARY
    FROM MM01.EMPLOYEE
        WHERE NOT (SALARY >= 50000) AND (HIREDATE > '1995-01-01')
```

A compound condition with a NOT operator that negates a set of predicates

```
SELECT EMPNO, HIREDATE, SALARY
    FROM MM01.EMPLOYEE
        WHERE NOT (SALARY >= 50000 AND HIREDATE > '1998-01-01')
```

A compound condition that's rephrased to eliminate the NOT operator

```
SELECT EMPNO, HIREDATE, SALARY
    FROM MM01.EMPLOYEE
        WHERE SALARY < 50000 AND HIREDATE <= '1998-01-01'
```

Description

- When parentheses are used, the conditions in the innermost sets of parentheses are evaluated first, followed by the conditions in outer sets.

- You should use parentheses to clarify the evaluation of any compound condition that is confusing.

- In general, you should avoid using NOT. This usually makes a WHERE clause easier to understand, and it will often improve performance too.

Figure 5-5   When and how to use parentheses in a compound condition

A COBOL program that uses advanced selection conditions

This chapter closes by presenting a COBOL program that displays customer information for each customer whose last name begins with the characters the user enters and who lives in the state the user enters. To keep it simple, this program runs under TSO. That way, you can concentrate on the DB2 coding that this program illustrates.

The interactive screen

Figure 5-6 presents an interactive terminal session for this customer inquiry program. For each inquiry, the user is asked to reply to two prompts. The first gets the search value for the customer's last name, and the second gets the search value for the state. After the user supplies these search values, the program gets the rows that satisfy the search conditions and displays one line on the terminal for each row in the result table.

In the first inquiry in this figure, the user entered the letter H in response to the customer name prompt and entered a blank line in response to the state code prompt. That directed the program to display all customers whose last names begin with the letter H and who live in any state. As you can see, that yielded three rows, two from California and one from Oregon.

The second inquiry in this figure shows that the user narrowed the selection by also specifying a state code. Here, the user again entered H for the customer last name, but this time entered CA for the state code. As a result, the program displays just the information for the California customers that start with the letter H.

To end the program, the user can enter 99 in response to either the name or state code prompt. And that's what the user did after the second inquiry.

An interactive session

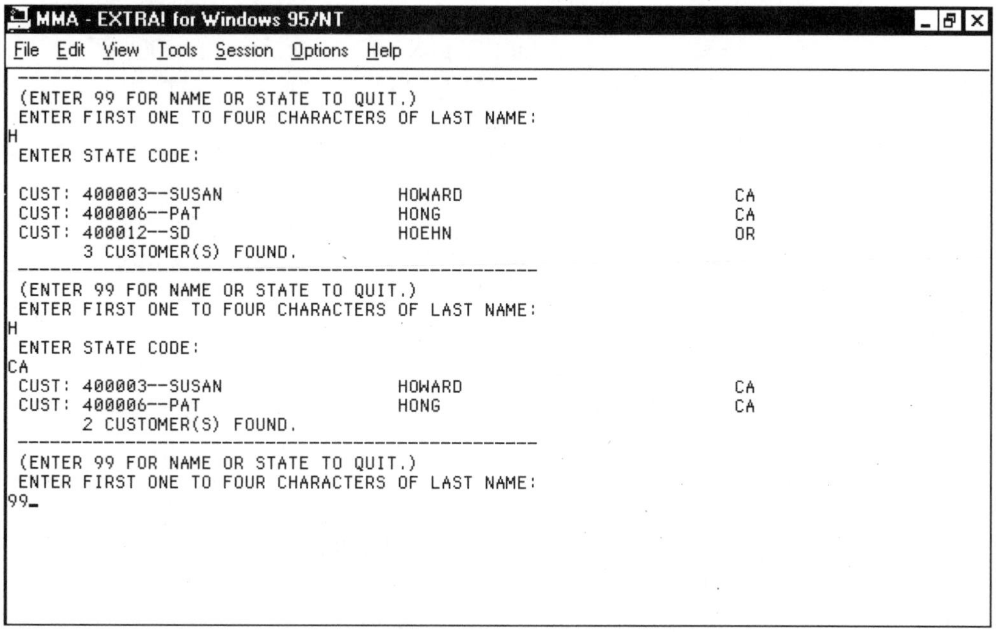

```
MMA - EXTRA! for Windows 95/NT                                    _ ☐ ✕
File  Edit  View  Tools  Session  Options  Help
-------------------------------------------------------
(ENTER 99 FOR NAME OR STATE TO QUIT.)
ENTER FIRST ONE TO FOUR CHARACTERS OF LAST NAME:
H
 ENTER STATE CODE:

 CUST: 400003--SUSAN           HOWARD               CA
 CUST: 400006--PAT             HONG                 CA
 CUST: 400012--SD              HOEHN                OR
     3 CUSTOMER(S) FOUND.
-------------------------------------------------------
(ENTER 99 FOR NAME OR STATE TO QUIT.)
ENTER FIRST ONE TO FOUR CHARACTERS OF LAST NAME:
H
 ENTER STATE CODE:
CA
 CUST: 400003--SUSAN           HOWARD               CA
 CUST: 400006--PAT             HONG                 CA
     2 CUSTOMER(S) FOUND.
-------------------------------------------------------
(ENTER 99 FOR NAME OR STATE TO QUIT.)
ENTER FIRST ONE TO FOUR CHARACTERS OF LAST NAME:
99_
```

Description

- In the first inquiry, the user enters the letter H in response to the customer name prompt and a blank in response to the state code prompt.

- In the second inquiry, the user enters the letter H in response to the customer name prompt and the letters CA in response to the state code prompt.

- In the third inquiry, the user enters 99 to end the program.

Figure 5-6   The interactive screen for the customer inquiry program

The structure chart

Figure 5-7 shows the structure chart for this program. Here, module 000 performs module 100 repeatedly until the user keys in 99 to end the program. Each time module 100 is performed, it performs module 110, which gets the user entries for last name and state and formats them for use in LIKE masks in a WHERE clause.

If the user hasn't entered 99 to end the program, module 100 then performs module 120 to open the cursor-controlled result table for those customers that satisfy the search conditions. After that, it performs module 130 repeatedly to display the data for each row in the result table. Last, it performs module 150 to close the cursor-controlled result table so the program is ready for the next set of user entries.

The DCLGEN output

The DCLGEN output for the CUSTOMER table that this program uses is the same as the output used by the program for the last chapter. Although you shouldn't need to review it, you can find it in figure 4-14.

The structure chart

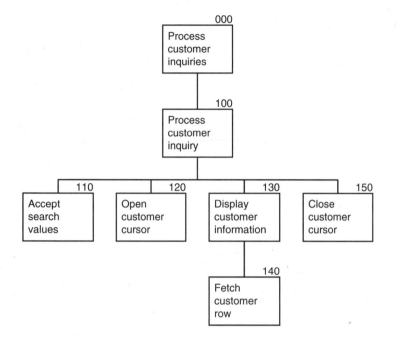

Description

- Module 000 performs module 100 repeatedly until the user keys in 99 to end the program.

- Module 100 performs module 110 to accept the search values. If the user doesn't enter 99, module 100 performs module 120 to open the cursor and then performs module 130 once for each row in the result table.

- Each time module 130 is performed, it performs module 140 to get the next row from the result table. It then displays the data for that row.

- When the FETCH operation in module 140 results in the end-of-table condition, module 100 doesn't display any data. Instead, it performs module 150 to close the cursor so the program can either start a new inquiry or end.

Figure 5-7   The structure chart for the customer inquiry program

The COBOL listing

Figure 5-8 presents the COBOL listing for this program. Since this program works much like the programs you've already seen, you shouldn't have much trouble following it. You should, however, focus on the two shaded blocks.

The shaded block on page 1 is the DECLARE CURSOR statement that's used to get the customer rows. Here, the WHERE clause contains two predicates connected by AND that include LIKE phrases. The first predicate causes DB2 to compare the contents of the CUSTOMER table's LNAME column to the host variable :NAME-STRING. The second predicate causes DB2 to compare the contents of the STATE column to the host variable :STATE-STRING. Before the program opens the cursor for each inquiry, the program must move the proper LIKE masks to these host variables.

The shaded block on page 2 is the paragraph for module 110 on the structure chart. This paragraph first sets the values of the two host variables to spaces. Next, it prompts the user to enter up to four search characters for the last name column. Then, the ACCEPT statement stores the value the user enters in the field NAME-STRING. Since this field is defined as a five-byte field, it's long enough to contain the one to four characters the user enters, plus a percent sign.

To combine the characters the user enters with the percent sign, the program uses a STRING statement. This statement takes the contents of NAME-STRING up to the delimiter character (a space) and appends five percent signs to it. Then, it stores the result right back in the NAME-STRING variable, which will truncate any characters after the first five.

If, for example, the user enters HE in response to the last-name prompt, the value in NAME-STRING starts with HE followed by three spaces. The STRING statement then converts this value to HE%%%% and stores it back into NAME-STRING, which truncates two percent signs. Later, when module 120 opens the cursor, this clause in the SELECT statement

```
WHERE LNAME LIKE :NAME-STRING
```

is effectively replaced by

```
WHERE LNAME LIKE 'HE%%%'
```

As a result, each row whose LNAME column value starts with HE satisfies this part of the condition.

Now, you may be wondering why the STRING statement doesn't append just one percent sign to the NAME-STRING field, like this:

```
STRING NAME-STRING '%' DELIMITED BY ' '
    INTO NAME-STRING
```

The reason is that this would lead to a mask with a trailing space whenever the user entered less than four characters, and that could affect the search results.

After module 110 does this processing for the last-name prompt, it does similar processing for the state code prompt. In this case, if the user doesn't enter anything for the state code, the program uses %% as the LIKE mask so any value in the STATE column matches this mask.

The customer inquiry program   **Page 1**

```
IDENTIFICATION DIVISION.
*
PROGRAM-ID.      NAMEINQ.
*
ENVIRONMENT DIVISION.
*
INPUT-OUTPUT SECTION.
*
FILE-CONTROL.
*
DATA DIVISION.
*
FILE SECTION.
*
WORKING-STORAGE SECTION.
*
 01   SWITCHES.
      05   END-OF-INQUIRIES-SW          PIC X     VALUE 'N'.
           88   END-OF-INQUIRIES                  VALUE 'Y'.
      05   END-OF-CUSTOMERS-SW          PIC X     VALUE 'N'.
           88   END-OF-CUSTOMERS                  VALUE 'Y'.
      05   VALID-CURSOR-SW              PIC X     VALUE 'Y'.
           88   VALID-CURSOR                      VALUE 'Y'.
*
 01   COUNT-FIELDS.
      05   CUSTOMER-COUNT              PIC S9(7)   COMP-3.
      05   EDITED-CUSTOMER-COUNT       PIC Z(6)9.
*
 01   SEARCH-STRINGS.
      05   NAME-STRING                 PIC X(5).
      05   STATE-STRING                PIC XX.
*
     EXEC SQL
         INCLUDE CUSTOMER
     END-EXEC.
*
     EXEC SQL
         INCLUDE SQLCA
     END-EXEC.
*
     EXEC SQL
         DECLARE CUSTCURS CURSOR FOR
             SELECT  CUSTNO, LNAME, FNAME, STATE
                 FROM MM01.CUSTOMER
                     WHERE LNAME LIKE :NAME-STRING
                     AND STATE LIKE :STATE-STRING
     END-EXEC.
*
```

Figure 5-8   The COBOL listing for the customer inquiry program (part 1 of 3)

The customer inquiry program   **Page 2**

```
PROCEDURE DIVISION.
*
000-PROCESS-CUST-INQUIRIES.
    PERFORM 100-PROCESS-CUST-INQUIRY
        UNTIL END-OF-INQUIRIES.
    STOP RUN.
*
100-PROCESS-CUST-INQUIRY.
    PERFORM 110-ACCEPT-SEARCH-VALUES.
    IF NOT END-OF-INQUIRIES
        MOVE 'Y' TO VALID-CURSOR-SW
        MOVE ZERO TO CUSTOMER-COUNT
        PERFORM 120-OPEN-CUSTOMER-CURSOR
        IF VALID-CURSOR
            MOVE 'N' TO END-OF-CUSTOMERS-SW
            PERFORM 130-DISPLAY-CUSTOMER-INFO
                UNTIL END-OF-CUSTOMERS
            PERFORM 150-CLOSE-CUSTOMER-CURSOR
            MOVE CUSTOMER-COUNT TO EDITED-CUSTOMER-COUNT
            DISPLAY EDITED-CUSTOMER-COUNT ' CUSTOMER(S) FOUND.'.
*
110-ACCEPT-SEARCH-VALUES.
    MOVE SPACE TO NAME-STRING.
    MOVE SPACE TO STATE-STRING.
    DISPLAY '-------------------------------------------------'.
    DISPLAY '(ENTER 99 FOR NAME OR STATE TO QUIT.)'.
    DISPLAY 'ENTER FIRST ONE TO FOUR CHARACTERS OF LAST NAME:'.
    ACCEPT NAME-STRING.
    IF NAME-STRING = '99'
        MOVE 'Y' TO END-OF-INQUIRIES-SW
    ELSE
        STRING NAME-STRING '%%%%' DELIMITED BY ' '
            INTO NAME-STRING
        DISPLAY 'ENTER STATE CODE: '
        ACCEPT STATE-STRING
        IF STATE-STRING = '99'
            MOVE 'Y' TO END-OF-INQUIRIES-SW
        ELSE
            STRING STATE-STRING '%%' DELIMITED BY ' '
                INTO STATE-STRING.
*
120-OPEN-CUSTOMER-CURSOR.
    EXEC SQL
        OPEN CUSTCURS
    END-EXEC.
    IF SQLCODE NOT = 0
        MOVE 'N' TO VALID-CURSOR-SW.
*
```

Figure 5-8   The COBOL listing for the customer inquiry program (part 2 of 3)

The customer inquiry program

Page 3

```
130-DISPLAY-CUSTOMER-INFO.
    PERFORM 140-FETCH-CUSTOMER-ROW.
    IF NOT END-OF-CUSTOMERS
        IF VALID-CURSOR
            DISPLAY 'CUST: ' CUSTNO '--' FNAME ' '
                    LNAME ' ' STATE.
*
140-FETCH-CUSTOMER-ROW.
    EXEC SQL
        FETCH CUSTCURS
            INTO :CUSTNO, :LNAME, :FNAME, :STATE
    END-EXEC.
    IF SQLCODE = 0
        ADD 1 TO CUSTOMER-COUNT
    ELSE
        MOVE 'Y' TO END-OF-CUSTOMERS-SW
        IF SQLCODE NOT = 100
            MOVE 'N' TO VALID-CURSOR-SW.
*
150-CLOSE-CUSTOMER-CURSOR.
    EXEC SQL
        CLOSE CUSTCURS
    END-EXEC.
*
```

Figure 5-8   The COBOL listing for the customer inquiry program (part 3 of 3)

Perspective

Now that you've finished this chapter, you should be able to code WHERE clauses that get the exact data you want from a database. By using the IN, BETWEEN, and LIKE phrases, you can code selection conditions in ways that are often simpler than their COBOL counterparts. And by avoiding the use of the NOT operator, you can further simplify your code and often improve performance.

If a user does complain about the performance of a program, you can sometimes improve the performance by eliminating the use of NOT and OR operators. Otherwise, the database administrator can sometimes add an index to a database that improves performance without reprogramming. If, for example, your program uses an OR operator to combine two conditions that are based on two different columns, an index that spans the columns will improve performance.

6

How to use column functions

In chapter 2, you learned how to use DB2 to perform basic arithmetic and concatenation operations as data is retrieved. Now, in this chapter, you can learn how to use DB2's functions for performing operations on the data in columns, like calculating averages and sums. And in the next chapter, you can learn how to use DB2's functions for performing operations on the data in rows, like converting data formats and manipulating text strings.

To start, this chapter introduces the two types of DB2 functions and shows you how to use the column functions. Then, it describes how to use the GROUP BY and HAVING clauses to apply column functions to specific groups of rows. This chapter ends by presenting a program that illustrates how functions can save coding time and improve program performance.

Introduction to DB2 functions

DB2's functions fall into two categories: column functions and scalar functions. A *column function* yields a single value that's derived from the data in one column for a number of rows. For instance, SUM is a column function that you can use to total the values in a single column for a group of rows. Because the purpose of a column function is to produce a single *aggregate value*, column functions are sometimes referred to as *aggregate functions*.

In contrast, a *scalar function* works within the context of a single row. The SUBSTR function, for example, does string manipulations of character data. Since scalar functions derive different values for each row, they usually produce multi-row result tables. To learn how to use the scalar functions, please refer to the next chapter.

The syntax of the column functions

Figure 6-1 presents the syntax for DB2's five column functions. When you code a DB2 function, you first specify a *function name* that tells DB2 what you want it to do. Then, you identify the data elements the function should operate upon. These data elements are called *operands*, or *arguments*.

The names of the column functions make it easy to tell what they do. AVG computes the average of the values in a numeric column, and SUM computes their total. MIN and MAX return the minimum and maximum values in a column, numeric or otherwise. And COUNT returns the number of rows that meet a selection condition.

When you code a function in an SQL statement in a COBOL program, you need to define the host variables so they can accept the results of the functions. To do that, you should follow the guidelines given in this figure for the COBOL pictures.

Although you can use the DISTINCT keyword with all five of the column functions, this keyword has no effect for the MIN and MAX functions. In contrast, this keyword does make a difference for AVG and SUM, but you normally should avoid using it. If, for example, you want to SUM a five-row column that has the value 100 in four of the rows and the value 1 in the fifth row, the SUM is only 101if you use DISTINCT, which probably isn't what you want.

The syntax of the column functions

Function syntax	COBOL picture for the result
AVG([ALL | DISTINCT] column-name) SUM([ALL | DISTINCT] column-name)	If the argument column has the SMALLINT or INTEGER data type: PIC S9(9) COMP If the argument column has the DECIMAL data type: PIC S9(n)v9(n) COMP-3
MIN([ALL | DISTINCT] column-name) MAX([ALL | DISTINCT] column-name)	The same data type as the argument.
COUNT([DISTINCT] column-name | *)	The INTEGER data type: PIC S9(9) COMP

Description

- If the keyword DISTINCT is specified, duplicate values aren't included. If ALL is specified, duplicate values are included. And if neither DISTINCT nor ALL is included, duplicate values are included.
- The AVG function returns the average of a set of numbers.
- The SUM function returns the sum of a set of numbers.
- The MIN function returns the minimum value in a set of values.
- The MAX function returns the maximum value in a set of values.
- The COUNT function returns the number of rows or values in a set of rows or values. The asterisk in the syntax means to count all the rows that meet the selection condition.

Figure 6-1   The syntax of the column functions

SELECT statements that use column functions

To illustrate the use of the column functions, figure 6-2 presents six examples. The first example shows how easy it is to total the values in the INVTOTAL column for all of the rows in a table. The second example shows how you can total these values for a specific customer. The third example shows how you can average these values for a specific customer. And the fourth example shows how to get the minimum and maximum values in the INVTOTAL column for a specific customer. Since all of these column functions create a one-row result table, you don't have to code the SELECT statement within a DECLARE CURSOR statement in a COBOL program.

The fifth example in this figure uses the COUNT function to get a count of the number of rows in the invoice table for a specific customer. Here, an asterisk (*) is used as the argument of the function, which tells DB2 to count all of the rows that meet the selection condition in its count.

In contrast, the sixth example uses a COUNT function to count the number of values in the INVCUST (customer number) column for all the rows in the table. Since the DISTINCT keyword is used, however, DB2 doesn't count rows that have duplicate values in that column. As a result, this statement counts the number of different customers that have invoice rows in the table.

A SUM function that totals the values in the INVTOTAL column for all of the rows of the invoice table

```
SELECT    SUM(INVTOTAL)
     INTO :TOTAL-BILLED
     FROM  MM01.INVOICE
```

A SUM function that totals the values in the INVTOTAL column for a specific customer

```
SELECT    SUM(INVTOTAL)
     INTO :TOTAL-BILLED
     FROM  MM01.INVOICE
         WHERE INVCUST = :CUSTOMER-NUMBER
```

An AVG function that gets the average of the values in the INVTOTAL column for a specific customer

```
SELECT    AVG(INVTOTAL)
     INTO :AVERAGE-BILLED
     FROM  MM01.INVOICE
         WHERE INVCUST = :CUSTOMER-NUMBER
```

MAX and MIN functions that determine the largest and smallest INVTOTAL value for a specific customer

```
SELECT    MAX(INVTOTAL), MIN(INVTOTAL)
     INTO :LARGEST-INVOICE, :SMALLEST-INVOICE
     FROM  MM01.INVOICE
         WHERE INVCUST = :CUSTOMER-NUMBER
```

A COUNT function that counts the number of rows for a specific customer

```
SELECT    COUNT(*)
     INTO :INVOICES-ISSUED
     FROM  MM01.INVOICE
         WHERE INVCUST = :CUSTOMER-NUMBER
```

A COUNT function that counts the number of customers who have one or more invoices in the invoice table

```
SELECT    COUNT(DISTINCT INVCUST)
     INTO :CUSTOMER-COUNT
     FROM  MM01.INVOICE
```

Figure 6-2   SELECT statements that use column functions

How to use the GROUP BY and HAVING clauses

Figure 6-3 presents the syntax of the GROUP BY and HAVING clauses that can be used with the column functions. When you use the GROUP BY clause in a SELECT statement, DB2 groups the rows by the values in the column name or names that are specified. Then, DB2 treats each group like an interim table and applies the column function to it. This creates a multi-row result table where each row contains one aggregate value for each group. Some examples will help this make sense.

The first example in this figure groups the rows in an invoice table by the customer number (INVCUST). The result table then consists of one row for each customer. The first column in each row contains the customer number; the second column contains the average invoice total.

The second example shows how to use the WHERE clause along with the GROUP BY clause. Here, the SELECT statement creates a result table that contains one row for each customer, but it averages only those rows with invoice totals greater than $1000. The ORDER BY clause in this statement sorts the result table by the average value.

If you want the result table to include only the rows for groups that meet specific conditions, you can code the HAVING clause after the GROUP BY clause. In the third example in this figure, the HAVING clause specifies that only customers whose average invoice total is greater than $1000 should be included in the result table. Note how this differs from the preceding example.

In the last example, both the WHERE and HAVING clauses are coded so the result table contains only rows for customers who have five or more invoices with totals greater than $1000. When DB2 runs this statement, it first generates an interim result table that contains the rows where the invoice total column's value is greater than 1000. Then, DB2 groups all the rows in the table for each customer. Last, it excludes the groups of rows with a count of five or fewer, and it applies the AVG function to each group that remains.

The syntax of the GROUP BY and HAVING clauses

```
GROUP BY column-name[, column-name]...
   [HAVING selection-condition]
```

A SELECT statement that computes the average invoice total for each customer

```
SELECT     INVCUST, AVG(INVTOTAL) AS AVG_TOTAL
    FROM   MM01.INVOICE
    GROUP BY INVCUST
```

A SELECT statement that computes the average invoice total by customer for invoices over $1000

```
SELECT     INVCUST, AVG(INVTOTAL) AS AVG_TOTAL
    FROM   MM01.INVOICE
        WHERE INVTOTAL > 1000
    GROUP BY INVCUST
        ORDER BY AVG_TOTAL
```

A SELECT statement that produces a result table with one row for each customer with an average invoice total over $1000

```
SELECT     INVCUST, AVG(INVTOTAL) AS AVG_TOTAL
    FROM   MM01.INVOICE
    GROUP BY INVCUST
        HAVING AVG(INVTOTAL) > 1000
        ORDER BY AVG_TOTAL
```

A SELECT statement that produces a result table with one row for each customer with more than 5 invoices over $1000

```
SELECT     INVCUST, AVG(INVTOTAL) AS AVG_TOTAL
    FROM   MM01.INVOICE
        WHERE INVTOTAL > 1000
    GROUP BY INVCUST
        HAVING COUNT(*) > 5
        ORDER BY AVG_TOTAL
```

Figure 6-3   The GROUP BY and HAVING clauses

A COBOL program that uses column functions

This chapter closes by presenting a COBOL program that uses column functions. To keep it simple, this program displays a list of summary sales information at a TSO terminal. That way, you can concentrate on the DB2 elements that this program illustrates.

The output display

Figure 6-4 shows the output displayed by this inquiry program. Here, one line is displayed for each customer. Within each line, you can see the customer number plus the total number of invoices issued to the customer, the total of the billings for those invoices, and the average invoice total. These last three values, of course, are derived by the use of column functions. The three asterisks after the last customer line are generated by TSO, not by this program.

The structure chart

The structure chart in this figure indicates how simple this program is. After module 100 opens a cursor-controlled table that gets the required data from the database, the program fetches each row in the table and displays its data. When the program reaches the end of the result table, it closes the cursor.

The output display

```
MMA - EXTRA! for Windows 95/NT                                    _ 🗗 ✕
File  Edit  View  Tools  Session  Options  Help
CUSTOMER       COUNT      TOTAL      AVERAGE
400011            7      3922.42      560.34
400012            3       582.67      194.22
400014            3       377.84      125.94
400015            3      3764.65     1254.88
400002            2       320.57      160.28
400003            2       371.30      185.65
400004            2       362.84      181.42
400010            2       295.00      147.50
400001            1       205.60      205.60
400013            1       178.23      178.23
*** _
```

The structure chart

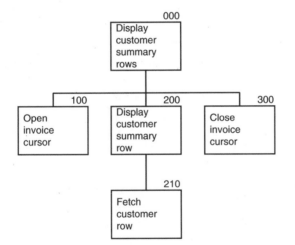

Notes

- The output displayed above is for an invoice table with rows for only ten different customers. This output is presented in descending count sequence within ascending customer number sequence.

- The structure chart for this program indicates that module 000 performs module 100 to open a cursor-controlled result table. Then, it performs module 200 to display one customer line for each row in the result table. Last, it performs module 300 to close the result table.

Figure 6-4   The output display and structure chart for the summary inquiry program

The COBOL listing

Figure 6-5 presents the COBOL source listing for this program. In the second shaded block in this figure, you can see the SELECT statement that gets all of the data needed for the screen display. If you want to refer to the DCLGEN output for the INVOICE table that's used by this SELECT statement, you can refer back to figure 4-14, but you shouldn't need to do that.

The SELECT clause in this statement specifies that the result table should contain four columns: INVCUST and the results of three functions. The GROUP BY clause specifies that the result table should contain one row for each customer. And the ORDER BY clause specifies that the rows in the result table should be sorted first by customer number, then by the count of the invoices for each customer in descending sequence. As a result, the customers who have the most invoices appear first. But when customers have the same number of invoices, DB2 sorts them into ascending order by customer number.

If you look at the first shaded block in this figure, you can see how the host variables are coded for the three columns whose values are generated by functions. For the AVG and SUM functions, the host variable has the same size and characteristics as the column the function processes. For the COUNT function, the host variable needs to be a fullword integer field.

Although this program displays summary information for all customers, you can easily add a HAVING clause to the SELECT statement if you want to limit the amount of data that's returned. If, for example, you want to display summary lines for only those customers whose average invoice total is more than some minimum, you could code:

```
SELECT   INVCUST AS INVCUST,   COUNT(*) AS INVCOUNT,
         AVG(INVTOTAL),        SUM(INVTOTAL)
      FROM MM01.INVOICE
         GROUP BY INVCUST
            HAVING AVG(INVTOTAL) > :MINIMUM-AVERAGE
         ORDER BY INVCOUNT DESC, INVCUST
```

In this case, the program has to set the value of the host variable MINIMUM-AVERAGE to a specific amount before it opens the cursor.

The summary inquiry program   **Page 1**

```
IDENTIFICATION DIVISION.
*
PROGRAM-ID.     SUMINQ.
*
ENVIRONMENT DIVISION.
*
INPUT-OUTPUT SECTION.
*
FILE-CONTROL.
*
DATA DIVISION.
*
FILE SECTION.
*
WORKING-STORAGE SECTION.
*
01   SWITCH.
     05   END-OF-CUSTOMERS-SW        PIC X   VALUE 'N'.
          88  END-OF-CUSTOMERS               VALUE 'Y'.
*
01   WORK-FIELDS.
     05   INVOICE-COUNT              PIC S9(9)     COMP.
     05   INVOICE-SUM                PIC S9(7)V99  COMP-3.
     05   INVOICE-AVG                PIC S9(7)V99  COMP-3.
     05   EDITED-INVOICE-COUNT       PIC Z(8)9.
     05   EDITED-INVOICE-SUM         PIC Z(6)9.99.
     05   EDITED-INVOICE-AVG         PIC Z(6)9.99.
*
     EXEC SQL
         INCLUDE INVOICE
     END-EXEC.
*
     EXEC SQL
         INCLUDE SQLCA
     END-EXEC.
*
     EXEC SQL
         DECLARE INVCURS CURSOR FOR
             SELECT  INVCUST AS INVCUST,   COUNT(*) AS INVCOUNT,
                     AVG(INVTOTAL),        SUM(INVTOTAL)
             FROM MM01.INVOICE
             GROUP BY INVCUST
             ORDER BY INVCOUNT DESC, INVCUST
     END-EXEC.
*
```

Figure 6-5   The COBOL listing for the summary inquiry program (part 1 of 2)

The rest of this program should be easy to follow. To display the data for each row in the result table, the code for module 200 performs module 210 to fetch the next row. Then, if there is another row, module 200 moves the function fields to edited fields and displays the customer number and edited fields. When there aren't any more rows, the program ends.

The summary inquiry program   **Page 2**

```
PROCEDURE DIVISION.
*
 000-DISPL-CUST-SUMMRY-ROWS.
*
     PERFORM 100-OPEN-INVOICE-CURSOR.
     IF NOT END-OF-CUSTOMERS
         DISPLAY 'CUSTOMER         COUNT       TOTAL      AVERAGE'
         PERFORM 200-DISPL-CUST-SUMMRY-ROW
             UNTIL END-OF-CUSTOMERS
         PERFORM 300-CLOSE-INVOICE-CURSOR.
     STOP RUN.
*
 100-OPEN-INVOICE-CURSOR.
*
     EXEC SQL
         OPEN INVCURS
     END-EXEC.
     IF SQLCODE NOT = 0
         MOVE 'Y' TO END-OF-CUSTOMERS-SW.
*
 200-DISPL-CUST-SUMMRY-ROW.
*
     PERFORM 210-FETCH-CUSTOMER-ROW.
     IF NOT END-OF-CUSTOMERS
         MOVE INVOICE-COUNT TO EDITED-INVOICE-COUNT
         MOVE INVOICE-AVG   TO EDITED-INVOICE-AVG
         MOVE INVOICE-SUM   TO EDITED-INVOICE-SUM
         DISPLAY INVCUST '             '
             EDITED-INVOICE-COUNT ' '
             EDITED-INVOICE-SUM   ' '
             EDITED-INVOICE-AVG.
*
 210-FETCH-CUSTOMER-ROW.
*
     EXEC SQL
         FETCH  INVCURS
         INTO  :INVCUST,      :INVOICE-COUNT,
               :INVOICE-AVG, :INVOICE-SUM
     END-EXEC.
     IF SQLCODE NOT = 0
         MOVE 'Y' TO END-OF-CUSTOMERS-SW.
*
 300-CLOSE-INVOICE-CURSOR.
*
     EXEC SQL
         CLOSE INVCURS
     END-EXEC.
*
```

Figure 6-5   The COBOL listing for the summary inquiry program (part 2 of 2)

Perspective

When you use DB2's column functions, you benefit in two ways. First, you save coding time because the SQL code is simpler than the COBOL code for the same purpose. Second, you improve program performance because only the results of the functions need to be retrieved from the database, not all the data that's needed to derive the results. For these reasons, you should use the column functions whenever they are appropriate.

In the next chapter, you can learn how to use DB2's scalar functions. As you will see, these functions are useful when you need to convert data from one form to another, when you need to manipulate the data within a string, or when you need to work with dates.

7

How to use the data manipulation features

In the last chapter, you learned how to use DB2's column functions. Now, in this chapter, you can learn to use its scalar functions. Since scalar functions work on DB2 data, this chapter starts by presenting the DB2 data types. Next, it presents the scalar functions for working with those data types. Last, it shows you how to use dates and times in expressions.

A review of the data types

The eleven DB2 data types can be divided into three categories: string, numeric, and date and time. The topics that follow present the data types in each of these categories.

String data types

Figure 7-1 presents the four data types for *string* (character) data. The CHAR and VARCHAR data types are for standard EBCDIC character data. They differ in that the CHAR data type provides for a fixed number of characters, while the VARCHAR type provides for a variable number.

In this figure, you can see typical COBOL pictures for receiving the contents of these data types. For the VARCHAR data type, the picture consists of two 49-level components that are subordinate to a group item. The first component is a halfword field that gives the length (number of characters) of the data that follows. The second component is the data itself. In your program, you must provide enough space for the largest value the column can contain.

Although both CHAR and VARCHAR data types normally are a maximum of 254 bytes, DB2 supports long VARCHAR columns of more than 32,000 bytes. In this case, though, a table row must fit on a single page in the table space where the table is stored, so the exact upper limit depends on the page size (either 4K or 32K) and on the size of the other columns in the table.

In contrast, the GRAPHIC and VARGRAPHIC data types are fixed-length and variable-length columns that contain *double-byte character set* (DBCS) data. In this format, two bytes of storage are required to store one character. This format can be used for special purposes, such as storing text in non-Western languages (like Japanese) or representing chemical structures.

The maximum length of a GRAPHIC column is 127 DBCS characters, or 254 bytes. To code the PICTURE clause for a DBCS item, you use DISPLAY-1 usage and G instead of X so the definition for a 40-character item is PIC G(40). For a VARGRAPHIC item, you code two 49-level components just as you do for a VARCHAR item, but you use DISPLAY-1 usage and G instead of X for the data component. Here again, DB2 provides for long items of more than 32,000 bytes, but the upper limit depends on the page size and on the size of the other columns in the table.

String data types

DB2 data type	Kind of data	Description
CHAR	Fixed-length character (EBCDIC) data	Up to 254 bytes of alphanumeric data. Defined in COBOL as PIC X(n) where *n* is the number of characters the column contains. A typical example is: `01   CUSTNO          PIC X(6).`

VARCHAR	Variable-length character (EBCDIC) data	A variable amount of alphanumeric data. The number of bytes in the data component is stored in a halfword. A typical COBOL example is:
		
		`01   NOTES.`
		`     49   NOTES-LEN   PIC S9(4) COMP.`
		`     49   NOTES-TEXT  PIC X(254).`
		
		The text component has a maximum length of 254 bytes in a regular VARCHAR column. In a LONG VARCHAR column, which is subject to some processing restrictions, the text component's length can be over 32,000 bytes. The exact maximum length depends on the table's page size and the sizes of the other columns in the table.

GRAPHIC	Fixed-length DBCS data	Up to 127 characters of Double Byte Character Set (DBCS) data. Defined in COBOL with DISPLAY-1 usage and PIC G(n) where *n* is the number of characters the column contains. A typical example is:
		
		`01   DBCS-NAME       PIC G(20)`
		`                     DISPLAY-1.`

VARGRAPHIC	Variable-length DBCS data	A variable amount of DBCS data. The number of characters in the data component is stored in a halfword. A typical COBOL example is:
		
		`01   EXPL.`
		`     49   EXPL-LEN    PIC S9(4) COMP.`
		`     49   EXPL-TEXT   PIC G(127)`
		`                      DISPLAY-1.`
		
		The text component has a maximum length of 127 characters in a regular VARGRAPHIC column. As with VARCHAR, a LONG VARGRAPHIC column can store more characters, but it's subject to some processing restrictions. The exact maximum length depends on the table's page size and the sizes of the other columns in the table.

Figure 7-1   String data types

Numeric data types

Figure 7-2 presents the data types for numeric data. The SMALLINT and INTEGER types are for binary data that represents whole numbers. As a result, the pictures used for their host variables must be coded with COMP usage.

In contrast, the DECIMAL data type provides for packed-decimal data with a specific number of digits and a specific number of digits to the right of the decimal point. The number of digits is called its *precision*, while the number of digits to the right of the decimal point is called the *scale* of the item. As a result, a DECIMAL item defined with a precision of 9 and a scale of 2 can contain a value up to 9,999,999.99. When you define a host variable for a DECIMAL column, you must use COMP-3 usage and a picture with an implied decimal point.

Although you'll use the first three data types often, you may never need to use the FLOAT data type, which provides for a *floating-point number*. Depending on how a database administrator defines a FLOAT column, it can contain a *single-precision number* (4 bytes) or a *double-precision number* (8 bytes). When you define a host variable for a FLOAT item in a COBOL program, you use COMP-1 or COMP-2 usage and you don't provide a picture.

Numeric data types

DB2 data type	Kind of data	Description
SMALLINT	Halfword integer data	A halfword integer contains whole-number values between –32,768 and 32,767. It is always defined in COBOL with COMP usage and PIC S9(4). A typical COBOL definition is: `10   INVCOUNT        PIC S9(4) COMP.`
INTEGER	Fullword integer data	A fullword integer contains whole-number values between –2,147,483,648 and 2,147,483,647. It is always defined in COBOL with COMP usage and PIC S9(9). A typical COBOL definition is: `10   INVCOUNT        PIC S9(9) COMP.`
DECIMAL(p,s)	Packed-decimal data	A decimal value contains an implicit decimal point. The value *p* (which can't be greater than 31, or prior to DB2 version 2.3, 15) specifies how many digits the number can contain, and the value *s* specifies how many of those digits are to the right of the implicit decimal point. The abbreviations *p* and *s* stand for precision and scale. A typical COBOL definition is: `10   INVTOTAL        PIC S9(7)V99 COMP-3.` This is an appropriate host variable definition for a column defined with DECIMAL(9,2).

FLOAT(n)	Floating-point data	A floating point number, either single-precision (if *n* is less than 22) or double-precision (if *n* is between 22 and 53). COBOL definitions do not include a PIC clause and are simply a field name followed by COMP-1 (for single-precision) or COMP-2 (for double-precision). Examples are:
		
		`10   SINGLE-PRECISION-NUMBER   COMP-1.`
		`10   DOUBLE-PRECISION-NUMBER   COMP-2.`

Figure 7-2   Numeric data types

Date and time data types

Figure 7-3 presents the three data types for date and time data. A DATE item consists of year, month, and day. A TIME item consists of hours, minutes, and seconds. And a TIMESTAMP item contains the components of both the DATE and TIME items, plus a microsecond component.

As you can see in this figure, these data types are character strings that are 10, 8, or 26 characters long. When you define the host variable for one of these data types, you can define an elementary character item that's large enough to hold the entire string. Or, you can define a group item that defines each component of the string. If your shop has changed DB2's default date and time formats, though, you'll have to adjust your host variables accordingly.

Incidentally, DB2 uses a more efficient format for storing date and time data than is indicated by the COBOL pictures for the host variables. When the data is retrieved by a COBOL program, though, it is converted to the COBOL format.

DCLGEN output and data for two tables that use some of these data types

The figures on the next two pages present the DCLGEN output for two tables that include some of the data types just described. In particular, the customer table in figure 7-4 includes four VARCHAR columns, and the invoice table in figure 7-5 includes a DATE column and four DECIMAL columns.

In the COBOL declarations for these tables, you should note how the declarations for the host variables match up with the declarations for the VARCHAR, DATE, and DECIMAL columns. For each VARCHAR column, two 49-level items are generated. The name of the first item is the name of the column followed by a hyphen and LEN; this field receives the length of the field that follows when the column is retrieved. The name of the second item is the name of the column followed by a hyphen and TEXT; this field receives the character data for the column.

These figures also present some data for these tables. This data is used to show how the scalar functions that are presented in the rest of this chapter work. As a result, you may occasionally want to refer back to these figures.

Date and time data types

DB2 data type	Kind of data	Description

DATE	Date	A 10-byte string. A typical example is:
		
		`01   INVDATE            PIC X(10).`
		
		The internal structure of a date item is yyyy-mm-dd. To identify the parts of a DB2 date, you can move the value to a group item like:
		
		`01   EDITED-DATE.`
		`     05   ED-YEAR      PIC X(4).`
		`     05   FILLER       PIC X.`
		`     05   ED-MONTH     PIC XX.`
		`     05   FILLER       PIC X.`
		`     05   ED-DAY       PIC XX.`

TIME	Time	An 8-byte string. A typical example is:
		
		`01   START-TIME         PIC X(8).`
		
		The internal structure of a time item is hh.mm.ss. To identify the parts of a DB2 time, you can move the value to a group item like:
		
		`01   EDITED-TIME.`
		`     05   ED-HOUR      PIC XX.`
		`     05   FILLER       PIC X.`
		`     05   ED-MINUTE    PIC XX.`
		`     05   FILLER       PIC X.`
		`     05   ED-SECOND    PIC XX.`

TIMESTAMP	Date and time	A 26-byte string. A typical example is:
		
		`01   START-DATE-TIME  PIC X(26).`
		
		The internal structure of a timestamp item is yyyy-mm-dd-hh.mm.ss.mmmmmm. To identify the parts of a DB2 timestamp, you can move the value to a group item like:
		
		`01   EDITED-TIMESTAMP.`
		`     05   ETS-YEAR     PIC X(4).`
		`     05   FILLER       PIC X.`
		`     05   ETS-MONTH    PIC XX.`
		`     05   FILLER       PIC X.`
		`     05   ETS-DAY      PIC XX.`
		`     05   FILLER       PIC X.`
		`     05   ETS-HOUR     PIC XX.`
		`     05   FILLER       PIC X.`
		`     05   ETS-MINUTE   PIC XX.`
		`     05   FILLER       PIC X.`
		`     05   ETS-SECOND   PIC XX.`
		`     05   FILLER       PIC X.`
		`     05   ETS-MSECOND  PIC X(6).`

Figure 7-3   Date and time data types

DCLGEN output for a customer table

```
*******************************************************************
* DCLGEN TABLE(MM01.VARCUST)                                      *
*        LIBRARY(MM01.DB2.DCLGENS(VARCUST))                       *
*        ACTION(REPLACE)                                          *
*        LANGUAGE(COBOL)                                          *
*        STRUCTURE(CUSTOMER-ROW)                                  *
*        QUOTE                                                    *
* ... IS THE DCLGEN COMMAND THAT MADE THE FOLLOWING STATEMENTS    *
*******************************************************************
       EXEC SQL DECLARE MM01.VARCUST TABLE
       ( CUSTNO                     CHAR(6) NOT NULL,
         FNAME                      VARCHAR(20) NOT NULL,
         LNAME                      VARCHAR(30) NOT NULL,
         CITY                       VARCHAR(20) NOT NULL,
         STATE                      CHAR(2) NOT NULL,
         ZIPCODE                    CHAR(10) NOT NULL,
         HOMEPH                     CHAR(16),
         WORKPH                     CHAR(16),
         NOTES                      VARCHAR(254)
       ) END-EXEC.
*******************************************************************
* COBOL DECLARATION FOR TABLE MM01.VARCUST                        *
*******************************************************************
  01   CUSTOMER-ROW.
       10 CUSTNO               PIC X(6).
       10 FNAME.
          49 FNAME-LEN         PIC S9(4) USAGE COMP.
          49 FNAME-TEXT        PIC X(20).
       10 LNAME.
          49 LNAME-LEN         PIC S9(4) USAGE COMP.
          49 LNAME-TEXT        PIC X(30).
       10 CITY.
          49 CITY-LEN          PIC S9(4) USAGE COMP.
          49 CITY-TEXT         PIC X(20).
       10 STATE                PIC X(2).
       10 ZIPCODE              PIC X(10).
       10 HOMEPH               PIC X(16).
       10 WORKPH               PIC X(16).
       10 NOTES.
          49 NOTES-LEN         PIC S9(4) USAGE COMP.
          49 NOTES-TEXT        PIC X(254).
*******************************************************************
* THE NUMBER OF COLUMNS DESCRIBED BY THIS DECLARATION IS 9        *
*******************************************************************
```

Test data for the table

CUSTNO	FNAME	LNAME	CITY	STATE	ZIPCODE	HOMEPH	WORKPH	NOTES
400001	KEITH	JONES	DALLAS	TX	75209	214-555-8029	.....	.....
400002	ARREN	ANELLI	DENVILLE	NJ	07834	.....	.....	.....
400003	SUSAN	HOWARD	REDWOOD CITY	CA	94063	415-555-4587	415-555-3298	.....
400004	CAROL	EVANS	GREAT LAKES	IL	60088	708-555-5484	.....	.....
400005	ELAINE	ROBERTS	CERRITOS	CA	90701	.....	.....	.....
400006	PAT	HONG	SAN FRANCISCO	CA	94114	.....	415-555-2436	.....
400007	PHIL	ROACH	DEARBORN HTS	MI	48125	.....	.....	.....
400008	TIM	JOHNSON	SO CHICAGO HTS	IL	60411	.....	708-555-4490	.....
400009	MARIANNE	BUSBEE	MOBILE	AL	36608	205-555-9934	.....	.....
400010	ENRIQUE	OTHON	RICHMOND	VA	23261	804-555-3437	804-555-9090	.....

Figure 7-4   DCLGEN output and data for a customer table

DCLGEN output for an invoice table

```
******************************************************************
* DCLGEN TABLE(MM01.INVOICE2)                                    *
*        LIBRARY(MM01.DB2.DCLGENS(INVOICE2))                     *
*        ACTION(REPLACE)                                         *
*        LANGUAGE(COBOL)                                         *
*        STRUCTURE(INVOICE-ROW)                                  *
*        QUOTE                                                   *
* ... IS THE DCLGEN COMMAND THAT MADE THE FOLLOWING STATEMENTS   *
******************************************************************
      EXEC SQL DECLARE MM01.INVOICE2 TABLE
      ( INVCUST                      CHAR(6) NOT NULL,
        INVNO                        CHAR(6) NOT NULL,
        INVDATE                      DATE NOT NULL,
        INVSUBT                      DECIMAL(9, 2) NOT NULL,
        INVSHIP                      DECIMAL(7, 2) NOT NULL,
        INVTAX                       DECIMAL(7, 2) NOT NULL,
        INVTOTAL                     DECIMAL(9, 2) NOT NULL,
        INVPROM                      CHAR(10) NOT NULL
      ) END-EXEC.
******************************************************************
* COBOL DECLARATION FOR TABLE MM01.INVOICE2                      *
******************************************************************
  01  INVOICE-ROW.
      10 INVCUST              PIC X(6).
      10 INVNO                PIC X(6).
      10 INVDATE              PIC X(10).
      10 INVSUBT              PIC S9(7)V9(2) USAGE COMP-3.
      10 INVSHIP              PIC S9(5)V9(2) USAGE COMP-3.
      10 INVTAX               PIC S9(5)V9(2) USAGE COMP-3.
      10 INVTOTAL             PIC S9(7)V9(2) USAGE COMP-3.
      10 INVPROM              PIC X(10).
******************************************************************
* THE NUMBER OF COLUMNS DESCRIBED BY THIS DECLARATION IS 8       *
******************************************************************
```

Test data for the table

INVCUST	INVNO	INVDATE	INVSUBT	INVSHIP	INVTAX	INVTOTAL	INVPROM
400009	062308	1997-12-22	200.00	4.45	.00	204.45	PCQ3
400002	062309	1997-12-22	15.00	.00	.00	15.00	PCQ3
400001	062310	1998-02-22	140.00	7.50	.00	147.50	PCQ3
400005	062311	1998-02-22	178.23	3.19	.00	181.42	PCQ3
400002	062312	1998-02-22	162.00	11.07	.00	173.07	PCQ3
400004	062313	1998-03-14	22.00	.50	.00	22.50	RXTY
400003	062314	1998-03-14	140.00	.00	9.80	149.80	RXTY
400004	062315	1998-03-14	178.23	3.19	.00	181.42	RXTY
400010	062316	1998-03-14	140.00	7.50	.00	147.50	RXTY
400003	062317	1998-03-17	289.00	9.00	.00	298.00	RXTY
400006	062318	1998-03-17	199.99	.00	.00	199.99	PCQ3
400007	062319	1998-03-17	178.23	3.19	.00	181.42	RXTY
400002	062320	1998-03-17	3245.90	160.00	.00	3405.90	RXTY
400001	062321	1998-04-03	200.00	5.60	.00	205.60	PCQ4
400005	062322	1998-04-03	15.00	.00	.00	15.00	PCQ4
400007	062323	1998-04-11	925.00	24.00	.00	949.00	PCQ4
400003	062324	1998-04-14	178.23	3.19	.00	181.42	PCQ4
400002	062325	1998-04-17	140.00	7.50	.00	147.50	PCQ3

Figure 7-5   DCLGEN output and data for an invoice table

How to use the scalar functions

Figure 7-6 presents the 21 scalar functions that you can use with DB2. One of these functions can be coded as either COALESCE or VALUE. The COALESCE name became available with DB2 version 4 because it conforms to the SQL standards.

Each scalar function produces a single-value result based on the *arguments* that you code in parentheses after the *function name*. Although some scalar functions can have multiple arguments that are separated by commas, most require only one.

The topics that follow present these functions in the sequence in which they're listed in this figure. For each function, you'll see the complete syntax, an explanation of that syntax, and an illustrative example. Because you won't be able to remember all of the details that are presented, we recommend that you read this portion of this chapter rather quickly with your focus on what each function does, not the coding details. Then, you can refer back to the details whenever you need to use one of these functions on the job.

The scalar functions

Function	Returns	Example
Used with string data		
HEX	A hexadecimal representation of its argument	`HEX(INVNO)`
LENGTH	The length of its argument	`LENGTH(LNAME)`
SUBSTR	A substring of a string	`SUBSTR(FNAME,1,1)`
VARGRAPHIC	A graphic string of its argument	`VARGRAPHIC(:MIXEDSTRING)`
Used with numeric data		
DECIMAL	A decimal representation of its first argument	`DECIMAL(INVTOTAL,11,4)`
DIGITS	A character string representation of its argument	`DIGITS(INVTOTAL)`
FLOAT	Floating-point representation of its argument	`FLOAT(SALARY)/COMM`
INTEGER	An integer representation of its argument	`INTEGER(AVG(SALARY)+.5)`
Used with null values		
VALUE or COALESCE	The first argument that is not null	`VALUE(VALUE1,0)` `COALESCE(PHONE,'NO PHONE')`
Used with date and time data		
CHAR	A string representation of its first argument	`CHAR(HIREDATE,USA)`
DAYS	An integer representation of its argument	`DAYS('1998-01-01')`
YEAR	The year part of its argument	`YEAR(BIRTHDATE)`
MONTH	The month part of its argument	`MONTH(CURRENT DATE)`
DAY	The day part of its argument	`DAY(DATE1 - DATE2)`
HOUR	The hour part of its argument	`HOUR(CURRENT TIME)`
MINUTE	The minute part of its argument	`MINUTE(CURRENT TIME)`
SECOND	The seconds part of its argument	`SECOND(CURRENT TIME)`
MICROSECOND	The microsecond part of its argument	`MICROSECOND(CURRENT TIMESTAMP)`
DATE	A date derived from its argument	`DATE('1998-06-16')`
TIME	A time derived from its argument	`TIME('13:00:00')`
TIMESTAMP	A timestamp derived from its argument or arguments	`TIMESTAMP(CURRENT DATE)`

Figure 7-6   A summary of the scalar functions

How to work with string data

Figure 7-7, which is in two parts, presents the four functions that can be used to work with string data. The HEX function returns the hexadecimal value of the expression that's coded as the argument. If the expression is a character item, the result is a character string that contains two bytes for each byte in the expression. If the expression is a graphic item, the result contains four bytes for each byte in the expression.

Although you probably won't ever need to use the HEX function in a COBOL program, it can be useful as a debugging tool when you submit queries from your terminal using SPUFI (see chapter 14) or the Query Management Facility. If, for example, you submit a SPUFI query like the one shown in this figure, you can review the hex code for the invoice number and invoice total columns in a result table. You can then determine whether the these columns contain valid data. This assumes, of course, that you know how to interpret hex code.

The LENGTH function returns the length of the value of the expression in the argument as a binary number. In the example for this function, the SELECT statement returns the last name, the length of the last name, and the first name of all the customers in California. In a COBOL program, of course, you don't need to get the length of a variable-length column because the length is automatically returned in one of the host variables. However, you may use this function in a SPUFI or QMF query.

For instance, the LENGTH function is often useful when you're working with a lengthy column like a NOTES column that has a maximum of 254 bytes and you don't have enough room to display or print all of the characters. If, for example, you only have enough room for 50 bytes of notes, you can start by using a SPUFI to find out how many customers are going to have truncated notes:

```
SELECT CUSTNO, NOTES
    FROM MM01.VARCUST
        WHERE LENGTH(NOTES) > 50
```

Then, if this number is within acceptable limits, you can add code to your program that checks the length of each customer's notes and displays a message when they are truncated.

The syntax of the HEX function

`HEX(expression)`

Returns the hexadecimal value of *expression*, but that value can't be longer than 254 EBCDIC characters or 127 DBCS characters.

If *expression* is a character item, the result of the function is a character string that contains two bytes for each byte in *expression*. If *expression* is a graphic data item, the result contains four bytes for each character it contains. The result may be null.

A SELECT statement that uses the HEX function

```
SELECT  A.LNAME,  B.INVNO,  HEX(B.INVNO) AS H_INVNO,
        B.INVTOTAL,  HEX(B.INVTOTAL) AS H_INVTOTAL
    FROM MM01.VARCUST A
        INNER JOIN MM01.INVOICE2 B
    ON INVCUST = CUSTNO
        WHERE STATE = 'IL'
```

The result table

LNAME	INVNO	H_INVNO	INVTOTAL	H_INVTOTAL
EVANS	062315	F0F6F2F3F1F5	181.42	000000000018142C
EVANS	062313	F0F6F2F3F1F3	22.50	000000000002250C

The syntax of the LENGTH function

`LENGTH(expression)`

Returns the length of the value of *expression*.

The result of the function is a fullword integer: PIC S9(9) COMP. The result may be null.

A SELECT statement that uses the LENGTH function

```
SELECT  LNAME,
        LENGTH(LNAME) AS LEN,
        FNAME
    FROM MM01.VARCUST
        WHERE STATE = 'CA'
```

The result table

LNAME	LEN	FNAME
HOWARD	6	SUSAN
ROBERTS	7	ELAINE
HONG	4	PAT

Figure 7-7   The functions for working with string data (part 1 of 2)

The SUBSTR function lets you extract a substring from a character expression. The first argument names the column you want to extract the substring from; the second argument gives the location of the first character you want to extract, and the third gives the number of characters you want to extract. As a result,

```
SUBSTR(FNAME,1,3)
```

returns the first three characters of the FNAME column.

If you omit the third argument, though, DB2 returns every character in the source string from the starting position through its end. So,

```
SUBSTR(FNAME,1)
```

Returns the entire value of the FNAME column.

If you supply a length value or if the source expression is a fixed-length column, DB2 returns the substring in a fixed-length column. If you don't specify a length and the source expression is a variable-length column, the result will be variable-length. You need to note this when you define a host variable for the data the function will return.

In the example for this function, the SELECT statement produces a single-column result table that contains the names of customers who live in California. To get the customer name in a single column, the column specification in the SELECT clause uses concatenation operators (| |) to combine a column, a comma, the result of the SUBSTR function (the first initial of the first name), and a period.

The VARGRAPHIC function is included just to make this figure complete, because chances are slim that you'll ever need to use this function in a COBOL program or a SPUFI. It can be used to convert a character string to the DBCS format as shown in this example.

The syntax of the SUBSTR function

```
SUBSTR(expression,start[,length])
```

Returns the characters from the string identified by the first argument, *expression*, beginning at the character identified by the second argument, *start*. The second argument must be a number (a binary integer) between 1 and the maximum length of the string identified by *expression*. The third argument, *length*, specifies how many characters should be returned in the result. It must be a number (a binary integer) ranging from 1 to the length of the string identified by *expression*. If *length* isn't specified, all of the characters in the first argument from the *start* position through its end are returned. The result may be null.

If *length* is specified or *expression* is fixed-length, the result of the function is a fixed-length character string: PIC X(n). Otherwise, the function returns the substring in a variable-length column, and you need to provide the same sort of two-level host variable you use for data from a VARCHAR column.

A SELECT statement that uses the SUBSTR function

```
SELECT   LNAME  || ', ' ||
         SUBSTR(FNAME,1,1) || '.' AS LNAME_FI
    FROM MM01.VARCUST
         WHERE STATE = 'CA'
```

The result table

LNAME_FI
HOWARD, S.
ROBERTS, E.
HONG, P.

The syntax of the VARGRAPHIC function

```
VARGRAPHIC(expression)
```

Returns a graphic string of the value of *expression*. *Expression* must be a character string with a maximum length no greater than 254 EBCDIC characters or 127 DBCS characters.

The result of the function is a variable-length graphic string. The result may be null.

A SELECT statement that uses the VARGRAPHIC function

```
EXEC SQL
    UPDATE TABLEX
        SET GRPHCOL = VARGRAPHIC(:MIXEDSTRING)
            WHERE CURRENT OF CRSNAME
END-EXEC.
```

Figure 7-7   The functions for working with string data (part 2 of 2)

How to work with numeric data

Figure 7-8, which is in two parts, presents four functions for working with numeric data. The DECIMAL function converts a numeric value to decimal format. The first argument gives the expression that identifies the value to be converted. The second argument gives the *precision* (total number of digits) for the decimal value. And the third argument gives the *scale* (number of digits to the right of the implied decimal point).

Although the precision and scale arguments are optional, you should always code them to make sure you get the intended results. Otherwise, the default precision and scale depend on the data type of the first argument.

When you code a COBOL host variable for the result of a DECIMAL function, you use COMP-3 (packed-decimal) usage. You must also be sure that the picture contains the correct number of digits on both sides of the assumed decimal point. For the example in this figure, you need to code PIC S9(7)V9(2) for the host variable for the first DECIMAL function and PIC S9(8)V9(7) for the host variable for the second DECIMAL function. If you specify a precision that's too small for the derived value, the statement will fail and DB2 will assign a value of -406 to SQLCODE. Although the result table in this example doesn't show leading zeros, they are there.

The DIGITS function returns a fixed-length character string of the digits that make up the absolute value of the argument, which must be a binary or decimal number. The length of the returned character string depends on the data type of the argument as summarized in this figure. As always, your host variable should be appropriate for the value that's returned.

In the example for this function, you can see how it is used to convert the numeric values in the INVTOTAL column to the character strings in the INVTOTAL_D column of the result table. Because the INVTOTAL column was defined as DECIMAL(9,2), the character strings in the INVTOTAL_D column are 9 characters long.

The syntax of the DECIMAL function

```
DECIMAL(expression[,precision[,scale]])
```

Returns a decimal representation of *expression*, the first argument. The second argument is the *precision* of the result and must be an integer value between 1 and 31. The third argument is the *scale* of the result and must be an integer value between 0 and *precision*.

To use the result of the function in a COBOL program, code a host variable with COMP-3 usage and with a PIC clause that accurately reflects the *precision* and *scale* of the number: PIC S9(precision – scale)V9(scale). The result may be null if *expression* is null.

A SELECT statement that uses the DECIMAL function

```
SELECT   INVNO,   INVTOTAL,
         DECIMAL(INVTOTAL,9,2) AS INVTOTAL_1,
         DECIMAL(INVTOTAL,15,7) AS INVTOTAL_2
    FROM MM01.INVOICE2
        WHERE INVCUST = '400003'
    ORDER BY INVNO
```

The result table

INVNO	INVTOTAL	INVTOTAL_1	INVTOTAL_2
062314	149.80	149.80	149.8000000
062317	298.00	298.00	298.0000000
062324	181.42	181.42	181.4200000

The syntax of the DIGITS function

```
DIGITS(expression)
```

Returns a character string of the digits that make up the absolute value of *expression*. The result doesn't include a decimal point or a sign. *Expression* must evaluate to a binary or decimal number.

The result of the function is a fixed-length character value: PIC X(n). The length depends on the data type of *expression*. If the data type of *expression* is SMALLINT, the length is 5; if it's INTEGER, the length is 10; if it's DECIMAL, the length is the precision of the decimal value. The result may be null.

A SELECT statement that uses the DIGITS function

```
SELECT INVNO,   INVTOTAL, DIGITS(INVTOTAL) AS INVTOTAL_D
    FROM MM01.INVOICE2
        WHERE INVCUST = '400001'
    ORDER BY INVNO
```

The result table

INVNO	INVTOTAL	INVTOTAL_D
062310	147.50	000014750
062321	205.60	000020560

Figure 7-8   The functions for working with numeric data (part 1 of 2)

The FLOAT function converts the number identified by the argument into a double-precision floating point number. To work with its result in COBOL, you code a host variable with no picture and COMP-2 usage. In case you aren't familiar with floating-point notation, its value is computed by multiplying the decimal number in front of the E by 10 raised to the power of the number after the E. Thus, the first number in the INVTOTAL_F column in the result table is .15 times 100, or 15.00, while the second number in this column is .17307 times 1000, or 173.07.

The INTEGER function requires a single numeric argument, and it returns a binary fullword whose value is the whole-number portion of the argument. Since this function truncates any fractional part of the argument, the result of INTEGER(1.999) is 1.

One use of the INTEGER function is to combine it with the AVG column function in a rounding operation like this:

```
SELECT INTEGER(AVG(SALARY)+.5)
    FROM MM01.EMPLOYEE
        WHERE DEPTNO = 'B12'
```

This gets the average salary of the employees in department B12 rounded to the nearest dollar.

The syntax of the FLOAT function

```
FLOAT(expression)
```

Returns the double-precision floating point equivalent of *expression*. *Expression* must be a number.

To use the result of the function in a COBOL program, code a host variable with COMP-2 usage. The result may be null.

A SELECT statement that uses the FLOAT function

```
SELECT  INVNO,  INVTOTAL,
        FLOAT(INVTOTAL) AS INVTOTAL_F
    FROM MM01.INVOICE2
        WHERE INVCUST = '400002'
    ORDER BY INVNO
```

The result table

INVNO	INVTOTAL	INVTOTAL_F
062309	15.00	+0.1500000000000E+02
062312	173.07	+0.1730700000000E+03
062320	3405.90	+0.3405900000000E+04
062325	147.50	+0.1475000000000E+03

The syntax of the INTEGER function

```
INTEGER(expression)
```

Returns only the whole-number part of *expression*. *Expression* must be a number.

The result of the function is a binary fullword: PIC S9(9) COMP. The result may be null.

A SELECT statement that uses the INTEGER function

```
SELECT  INVNO,  INVTOTAL,
        INTEGER(INVTOTAL) AS INVTOTAL_I
    FROM MM01.INVOICE2
        WHERE INVCUST = '400002'
    ORDER BY INVNO
```

The result table

INVNO	INVTOTAL	INVTOTAL_I
062309	15.00	15
062312	173.07	173
062320	3405.90	3405
062325	147.50	147

Figure 7-8   The functions for working with numeric data (part 2 of 2)

How to substitute values for nulls

In chapter 4, you were introduced to the VALUE (or COALESCE) function. This function lets you code SELECT statements so a null value isn't returned as the value of a column. Its syntax is presented in figure 7-9.

In simplest form, the VALUE function has two arguments, which are normally the name of a column whose value can be null and a literal value. Then, if the value of the column identified by the first argument is null, DB2 returns the literal value of the second argument.

You can also list more than two arguments in a VALUE function. To illustrate, suppose you want to produce a result table from a customer table that includes phone numbers for both home and work. The preferred number is the home number, but if that number isn't available, the work phone number is okay. If neither number is available, the result table should hold the literal 'NO PHONE NUMBER.'

The example is this figure produces this result table. Here, the first substitution value is a literal string concatenated with the contents of the HOMEPH column. If HOMEPH is null, though, the entire concatenation is treated as null and DB2 evaluates the next argument, which is a literal string concatenated with the contents of the WORKPH number. Then, if this concatenation is null, the function returns the literal 'NO PHONE NUMBER.'

If you want to insure that a VALUE function returns a non-null value, you should code a literal value or a column that doesn't allow nulls as the last argument. If you don't do that, this function can return a null value. In that case, you need to provide an indicator variable for its column as explained in the next chapter so you can test to see whether it contains a null value. On the other hand, there's no point in placing a literal value or a column that doesn't allow nulls anywhere but at the end of an argument list because DB2 will always ignore the remaining arguments once it finds a non-null value.

This function is especially valuable in a COBOL program that accesses DB2 tables that contain numeric columns with values that may be null. Then, if you code an arithmetic expression that refers to an item with a null value, the result of the expression is null, which usually isn't what you want. To avoid that, you can use the VALUE function to substitute zero for a null value, as demonstrated by the full outer join in figure 4-16.

The syntax of the VALUE function

```
VALUE(expression1,expression2[,expression3]…)
COALESCE(expression1,expression2[,expression3]…)
```

Returns the value of the first argument that isn't null scanning from left to right.
COALESCE is a synonym that can be used instead of VALUE.

A SELECT statement that uses the VALUE function

```
SELECT   CUSTNO,
         FNAME,
         LNAME,
         VALUE('(H): ' || HOMEPH,
               '(W): ' || WORKPH,
               'NO PHONE NUMBER') AS PHONE
      FROM MM01.VARCUST
      ORDER BY CUSTNO
```

The result table

CUSTNO	FNAME	LNAME	PHONE
400001	KEITH	JONES	(H): 214-555-8029
400002	ARREN	ANELLI	NO PHONE NUMBER
400003	SUSAN	HOWARD	(H): 415-555-4587
400004	CAROL	EVANS	(H): 708-555-5484
400005	ELANE	ROBERTS	NO PHONE NUMBER
400006	PAT	HONG	(W): 415-555-2436
400007	PHIL	ROACH	NO PHONE NUMBER
400008	TIM	JOHNSON	(W): 708-555-4490
400009	MARIANNE	BUSBEE	(H): 205-555-9934
400010	ENRIQUE	OTHON	(H): 804-555-3437

Figure 7-9   The function for substituting values for nulls

How to convert dates, times, and numbers to character strings

Figure 7-10 presents the syntax for the CHAR function. The first argument names the item you want to convert to a character string, while the second argument identifies the format DB2 should use when it constructs the character string for that item.

With the CHAR function, you can direct DB2 to return date and time character strings to your COBOL programs in different formats than the default. This default can either be DB2's general default, which is the ISO format, or your shop's site-specific default. As you can see in the table in this figure, this function provides for four standard formats plus the local format, which can be set up by your database administrator.

If you don't specify a format argument on the CHAR function, DB2 uses your system default. However, because the reason for using the CHAR function is to guarantee that the date or time will follow a specific format, you should always code the format argument. Then, if the system default changes, this function will still operate the way you want it to.

The first two examples in this figure illustrate the results produced by the CHAR function for the special DB2 registers named CURRENT DATE and CURRENT TIME. Here, the first two columns in each result table are the same, because DB2's system default, which is the ISO format, hasn't been changed.

The last example in this figure illustrates how to use the local format. To use it, though, an exit routine for date and time must be installed on your system. As this result table shows, our shop has an exit routine that uses the name of the month instead of the month number in a date. So the invoice date of 1997-12-22 in the function CHAR(INVDATE, LOCAL) produces the date in this format: December 22, 1997.

The syntax of the CHAR function

```
CHAR(expression[,format])
```

Returns a character string representation of the date, time, timestamp, or decimal value of *expression* in the format indicated by *format*. If *expression* is a timestamp or a decimal number, *format* isn't applicable and must not be specified. If *expression* is a date or time, *format* may be one of the arguments in the table that follows. The result may be null.

Format argument	Standard	Date format	Time format
ISO	International Standards Organization	yyyy-mm-dd	hh.mm.ss
USA	IBM American Standard	mm/dd/yyyy	hh:mm AM ǀ PM
EUR	IBM European Standard	dd.mm.yyyy	hh.mm.ss
JIS	Japanese Industrial Standard Christian Era	yyyy-mm-dd	hh:mm:ss
LOCAL		Site-specific	Site-specific

A SELECT statement that uses the CHAR function with a date value

```
SELECT   CURRENT DATE AS CURR_DATE,
         CHAR(CURRENT DATE,ISO) AS DATE_ISO,
         CHAR(CURRENT DATE,USA) AS DATE_USA,
         CHAR(CURRENT DATE,EUR) AS DATE_EUR,
         CHAR(CURRENT DATE,JIS) AS DATE_JIS
    FROM MM01.VARCUST
         WHERE CUSTNO = '400001'
```

The result table

CURR_DATE	DATE-ISO	DATE_USA	DATE_EUR	DATE_JIS
1998-06-18	1998-06-18	06/18/1998	18.06.1998	1998-06-18

A SELECT statement that uses the CHAR function with a time value

```
SELECT   CURRENT TIME AS CURR_TIME,
         CHAR(CURRENT TIME,ISO) AS TIME_ISO,
         CHAR(CURRENT TIME,USA) AS TIME_USA,
         CHAR(CURRENT TIME,EUR) AS TIME_EUR,
         CHAR(CURRENT TIME,JIS) AS TIME_JIS
    FROM MM01.VARCUST
         WHERE CUSTNO = '400001'
```

The result table

CURR_TIME	TIME-ISO	TIME_USA	TIME_EUR	TIME_JIS
15.49.37	15.49.37	03:49 PM	15.49.37	15:49:37

A SELECT statement that uses the CHAR function with LOCAL format

```
SELECT  INVCUST, INVNO, INVDATE, CHAR(INVDATE,LOCAL) AS LOC_DATE
    FROM MM01.INVOICE2
         WHERE INVCUST = '400009'
```

The result table

INVCUST	INVNO	INVDATE	LOC_DATE
400009	062308	1997-12-22	DECEMBER 22, 1997

Figure 7-10   The function for converting dates, times, and numbers to strings

How to determine the number of elapsed days represented by a date

One of the more useful scalar functions is the DAYS function, which is presented in figure 7-11. This function returns the number of days that have elapsed between December 31, 0000 and the date of its argument.

The most common use of this function is to determine the number of elapsed days between two dates. This is illustrated by the first example in this figure. Here, DB2 first evaluates each DAYS function by determining the number of elapsed days since December 31, 0000. Then, it subtracts the second value from the first, which means that 208 days have elapsed between 1999-07-18 and 1998-12-22.

The second example in this figure shows how you can use this function to calculate the age of an invoice. In this case, the number of elapsed days for each invoice is subtracted from the number of elapsed days for the current date.

The syntax of the DAYS function

`DAYS(expression)`

Returns the number of days that have elapsed between December 31, 0000 and *expression* as a binary integer: PIC S9(9) COMP. *Expression* may be a date, timestamp, or string that DB2 can interpret as a date. The result may be null.

A SELECT statement that determines the elapsed days between two dates

```
SELECT  DAYS('1999-07-18') - DAYS('1998-12-22') AS DAYS_DIF
    FROM MM01.VARCUST
        WHERE CUSTNO = '400001'
```

The elapsed days for the two dates

`729953 - 729745`

The result table

DAYS_DIF
208

A SELECT statement that determines the age of invoices

```
SELECT  INVNO,  INVCUST,  CURRENT DATE AS CURR_DATE,  INVDATE,
        DAYS(CURRENT DATE) - DAYS(INVDATE) AS DAYS_OLD
    FROM MM01.INVOICE2
    ORDER BY DAYS_OLD DESC, INVCUST
```

The result table on August 10, 1998

INVNO	INVCUST	CURR-DATE	INVDATE	DAYS_OLD
062309	400002	1998-08-10	1997-12-22	231
062308	400009	1998-08-10	1997-12-22	231
062310	400001	1998-08-10	1998-02-22	169
062312	400002	1998-08-10	1998-02-22	169
062311	400005	1998-08-10	1998-02-22	169
062314	400003	1998-08-10	1998-03-14	149
062315	400004	1998-08-10	1998-03-14	149
062313	400004	1998-08-10	1998-03-14	149
062316	400010	1998-08-10	1998-03-14	149
062320	400002	1998-08-10	1998-03-17	146
062317	400003	1998-08-10	1998-03-17	146
062318	400006	1998-08-10	1998-03-17	146
062319	400007	1998-08-10	1998-03-17	146
062321	400001	1998-08-10	1998-04-03	129
062322	400005	1998-08-10	1998-04-03	129
062323	400007	1998-08-10	1998-04-11	121
062324	400003	1998-08-10	1998-04-14	118
062325	400002	1998-08-10	1998-04-17	115

Figure 7-11   The function that determines the number of elapsed days

How to extract the components from dates and times

If you need to work with the components of a date or time in a numeric expression, you can use one of the functions listed in figure 7-12. These functions let you extract any part of a date, time, or timestamp item as a binary number. You can use the result of any of these functions directly in an arithmetic expression. In the example in this figure, you can see how these functions are used to extract components from DB2's CURRENT DATE and CURRENT TIMESTAMP registers

A typical use of these functions in a COBOL program is to retrieve invoice table rows that have an invoice month that's equal to the current month, but with the invoice year in the previous year. To do that, the SELECT statement can be coded like this:

```
SELECT *
    FROM MM01.INVOICE2
        WHERE MONTH(INVDATE) = MONTH(CURRENT DATE)
          AND  YEAR(INVDATE) =  YEAR(CURRENT DATE) - 1
```

The functions in this figure also let you extract component information from DB2 durations. Durations are involved in arithmetic operations that are performed directly on DB2 date and time data, and they are described in detail later in this chapter.

The syntax of the extraction functions

Syntax	Expression can be
YEAR(expression)	Date, timestamp, date duration, or timestamp duration
MONTH(expression)	Date, timestamp, date duration, or timestamp duration
DAY(expression)	Date, timestamp, date duration, or timestamp duration
HOUR(expression)	Time, timestamp, time duration, or timestamp duration
MINUTE(expression)	Time, timestamp, time duration, or timestamp duration
SECOND(expression)	Time, timestamp, time duration, or timestamp duration
MICROSECOND(expression)	Timestamp or timestamp duration

Each function returns the named component of the item in *expression* as a binary fullword: PIC S9(9) COMP. The result may be null.

A SELECT statement that uses the extraction functions

```
SELECT  CURRENT DATE AS C_DATE,
        YEAR(CURRENT DATE) AS C_YEAR,
        MONTH(CURRENT DATE) AS C_MONTH,
        DAY(CURRENT DATE) AS C_DAY,
        CURRENT TIMESTAMP AS C_TIME,
        HOUR(CURRENT TIMESTAMP) AS C_HOUR,
        MINUTE(CURRENT TIMESTAMP) AS C_MIN,
        SECOND(CURRENT TIMESTAMP) AS C_SEC
    FROM MM01.VARCUST
        WHERE CUSTNO = '400001'
```

The result table

C_DATE	C_YEAR	C_MONTH	C_DAY	C_TIME	C_HOUR	C_MIN	C_SEC
1998-06-18	1998	6	18	1998-06-18-15.02.25.550000	15	2	25

Figure 7-12   The functions for extracting components from dates and times

How to create a date, time, or timestamp item

Figure 7-13 presents the syntax for the DATE, TIME, and TIMESTAMP functions. These functions let you create a date, time, or timestamp item from other types of items.

In the first example in this figure, you can see how the DATE and TIME functions are used to create date and time items from DB2's CURRENT TIMESTAMP register. In the second example, you can see how the TIMESTAMP function is used to create a timestamp from date and time items. In the result tables, you can see that these functions use DB2's default formats for date, time, and timestamp.

One practical use of the DATE function in a COBOL program is to determine the due date of an invoice. To do that, you combine this function with the DAYS function. If, for example, an invoice is due 30 days after the invoice date, you can use a statement like this to get the due date:

```
DATE(DAYS(INVDATE) + 30)
```

Here, the DAYS function first converts the invoice date to the number of elapsed days since December 31, 0000. Then, 30 is added to this value. Last, the DATE function is used to convert this value back into the DATE format. (Later in this chapter, you'll see a more straightforward way to do this using durations.)

The syntax of the DATE, TIME, and TIMESTAMP functions

`DATE(expression)`

Returns a date item in default format. The result can be null. *Expression* can be a date, a timestamp, a positive number less than or equal to 3,652,059, a 10-character string representation of a date (yyyy-mm-dd), or a 7-character string representation of a date (yyyyddd) where yyyy represents the year and ddd represents the day of the year (between 1 and 366).

`TIME(expression)`

Returns a time item in default format. The result can be null. *Expression* can be a time, a timestamp, or an 8-character string representation of a time (hh.mm.ss).

`TIMESTAMP(expression1[,expression2])`

Returns a timestamp item. The result can be null. The TIMESTAMP function operates differently depending on whether you specify one argument or two.

If you only specify *expression1*, it can be a timestamp, a 26-character string representation of a timestamp (yyyy-mm-dd-hh.mm.ss.mmmmmm), or a 14-character string representation of a timestamp (yyyymmddhhmmss). When you use this form, the result is a timestamp that contains zeros for its microsecond component.

If you specify both *expression1* and *expression2*, *expression1* must be a date or a string representation of a date, and *expression2* must be a time or a string representation of a time. When you use this form, the result is a timestamp that contains zeros for its microsecond component.

A SELECT statement that uses the DATE and TIME functions

```
SELECT  CURRENT TIMESTAMP AS C_TIMESTAMP,
        DATE(CURRENT TIMESTAMP) AS C_DATE,
        TIME(CURRENT TIMESTAMP) AS C_TIME
    FROM MM01.VARCUST
        WHERE CUSTNO = '400001'
```

The result table

C_TIMESTAMP	C_DATE	C_TIME
1998-06-18-15.02.25.550000	1998-06-18	15.02.25

A SELECT statement that uses the TIMESTAMP function

```
SELECT  CURRENT TIMESTAMP AS C_TIMESTAMP,
        CURRENT DATE AS C_DATE,
        CURRENT TIME AS C_TIME,
        TIMESTAMP(CURRENT DATE, CURRENT TIME) AS N_TIMESTAMP
    FROM MM01.VARCUST
        WHERE CUSTNO = '400001'
```

The result table

C_TIMESTAMP	C_DATE	C_TIME	N_TIMESTAMP
1998-06-18-17.09.21.192134	1998-06-18	17.09.21	1998-06-18-17.09.21.000000

Figure 7-13   The functions for creating date, time, and timestamp items

How to use dates, times, and durations in expressions

So far in this chapter, you've learned how to use the scalar functions for working with dates, times, and durations. However, you can also use dates, times, and durations directly in some arithmetic expressions. Then, you can use those expressions in the column specifications and selection conditions of SELECT statements.

The rules, syntax, and formats for using dates, times, and durations in expressions

Figure 7-14 summarizes the ways you can use dates, times, and durations in arithmetic operations. As you can see, the only valid operations are addition or subtraction. Also, all of these operations involve a *duration*, which is simply an elapsed period of time. If, for example, you add a date and a duration, you get a different date. And if you subtract a date from a date, you get a duration.

When you code a duration in an expression, you can code the duration as a *labeled duration* using the syntax given in this figure. If, for example, you want to add a duration of 3 months to an invoice date, you can code it like this:

```
INVDATE + 3 MONTHS
```

Here, 3 MONTHS is the labeled duration, and the result of this expression will be a date item.

When an expression produces a duration, the result is a *decimal duration*, which come in two types. If an expression subtracts a date from a date, the result is a *date duration*. When an expression subtracts a time from a time, the result is a *time duration*. The formats for these durations are also given in this figure.

These formats are compatible with DB2's DECIMAL data type for time and date durations. So if you need to store a duration in a table, you use the DECIMAL data type. If you use a DECIMAL item in the context of a duration, DB2 interprets it as a duration. And if you need to retrieve a duration into a COBOL program, you do it through a packed-decimal host variable.

As you can see in this figure, though, a decimal duration isn't a single value. Instead, both date and time durations consist of three separate components. As a result, you usually shouldn't use these durations in standard arithmetic operations. If, for example, you add 7 to a date duration that contains the value 00010628 (1 year, 6 months, and 28 days), the result is 00010635 (1 year, 6 months, and 35 days). But this doesn't make sense because 35 days is more than one month.

Because DB2 can identify the components in a decimal duration, though, you can specify them as arguments in the functions that are presented in figure 7-12. Specifically, you can specify a date duration as the argument of the MONTH, DAY or YEAR function. And you can specify a time duration as the argument of the HOUR, MINUTE, or SECOND function.

Valid arithmetic operations involving date and time data

Addition operations	Result format
Date + duration	Date
Time + duration	Time
Timestamp + duration	Timestamp

Subtraction operations	Result format
Date – duration	Date
Time – duration	Time
Timestamp – duration	Timestamp
Date – date	Duration
Time – time	Duration

The syntax of labeled durations

n YEAR	or	n YEARS
n MONTH	or	n MONTHS
n DAY	or	n DAYS
n HOUR	or	n HOURS
n MINUTE	or	n MINUTES
n SECOND	or	n SECONDS
n MICROSECOND	or	n MICROSECONDS

The format of decimal durations

Date duration

DB2 column definition	DEC(8,0)
COBOL host variable	PIC S9(8) COMP-3
Format	yyyymmdd
Examples	00000000 = 0 years, 0 months, 0 days
	00000100 = 0 years, 1 month, 0 days
	00000115 = 0 years, 1 month, 15 days
	00010000 = 1 year, 0 months, 0 days
	00020600 = 2 years, 6 months, 0 days

Time duration

DB2 column definition	DEC(6,0)
COBOL host variable	PIC S9(6) COMP-3
Format	hhmmss
Examples	000000 = 0 hours, 0 minutes, 0 seconds
	000130 = 0 hours, 1 minute, 30 seconds
	120000 = 12 hours, 0 minutes, 0 seconds

Figure 7-14   The rules, syntax, and formats for using dates, times and durations

How to use dates and times in column specifications

Once you know how to code arithmetic expressions that operate on dates, times, or durations, you can use the expressions in the column specifications of a SELECT statement. Figure 7-15, for example, shows two SELECT statements that produce a list of invoices with the age of each invoice in the WEEKS_OLD column of the result table. Once you understand how dates can be used in column specifications, you can apply the same principles to the use of times.

The WEEKS_OLD column in the first example in this figure is produced by a column specification that's based on the expression

```
CURRENT DATE - INVDATE
```

which produces a date duration. This expression appears as the argument of the DAY, MONTH, and YEAR functions, which return just the day, month, and year component of the date duration as integers that can be used in arithmetic operations. The results of these functions are then used in simple expressions that calculate the number of weeks represented by the days, months, and years components of the duration. Last, those values are added together, and the INTEGER function truncates any decimal part of the sum.

The second example in this figure shows a simpler SELECT statement that produces a similar result table. Here, the DAYS function is applied to the CURRENT DATE and INVDATE values to determine the number of elapsed days each represents. Then, the elapsed days for the invoice date is subtracted from the elapsed days for the current date to determine how many days separate the two. Last, to determine the number of elapsed weeks between the two dates, the difference is divided by seven.

A SELECT statement that uses the DAY, MONTH, and YEAR functions

```
SELECT  INVNO,  INVCUST,  INVDATE,  CURRENT DATE AS CURR_DATE,
        INTEGER((  DAY(CURRENT DATE - INVDATE)) / 7    ) +
              ((MONTH(CURRENT DATE - INVDATE)) * 52/12) +
              (( YEAR(CURRENT DATE - INVDATE)) * 52  ) AS WEEKS_OLD
    FROM MM01.INVOICE2
    ORDER BY WEEKS_OLD DESC, INVNO
```

The result table

INVNO	INVCUST	INVDATE	CURR_DATE	WEEKS_OLD
062308	400009	1997-12-22	1998-08-10	32
062309	400002	1997-12-22	1998-08-10	32
062310	400001	1998-02-22	1998-08-10	23
062311	400005	1998-02-22	1998-08-10	23
062312	400002	1998-02-22	1998-08-10	23
062313	400004	1998-03-14	1998-08-10	20
062314	400003	1998-03-14	1998-08-10	20
062315	400004	1998-03-14	1998-08-10	20
062316	400010	1998-03-14	1998-08-10	20
062317	400003	1998-03-17	1998-08-10	20
062318	400006	1998-03-17	1998-08-10	20
062319	400007	1998-03-17	1998-08-10	20
062320	400002	1998-03-17	1998-08-10	20
062321	400001	1998-04-03	1998-08-10	18
062322	400005	1998-04-03	1998-08-10	18
062323	400007	1998-04-11	1998-08-10	17
062324	400003	1998-04-14	1998-08-10	16
062325	400002	1998-04-17	1998-08-10	16

A SELECT statement that uses the DAYS function to return a similar result table

```
SELECT  INVNO,  INVCUST,  INVDATE,  CURRENT DATE AS CURR_DATE,
        INTEGER ((DAYS(CURRENT DATE) - DAYS(INVDATE)) / 7) AS WEEKS_OLD
    FROM MM01.INVOICE2
    ORDER BY WEEKS_OLD DESC, INVNO
```

Figure 7-15   How to use dates in column specifications

How to use dates and times in selection conditions

You can also code expressions that contain dates, times, and durations in selection conditions. This is illustrated by the examples in figure 7-16. Here, the first example shows how to use labeled durations in a WHERE clause to retrieve rows from the invoice table that are between a year and a year and a month old.

This is like the example presented earlier in this chapter that uses the MONTH and YEAR functions to retrieve rows from the current month in the previous year:

```
SELECT *
    FROM MM01.INVOICE2
        WHERE MONTH(INVDATE) = MONTH(CURRENT DATE)
        AND   YEAR(INVDATE) =  YEAR(CURRENT DATE) - 1
```

However, that's a little different from retrieving rows that are between one year and one year and one month old. If, for example, the statement above were executed on March 15, 1998, it would return invoices with dates between 1997-03-01 and 1997-03-31. In contrast, the first example in this figure would return invoices with dates between 1997-02-15 and 1997-03-15.

The second example in this figure is an SQL statement that uses a union to combine the result tables generated by four SELECT statements. Here, each SELECT statement uses one or two arithmetic expressions involving dates in its WHERE clause. This is one way to select the data for a report like an aged accounts payable listing. Although the traditional COBOL approach has been to do the aging in COBOL, not DB2, you should now be able to see how changing that approach could simplify the program.

Exceptional situations when working with dates and times

In general, dates, times, and durations work the way you want them to when you use them in expressions. However, there are a few exceptions.

For times, the only exception occurs when you add the labeled duration 24 HOURS to 00.00.00, which gives 24.00.00. However, this usually doesn't present a problem. Otherwise, adding 24 HOURS to a time gives the same time, which is what you expect.

For dates, exceptions occur when working with months that have differing numbers of days. If, for example, you subtract the labeled duration 1 MONTH from July 31, 1998, you get June 30, 1998 because June has only 30 days. Similarly, if you add one month to January 31, you get either February 28 or February 29, depending on whether the year is a leap year. Whenever an expression yields a date result that has been changed in this way, DB2 sets the value of the SQLWARN6 field in the communication area to W.

Labeled durations used in a single selection condition

```
SELECT   *
    FROM MM01.INVOICE2
         WHERE INVDATE BETWEEN (CURRENT DATE - 1 YEAR - 1 MONTH)
                           AND (CURRENT DATE - 1 YEAR)
```

Labeled durations used in four selection conditions

```
SELECT  'OVER 90 DAYS' AS DAYS_OLD,
        INVNO, INVDATE, CURRENT DATE AS CURR_DATE, INVTOTAL, INVCUST
    FROM MM01.INVOICE2
         WHERE INVDATE < CURRENT DATE - 90 DAYS
UNION ALL
    SELECT  '75 - 90 DAYS' AS DAYS_OLD,
        INVNO, INVDATE, CURRENT DATE AS CURR_DATE, INVTOTAL, INVCUST
    FROM MM01.INVOICE2
         WHERE (INVDATE >= CURRENT DATE - 90 DAYS) AND
               (INVDATE <  CURRENT DATE - 75 DAYS)
UNION ALL
    SELECT  '60 - 75 DAYS' AS DAYS_OLD,
        INVNO, INVDATE, CURRENT DATE AS CURR_DATE, INVTOTAL, INVCUST
    FROM MM01.INVOICE2
         WHERE (INVDATE >= CURRENT DATE - 75 DAYS) AND
               (INVDATE <  CURRENT DATE - 60 DAYS)
UNION ALL
    SELECT  '30 - 60 DAYS' AS DAYS_OLD,
        INVNO, INVDATE, CURRENT DATE AS CURR_DATE, INVTOTAL, INVCUST
    FROM MM01.INVOICE2
         WHERE (INVDATE >= CURRENT DATE - 60 DAYS) AND
               (INVDATE <  CURRENT DATE - 30 DAYS)
ORDER BY INVDATE, INVNO
```

The result table

DAYS_OLD	INVNO	INVDATE	CURR_DATE	INVTOTAL	INVCUST
OVER 90 DAYS	062308	1997-12-22	1998-07-01	204.45	400009
OVER 90 DAYS	062309	1997-12-22	1998-07-01	15.00	400002
OVER 90 DAYS	062310	1998-02-22	1998-07-01	147.50	400001
OVER 90 DAYS	062311	1998-02-22	1998-07-01	181.42	400005
OVER 90 DAYS	062312	1998-02-22	1998-07-01	173.07	400002
OVER 90 DAYS	062313	1998-03-14	1998-07-01	22.50	400004
OVER 90 DAYS	062314	1998-03-14	1998-07-01	149.80	400003
OVER 90 DAYS	062315	1998-03-14	1998-07-01	181.42	400004
OVER 90 DAYS	062316	1998-03-14	1998-07-01	147.50	400010
OVER 90 DAYS	062317	1998-03-17	1998-07-01	298.00	400003
OVER 90 DAYS	062318	1998-03-17	1998-07-01	199.99	400006
OVER 90 DAYS	062319	1998-03-17	1998-07-01	181.42	400007
OVER 90 DAYS	062320	1998-03-17	1998-07-01	3405.90	400002
75 – 90 DAYS	062321	1998-04-03	1998-07-01	205.60	400001
75 – 90 DAYS	062322	1998-04-03	1998-07-01	15.00	400005
75 – 90 DAYS	062323	1998-04-11	1998-07-01	949.00	400007
75 – 90 DAYS	062324	1998-04-14	1998-07-01	181.42	400003
60 – 75 DAYS	062325	1998-04-17	1998-07-01	147.50	400002

Figure 7-16   How to use dates in selection conditions

Perspective

In this chapter, you have learned how to use the eleven DB2 data types and the 21 scalar functions. Although you may use only a few of these functions in your COBOL programs, you'll find most of them useful in SPUFI and QMF sessions. When you need them, just refer back to the figures in this chapter for the coding details.

In the next chapter, you can learn more about working with variable-length columns, which are frequently used in business databases. You can also learn more about working with nulls. As you will see, this information is closely related to some of the data types and functions presented in this chapter.

8

How to use variable-length data and nulls

In chapters 1 through 6, all of the DB2 table examples have used fixed-length columns that don't allow null values. In practice, though, variable-length (VARCHAR) columns are frequently used, and null values are allowed in some columns. As a result, a DB2 programmer needs to know how to work with variable-length data and nulls, and that's what this chapter teaches you.

In case you haven't already done so, though, you should read the first few pages of chapter 7 before you start this chapter. Those pages introduce you to the eleven data types that you can use with DB2, including the VARCHAR data type.

How to work with variable-length data

When you use variable-length columns in a table, DB2 does most of the work as you retrieve them. When you update or delete rows with variable-length columns, though, you need to pass the appropriate length values to DB2 through the host variables. In the topics that follow, you'll learn how to retrieve, update, and insert rows with variable-length columns.

A customer table with variable-length columns

Figure 8-1 presents the DCLGEN output for a customer table that has four VARCHAR columns. In the COBOL declarations for the host variables, you can see that the host variable for each of these columns consists of a length portion and a text portion. The text portion provides for the maximum number of characters that the column can contain, while the length portion gives the number of characters in the text portion when the data in the column is retrieved.

The NOTES column in this table declaration provides for the maximum number of characters that a VARCHAR column can contain. A column like this typically contains one or more notes or comments that are related to that row. Unlike the other VARCHAR columns in this example, NOT NULL isn't coded for the NOTES column, which means that the column can be null.

A table declaration that includes variable-length columns and columns that can be null

```
******************************************************************
* DCLGEN TABLE(MM01.VARCUST)                                     *
*       LIBRARY(MM01.DB2.DCLGENS(VARCUST))                       *
*       ACTION(REPLACE)                                          *
*       LANGUAGE(COBOL)                                          *
*       STRUCTURE(CUSTOMER-ROW)                                  *
*       QUOTE                                                    *
* ... IS THE DCLGEN COMMAND THAT MADE THE FOLLOWING STATEMENTS   *
******************************************************************
      EXEC SQL DECLARE MM01.VARCUST TABLE
      ( CUSTNO                     CHAR(6) NOT NULL,
        FNAME                      VARCHAR(20) NOT NULL,
        LNAME                      VARCHAR(30) NOT NULL,
        CITY                       VARCHAR(20) NOT NULL,
        STATE                      CHAR(2) NOT NULL,
        ZIPCODE                    CHAR(10) NOT NULL,
        HOMEPH                     CHAR(16),
        WORKPH                     CHAR(16),
        NOTES                      VARCHAR(254)
      ) END-EXEC.
******************************************************************
* COBOL DECLARATION FOR TABLE MM01.VARCUST                       *
******************************************************************
  01  CUSTOMER-ROW.
      10 CUSTNO            PIC X(6).
      10 FNAME.
         49 FNAME-LEN      PIC S9(4) USAGE COMP.
         49 FNAME-TEXT     PIC X(20).
      10 LNAME.
         49 LNAME-LEN      PIC S9(4) USAGE COMP.
         49 LNAME-TEXT     PIC X(30).
      10 CITY.
         49 CITY-LEN       PIC S9(4) USAGE COMP.
         49 CITY-TEXT      PIC X(20).
      10 STATE             PIC X(2).
      10 ZIPCODE           PIC X(10).
      10 HOMEPH            PIC X(16).
      10 WORKPH            PIC X(16).
      10 NOTES.
         49 NOTES-LEN      PIC S9(4) USAGE COMP.
         49 NOTES-TEXT     PIC X(254).
******************************************************************
* THE NUMBER OF COLUMNS DESCRIBED BY THIS DECLARATION IS 9       *
******************************************************************
```

Figure 8-1   The DCLGEN output for a customer table

How variable-length data is returned to your program

Figure 8-2 illustrates how variable-length data is returned to your program by SELECT statements, and this works the same for FETCH statements. For the first SELECT statement in the first example, the city name (SAN FRANCISCO) is stored in CITY-TEXT, while the length of that name (13) is stored in CITY-LEN. For the second SELECT statement in this first example, DALLAS is stored in CITY-TEXT and 6 in CITY-LENGTH.

Note in this first example that the last seven characters of the previous city name (ANCISCO) remain in the CITY-TEXT field after the second SELECT statement has been run. In other words, DB2 doesn't replace the entire text portion of a host variable with the next value that's retrieved. If this is a problem in your program, the solution is to move spaces to CITY-TEXT prior to retrieving it as shown in the second example in this figure. In some programs, though, you'll use the length to extract the right number of characters from the text portion of the field so the extra data in the field won't matter.

Example 1: CITY-TEXT isn't reset to spaces

```
MOVE SPACE TO CITY-TEXT.
    .
    .
    .
EXEC SQL
    SELECT    CITY
        FROM  MM01.VARCUST
        INTO  :CITY
        WHERE CUSTNO = '400006'
END-EXEC.
    .
    .
EXEC SQL
    SELECT    CITY
        FROM  MM01.VARCUST
        INTO  :CITY
        WHERE CUSTNO = '400001'
END-EXEC.
    .
    .
```

CITY-LEN	CITY-TEXT
?	

CITY-LEN	CITY-TEXT
13	SAN FRANCISCO

CITY-LEN	CITY-TEXT
6	DALLASANCISCO

Example 2: CITY-TEXT is reset to spaces

```
MOVE SPACE TO CITY-TEXT.
    .
    .
EXEC SQL
    SELECT    CITY
        FROM  MM01.VARCUST
        INTO  :CITY
        WHERE CUSTNO = '400006'
END-EXEC.
    .
    .
MOVE SPACE TO CITY-TEXT.
    .
    .
    .
    .
EXEC SQL
    SELECT    CITY
        FROM  MM01.VARCUST
        INTO  :CITY
        WHERE CUSTNO = '400001'
END-EXEC.
    .
    .
```

CITY-LEN	CITY-TEXT
?	

CITY-LEN	CITY-TEXT
13	SAN FRANCISCO

CITY-LEN	CITY-TEXT
13	

CITY-LEN	CITY-TEXT
6	DALLAS

Figure 8-2   How variable-length data is returned to your program

A subprogram that determines the length of a character string

When you retrieve variable-length data, DB2 automatically puts the length and text values in the host variables. But when you update or add variable-length data to a table, your COBOL program must put the length values in the host variables before you issue an UPDATE or INSERT statement. This means that you must use COBOL to determine what the length values are.

If your shop uses variable-length columns, it probably has a subprogram that your programs can call to determine the length of a variable-length field. It's also possible that your shop has a customized DB2 exit routine that determines the sizes of variable-length fields in a way that's transparent to your COBOL programs. So be sure to check with your colleagues or DBA to determine what's available before you write your own subprogram.

If nothing is available, though, figure 8-3 illustrates a relatively simple subprogram that determines what the length of a character field is. It puts the character field in an array, and then works backwards through the array, subtracting one from the text length for each space that it finds, until it finds a non-blank character. At that point, the text length is the length of the data.

When you call this subprogram, you have to pass two fields to it: (1) the length of the field that the subprogram is going to evaluate and (2) the field itself. Then, when the subprogram is finished, the first field contains the length of the data in the second field. In other words, the program passes the length of the container (the field), and the subprogram returns the length of the contents of the container (the data in the field).

This is illustrated by the CALL statement at the bottom of this figure, which passes FNAME-LEN and FNAME-TEXT to the program. Before this statement is executed, a MOVE statement moves the length of the FNAME-TEXT field to FNAME-LEN. Although this statement could move the actual length of the text field as in

```
MOVE 20 TO FNAME-LEN
```

it uses the special register named LENGTH to move the length of the FNAME-TEXT field to FNAME-LEN. Then, if the length of that DB2 column is changed by the DBA at some later date, the COBOL code doesn't have to be changed (although you still need to precompile, complile, bind, and link the program). When the subprogram finishes, FNAME-LEN contains the length of the data in FNAME-TEXT.

The STRLEN subprogram

```
IDENTIFICATION DIVISION.
*
PROGRAM-ID.     STRLEN.
*
ENVIRONMENT DIVISION.
*
DATA DIVISION.
*
WORKING-STORAGE SECTION.
*
01  SWITCH.
*
    05  LENGTH-DETERMINED-SW     PIC X  VALUE 'N'.
        88  LENGTH-DETERMINED           VALUE 'Y'.
*
LINKAGE SECTION.
*
01  TEXT-LENGTH                  PIC S9(4) COMP.
*
01  WORK-TABLE.
*
    05  WT-CHARACTER             OCCURS 1 TO 254 TIMES
                                 DEPENDING ON TEXT-LENGTH
                                 PIC X.
*
PROCEDURE DIVISION USING TEXT-LENGTH
                        WORK-TABLE.
*
000-DETERMINE-STRING-LENGTH.
*
    MOVE 'N' TO LENGTH-DETERMINED-SW.
    PERFORM 100-EXAMINE-LAST-CHARACTER
        UNTIL LENGTH-DETERMINED.
*
000-EXIT.
*
    EXIT PROGRAM.
*
100-EXAMINE-LAST-CHARACTER.
*
    IF WT-CHARACTER(TEXT-LENGTH) = SPACE
        SUBTRACT 1 FROM TEXT-LENGTH
    ELSE
        MOVE 'Y' TO LENGTH-DETERMINED-SW.
    IF TEXT-LENGTH = 0
        MOVE 'Y' TO LENGTH-DETERMINED-SW.
*
```

The code for calling the STRLEN subprogram

```
MOVE LENGTH OF FNAME-TEXT TO FNAME-LEN.
CALL 'STRLEN' USING FNAME-LEN
                    FNAME-TEXT.
```

Figure 8-3   A subprogram that determines the length of a character string

How to work with nulls

When a table column is declared as NOT NULL, DB2 doesn't let you use a null value for that column when you update or insert a row. When a table column isn't defined as not null, though, the column can either contain data or be null. In that case, you need to use an indicator variable in your COBOL program to determine whether a column value is null.

How to use indicator variables

Figure 8-4 shows how to use *indicator variables*. For each host variable that can be null, you start by defining an indicator variable that tells whether the value is null. Next, you use that indicator variable in the INTO clause of a SELECT or FETCH statement. Then, when DB2 runs the statement, it returns the appropriate value in the indicator variable: -1 if the related value is null; 0 if the related value isn't null. Your COBOL program can use this value to determine how the related value should be processed.

When you use an UPDATE or INSERT statement that writes a null value to the database, this process works in reverse. First, you need to put a value of -1 in the indicator variable for the host variable that's going to be null. Next, you issue the UPDATE or INSERT statement. Then, when DB2 runs the statement, it uses the indicator variable to determine whether a null value should be stored in the related field. This process is necessary because you can't move a null value into a host variable when using COBOL.

Incidentally, starting with version 4, the DCLGEN output can be set up so indicator variables are generated for the columns in the host structure. However, one variable is generated for each column, whether or not it can be null. Worse, the indicator variables are generated in this format:

```
01  IVARCUST.
    10  INDSTRUC   PIC S9(4) USAGE COMP OCCURS 9 TIMES.
```

Since this makes it hard to tell which variable applies to which column, you can improve the readability of your code by defining your own indicator variables. That's why we recommend that you avoid using this option.

Indicator host variables

```
01   IND-VARIABLES.
*
     05   IND-HOMEPH            PIC S9(4) COMP.
     05   IND-WORKPH            PIC S9(4) COMP.
     05   IND-NOTES             PIC S9(4) COMP.
*
```

A SELECT statement that uses indicator host variables

```
EXEC SQL
    SELECT *
        INTO :CUSTNO,
             :FNAME,
             :LNAME,
             :CITY,
             :STATE,
             :ZIPCODE,
             :HOMEPH:IND-HOMEPH,
             :WORKPH:IND-WORKPH,
             :NOTES:IND-NOTES
        FROM   MM01.VARCUST
        WHERE CUSTNO = :CUSTNO
END-EXEC
```

Description

- An *indicator variable* is a halfword binary field that tells whether the field it applies to is null. If the indicator variable has a value of -1, it means that the related field is null; if the value is zero, the related field isn't null.

- When working with fields that can be null, you need to define an indicator variable for each field as shown above.

- When you retrieve a column with an indicator variable, DB2 puts the appropriate value in the indicator. When you update or insert a column with a null value, your program needs to put -1 in the indicator variable because you can't move a null value into a host variable using COBOL.

- To refer to an indicator variable in the INTO clause of a SELECT or FETCH statement, you code the column name, a colon, and the name of the indicator variable with no intervening spaces as shown above.

- If you don't supply an indicator variable for a column and an SQL statement retrieves a row with a null value in that column, the statement will fail with an SQLCODE value of -305.

- DB2 returns values other than 0 and -1 in an indicator variable in two exceptional cases. If a value is null because of a conversion error, DB2 returns -2. If DB2 has to truncate the value it returns to a host variable, it returns the original length in the indicator variable as a positive value (this shouldn't happen if you define the host variable correctly).

Figure 8-4   How to use indicator variables

How nulls can affect SQL statements

When you use columns that can be null in a program, you need to be aware of the ways nulls can affect your SQL statements. First, when a null value is sorted or grouped by the ORDER BY or GROUP BY clauses, all nulls are treated as the last items in the collating sequence. This is illustrated by the first example in figure 8-5. In all of these examples, a null value is represented by a series of hyphens, which is the way they appear in a SPUFI query.

Second, when DB2 evaluates a selection condition that contains a null value, DB2 doesn't evaluate the condition as either true or false. Instead, DB2 evaluates it as "unknown." As a result, the unknown rows aren't included in selection conditions that require true or false evaluations. This is illustrated by second and third examples in figure 8-5. As you can see, a null isn't treated as equal to zero or not equal to zero.

Third, because NULL isn't really a value, you can't code it in a condition like this:

```
WHERE HOMEPH = NULL
```

However, you can code

```
WHERE HOMEPH IS NULL
```

This is illustrated by the fourth example in this figure. You can also code IS NOT NULL.

Fourth, DB2 ignores null values when it evaluates column functions. In particular, this can cause problems when you use the AVG function, as illustrated by the fifth example in this figure. Here, the COUNT of the rows and the SUM of the NUM column produce the expected results, but the average isn't the sum divided by the row count. Instead, it is the average of just those values in the NUM column that aren't null.

Last, when DB2 evaluates an arithmetic expression that contains a null, it returns a null value for the entire expression. If a numeric column is defined as NOT NULL, of course, this can't happen. But otherwise, you may need to code your SQL statements so they avoid this problem.

A SELECT statement that retrieves every row in a table

```
SELECT KEY, NUM
    FROM MM01.DEMO
    ORDER BY NUM
```

KEY	NUM
07	-50.00
09	.00
01	.00
03	.00
04	100.00
05	150.00
02	150.00
06	200.00
10	----------
08	----------

A SELECT statement that retrieves rows with zero values

```
SELECT KEY, NUM
    FROM MM01.DEMO
    WHERE NUM = 0
```

KEY	NUM
01	.00
03	.00
09	.00

A SELECT statement that retrieves rows with non-zero values

```
SELECT KEY, NUM
    FROM MM01.DEMO
    WHERE NUM <> 0
```

KEY	NUM
02	150.00
04	100.00
05	150.00
06	200.00
07	-50.00

A SELECT statement that retrieves rows with null values

```
SELECT KEY, NUM
    FROM MM01.DEMO
    WHERE NUM IS NULL
```

KEY	NUM
08	----------
10	----------

A SELECT statement that uses column functions

```
SELECT COUNT(*) AS COUNT,
    SUM(NUM) AS SUM,
    AVG(NUM) AS AVERAGE
    FROM MM01.DEMO
```

COUNT	SUM	AVERAGE
10	550.00	68.7500

Figure 8-5   How nulls can affect SQL statements

A COBOL program that updates a table that has variable-length data and nulls

This chapter concludes by presenting a COBOL program that maintains the rows in a customer table that includes variable-length columns and columns that allow nulls. This is an enhanced version of the program that was presented in chapter 3. It gets transaction data from the records in a VSAM entry-sequenced data set, and it uses this data to update the rows in the customer table.

The transaction record

Figure 8-6 presents the COBOL description for the transaction record that's used by this program. The first field in each record contains A (for Add), R (for Replace), or D (for Delete) to indicate what type of transaction the record represents. The remaining fields contain the data that should be used for adding a new row to the table or updating an existing row.

The DCLGEN output for the customer table

If you refer back to figure 8-1, you can see the DCLGEN output for the customer table. For each of the four VARCHAR columns, the program will have to determine the length of the related field in the transaction record and then set the length of the host variable to that number. For each field that can be null, the program will have to determine whether the related field in the transaction record is blank, which means the table column should be set to null. Then, the program will have to set that column's indicator variable to -1.

The structure chart

Figure 8-6 also presents the structure chart for this program. To keep this program simple, this program doesn't include COMMIT and ROLLBACK processing so this chart doesn't include modules for those tasks. To provide for the nulls and lengths, though, this chart has module 130, which is called by both module 120 and module 140. Otherwise, this chart is like the one for the simple version of the update program in chapter 3.

The transaction record

```
01  CUSTOMER-TRANSACTION-RECORD.
*
    05  CTR-TRANSACTION-CODE    PIC X.
    05  CTR-TRANSACTION-DATA.
        10  CTR-CUSTNO          PIC X(6).
        10  CTR-FNAME           PIC X(20).
        10  CTR-LNAME           PIC X(30).
        10  CTR-CITY            PIC X(20).
        10  CTR-STATE           PIC XX.
        10  CTR-ZIPCODE         PIC X(10).
        10  CTR-HOMEPH          PIC X(16).
        10  CTR-WORKPH          PIC X(16).
        10  CTR-NOTES           PIC X(254).
```

The structure chart

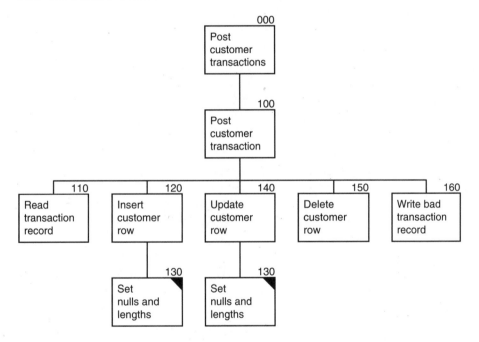

Figure 8-6   The transaction record and structure chart for the update program

The COBOL listing

Figure 8-7 presents the four-page COBOL listing for this program. At the top of page 2, you can see the definitions for the three indicator variables used by this program. Also, in module 100 on page 2, you can see how the fields in the transaction record are moved to the host variables. Otherwise, the code on the first two pages is like the code in the program in chapter 3 so you shouldn't have any trouble following it.

On page 3, module 120 starts by performing module 130. That module starts by calling the STRLEN subprogram that's in figure 8-3 once for each of the first three VARCHAR columns. Each time this subprogram is called, two fields are passed to it: a length field that contains the length of the text field to be evaluated and the text field itself. When the subprogram finishes, the length of the data in the text field is stored in the length field.

To illustrate, suppose the first value in FNAME-TEXT is CURTIS. To start, module 130 moves the LENGTH of FNAME-TEXT to FNAME-LEN. Since the length of FNAME-TEXT in the DCLGEN output in figure 8-1 is 20, this means that FNAME-LEN has a value of 20 when it is passed to the subprogram. When the subprogram is finished, though, this starting value is replaced by the length of the data in FNAME-TEXT, which is 6. At this point, the host variables for the FNAME column are both set up properly for an UPDATE or INSERT statement.

After the three calls to the subprogram, module 130 continues by using IF statements to set the indicator variables for the three fields that can be null. For all three fields, if the field contains a space, the indicator is set to -1 so the column will be treated as a null. Otherwise, the indicator is set to 0.

Because the third IF statement in this group is for a variable-length field that can be null, it also needs to move the length of the field to the length host variable if the field isn't null. To do that, the ELSE clause calls the STRLEN subprogram in the same way that this module calls this subprogram for the other VARCHAR columns.

Once module 130 does its processing, the program continues with the next statement in module 120. This is an INSERT statement that adds a row with nine columns to the customer table. Here, you can see how the indicator variables are coded for the three fields that require them.

The COBOL listing

Page 1

```
IDENTIFICATION DIVISION.
*
PROGRAM-ID.          VNCUPDT.
*
ENVIRONMENT DIVISION.
*
INPUT-OUTPUT SECTION.
*
FILE-CONTROL.
*
    SELECT CUSTTRAN ASSIGN TO UT-S-CUSTTRAN.
    SELECT BADTRAN  ASSIGN TO UT-S-BADTRAN.
*
DATA DIVISION.
*
FILE SECTION.
*
FD  CUSTTRAN
    LABEL RECORDS ARE STANDARD
    RECORD CONTAINS 375 CHARACTERS.
*
01  CUSTOMER-TRANSACTION-RECORD.
*
    05  CTR-TRANSACTION-CODE     PIC X.
    05  CTR-TRANSACTION-DATA.
        10  CTR-CUSTNO           PIC X(6).
        10  CTR-FNAME            PIC X(20).
        10  CTR-LNAME            PIC X(30).
        10  CTR-CITY             PIC X(20).
        10  CTR-STATE            PIC XX.
        10  CTR-ZIPCODE          PIC X(10).
        10  CTR-HOMEPH           PIC X(16).
        10  CTR-WORKPH           PIC X(16).
        10  CTR-NOTES            PIC X(254).
*
FD  BADTRAN
    LABEL RECORDS ARE STANDARD
    RECORD CONTAINS 375 CHARACTERS.
*
01  BAD-TRANSACTION-RECORD.
*
    05  BTR-TRANSACTION-CODE     PIC X.
    05  BTR-TRANSACTION-DATA     PIC X(374).
*
WORKING-STORAGE SECTION.
*
01  SWITCHES.
*
    05  END-OF-TRANSACTIONS-SW   PIC X     VALUE 'N'.
        88  END-OF-TRANSACTIONS            VALUE 'Y'.
    05  VALID-TRANSACTION-SW     PIC X     VALUE 'Y'.
        88  VALID-TRANSACTION              VALUE 'Y'.
*
```

Figure 8-7   The COBOL listing for the update program (part 1 of 4)

The COBOL listing

```
01  INDICATORS.
*
    05  IND-HOMEPH              PIC S9(4) COMP.
    05  IND-WORKPH              PIC S9(4) COMP.
    05  IND-NOTES              PIC S9(4) COMP.
*

    EXEC SQL
        INCLUDE VARCUST
    END-EXEC.
*

    EXEC SQL
        INCLUDE SQLCA
    END-EXEC.
*
 PROCEDURE DIVISION.
*
 000-POST-CUST-TRANSACTIONS.
*
    OPEN INPUT   CUSTTRAN
         OUTPUT  BADTRAN.
    PERFORM 100-POST-CUST-TRANSACTION
        UNTIL END-OF-TRANSACTIONS.
    CLOSE CUSTTRAN
          BADTRAN.
    STOP RUN.
*
 100-POST-CUST-TRANSACTION.
*
    MOVE 'Y' TO VALID-TRANSACTION-SW.
    PERFORM 110-READ-TRANSACTION-RECORD.
    IF NOT END-OF-TRANSACTIONS
        MOVE CTR-CUSTNO   TO CUSTNO
        MOVE CTR-FNAME    TO FNAME-TEXT
        MOVE CTR-LNAME    TO LNAME-TEXT
        MOVE CTR-CITY     TO CITY-TEXT
        MOVE CTR-STATE    TO STATE
        MOVE CTR-ZIPCODE  TO ZIPCODE
        MOVE CTR-HOMEPH   TO HOMEPH
        MOVE CTR-WORKPH   TO WORKPH
        MOVE CTR-NOTES    TO NOTES-TEXT
        EVALUATE CTR-TRANSACTION-CODE
            WHEN 'A'     PERFORM 120-INSERT-CUSTOMER-ROW
            WHEN 'R'     PERFORM 140-UPDATE-CUSTOMER-ROW
            WHEN 'D'     PERFORM 150-DELETE-CUSTOMER-ROW
            WHEN OTHER MOVE 'N' TO VALID-TRANSACTION-SW
        END-EVALUATE
        IF NOT VALID-TRANSACTION
            PERFORM 160-WRITE-BAD-TRANSACTION.
*
 110-READ-TRANSACTION-RECORD.
*
    READ CUSTTRAN
        AT END
            MOVE 'Y' TO END-OF-TRANSACTIONS-SW.
*
```

Figure 8-7   The COBOL listing for the update program (part 2 of 4)

The COBOL listing

```
120-INSERT-CUSTOMER-ROW.
*
    PERFORM 130-SET-NULLS-AND-LENGTHS.
    EXEC SQL
        INSERT INTO MM01.VARCUST
            (  CUSTNO,              FNAME,
               LNAME,               CITY,
               STATE,               ZIPCODE,
               HOMEPH,              WORKPH,
               NOTES)
        VALUES (:CUSTNO,            :FNAME,
               :LNAME,              :CITY,
               :STATE,              :ZIPCODE,
               :HOMEPH:IND-HOMEPH,  :WORKPH:IND-WORKPH,
               :NOTES:IND-NOTES)
    END-EXEC.
    IF SQLCODE NOT = 0
        MOVE 'N' TO VALID-TRANSACTION-SW.
*
130-SET-NULLS-AND-LENGTHS.
*
    MOVE LENGTH OF FNAME-TEXT TO FNAME-LEN.
    CALL 'STRLEN' USING FNAME-LEN
                        FNAME-TEXT.
*
    MOVE LENGTH OF LNAME-TEXT TO LNAME-LEN.
    CALL 'STRLEN' USING LNAME-LEN
                        LNAME-TEXT.
*
    MOVE LENGTH OF CITY-TEXT TO CITY-LEN.
    CALL 'STRLEN' USING CITY-LEN
                        CITY-TEXT.
*
    IF HOMEPH = SPACE
        MOVE -1 TO IND-HOMEPH
    ELSE
        MOVE 0  TO IND-HOMEPH.
*
    IF WORKPH = SPACE
        MOVE -1 TO IND-WORKPH
    ELSE
        MOVE 0  TO IND-WORKPH.
*
    IF NOTES-TEXT = SPACE
        MOVE -1 TO IND-NOTES
    ELSE
        MOVE 0  TO IND-NOTES
        MOVE LENGTH OF NOTES-TEXT TO NOTES-LEN
        CALL 'STRLEN' USING NOTES-LEN
                           NOTES-TEXT.
*
```

Figure 8-7   The COBOL listing for the update program (part 3 of 4)

On the last page of this COBOL listing, you can see that module 140 works much like module 120. First, it calls module 130 to set the length values and indicator variables properly. Then, it issues an UPDATE statement to update a customer row. Here again, you can see how the indicator variables are coded.

The COBOL listing   **Page 4**

```
140-UPDATE-CUSTOMER-ROW.
*
        PERFORM 130-SET-NULLS-AND-LENGTHS.
        EXEC SQL
            UPDATE MM01.VARCUST
                SET CUSTNO  = :CUSTNO,
                    FNAME   = :FNAME,
                    LNAME   = :LNAME,
                    CITY    = :CITY,
                    STATE   = :STATE,
                    ZIPCODE = :ZIPCODE,
                    HOMEPH  = :HOMEPH:IND-HOMEPH,
                    WORKPH  = :WORKPH:IND-WORKPH,
                    NOTES   = :NOTES:IND-NOTES
                WHERE   CUSTNO = :CUSTNO
        END-EXEC.
        IF SQLCODE NOT = 0
            MOVE 'N' TO VALID-TRANSACTION-SW.
*
 150-DELETE-CUSTOMER-ROW.
*
        EXEC SQL
            DELETE FROM MM01.VARCUST
                WHERE CUSTNO = :CUSTNO
        END-EXEC.
        IF SQLCODE NOT = 0
            MOVE 'N' TO VALID-TRANSACTION-SW.
*
 160-WRITE-BAD-TRANSACTION.
*
        WRITE BAD-TRANSACTION-RECORD
            FROM CUSTOMER-TRANSACTION-RECORD.
*
```

Figure 8-7   The COBOL listing for the update program (part 4 of 4)

Perspective

If you've been spoiled by how easy DB2 makes complex tasks like joins and column functions, you may be surprised at the coding that's required for the use of variable-length columns and nulls. To some extent, that's because COBOL was developed long before DB2 was. As a result, COBOL doesn't provide for nulls and doesn't handle variable-length data the same way DB2 does. Perhaps these differences will be resolved by future releases of COBOL or DB2.

9

How to use subqueries

A *subquery* is a SELECT statement that's nested inside another SQL statement. You can use a subquery whenever one SQL statement depends on the results of another. In this case, DB2 creates an intermediate result table for the subquery that can then be processed by the outer SQL statement.

How to code subqueries

If you know how to code SELECT statements, you already know how to code a subquery because it's just a SELECT statement nested within another SQL statement. As a result, the trick in using subqueries is knowing where and how to nest them. Before you learn that, though, this chapter shows you how the use of a subquery can simplify coding.

How the use of a subquery can simplify coding

Figure 9-1 shows two examples of coding that produce a result table that has one row for each invoice with an invoice total greater than the average invoice total for all the invoices. To do that, you need to first run a SELECT statement that uses the AVG function to calculate the average invoice amount for all the rows in the invoice table. Once the average is computed, it can be used in a SELECT statement that selects all the rows with invoice totals greater than that average.

In the first example in this figure, you can see how this is done without using a subquery statement. Here, the second EXEC SQL statement is executed first. It produces a one-row, one-column table that contains the computed average of all the invoice totals in the table. Then, the OPEN INVCURS statement is executed, which runs the SELECT statement in the DECLARE CURSOR statement that selects all the invoice rows with totals greater than the average. After that, the program can use a FETCH statement to retrieve the rows in the cursor-controlled result table, one row at a time.

In the second example in this figure, you can see how the use of a subquery can simplify this coding. Here, the subquery (shaded) is coded within the WHERE clause of the SELECT statement that's in a DECLARE CURSOR statement. When DB2 opens the cursor, it first processes the subquery to calculate the average. Then, it uses that value to retrieve just the rows that meet the selection condition in the outer SELECT.

When you code a subquery within a SELECT statement, you're actually *nesting* one SELECT statement, the subquery, within another. To complicate matters, DB2 lets you continue this nesting many layers deep. In other words, you can code one subquery within another. In practice, though, you should limit the number of levels of nesting because just a few levels can make a statement hard to understand. This will also improve system performance because each level of nesting requires additional system resources.

Similarly, you should use a join instead of a subquery whenever that's possible. This will usually make the statement easier to understand. It is also likely to improve system performance because joins make better use of indexes than subqueries do.

Of course, you can't always replace a statement that uses a subquery with a join. Also, because a join returns a read-only result table, you can't replace a subquery with a join when you need to update or delete rows in the result table.

Example 1: SQL statements without a subquery

```
EXEC SQL
    DECLARE INVCURS CURSOR FOR
        SELECT INVNO, INVCUST, INVTOTAL
            FROM MM01.INVOICE
            WHERE INVTOTAL > :COMPUTED-AVERAGE
END-EXEC.
.
.
EXEC SQL
    SELECT AVG(INVTOTAL)
        FROM MM01.INVOICE
        INTO :COMPUTED-AVERAGE
END-EXEC.
EXEC SQL
    OPEN INVCURS
END-EXEC.
```

Example 2: SQL statements with a subquery

```
EXEC SQL
    DECLARE INVCURS CURSOR FOR
        SELECT INVNO, INVCUST, INVTOTAL
            FROM MM01.INVOICE
            WHERE INVTOTAL >
                (SELECT AVG(INVTOTAL)
                    FROM MM01.INVOICE)
END-EXEC.
.
.
EXEC SQL
    OPEN INVCURS
END-EXEC.
```

Description

- Both examples above produce the same result table. This table has one row for each invoice row that has an invoice total greater than the average invoice total for all of the invoice rows.

- Although coding with a subquery uses more DB2 resources than coding without one, the use of a subquery often simplifies the coding. In addition, the use of a subquery sometimes lets you do processing that can't be done any other way.

Coding guidelines

- Although you can *nest* subqueries many layers deep, you should limit the number of nesting levels whenever that's possible. That will make your statements easier to understand, and it will also improve system performance.

- Whenever possible, use a join instead of a subquery because (1) it is usually easier to understand, and (2) a join is likely to be more efficient because it makes better use of indexes.

Figure 9-1   How the use of a subquery can simplify coding

How to code predicates that use subqueries

Figure 9-2, which is in two parts, presents the rules, syntax, and examples for coding subqueries within SELECT statements. In general, you code a subquery just like any other SELECT statement with two exceptions. First, a simple comparison subquery must return a one-column result table. Second, a subquery can't include the ORDER BY clause, although the outer SELECT statement can.

When you code a subquery as part of a simple comparison, the subquery must return a one-row, one-column result table. That's illustrated by the first example in this figure (which is the same as the example in the previous figure). To illustrate how this statement works, suppose the subquery returns an average invoice total value of $500. Then, the outer SELECT statement produces a result table that contains one row for each invoice with an invoice total greater than $500, sorted by INVNO.

When you code a subquery in an IN phrase, the subquery can return a one-column result table with more than one row. This table then provides a list of values that are matched with the value of the first expression in the condition, as illustrated by the second example in this figure. Here, the subquery produces a result table that contains the customer numbers (INVCUST) of those customers that have a row in the invoice table with an invoice total greater than or equal to $200.

In this example, there are seven customer numbers in the intermediate result table, and customer '400011' appears three times because that customer has three invoice totals greater than or equal to $200. When the outer SELECT statement is run, you can visualize these intermediate values in its IN clause as shown in this figure. In other words, the outer SELECT statement produces a result table with one customer row for each customer with a customer number (CUSTNO) equal to one of the customer numbers in the subquery's result table.

The rules for coding a subquery within a SELECT statement

- The result table produced by a subquery must contain only one column.
- A subquery can't include the ORDER BY clause, although the outer SELECT statement can.

A subquery in a simple comparison

```
WHERE column-specification operator (subquery)
```

Example

```
SELECT   INVNO, INVCUST, INVTOTAL
    FROM MM01.INVOICE
    WHERE INVTOTAL >
        (SELECT AVG(INVTOTAL)
            FROM MM01.INVOICE)
    ORDER BY INVNO
```

A subquery in an IN phrase

```
WHERE column-specification [NOT] IN (subquery)
```

Example

```
SELECT   CUSTNO, FNAME, LNAME
    FROM MM01.CUSTOMER
    WHERE CUSTNO IN
        (SELECT   INVCUST
            FROM  MM01.INVOICE
            WHERE INVTOTAL >= 200)
```

Intermediate result table of the subquery

```
400011
400015
400001
400011
400012
400003
400011
```

The subquery substituted by the intermediate result table

```
SELECT   CUSTNO, FNAME, LNAME
    FROM MM01.CUSTOMER
    WHERE CUSTNO IN
        ('400011','400015','400001','400011','400012','400003','4000011')
```

The result table

CUSTNO	FNAME	LNAME
400001	KEITH	JONES
400003	SUSAN	HOWARD
400011	WILLIAM C	FERGUSON
400012	SD	HOEHN
400015	VIVIAN	GEORGE

Figure 9-2   How to code predicates that use subqueries (part 1 of 2)

When you code a subquery with the keywords ANY, SOME, or ALL, the values returned by the subquery are compared with the value of the first expression in the condition. If you use ANY or SOME, the condition must be true when the value of the first expression is compared with any one of the values returned by the subquery. This is illustrated by the first example in this figure, which returns the same result table as the previous example. Here again, the subquery returns a table of customer numbers, and the outer SELECT returns a result table with one row for each customer with a customer number equal to at least one of the numbers in the subquery's result table.

In contrast, if you use the word ALL, the condition must be true for every value in the subquery's result table. Note, however, that the operator used with ANY, SOME, or ALL doesn't have to be an equal sign. So, for example, you can use the word ALL in a predicate that is true when the value in the first expression is greater than *all* of the values in the subquery's result table.

Incidentally, if you try to replace this example with the join statement shown here, the results won't be the same. As you can see, the result table of the join operation includes the duplicate rows for customer '400011'. So, you can't always replace a subquery with alternative coding.

A subquery used with the keywords ANY, SOME, or ALL

```
WHERE column-specification operator {ANY | SOME | ALL} (subquery)
```

Example

```
SELECT    CUSTNO, FNAME, LNAME
    FROM MM01.CUSTOMER
    WHERE CUSTNO = ANY
        (SELECT    INVCUST
            FROM   MM01.INVOICE
            WHERE INVTOTAL >= 200)
```

The result table

CUSTNO	FNAME	LNAME
400001	KEITH	JONES
400003	SUSAN	HOWARD
400011	WILLIAM C	FERGUSON
400012	SD	HOEHN
400015	VIVIAN	GEORGE

A join that might replace the above subquery

```
SELECT CUSTNO, FNAME, LNAME
    FROM MM01.CUSTOMER
        INNER JOIN MM01.INVOICE
    ON CUSTNO = INVCUST
    WHERE INVTOTAL >= 200
```

The result table

CUSTNO	FNAME	LNAME
400001	KEITH	JONES
400003	SUSAN	HOWARD
400011	WILLIAM C	FERGUSON
400011	WILLIAM C	FERGUSON
400011	WILLIAM C	FERGUSON
400012	SD	HOEHN
400015	VIVIAN	GEORGE

Description

- When you use a subquery in a simple comparison, it must return a one-column, one-row result table.

- When you use a subquery in an IN phrase or with the keywords ANY, SOME, or ALL, it can return more than one row.

- When you use ANY, SOME, or ALL, you code the keyword after a comparison operator. With ANY or SOME, the condition must be true for any one of the values returned by the subquery. With ALL, the condition must be true for all of the values returned by the subquery.

Figure 9-2   How to code predicates that use subqueries (part 2 of 2)

How to code correlated subqueries

Before you learn how to code *correlated subqueries*, you should know that they aren't as efficient or as easy to interpret as basic subqueries and joins. That's why you should avoid using them whenever you can. Although you had to use correlated subqueries to join tables with unmatched rows with earlier DB2 versions, you can replace most of those correlated subqueries with outer joins when you use version 4.

In case you do need to use or maintain a correlated subquery, though, figure 9-3 shows you how to code one. To correlate the subquery with the outer SELECT, you code a synonym for the table in the outer SELECT that the subquery is going to be correlated with. This synonym, called a *correlation name*, is used in the subquery to qualify a column reference, called a *correlation reference*. This subquery is coded in the WHERE clause of the outer SELECT after the keyword EXISTS. Then, when the entire statement is executed, the correlated subquery is performed once for each row the outer SELECT processes. In contrast, a basic subquery is executed in its entirety before the outer SELECT is executed.

To illustrate the use of a correlated subquery, the first example in this figure uses A as the correlation name for the customer table. This name is then used to create the correlation reference (A.CUSTNO) in the WHERE clause of the subquery. Although this statement makes logical sense without this correlation name and reference, DB2 requires this coding for a correlated subquery.

To process this statement, DB2 runs the correlated subquery for each row in the customer table. If there are no invoices in the invoice table for the current customer row (NOT EXISTS), DB2 constructs one row in the result table consisting of the first name and last name columns. When DB2 finishes processing, the result table contains the names of all customers that don't have any invoice rows in the invoice table.

As the second example in this figure shows, however, this same processing can be done by using a basic subquery. Because a basic subquery is easier to code and will probably run more efficiently, this is a better way to do this processing.

The third example in this figure shows the use of a correlated subquery that correlates two uses of the same table. Here, OUTR is used as the correlation name for the invoice table, and INNR is used as a synonym for the same invoice table in the correlated subquery. Then, in the WHERE clause of the subquery, the customer number (INVCUST) in the inner select is compared with the customer number in the outer SELECT while the AVG function for the current customer number is computed.

When DB2 processes this statement, it works through the invoice table one row at a time. For each row, DB2 runs the subquery to calculate the average invoice total for the current customer number. Then, DB2 runs the outer SELECT to determine whether the invoice total in the current row is greater than that average. If it is, one invoice row is added to the result table.

The syntax of a correlated subquery with the EXISTS keyword

```
WHERE [NOT] EXISTS (correlated-subquery)
```

A correlated subquery that correlates values from two different tables

```
SELECT    FNAME, LNAME
    FROM  MM01.CUSTOMER A
    WHERE NOT EXISTS
        (SELECT *
            FROM MM01.INVOICE
            WHERE INVCUST = A.CUSTNO)
```

A basic subquery that does the same processing as the first example

```
SELECT    FNAME, LNAME
    FROM MM01.CUSTOMER
    WHERE CUSTNO NOT IN
        (SELECT INVCUST
            FROM MM01.INVOICE)
```

A correlated subquery that correlates values from the same table

```
SELECT    INVNO, INVCUST, INVTOTAL
    FROM  MM01.INVOICE OUTR
    WHERE INVTOTAL >
        (SELECT AVG(INVTOTAL)
            FROM MM01.INVOICE INNR
            WHERE INNR.INVCUST =
                OUTR.INVCUST)
```

Description

- Unlike a basic subquery, a *correlated subquery* doesn't work independently of the outer SELECT. Instead, a correlated subquery is performed once for *each row* the outer SELECT processes.

- A correlated subquery with the EXISTS keyword doesn't name any column because no data is transferred when you use EXISTS. Instead, an asterisk is commonly used in place of a column name.

- To correlate the table in the subquery with the table in the outer SELECT, you need to define a synonym for the table in the outer SELECT and use it as a qualifier in the subquery. When you use a synonym in this context, it's called a *correlation name*, and the connection it makes is called a *correlated reference*.

- Because correlated subqueries often require substantial system resources, you should use a join or a basic subquery whenever that's possible.

Figure 9-3   How to code correlated subqueries

How to code INSERT, UPDATE, and DELETE statements that use subqueries

When you use subqueries in INSERT, UPDATE, and DELETE statements, you can't base the subquery on the same table that you're modifying. On the other hand, you don't have to limit the result table produced by a subquery to a single column. Other than those differences, though, you can use subqueries in these statements in much the same way that you use them in SELECT statements. This is illustrated by the examples in figure 9-4.

In the first example, the subquery selects all the columns for all the customers in the customer table with CUSTNO values greater than 300000 and STATUS values of INACTIVE. Then, the INSERT statement inserts the rows in that result table into a table named OLDCUST. This can be referred to as a *mass insert*.

In the second and third examples, those rows in the customer table that don't have matching rows in the invoice table are inserted in an inactive table. In both examples, which get the same results, one subquery is nested within another. However, since the second example uses NOT with IN, DB2 won't use the available indexes with this statement (you may recall this from chapter 5). Even so, the second example will probably run more efficiently than the third because it uses a correlated subquery.

In the fourth example, the subquery selects all of the customer numbers (INVCUST) in the invoice table. Then, the UPDATE statement changes the value of the STATUS column to ACTIVE in each row in the customer table that has a customer number equal to one of those in the subquery's result table.

In the fifth example, the subquery again selects all of the customer numbers in the invoice table. Then, the DELETE statement deletes all of the rows in the customer table that don't have a customer number equal to one of those in the subquery's result table.

Note in these examples that you don't put parentheses around the first SELECT statement used in an INSERT statement because that's a syntax error. You do, however, need to put parentheses around any subqueries nested in that SELECT statement. You also have to put parentheses around subqueries used in the WHERE clauses of UPDATE and DELETE statements.

Subquery differences for INSERT, DELETE, and UPDATE statements

- You can't base a subquery on the same table that you're modifying.
- You don't have to limit the result table of a subquery to a single column.
- You don't and can't put parentheses around the first SELECT statement in an INSERT statement.

An INSERT statement that uses a subquery with a compound predicate

```
INSERT INTO MM01.OLDCUST
    SELECT *
        FROM MM01.CUSTOMER
        WHERE CUSTNO < '300000'
          AND STATUS = 'INACTIVE'
```

An INSERT statement that uses a subquery in an IN phrase

```
INSERT INTO MM01.INACTIVE
    SELECT *
        FROM MM01.CUSTOMER
        WHERE CUSTNO NOT IN
            (SELECT INVCUST
                FROM MM01.INVOICE)
```

An INSERT statement that uses a correlated subquery

```
INSERT INTO MM01.INACTCST
    SELECT *
        FROM MM01.CUSTOMER A
        WHERE NOT EXISTS
            (SELECT *
                FROM MM01.INVOICE
                WHERE INVCUST = A.CUSTNO)
```

An UPDATE statement that uses a subquery in an IN phrase

```
UPDATE MM01.CUSTOMER
    SET STATUS = 'ACTIVE'
    WHERE CUSTNO IN
        (SELECT INVCUST
            FROM MM01.INVOICE)
```

A DELETE statement that uses a subquery in a NOT IN phrase

```
DELETE FROM MM01.CUSTOMER
    WHERE CUSTNO NOT IN
        (SELECT INVCUST
            FROM MM01.INVOICE)
```

Figure 9-4   How to code INSERT, DELETE, and UPDATE statements that use subqueries

An update program that uses subqueries

To illustrate the use of subqueries, the COBOL program that follows is an update, or maintenance, program that moves data from three active tables to three history tables. That way, the number of rows in the active tables are kept to reasonable numbers so the daily use of these tables is more efficient than it would be if all the data was kept in these tables.

The seven tables used by this program

Figure 9-5 presents the CREATE TABLE statements for the six tables that are updated by this program as well as a work table that's used by this program. As you can see, the three active tables are an invoice table with one row for each invoice; a line item table with one row for each billing line on an invoice; and a payment table with one row for each payment, credit, or adjustment that applies to an invoice. Although the three history tables have the same columns as the active tables, they hold the data that is no longer active.

When the values in the PAYAMT column in all the rows in the payment table for an invoice add up to the amount in the INVTOTAL column in the related invoice row, the invoice is considered to be paid in full. At that point, the invoice row in the invoice table and all related rows in the line item and payment tables can be moved from the active tables to the inactive tables.

The work table described in this figure isn't an essential part of the database. In fact, it's only purpose is to provide temporary storage for the data that is moved from the active invoice table to the history table. You'll see how this works in a moment.

Invoice table

```
CREATE TABLE MM01.INVOICE
   (INVCUST   CHAR(6)       NOT NULL,
    INVNO     CHAR(6)       NOT NULL,
    INVDATE   DATE          NOT NULL,
    INVSUBT   DECIMAL(9,2)  NOT NULL,
    INVSHIP   DECIMAL(7,2)  NOT NULL,
    INVTAX    DECIMAL(7,2)  NOT NULL,
    INVTOTAL  DECIMAL(9,2)  NOT NULL,
    INVPROM   CHAR(10)      NOT NULL)
 IN DATABASE MMADBV
```

Line item table

```
CREATE TABLE MM01.LINEITEM
   (LIINVNO   CHAR(6)       NOT NULL,
    LIPCODE   CHAR(10)      NOT NULL,
    LIQTY     DECIMAL(7)    NOT NULL,
    LIPRICE   DECIMAL(7,2)  NOT NULL,
    LIDISC    DECIMAL(7,2)  NOT NULL)
 IN DATABASE MMADBV
```

Payment table

```
CREATE TABLE MM01.PAYMENT
   (PAYINVNO  CHAR(6)       NOT NULL,
    PAYDATE   DATE          NOT NULL,
    PAYAMT    DECIMAL(9,2)  NOT NULL,
    PAYCHECK  CHAR(20),
    PAYCCARD  CHAR(20),
    PAYEXP    CHAR(5),
    PAYNOTE   VARCHAR(254))
 IN DATABASE MMADBV
```

Work table

```
CREATE TABLE MM01.WORKTABLE
   (INVCUST   CHAR(6)       NOT NULL,
    INVNO     CHAR(6)       NOT NULL,
    INVDATE   DATE          NOT NULL,
    INVSUBT   DECIMAL(9,2)  NOT NULL,
    INVSHIP   DECIMAL(7,2)  NOT NULL,
    INVTAX    DECIMAL(7,2)  NOT NULL,
    INVTOTAL  DECIMAL(9,2)  NOT NULL,
    INVPROM   CHAR(10)      NOT NULL)
 IN DATABASE MMADBV
```

Invoice history table

```
CREATE TABLE MM01.INVHIST
   (INVCUST   CHAR(6)       NOT NULL,
    INVNO     CHAR(6)       NOT NULL,
    INVDATE   DATE          NOT NULL,
    INVSUBT   DECIMAL(9,2)  NOT NULL,
    INVSHIP   DECIMAL(7,2)  NOT NULL,
    INVTAX    DECIMAL(7,2)  NOT NULL,
    INVTOTAL  DECIMAL(9,2)  NOT NULL,
    INVPROM   CHAR(10)      NOT NULL)
 IN DATABASE MMADBV
```

Line item history table

```
CREATE TABLE MM01.LIHIST
   (LIINVNO   CHAR(6)       NOT NULL,
    LIPCODE   CHAR(10)      NOT NULL,
    LIQTY     DECIMAL(7)    NOT NULL,
    LIPRICE   DECIMAL(7,2)  NOT NULL,
    LIDISC    DECIMAL(7,2)  NOT NULL)
 IN DATABASE MMADBV
```

Payment history table

```
CREATE TABLE MM01.PAYHIST
   (PAYINVNO  CHAR(6)       NOT NULL,
    PAYDATE   DATE          NOT NULL,
    PAYAMT    DECIMAL(9,2)  NOT NULL,
    PAYCHECK  CHAR(20),
    PAYCCARD  CHAR(20),
    PAYEXP    CHAR(5),
    PAYNOTE   VARCHAR(254))
 IN DATABASE MMADBV
```

Figure 9-5   The CREATE TABLE statements for seven tables used by the update program

The structure chart

Figure 9-6 presents the structure chart for this program. Here, module 200 produces a work table with one row for each invoice that has been paid in full. Then, modules 300, 400, and 500 move the data for those invoices from the active to the history tables.

The structure chart

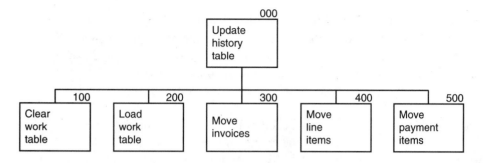

Description

- Unlike the other programs in this book, module 000 doesn't repeatedly perform one module at the next level to do the primary processing of the program. Instead, it performs each of its subordinates one time in sequence from module 100 to module 500.

- After module 100 clears the work table, module 200 selects all of the invoices that are paid in full and stores them in the work table. Then, modules 300, 400, and 500 move the rows related to the paid invoices from the active tables to the history tables.

Figure 9-6   The structure chart for the update program

The COBOL listing

If you look at the first page of the COBOL listing in figure 9-7, you may be surprised to see that it doesn't have INCLUDE statements that include the DCLGEN output for the seven tables used by this program. This output isn't necessary, because this program doesn't retrieve, update, or add any data to the tables. As a result, host variables aren't needed, and neither is the DCLGEN output.

In module 000, you can see that each of the subordinate modules is performed only one time. If the DB2 statements in one of these modules fails, however, the UPDATE-UNSUCCESSFUL condition is turned on. Then, no other module is performed and the program ends.

You can see how this condition is turned on in module 100. Here, the SQL DELETE statement deletes all of the rows in the work table. If this isn't done successfully (SQLCODE less than zero), though, the program displays an error message and turns the error condition on. You'll see similar error-handling code after each of the other SQL statements in this program.

The update program

```
IDENTIFICATION DIVISION.
*
PROGRAM-ID.      UPDTHST1.
*
ENVIRONMENT DIVISION.
*
DATA DIVISION.
*
WORKING-STORAGE SECTION.
*
01  SWITCH.
*
    05  UPDATE-SUCCESSFUL-SW     PIC X     VALUE 'Y'.
        88  UPDATE-SUCCESSFUL              VALUE 'Y'.
*
    EXEC SQL
        INCLUDE SQLCA
    END-EXEC.
*
PROCEDURE DIVISION.
*
000-UPDATE-HISTORY-TABLES.
*
    PERFORM 100-CLEAR-WORK-TABLE.
    IF UPDATE-SUCCESSFUL
        PERFORM 200-LOAD-WORK-TABLE.
    IF UPDATE-SUCCESSFUL
        PERFORM 300-MOVE-INVOICES.
    IF UPDATE-SUCCESSFUL
        PERFORM 400-MOVE-LINE-ITEMS.
    IF UPDATE-SUCCESSFUL
        PERFORM 500-MOVE-PAYMENT-ITEMS.
    IF UPDATE-SUCCESSFUL
        DISPLAY 'UPDATE COMPLETED SUCCESSFULLY.'.
    STOP RUN.
*
100-CLEAR-WORK-TABLE.
*
    EXEC SQL
        DELETE FROM MM01.WORKTABLE
    END-EXEC.
    IF SQLCODE < 0
        DISPLAY 'DELETE IN MODULE 100 FAILED.'
        DISPLAY 'SQLCODE = ' SQLCODE
        MOVE 'N' TO UPDATE-SUCCESSFUL-SW.
*
```

Figure 9-7   The COBOL listing for the update program (part 1 of 3)

In module 200 on page 2 of this listing, you can see the INSERT statement that produces a work table with one invoice row for each invoice that has been paid in full. To produce this table, the INSERT statement uses a subquery within a subquery. Here, the outer subquery selects all the columns (*) in the invoice table, and it gives this invoice table the correlation name A. Then, the inner subquery computes the sum of all the payment amounts (PAYAMT) in the rows of the payment table that have the same invoice number as the current invoice. To do that, the inner subquery uses A.INVNO as the correlation reference.

Because the inner subquery is correlated with the outer subquery, it's processed once for each row DB2 processes in the outer subquery. Then, all the invoice rows in the final result table are inserted into the work table. These are the rows that should be moved to the invoice history table.

After module 200 creates the work table, an INSERT statement in module 300 directs DB2 to insert every row in the work table into the related history table. Then, if that statement is successful, a DELETE statement uses a subquery to delete every row in the invoice table that has a related row in the work table. This combination of inserting and deleting has the effect of moving the paid invoice rows from the active invoice table to the invoice history table.

Similarly, the purpose of module 400 is to move the paid line item rows from the active table to the history table. To do that, this module starts with an INSERT statement that contains a subquery within a subquery. The inner subquery produces an intermediate table that has one customer number (INVNO) for each row in the work table. Then, the outer subquery produces a result table that contains all the columns for all the rows in the line item table that have a customer number equal to one of those in the intermediate table. Last, the INSERT statement inserts the rows of that result table into the line item history table. If that's successful, the DELETE statement that follows deletes all the related rows from the active line item table.

The update program   **Page 2**

```
200-LOAD-WORK-TABLE.
*
    EXEC SQL
        INSERT INTO MM01.WORKTABLE
            SELECT *
                FROM  MM01.INVOICE A
                WHERE INVTOTAL =
                    (SELECT SUM(PAYAMT)
                        FROM MM01.PAYMENT
                        WHERE PAYINVNO = A.INVNO)
    END-EXEC.
    IF SQLCODE < 0
        DISPLAY 'INSERT IN MODULE 200 FAILED.'
        DISPLAY 'SQLCODE = ' SQLCODE
        MOVE 'N' TO UPDATE-SUCCESSFUL-SW.
*
300-MOVE-INVOICES.
*
    EXEC SQL
        INSERT INTO MM01.INVHIST
            SELECT *
                FROM  MM01.WORKTABLE
    END-EXEC.
    IF SQLCODE < 0
        DISPLAY 'INSERT IN MODULE 300 FAILED.'
        DISPLAY 'SQLCODE = ' SQLCODE
        MOVE 'N' TO UPDATE-SUCCESSFUL-SW
    ELSE
        EXEC SQL
            DELETE FROM MM01.INVOICE
                WHERE INVNO IN
                    (SELECT INVNO
                        FROM MM01.WORKTABLE)
        END-EXEC
        IF SQLCODE < 0
            DISPLAY 'DELETE IN MODULE 300 FAILED.'
            DISPLAY 'SQLCODE = ' SQLCODE
            MOVE 'N' TO UPDATE-SUCCESSFUL-SW.
*
400-MOVE-LINE-ITEMS.
*
    EXEC SQL
        INSERT INTO MM01.LIHIST
            SELECT *
                FROM  MM01.LINEITEM
                WHERE LIINVNO IN
                    (SELECT INVNO
                        FROM MM01.WORKTABLE)
    END-EXEC.
```

Figure 9-7   The COBOL listing for the update program (part 2 of 3)

On the last page of this COBOL listing, you can see that the coding for module 500 works much like the coding for module 400. First, an INSERT statement selects the rows in the active payment table that are related to the rows in the work table by invoice number and inserts them into the payment history table. Then, if that's successful, a DELETE statement deletes the same rows from the active payment table. This completes the updating that's required and the program ends.

The update program

```
        IF SQLCODE < 0
            DISPLAY 'INSERT IN MODULE 400 FAILED.'
            DISPLAY 'SQLCODE = ' SQLCODE
            MOVE 'N' TO UPDATE-SUCCESSFUL-SW
        ELSE
            EXEC SQL
                DELETE FROM MM01.LINEITEM
                    WHERE LIINVNO IN
                        (SELECT INVNO
                            FROM MM01.WORKTABLE)
            END-EXEC
            IF SQLCODE < 0
                DISPLAY 'DELETE IN MODULE 400 FAILED.'
                DISPLAY 'SQLCODE = ' SQLCODE
                MOVE 'N' TO UPDATE-SUCCESSFUL-SW.
*
    500-MOVE-PAYMENT-ITEMS.
*
        EXEC SQL
            INSERT INTO MM01.PAYHIST
                SELECT *
                    FROM  MM01.PAYMENT
                    WHERE PAYINVNO IN
                        (SELECT INVNO
                            FROM MM01.WORKTABLE)
        END-EXEC.
        IF SQLCODE < 0
            DISPLAY 'INSERT IN MODULE 500 FAILED.'
            DISPLAY 'SQLCODE = ' SQLCODE
            MOVE 'N' TO UPDATE-SUCCESSFUL-SW
        ELSE
            EXEC SQL
                DELETE FROM MM01.PAYMENT
                    WHERE PAYINVNO IN
                        (SELECT INVNO
                            FROM MM01.WORKTABLE)
            END-EXEC
            IF SQLCODE < 0
                DISPLAY 'DELETE IN MODULE 500 FAILED.'
                DISPLAY 'SQLCODE = ' SQLCODE
                MOVE 'N' TO UPDATE-SUCCESSFUL-SW.
*
```

Figure 9-7   The COBOL listing for the update program (part 3 of 3)

An enhanced update program

The COBOL program that you've just reviewed doesn't rely on DB2's features for maintaining referential integrity. As a result, the program is responsible for inserting the new rows into the history tables as well as deleting the old rows from the active tables. In contrast, the program that follows lets DB2 delete the old rows in those active tables that are subordinate to the invoice table.

The enhanced CREATE TABLE statements

Figure 9-8 presents the enhanced versions of the CREATE TABLE statements for the three active tables. As you can see, each of these statements includes a FOREIGN KEY clause that relates the table to a parent table. This clause also uses the CASCADE option for deletions of related rows in the parent table. This means that if a row in the parent table is deleted, all related rows in the subordinate table are also deleted.

In terms of this program, this means that deleting a row in the invoice table will also delete the related rows in the line item and payment tables. This, of course, will simplify the code in the COBOL program. For this program, the FOREIGN KEY clause in the invoice table is irrelevant because it describes the relationship between the invoice table and its parent table, the customer table, which isn't used by this program.

If you wonder why enhanced history tables aren't included in this figure with FOREIGN KEY clauses that take advantage of DB2's support for referential integrity, it's because this support isn't free. In fact, DB2 uses a substantial amount of system resources for enforcing referential integrity. In this case, since the history tables aren't going to be subject to much update and delete activity, it is probably a waste of system resources to define primary and foreign keys for them.

The modified structure chart

Figure 9-8 also presents the modified structure chart for this program. Because the CASCADE option is specified for the line item and payment tables, you can't delete the old invoice rows in module 300 as in the previous version of this program. If you did, that would also delete the rows in the line item and payment tables before they were added to their related history tables. Unlike the previous version of this chart, then, all the deletions for all the tables are done by module 600 and only insertions are done by modules 300, 400, and 500.

Invoice table

```
CREATE TABLE MM01.INVOICE
    (INVCUST   CHAR(6)       NOT NULL,
     INVNO     CHAR(6)       NOT NULL,
     INVDATE   DATE          NOT NULL,
     INVSUBT   DECIMAL(9,2)  NOT NULL,
     INVSHIP   DECIMAL(7,2)  NOT NULL,
     INVTAX    DECIMAL(7,2)  NOT NULL,
     INVTOTAL  DECIMAL(9,2)  NOT NULL,
     INVPROM   CHAR(10)      NOT NULL,
     PRIMARY KEY (INVNO)
     FOREIGN KEY CUSTNO (INVCUST)
         REFERENCES MM01.CUSTOMER
         ON DELETE CASCADE)
    IN DATABASE MMADBV
```

Payment table

```
CREATE TABLE MM01.PAYMENT
    (PAYINVNO  CHAR(6)       NOT NULL,
     PAYDATE   DATE          NOT NULL,
     PAYAMT    DECIMAL(9,2)  NOT NULL,
     PAYCHECK  CHAR(20),
     PAYCCARD  CHAR(20),
     PAYEXP    CHAR(5),
     PAYNOTE   VARCHAR(254),
     FOREIGN KEY INVNO (PAYINVNO)
         REFERENCES MM01.INVOICE
         ON DELETE CASCADE)
    IN DATABASE MMADBV
```

Line item table

```
CREATE TABLE MM01.LINEITEM
    (LIINVNO   CHAR(6)       NOT NULL,
     LIPCODE   CHAR(10)      NOT NULL,
     LIQTY     DECIMAL(7)    NOT NULL,
     LIPRICE   DECIMAL(7,2)  NOT NULL,
     LIDISC    DECIMAL(7,2)  NOT NULL,
     FOREIGN KEY INVNO (LIINVNO)
         REFERENCES MM01.INVOICE
         ON DELETE CASCADE)
    IN DATABASE MMADBV
```

The structure chart

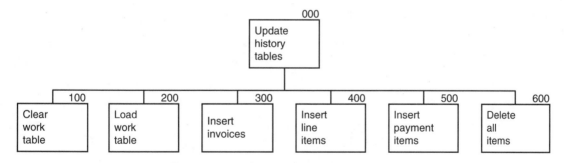

Figure 9-8   The enhanced CREATE TABLE statements and the modified structure chart

The enhanced COBOL listing

Figure 9-9 presents the COBOL listing for the enhanced update program. Because this program is so similar to the previous one, you shouldn't have much trouble understanding it. The main difference is that all of the deletions are done by a single DELETE statement in module 600 that deletes the old rows in the invoice table. Because these deletions are cascaded to the related tables, the related rows in those tables are also deleted.

The enhanced update program

```
 IDENTIFICATION DIVISION.
*
 PROGRAM-ID.      UPDTHST2.
*
 ENVIRONMENT DIVISION.
*
 DATA DIVISION.
*
 WORKING-STORAGE SECTION.
*
 01  SWITCH.
*
     05  UPDATE-SUCCESSFUL-SW     PIC X     VALUE 'Y'.
         88  UPDATE-SUCCESSFUL              VALUE 'Y'.
*
     EXEC SQL
         INCLUDE SQLCA
     END-EXEC.
*
 PROCEDURE DIVISION.
*
 000-UPDATE-HISTORY-TABLES.
*
     PERFORM 100-CLEAR-WORK-TABLE.
     IF UPDATE-SUCCESSFUL
         PERFORM 200-LOAD-WORK-TABLE.
     IF UPDATE-SUCCESSFUL
         PERFORM 300-INSERT-INVOICES.
     IF UPDATE-SUCCESSFUL
         PERFORM 400-INSERT-LINE-ITEMS.
     IF UPDATE-SUCCESSFUL
         PERFORM 500-INSERT-PAYMENT-ITEMS.
     IF UPDATE-SUCCESSFUL
         PERFORM 600-DELETE-ALL-ITEMS.
     IF UPDATE-SUCCESSFUL
         DISPLAY 'UPDATE COMPLETED SUCCESSFULLY.'.
     STOP RUN.
*
```

Figure 9-9   The COBOL listing for the enhanced update program (part 1 of 3)

The enhanced update program

```
100-CLEAR-WORK-TABLE.
*
    EXEC SQL
        DELETE FROM MM01.WORKTABLE
    END-EXEC.
    IF SQLCODE < 0
        DISPLAY 'DELETE IN MODULE 100 FAILED.'
        DISPLAY 'SQLCODE = ' SQLCODE
        MOVE 'N' TO UPDATE-SUCCESSFUL-SW.
*
 200-LOAD-WORK-TABLE.
*
    EXEC SQL
        INSERT INTO MM01.WORKTABLE
            SELECT *
                FROM  MM01.INVOICE A
                WHERE INVTOTAL =
                    (SELECT SUM(PAYAMT)
                        FROM MM01.PAYMENT
                        WHERE PAYINVNO = A.INVNO)
    END-EXEC.
    IF SQLCODE < 0
        DISPLAY 'INSERT IN MODULE 200 FAILED.'
        DISPLAY 'SQLCODE = ' SQLCODE
        MOVE 'N' TO UPDATE-SUCCESSFUL-SW.
*
 300-INSERT-INVOICES.
*
    EXEC SQL
        INSERT INTO MM01.INVHIST
            SELECT *
                FROM  MM01.WORKTABLE
    END-EXEC.
    IF SQLCODE < 0
        DISPLAY 'INSERT IN MODULE 300 FAILED.'
        DISPLAY 'SQLCODE = ' SQLCODE
        MOVE 'N' TO UPDATE-SUCCESSFUL-SW.
*
```

Figure 9-9   The COBOL listing for the enhanced update program (part 2 of 3)

The enhanced update program   **Page 3**

```
 400-INSERT-LINE-ITEMS.
*
     EXEC SQL
         INSERT INTO MM01.LIHIST
             SELECT *
                 FROM   MM01.LINEITEM
                 WHERE LIINVNO IN
                     (SELECT INVNO
                         FROM MM01.WORKTABLE)
     END-EXEC.
     IF SQLCODE < 0
         DISPLAY 'INSERT IN MODULE 400 FAILED.'
         DISPLAY 'SQLCODE = ' SQLCODE
         MOVE 'N' TO UPDATE-SUCCESSFUL-SW.
*
 500-INSERT-PAYMENT-ITEMS.
*
     EXEC SQL
         INSERT INTO MM01.PAYHIST
             SELECT *
                 FROM   MM01.PAYMENT
                 WHERE PAYINVNO IN
                     (SELECT INVNO
                         FROM MM01.WORKTABLE)
     END-EXEC.
     IF SQLCODE < 0
         DISPLAY 'INSERT IN MODULE 500 FAILED.'
         DISPLAY 'SQLCODE = ' SQLCODE
         MOVE 'N' TO UPDATE-SUCCESSFUL-SW.
*
 600-DELETE-ALL-ITEMS.
*
     EXEC SQL
         DELETE FROM MM01.INVOICE
             WHERE INVNO IN
                 (SELECT INVNO
                     FROM MM01.WORKTABLE)
     END-EXEC.
     IF SQLCODE < 0
         DISPLAY 'DELETE IN MODULE 600 FAILED.'
         DISPLAY 'SQLCODE = ' SQLCODE
         MOVE 'N' TO UPDATE-SUCCESSFUL-SW.
*
```

Figure 9-9   The COBOL listing for the enhanced update program (part 3 of 3)

Perspective

Although the programs in this chapter do a good job of illustrating the use of subqueries, they represent just one way to do this type of updating. Instead of using a work table, for example, you can use INSERT statements like the one in module 200 to insert the appropriate rows directly into the related history tables. Because correlated subqueries aren't efficient, though, this could degrade the program's performance at the same time that it increases the complexity of the code.

Another approach to this type of updating is to first produce a cursor-controlled result table with one row for each invoice to be moved. Then, you can fetch one row at a time, and insert and delete the related rows in the base tables. The benefit of this approach is that you can do additional processing for each invoice, such as printing a line on a report to document its status change. However, this approach will also make the COBOL program longer and less efficient.

As you design a program like this, remember that you should generally avoid the use of subqueries and especially correlated subqueries because they usually aren't as efficient as joins. As a result, although subqueries occasionally help you do a job that's hard to do any other way, you'll probably use them infrequently. That's particularly true since the explicit language for inner and outer joins became available with DB2 version 4.

10

How to use the features for error processing

In the other chapters in this book, all of the example programs do minimal error processing. Usually, they just use an IF statement to check the SQLCODE value after each SQL statement to see whether it is negative, which means an error has occurred. Then, if an error has occurred, they set a switch so a simple error message is displayed and the program ends.

In practice, though, most COBOL programs provide more error processing than that. At the least, for example, a COBOL program is likely to display a more detailed error message before it ends. In addition, a COBOL program may check for a variety of error conditions. In this chapter, you'll learn how to use the other DB2 features for error processing.

The DB2 features for error processing

To facilitate error processing, DB2 provides the SQL communication area, a subprogram named DSNTIAR for reporting errors, and a WHENEVER statement. After the topics that follow present these features, you'll see a COBOL program that shows them in use.

The most useful fields in the SQL communication area

All of the programs in the other chapters of this book use only the SQLCODE field in the SQL communication area. As you should recall, a zero value in this field means that the preceding SQL statement ran successfully. A negative value means it didn't run successfully. And a positive value of 100 means a statement like a FETCH or UPDATE statement couldn't find the next row or the specified row. For a complete list of the SQLCODE values that are returned by DB2, please refer to appendix B.

In figure 10-1, though, you can see that some of the other fields in the SQL communication area are also of use to the COBOL programmer. For instance, the third field in the SQLERRD array returns the number of rows affected by an INSERT, DELETE, or UPDATE statement.

DB2 uses the SQLWARN fields to report some unusual conditions that aren't considered to be errors. If the SQLWARN0 field contains a W value, it means that one or more of the other SQLWARN fields also contains a W. If, for example, the SQLWARN1 field contains a W value, it means that one of the host variables isn't large enough to receive all the data in the related column. This probably means that you didn't use DCLGEN output for the host variable and it isn't defined with the right size.

If the SQLWARN2 field contains a W, it means that null values weren't used in one of the column functions (see chapter 6). Normally, however, this only affects the results of an AVG function.

If the SQLWARN3 field contains a W, it means that the number of columns and host variables don't match. This can happen when you code statements that don't explicitly name all of the columns that they process, as in a SELECT * statement or in an INSERT statement without a list of column names.

The SQLWARN4 field applies only to UPDATE and DELETE statements that are processed dynamically. Since dynamic SQL is covered in the second book in this series, this probably doesn't have any meaning to you now.

The SQLWARN6 field is set to W when an arithmetic expression produces a date or timestamp item whose value had to be adjusted due to a differing number of days in different months. This is described under "Exceptional conditions when working with dates and times" near the end of chapter 7, but it isn't normally a problem.

The COBOL code for the SQL communication area

```
01  SQLCA.
    05 SQLCAID     PIC X(8).
    05 SQLCABC     PIC S9(9) COMP-4.
    05 SQLCODE     PIC S9(9) COMP-4.
    05 SQLERRM.
        49 SQLERRML PIC S9(4) COMP-4.
        49 SQLERRMC PIC X(70).
    05 SQLERRP     PIC X(8).
    05 SQLERRD     OCCURS 6 TIMES
                   PIC S9(9) COMP-4.
    05 SQLWARN.
        10 SQLWARN0 PIC X.
        10 SQLWARN1 PIC X.
        10 SQLWARN2 PIC X.
        10 SQLWARN3 PIC X.
        10 SQLWARN4 PIC X.
        10 SQLWARN5 PIC X.
        10 SQLWARN6 PIC X.
        10 SQLWARN7 PIC X.
    05 SQLEXT.
        10 SQLWARN8 PIC X.
        10 SQLWARN9 PIC X.
        10 SQLWARNA PIC X.
        10 SQLSTATE PIC X(5).
```

Field	Data type	Description
SQLCODE	Binary fullword	SQL return code
SQLERRD(3)	Binary fullword	Number of rows affected by an INSERT, DELETE, or UPDATE statement
SQLERRD(5)	Binary fullword	Contains the column (position) of the syntax error for a dynamic SQL statement
SQLWARN0	1-byte string	Contains W if any other SQLWARN field contains W
SQLWARN1	1-byte string	Contains W if a string was truncated when stored in a host variable
SQLWARN2	1-byte string	Contains W if null values were excluded during the processing of a column function
SQLWARN3	1-byte string	Contains W if the number of columns and host variables don't match
SQLWARN4	1-byte string	Contains W if an UPDATE or DELETE statement issued dynamically doesn't have a WHERE clause
SQLWARN6	1-byte string	Contains W if an arithmetic operation produces an unusual date or timestamp
SQLSTATE	5 byte string	Contains a return code indicating the status of the most recent SQL statement

Figure 10-1   The most useful fields in the SQL communication area

Last, the SQLSTATE field is similar to the SQLCODE field in that it contains a return code indicating the status of the most recent SQL statement. Although the SQLCODE field is unique to DB2 for MVS, the SQLSTATE field can be used across DB2 (and ANSI-compliant SQL) platforms. So, if your DB2 application runs on DB2 for MVS, DB2 for OS/2, and DB2 for Windows NT, your COBOL programs should check the SQLSTATE field. You can find a complete list of SQLSTATE values in appendix B.

How to use the DSNTIAR subprogram for reporting errors

DSNTIAR is an error-reporting subprogram that comes with DB2. It takes data from the communication area, adds explanatory text, and formats it in a readable form. Then, your COBOL program can display the message or save it on disk. In figure 10-2, you can learn how to use this subprogram.

When you call this subprogram, you pass three arguments to it: the SQL communication area, the area that should receive the formatted message, and the length of each of the lines in the message area. In this figure, you can see one way that the second and third arguments can be defined. Here, the third argument (ERROR-LINE-LENGTH) supplies a length value of 80 for each line that's returned by the subprogram. Although this value can be from 72 to 240, a value of 79 or 80 is appropriate if you intend to display the message on a terminal. If your shop uses DSNTIAR, it probably has a standard for what the length value should be so find out what that is.

Because DSNTIAR returns a variable-length message, the second argument that you define in your COBOL program must consist of both a length and a data component. You can see how these components are defined within the ERROR-MESSAGE field in this figure. Since the length of each line has been set at 80 by the third argument and the message can consist of up to ten lines, the total length of the data component must be 10 times 80, or 800 characters. To make it easy to get the data for each of these lines, the data component has been defined as an indexed area consisting of ten 80-character fields. You'll see one way that these fields can be used in the COBOL program at the end of this chapter.

In this figure, you can see the possible return codes generated when a COBOL program calls DSNTIAR. Since this return code is different than the return codes generated for each step of your jobs, make sure to display all return codes other than zero. You'll see how you can do this in a moment.

This figure also shows the output produced by DSNTIAR after an unsuccessful SELECT statement. (You'll rarely see a COBOL program call DSNTIAR after a successful execution of an SQL statement.) Here, the output shows more than just the SQLCODE value and its meaning. It also shows the values of the SQLERRD fields in two different formats including hex. In most DB2 shops, though, interpreting this extra data is more the responsibility of the database administrator than of the COBOL programmer. As a result, this book doesn't summarize what the values in each SQLERRD field mean.

Call statement in the Procedure Division

```
CALL 'DSNTIAR' USING SQLCA
                     ERROR-MESSAGE
                     ERROR-LINE-LENGTH.
```

Related field definitions in the working-storage section

```
01  ERROR-MESSAGE.
    05  ERROR-MESSAGE-LENGTH    PIC S9(4)   COMP    VALUE +800.
    05  ERROR-MESSAGE-LINE      PIC X(80)   OCCURS 10 TIMES
                                            INDEXED BY EML-INDEX.
*
01  ERROR-LINE-LENGTH           PIC S9(9)   COMP    VALUE +80.
```

DSNTIAR return codes

Code	Meaning
0	Successful execution.
4	More data was available than could fit into the provided message area.
8	The logical record length was not between 72 and 240, inclusive.
12	The message area was not large enough, or the message length was 240 or greater.
16	Error in TSO message routine.
20	Module DSNTIA1 couldn't be loaded.
24	SQLCA data error.

Sample DSNTIAR output after an unsuccessful SELECT statement

```
DSNT404I SQLCODE = 100, NOT FOUND:  ROW NOT FOUND FOR FETCH, UPDATE,
         OR DELETE, OR THE RESULT OF A QUERY IS AN EMPTY TABLE
DSNT415I SQLERRP = DSNXRFCH SQL PROCEDURE DETECTING ERROR
DSNT416I SQLERRD = 110  0  0  1  0  0 SQL DIAGNOSTIC INFORMATION
DSNT416I SQLERRD = X'FFFFFF92'  X'00000000'  X'00000000' X'FFFFFFFF'
         X'00000000'  X'00000000' SQL DIAGNOSTIC INFORMATION
```

Description

- DSNTIAR is an error-reporting subprogram that comes with DB2. It takes data from the DB2 communication area, adds explanatory text, and formats it in a more readable form.

- The DSNTIAR subprogram requires three arguments: (1) the name of the SQL communication area; (2) the name of the data area that will receive the formatted message from DSNTIAR; and (3) the name of a binary fullword field that contains the length of the message lines that DSNTIAR will return (this length must be between 72 and 240).

- DSNTIAR returns the message as a variable-length field. As a result, the group field used for the second argument must contain (1) a length component and (2) a data component.

- Since DSNTIAR can return a maximum of 10 message lines, the data component of the second argument must provide for 10 lines. To make it easy to access each of these lines, you can code an indexed data area that occurs 10 times as shown above.

Figure 10-2   How to use the DSNTIAR subprogram for reporting errors

How to use the WHENEVER statement

Instead of using a COBOL IF statement to check for error conditions, many COBOL programs use the DB2 WHENEVER statement to check for them. Although this statement is limited, it provides an easy way to branch to an exit paragraph when a serious SQL error occurs. The exit paragraph can then display or save an error message and end the program.

Figure 10-3 presents the syntax for the WHENEVER statement. It is normally used with the keyword SQLERROR so its action takes place whenever SQLCODE has a negative value. Then, it uses the GOTO or GO TO keywords to branch to a paragraph. This is illustrated by the first example in this figure:

```
WHENEVER SQLERROR GO TO DB2-ERROR-EXIT.
```

In some COBOL shops, this is the standard way to handle serious SQL errors.

When you code a WHENEVER statement, you must realize that it applies to all SQL statements that follow it, but none that precede it. In fact, the WHENEVER statement is a precompiler statement that causes error-processing code to be inserted after each SQL statement that follows it. So if you want the WHENEVER statement to apply to all of the SQL statements in a program, you code it at the start of the first paragraph in the program.

Because the WHENEVER statement doesn't provide a way to return to the statement that follows the SQL statement that caused the error, it violates the principles of structured programming. In addition, the three types of errors that it can detect are often too general for practical use. For instance, the error that occurs when a program tries to add a row to a table with a duplicate key should probably be handled differently than the error that occurs when the program tries to access a table that's damaged or missing. For these reasons, the WHENEVER statement is usually found only in COBOL programs prior to DB2 version 3.0. It's almost always safer to check the SQLCODE after each SQL statement and continue processing accordingly.

The syntax of the WHENEVER statement

```
EXEC SQL
    WHENEVER {SQLERROR | SQLWARNING | NOT FOUND}
        {{GOTO | GO TO} paragraph-name | CONTINUE}
END-EXEC.
```

Keyword	Meaning
SQLERROR	SQLCODE has a negative value.
SQLWARNING	SQLCODE has a positive value other than +100 or SQLWARN0 is W.
NOT FOUND	SQLCODE has a value of +100.
GOTO or GO TO	Branch to the paragraph name that follows.
CONTINUE	Continue with the statement that follows the SQL statement that caused the error condition.

Typical WHENEVER statements

```
WHENEVER SQLERROR GO TO DB2-ERROR-EXIT.

WHENEVER SQLWARNING GOTO DB2-WARNING-EXIT.

WHENEVER NOT FOUND CONTINUE.
```

Description

- The WHENEVER statement lets you specify the action that the program should take whenever a specific DB2 condition is caused by any SQL statement that follows the WHENEVER statement.

- One of the problems with the WHENEVER statement is that its GO TO clause branches to a COBOL paragraph without providing a means to return to the statement that follows the SQL statement that caused the error condition. As a result, this statement is normally used to branch to a paragraph that displays an error message and ends the program.

- The WHENEVER statement is usually found in COBOL programs prior to DB2 version 3.0. It's almost always safer to code specific SQLCODE checks after each SQL statement and process accordingly. Additionally, you should avoid coding the GO TO verb as used by the WHENEVER statement.

Figure 10-3   How to use the WHENEVER statement

A COBOL program with enhanced error processing

The next three figures present a COBOL program that uses some of the error-processing features just presented. It is an enhanced version of the second update program in the previous chapter. So if you haven't already read that chapter, you may want to do so before you study the program that follows.

The seven DB2 tables

Figure 10-4 presents the seven tables used by this update program. If you've read the previous chapter, you know that this program updates these tables by moving the rows for paid invoices from the invoice, line item, and payment tables to the related history tables. The work table is used to do this in an efficient way.

Invoice table

```
CREATE TABLE MM01.INVOICE
  ( INVCUST   CHAR(6)        NOT NULL,
    INVNO     CHAR(6)        NOT NULL,
    INVDATE   DATE           NOT NULL,
    INVSUBT   DECIMAL(9,2)   NOT NULL,
    INVSHIP   DECIMAL(7,2)   NOT NULL,
    INVTAX    DECIMAL(7,2)   NOT NULL,
    INVTOTAL  DECIMAL(9,2)   NOT NULL,
    INVPROM   CHAR(10)       NOT NULL,
    PRIMARY KEY (INVNO)
    FOREIGN KEY CUSTNO (INVCUST)
      REFERENCES MM01.CUSTOMER
      ON DELETE CASCADE )
IN DATABASE MMADBV
```

Invoice history table

```
CREATE TABLE MM01.INVHIST
  ( INVCUST   CHAR(6)        NOT NULL,
    INVNO     CHAR(6)        NOT NULL,
    INVDATE   DATE           NOT NULL,
    INVSUBT   DECIMAL(9,2)   NOT NULL,
    INVSHIP   DECIMAL(7,2)   NOT NULL,
    INVTAX    DECIMAL(7,2)   NOT NULL,
    INVTOTAL  DECIMAL(9,2)   NOT NULL,
    INVPROM   CHAR(10)       NOT NULL )
IN DATABASE MMADBV
```

Line item table

```
CREATE TABLE MM01.LINEITEM
  ( LIINVNO   CHAR(6)        NOT NULL,
    LIPCODE   CHAR(10)       NOT NULL,
    LIQTY     DECIMAL(7)     NOT NULL,
    LIPRICE   DECIMAL(7,2)   NOT NULL,
    LIDISC    DECIMAL(7,2)   NOT NULL,
    FOREIGN KEY INVNO (LIINVNO)
      REFERENCES MM01.INVOICE
      ON DELETE CASCADE )
IN DATABASE MMADBV
```

Line item history table

```
CREATE TABLE MM01.LIHIST
  ( LIINVNO   CHAR(6)        NOT NULL,
    LIPCODE   CHAR(10)       NOT NULL,
    LIQTY     DECIMAL(7)     NOT NULL,
    LIPRICE   DECIMAL(7,2)   NOT NULL,
    LIDISC    DECIMAL(7,2)   NOT NULL )
IN DATABASE MMADBV
```

Payment table

```
CREATE TABLE MM01.PAYMENT
  ( PAYINVNO  CHAR(6)        NOT NULL,
    PAYDATE   DATE           NOT NULL,
    PAYAMT    DECIMAL(9,2)   NOT NULL,
    PAYCHECK  CHAR(20),
    PAYCCARD  CHAR(20),
    PAYEXP    CHAR(5),
    PAYNOTE   VARCHAR(254),
    FOREIGN KEY INVNO (PAYINVNO)
      REFERENCES MM01.INVOICE
      ON DELETE CASCADE )
IN DATABASE MMADBV
```

Payment history table

```
CREATE TABLE MM01.PAYHIST
  ( PAYINVNO  CHAR(6)        NOT NULL,
    PAYDATE   DATE           NOT NULL,
    PAYAMT    DECIMAL(9,2)   NOT NULL,
    PAYCHECK  CHAR(20),
    PAYCCARD  CHAR(20),
    PAYEXP    CHAR(5),
    PAYNOTE   VARCHAR(254) )
IN DATABASE MMADBV
```

Work table

```
CREATE TABLE MM01.WORKTABLE
  ( INVCUST   CHAR(6)        NOT NULL,
    INVNO     CHAR(6)        NOT NULL,
    INVDATE   DATE           NOT NULL,
    INVSUBT   DECIMAL(9,2)   NOT NULL,
    INVSHIP   DECIMAL(7,2)   NOT NULL,
    INVTAX    DECIMAL(7,2)   NOT NULL,
    INVTOTAL  DECIMAL(9,2)   NOT NULL,
    INVPROM   CHAR(10)       NOT NULL )
IN DATABASE MMADBV
```

Figure 10-4   The CREATE TABLE statements for seven tables

The messages displayed by an unsuccessful test run

Figure 10-5 presents the messages that are displayed by this update program when a serious SQL error occurs. To force the error that led to this display, I changed the table name in the DELETE statement in module 600 from MM01.INVOICE, which is correct, to MM01.XXXXXXX, which is invalid. Then, to identify this version of the program, I changed the program name to UPDTHSTX.

The third line in the output for this program identifies the program that is running: UPDTHSTX. This line is followed by two lines that are displayed by a system abend subprogram named ILBOABN0 that's called to end the update program. The second line of this output (the fifth overall) shows that the user abend code is 2280. This is a code supplied by the program that should quickly tell what type of error has occurred.

The next five lines are messages that were displayed by the program for SQL statements that ran successfully. At this point, though, the program fails. Then, the next line is an error message prepared by the program that tells what the SQLCODE value is, what table was involved, and in what paragraph the error occurred. Here, you can see that the error occurred in the paragraph named 600-DELETE-ALL-ITEMS.

This message is followed by ten lines that display the message returned by the DSNTIAR subprogram (although the last four lines are blank). In the first line of this output, you can see that MM01.XXXXXXX is an undefined name. This, of course, identifies the problem that forced the SQL error. After the DSNTIAR message lines, the display continues with the values of some of the fields in the SQL communication area.

This output, of course, will vary depending on what the error is. But this should give you an idea of the type of error reporting that this enhanced update program does.

The structure chart

Figure 10-5 also presents the structure chart for this program. This is the same as the structure chart used for the second update program in the previous chapter, but it includes one new module. Here, module 990 is a standard error-handling routine for SQL errors that displays the required error messages and calls the abend subprogram. To learn more about a standard error-handling routine, please turn the page.

The messages displayed by an unsuccessful run of the update program

```
MMA - EXTRA! for Windows 95/NT                            _ □ ×
File  Edit  View  Tools  Session  Options  Help

   Display  Filter  View  Print  Options  Help
--------------------------------------------------------------------
 SDSF OUTPUT DISPLAY MM01X    JOB00061  DSID   102 LINE 4      COLUMNS 02- 81
 COMMAND INPUT ===> _                                  SCROLL ===> CSR
 RUN  PROGRAM(UPDTHSTX) PLAN(MM01PLAN) LIB('MM01.DB2.LOADLIB')
IKJ56641I DSN      ENDED DUE TO ERROR+
IKJ56641I USER ABEND CODE 2280  REASON CODE 00000000
0000000004 ROWS DELETED FROM WORKTABLE.
0000000004 ROWS INSERTED INTO WORKTABLE.
0000000004 ROWS INSERTED INTO INVHIST.
0000000004 ROWS INSERTED INTO LIHIST.
0000000004 ROWS INSERTED INTO PAYHIST.
SQLCODE IS -204      MM01.INVOICE      600-DELETE-ALL-ITEMS
 DSNT408I SQLCODE = -204, ERROR:  MM01.XXXXXXX IS AN UNDEFINED NAME
 DSNT418I SQLSTATE   = 42704 SQLSTATE RETURN CODE
 DSNT415I SQLERRP    = DSNXOTL SQL PROCEDURE DETECTING ERROR
 DSNT416I SQLERRD    = -500  0  0  -1  0  0 SQL DIAGNOSTIC INFORMATION
 DSNT416I SQLERRD    = X'FFFFFE0C'  X'00000000'  X'00000000'  X'FFFFFFFF'
          X'00000000'  X'00000000' SQL DIAGNOSTIC INFORMATION



SQLERRMC    MM01.XXXXXXX
```

The structure chart for the update program

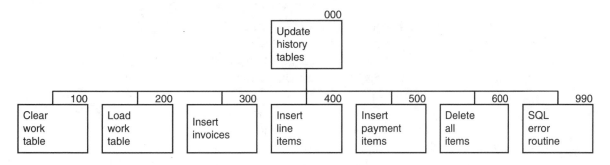

Notes

- Module 990 is a standard module used to display error messages like those shown in the display above whenever a serious SQL error occurs

- To force the error display in this example, the DELETE statement in module 600 was changed so it refers to a table named MM01.XXXXXXX instead of the correct MM01.INVOICE. The program name was also changed to UPDTHSTX.

- The fourth and fifth lines in this example are displayed by a system abend program named ILBOABN0 that's called by module 990. The next five lines are displayed by modules 100 through 500 to indicate normal processing before the abend. The remaining lines are displayed by module 990 to help identify the cause of the error.

Figure 10-5   The error message display and structure chart for the update program

A standard error-handling routine

Figure 10-6 presents a standard error-handling routine for SQL errors that can be copied into any COBOL program. Today, most COBOL shops use a standard routine like this, so you should find out what's available in your shop and use it. If your shop doesn't have a routine like this, of course, you can modify the one in this figure to suit your specific requirements.

The first statement in this routine displays an error message prepared by the program. This message includes the SQLCODE value, the name of the table or tables used in the SQL statement, and the name of the paragraph that the error occurs in. In a moment, when you review the complete COBOL listing for the update program, you can see how this information is moved into the error message by each paragraph that includes an SQL statement.

The second statement in this routine calls the DSNTIAR subprogram, as explained in figure 10-2. If the subprogram runs successfully, this routine displays its ten message lines. But if a non-zero return code is passed back from the subprogram, this routine displays an error message that includes the return code.

Next, this error routine displays the eight fields in the SQL communication area that are presented in figure 10-1. In practice, though, you may want to display the values for more of these fields so they can be used by the database administrator when an unusual error occurs.

After these error messages are displayed, this routine runs an SQL ROLL-BACK statement to roll back any transactions that haven't been committed. Then, if this statement isn't successful, an error message is displayed.

Last, this routine calls the ILBOABN0 subprogram to end the program. By this time, the program has moved the appropriate value into ABND-CODE, which is passed to the subprogram. This value is then displayed by the subprogram as the user abend code (see the fifth program line in the previous figure). This subprogram also makes a storage dump available to the programmer.

If you're not familiar with ILBOABN0, it's an abend subprogram supplied by IBM to abend a job. This subprogram puts the code you supply as a parameter into the USER ABEND CODE of the abending step of the job. Because this error routine calls the subprogram dynamically, your job must include the library where ILBOABN0 resides in its STEPLIB. In our shop, ILBOABN0 resides in SYS1.COB2LIB.

In the four shops that I've worked as a COBOL programmer, each one had a similar error routine. In addition, they all used standard error numbers for specific abends. For example, if a job abended during an SQL INSERT statement, the abend code passed to ILBOABN0 was +2270; if a job abended during a DELETE statement, the code was +2280; and so on. That way, when an abend occurred and you were called at 2:00 a.m. to fix the problem, the operator would tell you something like "Job RC9900 abended in STEP010 with a user abend code of +2270." Then, you would know immediately what kind of abend you were dealing with.

A standard error-handling routine

```
990-SQL-ERROR-ROUTINE.
*
    DISPLAY PROGRAM-ERROR-MESSAGE.
    CALL 'DSNTIAR' USING SQLCA
                        ERROR-MESSAGE
                        ERROR-LINE-LENGTH.
    IF RETURN-CODE IS EQUAL TO ZERO
        PERFORM
            VARYING EML-INDEX FROM 1 BY 1
            UNTIL EML-INDEX > 10
                DISPLAY ERROR-MESSAGE-LINE(EML-INDEX)
        END-PERFORM
    ELSE
        DISPLAY 'DSNTIAR ERROR - RETURN CODE = ' RETURN-CODE.
    DISPLAY 'SQLERRD3   ' SQLERRD(3).
    DISPLAY 'SQLERRD5   ' SQLERRD(5).
    DISPLAY 'SQLWARN0   ' SQLWARN0.
    DISPLAY 'SQLWARN1   ' SQLWARN1.
    DISPLAY 'SQLWARN2   ' SQLWARN2.
    DISPLAY 'SQLWARN3   ' SQLWARN3.
    DISPLAY 'SQLWARN4   ' SQLWARN4.
    DISPLAY 'SQLWARN6   ' SQLWARN6.
    EXEC SQL
        ROLLBACK
    END-EXEC.
    IF SQLCODE NOT EQUAL ZERO
        DISPLAY 'INVALID ROLLBACK'
        MOVE SQLCODE TO ROLLBACK-SQLCODE
        DISPLAY ROLLBACK-ERROR-MESSAGE.
    CALL 'ILBOABN0' USING ABND-CODE.
```

What a standard error-handling routine should do

- Display an error message created by the program so you can quickly tell what happened.

- Call the DSNTIAR subprogram and display its error message. If this subprogram doesn't run successfully, display an appropriate error message.

- Display some or all of the fields in the SQL communication area (SQLCA).

- Issue a ROLLBACK statement to roll back all of the transactions that haven't been committed. If the ROLLBACK is unsuccessful, display an appropriate error message. (Although the ROLLBACK statement isn't required because an implicit rollback occurs when a program ends abnormally, it's a good practice to include this ROLLBACK statement.)

- Call an abend subprogram to end the program.

Figure 10-6   How to code a standard error-handling routine

The COBOL listing

Figure 10-7 presents the four pages of the COBOL listing for this program with the error-processing code shaded. This code either replaces or is in addition to the error-processing code for the second update program in the previous chapter.

In the Identification Division of this program, you can see how comments are used to document the codes that are used for identifying abends. This is particularly useful if you're using codes that aren't standard in your COBOL shop.

In the working-storage section, you can see the COBOL definitions for all the fields required by module 990. This includes the fields for the program error message, the DSNTIAR error message, the ROLLBACK error message, and the abend code that's passed to the ILBOABN0 subprogram. These standard fields can be copied into the working-storage section and module 990 can be copied into the Procedure Division.

On pages 2 and 3, you can see how each paragraph issues an SQL statement and then checks the SQL return code. If SQLCODE is less than zero, each paragraph moves the SQLCODE value, the name of the table in the SQL statement, and the paragraph name into the elementary fields in the PRO-GRAM-ERROR-MESSAGE group item. In addition, each paragraph moves the appropriate user abend code into ABND-CODE. Each of these paragraphs then performs paragraph 990, which is the standard error routine. If on the other hand, the SQL statement is performed successfully, each paragraph displays the number of rows affected by the statement.

The update program   **Page 1**

```
IDENTIFICATION DIVISION.
*
 PROGRAM-ID.     UPDTHST3.
*
*USER ABEND CODES:   2200   DSNTIAR SUBPROGRAM ERROR
*                    2270   INSERT STATEMENT ERROR
*                    2280   DELETE STATEMENT ERROR
*
 ENVIRONMENT DIVISION.
*
 DATA DIVISION.
*
 WORKING-STORAGE SECTION.
*
 01  SQL-ERROR-ROUTINE-FIELDS.
*
     05  PROGRAM-ERROR-MESSAGE.
         10  FILLER              PIC X(11)    VALUE 'SQLCODE IS '.
         10  PEM-SQLCODE         PIC -999.
         10  FILLER              PIC X(5)     VALUE SPACES.
         10  PEM-TABLE           PIC X(18)    VALUE SPACES.
         10  FILLER              PIC X(2)     VALUE SPACES.
         10  PEM-PARAGRAPH       PIC X(30)    VALUE SPACES.
*
     05  DSNTIAR-ERROR-MESSAGE.
         10  DEM-LENGTH          PIC S9(4)    COMP    VALUE +800.
         10  DEM-MESSAGE         PIC X(80)    OCCURS 10 TIMES
                                              INDEXED BY DEM-INDEX.
*
     05  DSNTIAR-LINE-LENGTH     PIC S9(9)    COMP    VALUE +80.
*
     05  ROLLBACK-ERROR-MESSAGE.
         10  FILLER              PIC X(20)
                                 VALUE 'ROLLBACK SQLCODE IS '.
         10  REM-SQLCODE         PIC -999.
*
     05  ABND-CODE               PIC S9(4)    COMP    VALUE +00.
*
     EXEC SQL
         INCLUDE SQLCA
     END-EXEC.
*
 PROCEDURE DIVISION.
*
 000-UPDATE-HISTORY-TABLES.
*
     PERFORM 100-CLEAR-WORK-TABLE.
     PERFORM 200-LOAD-WORK-TABLE.
     PERFORM 300-INSERT-INVOICES.
     PERFORM 400-INSERT-LINE-ITEMS.
     PERFORM 500-INSERT-PAYMENT-ITEMS.
     PERFORM 600-DELETE-ALL-ITEMS.
     DISPLAY 'UPDATE COMPLETED SUCCESSFULLY.'.
     STOP RUN.
```

Figure 10-7   The COBOL listing for the update program (part 1 of 4)

The update program

```
*
 100-CLEAR-WORK-TABLE.
*
     EXEC SQL
         DELETE FROM MM01.WORKTABLE
     END-EXEC.
     IF SQLCODE < 0
         MOVE SQLCODE                    TO PEM-SQLCODE
         MOVE 'MM01.WORKTABLE'           TO PEM-TABLE
         MOVE '100-CLEAR-WORK-TABLE'     TO PEM-PARAGRAPH
         MOVE +2280 TO ABND-CODE
         PERFORM 990-SQL-ERROR-ROUTINE
     ELSE
         DISPLAY SQLERRD(3) ' ROWS DELETED FROM WORKTABLE.'.
*
 200-LOAD-WORK-TABLE.
*
     EXEC SQL
         INSERT INTO MM01.WORKTABLE
             SELECT *
                 FROM  MM01.INVOICE A
                 WHERE INVTOTAL =
                     (SELECT SUM(PAYAMT)
                         FROM MM01.PAYMENT
                         WHERE PAYINVNO = A.INVNO)
     END-EXEC.
     IF SQLCODE < 0
         MOVE SQLCODE                    TO PEM-SQLCODE
         MOVE 'MM01.WORKTABLE'           TO PEM-TABLE
         MOVE '200-LOAD-WORK-TABLE'      TO PEM-PARAGRAPH
         MOVE +2270 TO ABND-CODE
         PERFORM 990-SQL-ERROR-ROUTINE
     ELSE
         DISPLAY SQLERRD(3) ' ROWS INSERTED INTO WORKTABLE.'.
*
 300-INSERT-INVOICES.
*
     EXEC SQL
         INSERT INTO MM01.INVHIST
             SELECT *
                 FROM  MM01.WORKTABLE
     END-EXEC.
     IF SQLCODE < 0
         MOVE SQLCODE                    TO PEM-SQLCODE
         MOVE 'MM01.INVHIST'             TO PEM-TABLE
         MOVE '300-INSERT-INVOICES'      TO PEM-PARAGRAPH
         MOVE +2270 TO ABND-CODE
         PERFORM 990-SQL-ERROR-ROUTINE
     ELSE
         DISPLAY SQLERRD(3) ' ROWS INSERTED INTO INVHIST.'.
```

Figure 10-7   The COBOL listing for the update program (part 2 of 4)

The update program   **Page 3**

```
*
 400-INSERT-LINE-ITEMS.
*
     EXEC SQL
         INSERT INTO MM01.LIHIST
             SELECT *
                 FROM   MM01.LINEITEM
                 WHERE LIINVNO IN
                     (SELECT INVNO
                         FROM MM01.WORKTABLE)
     END-EXEC.
     IF SQLCODE < 0
         MOVE SQLCODE                      TO PEM-SQLCODE
         MOVE 'MM01.LIHIST'                TO PEM-TABLE
         MOVE '400-INSERT-LINE-ITEMS'  TO PEM-PARAGRAPH
         MOVE +2270 TO ABND-CODE
         PERFORM 990-SQL-ERROR-ROUTINE
     ELSE
         DISPLAY SQLERRD(3) ' ROWS INSERTED INTO LIHIST.'.
*
 500-INSERT-PAYMENT-ITEMS.
*
     EXEC SQL
         INSERT INTO MM01.PAYHIST
             SELECT *
                 FROM   MM01.PAYMENT
                 WHERE PAYINVNO IN
                     (SELECT INVNO
                         FROM MM01.WORKTABLE)
     END-EXEC.
     IF SQLCODE < 0
         MOVE SQLCODE                      TO PEM-SQLCODE
         MOVE 'MM01.PAYHIST'               TO PEM-TABLE
         MOVE '500-INSERT-PAYMENT-ITEMS' TO PEM-PARAGRAPH
         MOVE +2270 TO ABND-CODE
         PERFORM 990-SQL-ERROR-ROUTINE
     ELSE
         DISPLAY SQLERRD(3) ' ROWS INSERTED INTO PAYHIST.'.
*
 600-DELETE-ALL-ITEMS.
*
     EXEC SQL
         DELETE FROM MM01.INVOICE
             WHERE INVNO IN
                 (SELECT INVNO
                     FROM MM01.WORKTABLE)
     END-EXEC.
     IF SQLCODE < 0
         MOVE SQLCODE                      TO PEM-SQLCODE
         MOVE 'MM01.INVOICE'               TO PEM-TABLE
         MOVE '600-DELETE-ALL-ITEMS'   TO PEM-PARAGRAPH
         MOVE +2280 TO ABND-CODE
         PERFORM 990-SQL-ERROR-ROUTINE
     ELSE
         DISPLAY SQLERRD(3) ' ROWS DELETED FROM INVOICE.'.
```

Figure 10-7   The COBOL listing for the update program (part 3 of 4)

On page 4 you can see the paragraph for the SQL error routine. Although it is similar to the one in figure 10-6, it uses the names defined in the working-storage section of this program. It also displays more of the field values in the SQL communication area. By using the same SQL error routine in all of your COBOL programs, you not only minimize the amount of code you have to write, but you also make it easier to recover from an abend because you'll be familiar with the output displayed by the abending job.

The update program

```
*
990-SQL-ERROR-ROUTINE.
*
    DISPLAY PROGRAM-ERROR-MESSAGE.
    CALL 'DSNTIAR' USING SQLCA
                         DSNTIAR-ERROR-MESSAGE
                         DSNTIAR-LINE-LENGTH.
    IF RETURN-CODE IS EQUAL TO ZERO
        PERFORM
            VARYING DEM-INDEX FROM 1 BY 1
            UNTIL DEM-INDEX > 10
                DISPLAY DEM-MESSAGE(DEM-INDEX)
        END-PERFORM
    ELSE
        DISPLAY 'DSNTIAR ERROR - RETURN CODE = ' RETURN-CODE.
    DISPLAY 'SQLERRMC    ' SQLERRMC.
    DISPLAY 'SQLERRD1    ' SQLERRD(1).
    DISPLAY 'SQLERRD2    ' SQLERRD(2).
    DISPLAY 'SQLERRD3    ' SQLERRD(3).
    DISPLAY 'SQLERRD4    ' SQLERRD(4).
    DISPLAY 'SQLERRD5    ' SQLERRD(5).
    DISPLAY 'SQLERRD6    ' SQLERRD(6).
    DISPLAY 'SQLWARN0    ' SQLWARN0.
    DISPLAY 'SQLWARN1    ' SQLWARN1.
    DISPLAY 'SQLWARN2    ' SQLWARN2.
    DISPLAY 'SQLWARN3    ' SQLWARN3.
    DISPLAY 'SQLWARN4    ' SQLWARN4.
    DISPLAY 'SQLWARN5    ' SQLWARN5.
    DISPLAY 'SQLWARN6    ' SQLWARN6.
    DISPLAY 'SQLWARN7    ' SQLWARN7.
    DISPLAY 'SQLWARN8    ' SQLWARN8.
    DISPLAY 'SQLWARN9    ' SQLWARN9.
    DISPLAY 'SQLWARNA    ' SQLWARNA.
    EXEC SQL
        ROLLBACK
    END-EXEC.
    IF SQLCODE NOT EQUAL ZERO
        DISPLAY 'INVALID ROLLBACK'
        MOVE SQLCODE TO REM-SQLCODE
        DISPLAY ROLLBACK-ERROR-MESSAGE.
    CALL 'ILBOABN0' USING ABND-CODE.
```

Figure 10-7   The COBOL listing for the update program (part 4 of 4)

Perspective

This chapter has shown how to use the DSNTIAR subprogram, the WHENEVER statement, a standard error-handling routine, and the ILBOABN0 subprogram for abending a program. This chapter has also shown how to use more of the fields in the SQL communication area. By using these features, you should be able to do the error processing for any COBOL program that you develop.

11

How to maximize locking efficiency

With each new release, DB2 adds language and features that are designed to improve the performance of the programs that access and update the data in DB2 databases. To a large extent, this performance depends on the *locking* features that DB2 provides. These features help insure the integrity of the data in a database by locking a row while it's being updated so other programs or users can't change it before it's committed to the database. Unfortunately, locking also limits the number of programs or users that can access the data at the same time, which isn't desirable. That's why you need to develop programs that maximize locking efficiency.

Today, COBOL programmers need to know how locking works, even though DB2 acquires and releases all locks automatically. In particular, you need to know enough about locking to discuss its effects intelligently with your database administrator. You need to know how table space definitions and binding parameters affect locking. And you need to know how to use the COBOL constructs that override the automatic locking that's done by DB2. So that's what the focus of this chapter is.

Introduction to locking

To protect the data in a database, DB2 uses a sophisticated set of *locking* features. In particular, a DB2 *lock* prevents one program from accessing data that has been changed, but not yet committed, by another program. This, however, has a negative effect on the number of programs and users that can access the data in shared DB2 tables at the same time, which is the *concurrency* of the system. The conflicting goals of DB2 are (1) to maintain the integrity of the data in a database by locking data whenever that's necessary and (2) to maximize the concurrency of a system so the users can quickly access the data they want.

How DB2 uses locks to protect shared data

To illustrate how locking works, figure 11-1 presents an example. In the first diagram, program 2 and program 3 are concurrently accessing shared data. These programs are said to "hold" or "own" a *shared lock* (S) on the data. Since program 1 is attempting to update that data, it has an *update lock* (U), but it must wait until programs 2 and 3 are finished before it can continue.

In the second diagram, program 2 and 3 have finished, which releases their holds on the data. Then, DB2 can *promote* program 3's update lock to an *exclusive lock* (X) so it can update the shared data. At this point, no other programs can read or update this shared data.

In the third diagram, program 1 has either ended or executed a COMMIT statement, thus releasing its hold on the shared data. At that point, other programs can again access the data.

The locking process in this figure is controlled by DB2's *Intersystem Resource Lock Manager* (*IRLM*). Whenever practical, though, DB2 tries to lock pages without using IRLM by using a *latch*. Although true locks are always set in the IRLM, latches are set internally by DB2 without using the IRLM, thus eliminating some of the overhead associated with locks.

Prior to DB2 version 3, latches could be used to lock internal DB2 resources only, not table data. With DB2 version 3 and later, though, DB2 can use latches for table data too. As a result, latches are used more frequently by DB2. In this chapter, the term *lock* is used to refer to both locks and latches because the concepts are the same for both.

An update lock waiting for shared locks to be released

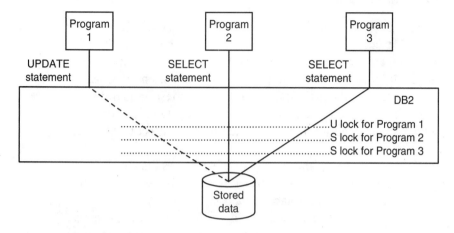

An update lock that's been promoted to an exclusive lock

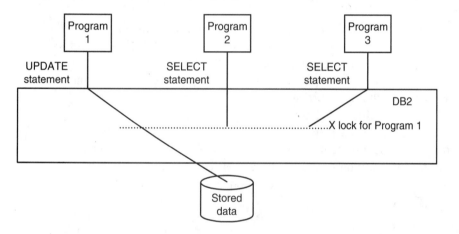

After the exclusive lock is released, other programs can access the data

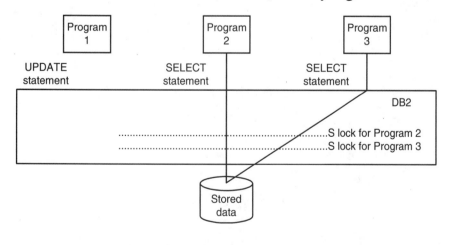

Figure 11-1   How DB2 uses locks to protect shared data

The three types of table spaces

When you use DB2, each table is stored in a DB2 table space. This space defines the physical structure of the VSAM data sets that are used for storing DB2 tables. Although a database administrator usually creates the table spaces for a production environment, application programmers are often responsible for creating and maintaining the table spaces for their own test or quality assurance environments. Even if you don't create your own table spaces, though, you need to understand what they are and how they affect locking and concurrency.

In figure 11-2, you can see the three types of table spaces that you can create. As you can see, all three types are divided into equal-sized units called *pages*, and each page contains rows of table data.

In a *segmented table space*, the space is divided into units called *segments*, and each segment can contain the rows from only one table. For most applications, this is the most efficient type of table space because it maximizes concurrency.

In a *partitioned table space*, the space is divided into units called *partitions*, and each partition contains part of one table. This type of table space is appropriate for large tables that contain one million or more pages.

In a *simple table space*, the space is divided into pages without any higher level structure. In addition, a simple table space can contain data from more than one table. Because this can seriously reduce concurrency, most applications that use simple table spaces were developed before DB2 version 2.1. So if you run across an application that still uses simple table spaces, you should talk with your database administrator about converting them to segmented table spaces. By doing this, you will improve concurrency as well as the response times for your users.

A segmented table space

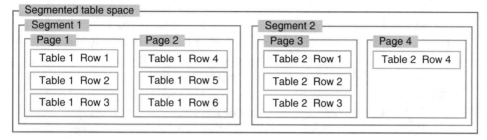

Description

- A segmented table space is the most efficient type of table space for most tables.
- The space is divided into equal-sized groups of pages called *segments*, and each segment can contain rows from only one table.

A partitioned table space

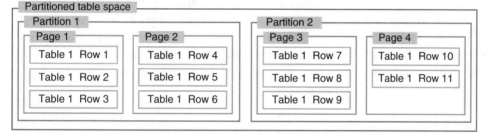

Description

- Partitioned table spaces are best suited for tables that must store one million or more data pages. Each partitioned table space can contain only one table.
- The space is divided into components called *partitions*, with each partition residing on a separate VSAM data set.

A simple table space

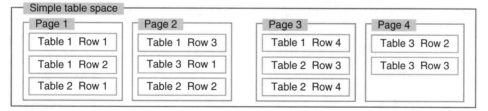

Description

- Most COBOL programs that use simple table spaces were developed prior to DB2 version 2.1. Today, simple table spaces are almost obsolete.
- Because data rows from different tables can reside on the same page, concurrent access to tables in the same table space can cause lengthy response delays.

Figure 11-2   The three types of DB2 table spaces

Lock size and lock escalation

When DB2 locks data that's in a table in a segmented table space, the *lock size* can be (1) a table space, (2) a table, or (3) a page or row. In contrast, when DB2 locks data in a simple or partitioned table space, it can lock (1) a table space or (2) a page or row. This is summarized by figure 11-3.

One of the factors that determines the lock size that's used is the LOCKSIZE option that's set when a table space is defined. Although this can be set to ROW, PAGE, TABLE, or TABLESPACE, the ANY option should be used for most table spaces. Then, DB2 selects the optimum lock size for each processing situation. In most cases, that size is a page, which means that less data is locked and more concurrency is possible.

When the number of locks at one level reaches a preset default, DB2 will *escalate* the lock to another level. If, for example, the number of page locks in a segmented table space exceeds the default, DB2 will escalate the locks to a table lock. Or, if the number of page locks in a partitioned table space exceeds the default, DB2 will escalate the locks to a table space lock. By increasing the lock size, DB2 reduces the overhead that's required for managing the page locks, but this also reduces concurrency.

Although DB2 can use row locks when the lock size option for a table is set to ANY, it rarely uses them. One reason is that row locks are so restrictive that they are prone to lock escalation.

The hierarchy of locks

Segmented table space

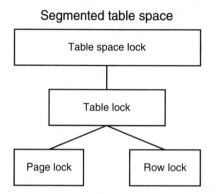

Simple table space or partitioned table space

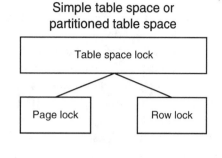

Description

- When a table space is defined or altered, the LOCKSIZE clause specifies a default *lock size* for the table space. This size can be ROW, PAGE, TABLE, TABLESPACE, or ANY.

- When the LOCKSIZE(ANY) option is used, DB2 selects the optimum lock size for each processing situation. In most cases, this means that DB2 selects page level locking. But if the number of pages that are locked exceeds an installation default, DB2 automatically does a *lock escalation*, which means that it locks a larger unit.

- In a non-segmented table space, a page or row lock is escalated to the table space level. In a segmented table space, a page or row lock is first escalated to a table and then, if necessary, to a table space.

- DB2 can take locks at any level without taking a lock at a lower level. However, before DB2 takes a lock at a lower level, it takes a compatible lock at a higher-level.

- Because row locks and page locks are on the same level in the hierarchy, DB2 doesn't have to take a page lock before it takes a row lock.

Figure 11-3   Lock size and lock escalation

Lock mode and lock promotion

In figure 11-1, you were introduced to three *lock modes*: S, U, and X. But with DB2, it's more complicated than that. In figure 11-4, you can see the six lock modes that are used for table and table space locks, as well as the three modes that are used for page and row locks.

The mode of a lock determines what the program that owns the lock and what concurrent programs can do with the locked resource. If, for example, DB2 applies an IX lock to a table space, both the lock owner and concurrent programs can read and change the data in the tables in that space. This lasts until one of the programs acquires a U-lock on a page or row. But even then, the other programs can read, but not change, the data in that page or row. And even when a U-lock on a page or row is *promoted* to an X-lock, the other programs can read the data in that page or row if they are bound with a UR isolation level, which is explained in the next figure. If they aren't bound with that level, they just have to wait until the X-lock is released.

The modes of table and table space locks

Lock mode	Lock owner can	Concurrent program can	Promotion possibilities
IS (Intent Share)	Read but not change data	Read and change data	S-lock on a page or row
IX (Intent Exclusive)	Read and change data	Read and change data	S- or U-lock on a page or row
S (Share)	Read but not change data	Read but not change data	
U (Update)	Read but not change data until the lock is promoted to an X-lock	Acquire S-lock and read data, but can't acquire a U-lock.	X-lock on a table or table space so there's no need for a page or row lock
SIX (Share with Intent Exclusive)	Read and change data	Read but not change data	X-lock on a page or row
X (Exclusive)	Read and change data	Read data, but only if the program uses UR isolation (see figure 11-5)	No need for page or row locks

The modes of page and row locks

Lock mode	Lock owner can	Concurrent program can	Promotion possibilities
S (Share)	Read but not change data	Acquire S-lock or U-lock, or read data without acquiring a lock	U-lock
U (Update)	Read but not change data until the lock is promoted to an X-lock	Acquire S-lock and read data, but can't acquire a U-lock.	X-lock, but this can cause a suspension if a concurrent program holds an S-lock
X (Exclusive)	Read and change data	Read data, but only if the program uses UR isolation (see figure 11-5)	

Description

- DB2 sets and *promotes* the locks automatically based on the options that were used when the table space and table were defined and the options that were used when the program package and plan were bound.

- Before an S-lock is acquired for a page or a row, DB2 acquires an IS- or IX-lock for the related table or table space. Before an X-lock is acquired for a page or row, DB2 acquires an IX- or SIX-lock for the related table or table space.

- These modes are listed in sequence from those that require the least control over DB2 resources to those requiring the most control.

Figure 11-4   Lock mode and lock promotion

Lock duration

The *duration* of a lock is the length of time that the lock is held, which is measured from the time the lock is acquired to the time it's released. This is affected by three parameters that are set when a program is bound into a *plan*. In the next chapter, you can learn more about binding both plans and *packages,* but this chapter introduces you to the bind parameters that affect locking.

In figure 11-5, you can see the DB2I panel that's used for setting the defaults for a bind plan. In option 3, you set the RELEASE parameter. And in option 8, you set the ACQUIRE parameter. These parameters have a large effect on when a table or table space lock is acquired.

For a batch program, you normally use the ALLOCATE option for the ACQUIRE parameter and the DEALLOCATE option for the RELEASE parameter. Then, the table or table space lock is acquired when the bind plan is allocated, and the lock is released when the bind plan is terminated. These options will improve the run-time of most batch programs without degrading concurrency.

In contrast, the USE and COMMIT options are better for interactive programs. With those options, a table or table space lock is acquired when it's needed and released when a commit occurs. This maximizes concurrency with minimal effect on program performance.

Figure 11-5 also summarizes the four *isolation levels* that can be set for the programs that are bound to a plan. These levels have an effect on the page and row locks that are acquired by a program. In general, the various levels offer more or less concurrency at the cost of more or less protection from other application programs. As a result, the values you choose should be based primarily on the needs of the application.

The isolation levels in this figure are in sequence from the one offering the most isolation and least concurrency (RR) to that the one offering the least isolation and most concurrency (UR). The one that should be used for most programs is CS, or Cursor Stability, which should maximize concurrency at the same time that it insures data integrity. When this isolation level is used, read-only page locks are released as soon as another page is accessed.

With DB2 version 4.0, the UR isolation level provides *read-through locks,* which are also know as *dirty reads* or *uncommitted reads.* These locks help overcome some concurrency problems. When an application program uses an uncommitted read, though, it may read data that has been changed, but not yet committed. Then, if the change is rolled back, the program has read data that is different than the current data in the database. Whenever this is acceptable, though, the UR level can improve performance.

The Defaults For Bind Plan panel

```
 MMA - EXTRA! for Windows 95/NT                                    _ ⊡ ⊠
 File  Edit  View  Tools  Session  Options  Help
                     DEFAULTS FOR BIND PLAN              SSID: DSN
 COMMAND ===> _

 Change default options as necessary:

  1   ISOLATION LEVEL ......... ===> CS        (RR, RS, CS, or UR)
  2   VALIDATION TIME ......... ===> BIND      (RUN or BIND)
  3   RESOURCE RELEASE TIME ... ===> COMMIT    (COMMIT or DEALLOCATE)
  4   EXPLAIN PATH SELECTION .. ===> YES       (NO or YES)
  5   DATA CURRENCY ........... ===> NO        (NO or YES)
  6   PARALLEL DEGREE ......... ===> ANY       (1 or ANY)
  7   DYNAMIC RULES ........... ===> RUN       (RUN or BIND)
  8   RESOURCE ACQUISITION TIME ===> USE       (USE or ALLOCATE)
  9   DEFER PREPARE ........... ===> NO        (NO or YES)
 10   SQLRULES ................ ===> DB2       (DB2 or STD)
 11   DISCONNECT .............. ===> EXPLICIT  (EXPLICIT, AUTOMATIC,
                                                 or CONDITIONAL)
```

Bind parameters that affect table and table space locks

Parameter	Locks are acquired or released	Recommendation
ACQUIRE(ALLOCATE)	When plan is allocated	Use for batch processing
ACQUIRE(USE)	As they are needed	Use for on-line processing
RELEASE(DEALLOCATE)	When plan is terminated	Use for batch processing
RELEASE(COMMIT)	When a commit occurs	Use for on-line processing

Bind parameters that affect page and row locks

Isolation level	Description
RR (Repeatable Read)	The program can read the same pages or rows more than once without allowing inserts, updates, or changes by other programs. All rows and pages are locked, even if they don't satisfy the predicate of the executing SQL statement. And the locks are held until the data is committed.
RS (Read Stability)	The program can read the same pages or rows more than once without allowing qualifying rows (those that satisfy the predicate) to be updated or deleted by other programs. However, other programs can insert new rows or update non-qualifying rows.
CS (Cursor Stability)	This provides for maximum concurrency with data integrity. After the program leaves a row or page, though, another program can change the data. This option should be used for most packages and plans.
UR (Uncommitted Read)	The program acquires few locks with the risk of reading uncommitted data. You can use this for working with a table that is rarely updated.

Note

- The isolation levels are in sequence from the one offering the most isolation (and least concurrency) to the one offering the least isolation.

Figure 11-5   Bind parameters that affect lock duration

Suspensions, timeouts, and deadlocks

DB2 *suspends* a program when it requests a lock that is already held by another program and cannot be shared. In most cases, the program resumes processing when the conflicting lock is released. If a program is suspended for longer than a preset time interval, though, a *timeout* occurs. This timeout interval is set by the database administrator through the IRLM.

When a timeout occurs, DB2 issues two messages to the console and returns an SQLCODE of -911 or -913. If the code is -911, it means that DB2 automatically rolled back the program's last unit of work. If the code is -913, it means that DB2 didn't issue a rollback for the program. However, if the program uses a standard error handling routine like the one in the last chapter, it will attempt a rollback when it encounters an error.

In contrast to a suspension or timeout, a *deadlock* (also known as a *deadly embrace*) occurs when two or more programs hold locks on data that the others need and without which they cannot proceed. This is illustrated by the example in figure 11-6. Here, each program requires an exclusive lock on a page that the other program is already holding with an exclusive lock. To break this deadlock, DB2 rolls back the current unit of work for one of the programs after the preset time interval for deadlocks and then terminates that program (the *victim*) with a -911 or -913 SQLCODE. That will free the locks and allow the remaining program to continue.

A deadlock example

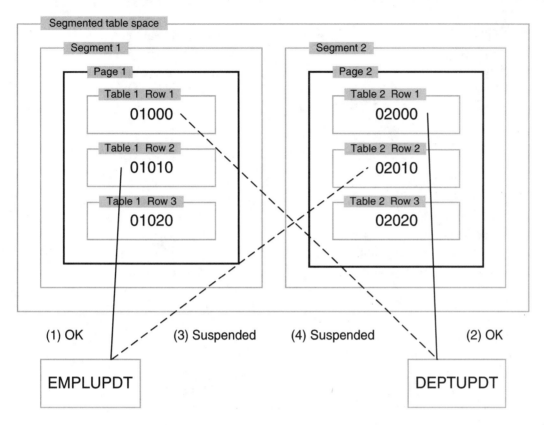

(1) OK	(3) Suspended	(4) Suspended	(2) OK

EMPLUPDT   **DEPTUPDT**

How a deadlock can occur

1. EMPLUPDT and DEPTUPDT are two programs. EMPLUPDT accesses Table 1 and acquires an exclusive lock for Page 1, which contains record 01010 in Row 2.

2. DEPTUPDT accesses Table 2 and acquires an exclusive lock for Page 2, which contains record 02000 in Row 1.

3. EMPLUPDT requests a lock for Page 2 of Table 2 while still holding the lock on Page 1 of Table 1. The program is suspended because DEPTUPDT is holding an exclusive lock on Page 2.

4. DEPTUPDT requests a lock for Page 1 of Table 1 while still holding the lock on Page 2 of Table 2. The program is suspended because EMPLUPDT is holding an exclusive lock on Page 1. *This is a deadlock.*

The resolution of the deadlock

- After the preset time interval for deadlocks, DB2 rolls back the current unit of work for one of the programs and terminates the program (the *victim*). That frees its locks and allows the remaining program to continue.

Figure 11-6   A deadlock

COBOL constructs that affect locking

In general, DB2 handles locking and concurrency automatically based on the options that are set when a table space is defined and when a program package or plan is bound. In addition, though, COBOL provides three constructs that affect locking. These are the WITH clause, the WITH HOLD clause, and the LOCK TABLE statement.

The WITH clause

Figure 11-7 presents an example of a SELECT statement that uses the WITH clause. Here, the isolation level that's specified in the clause overrides the isolation level that the plan or package was bound with. However, the new isolation level is in effect only for the statement in which it appears.

If your shop has any kind of review process when new or updated programs are put into production, you should be prepared to explain why this override is necessary to the database administrator. Better yet, talk with your database administrator about the override before attempting to put the program into production.

In this example, the WITH clause calls for Uncommitted Read isolation on the assumption that the MAX, MIN, and AVG functions aren't going to be affected much by a change that takes place after a dirty read. Since this can improve both processing time and concurrency while the statement is running, you shouldn't have any trouble explaining your override. In contrast, if you override CS isolation with RR isolation, your explanation will be far more difficult.

The WITH HOLD clause

Figure 11-7 also presents an example of a DECLARE CURSOR statement that uses the WITH HOLD clause. When that clause is specified, the cursor position is maintained past a commit point, even if the plan was bound with ISOLATION(CS) or RELEASE(COMMIT). Then, you can access the next row in the cursor-controlled table by issuing a simple FETCH statement. Although this can simplify the coding in your COBOL program, it also increases lock duration, which can lead to suspensions and timeouts.

Whenever you use this clause, then, you should monitor your program and the programs that run with it to determine whether response times are satisfactory. Because the DB2 environment is dynamic, this monitoring should be done at least on a monthly basis. Then, if the response times become unsatisfactory, you can modify the program so it doesn't use the WITH HOLD clause.

An SQL statement that uses the WITH clause

```
SELECT MAX(SALARY) AS MAX_SAL,
       MIN(SALARY) AS MIN_SAL,
       AVG(SALARY) AS AVG_SAL
    FROM MM01.EMPLOYEE
       WITH UR
```

Description

- The WITH clause can be used to override the isolation level of a bound plan or package.
- The WITH clause can be used in SELECT statements, SELECT INTO statements, searched deletes, searched updates, and INSERT statements that use a subquery.
- The WITH clause can't be used in subqueries except in INSERT statements.
- The isolation level in the WITH clause is in effect only for the statement in which it appears.

An SQL statement that uses the WITH HOLD clause

```
EXEC SQL
    DECLARE EMPLCURS CURSOR WITH HOLD FOR
        SELECT EMPNO, DEPTNO, LNAME, FNAME, EXT
        FROM MM01.EMPLOYEE
            WHERE DEPTNO = 'B12'
        ORDER BY EMPNO
END-EXEC.
```

Description

- When you code the WITH HOLD clause, the cursor position is maintained past a commit point. Thus, the locks needed to maintain that position aren't released, even if they were acquired with ISOLATION(CS) or RELEASE(COMMIT).
- You should code the WITH HOLD clause only for cursors that need to be accessed after a COMMIT has been taken.
- Because the use of the WITH HOLD clause can increase the number of suspensions and timeouts, you should monitor any program that uses it to see whether the decrease in concurrency is justified by the improvement in program performance.
- If the WITH HOLD clause reduces the concurrency to an unsatisfactory level, you can remove the clause and rewrite the code so it uses a second cursor that maintains the location of the last row that was processed when the first cursor is closed.

Figure 11-7   How to use the WITH and WITH HOLD clauses

The LOCK TABLE statement

Figure 11-8 presents the LOCK TABLE statement. The size of the lock that DB2 applies when this statement is executed depends on whether or not the table resides in a segmented table space. If it does, DB2 applies a table lock to the table specified. Otherwise, DB2 locks all of the tables in that table space, even though you named only one table.

The most common use of this statement is in a high-priority program that needs to run with maximum efficiency. If you lock a table in exclusive mode, for example, your program will run as efficiently as possible because other programs won't be able to access the data in the table unless they are bound with UR isolation. In contrast, if you lock a table in share mode, concurrency won't suffer as much and the program won't run as efficiently.

You can also use this statement in a program after a DB2 monitor determines that the program frequently sets many row or page locks on a table, which are eventually escalated to table or table space locks. Then, the LOCK TABLE statement can save the overhead that's required by the row or page locks by locking the entire table from the start. For this type of program, you don't code the LOCK TABLE statement in the initial version of the program that's put into production. You only add the LOCK TABLE statement when the data provided by the DB2 monitor indicates that the use of this statement will improve performance.

When you use the LOCK TABLE statement, you should realize that concurrency probably isn't an issue if your program runs in batch mode during off-hours or if it processes tables that aren't accessed by interactive programs. In those situations, an exclusive table lock should maximize program performance with little or no degradation of other programs.

The two forms of the LOCK TABLE statement

```
LOCK TABLE table-name IN SHARE MODE
LOCK TABLE table-name IN EXCLUSIVE MODE
```

When the acquired locks are released

Bind option	Releases locks
RELEASE(COMMIT)	At the next commit point. Then, page or row locking resumes in the next unit of work.
RELEASE(DEALLOCATE)	Only when the program ends.

The modes of the locks acquired by the LOCK TABLE statement

LOCK TABLE IN	Non-segmented table space	Segmented table space
SHARE MODE	S or SIX	S or SIX for a table IS for a table space
EXCLUSIVE MODE	X	X for a table IX for a table space

Description

- The LOCK TABLE statement is appropriate in a high-priority program.
- The LOCK TABLE statement is also appropriate in a program that frequently acquires many row or page locks for a table before these locks are escalated to a table or table space lock. This is usually determined by a DB2 monitor after the program is put into production.
- If the table specified in this statement isn't in a segmented table space, DB2 applies the lock to all of the tables in the table space, not just the one named.

Figure 11-8   How to use the LOCK TABLE statement

Perspective

This chapter has introduced the basic concepts, terms, and skills that every COBOL programmer needs for dealing with locking and concurrency. At the least, this knowledge will help you talk intelligently with your database administrator. It also provides the background you need for defining table spaces and setting binding parameters.

You need to realize, though, that what you've learned is just an introduction to this complicated subject. As you progress as a DB2 programmer, you'll eventually discover that you need to know more about it. That's why *Part 2* of *DB2 for the COBOL Programmer* presents more information about how DB2 manages locking and concurrency and what you can do to optimize it.

Once when I was working as a production support analyst, for example, a user called to complain about a bad response time. After she changed some information on her screen, she told me that she was pressing the Enter key and that she would tell me when the transaction was finished. When she finally responded, a full two and a half minutes had gone by. She said that this was common and that other users were furious about their response times too.

After we met with the application programmers and the database administrator for this group of applications, we decided to convert all of the Type 1 indexes to Type 2 indexes, which had just become available with DB2 version 4.0. Incredibly, this relatively simple change reduced the response time to under 2 seconds on a light day and under 4 seconds on a heavy day. In *Part 2*, you can learn how indexes affect locking...and much more.

Section 3

Program development skills

This section presents the skills you need for preparing and testing a COBOL program that uses DB2 data. In chapter 12, for example, you can learn how to use a TSO facility called DB2I to create DCLGEN output. You can also learn how to use DB2I to precompile, bind, compile, link-edit, and run a program.

In chapter 13, you can learn how to do some of these program development tasks without using DB2I. You can do that by submitting batch jobs for program development through MVS JCL. Since these are the same types of jobs that are submitted by DB2I, you should read chapter 12 before you read chapter 13.

In chapter 14, you can learn how to use a DB2I facility called SPUFI to run SQL statements at a TSO terminal for immediate processing. You can use SPUFI to test the operation of SQL statements before you use them in your COBOL programs. You can also use SPUFI to create the tables that you need for testing your programs.

Last, in chapter 15, you can learn how to use QMF to update DB2 tables. This is the most efficient way to add or change rows in the DB2 tables that you create with SPUFI. When you complete this section, you'll have the skills you need to create DB2 tables, add data to those tables, and prepare and run your DB2 COBOL programs.

12

How to use DB2I to prepare and run programs

To prepare and run DB2 programs interactively through TSO, you use a DB2 program called *DB2 Interactive*, or *DB2I*. This program makes it easy to prepare DCLGEN output as well as precompile, bind, compile, link, and run a COBOL program. In this chapter, you'll learn how to do all of those tasks.

Note, however, that you can't use DB2I for program development in all COBOL shops because it uses too many resources. And in other shops, you can use DB2I for some tasks but not all. In either case, you need to know how to develop and test programs outside of DB2I, which is presented in the next chapter.

An introduction to program development with DB2I

When you develop a COBOL program that accesses a DB2 database, you have to do several tasks that aren't required when you develop a COBOL program that uses VSAM files. These tasks are made easier by the use of DB2I. As you will see, DB2I is just a set of ISPF panels that let you perform DB2 program-development tasks in an interactive environment.

The steps in program development

Figure 12-1 presents the steps that you need to follow when you prepare a COBOL program that accesses a DB2 database. After you've entered the source program into the system, the first step is to run the *DB2 precompiler* on the source program. This produces two output files. The first is a *modified source program* in which each of the SQL statements has been translated into the COBOL statements that invoke the appropriate DB2 interface functions. Although the precompiler leaves the original SQL statements in the source program, it converts them to comments so they will be ignored by the COBOL compiler. If you want to see what this looks like, appendix A presents the listing of the modified source program for the inquiry program presented in the first chapter.

The second file produced by the precompiler is a *database request module*, or *DBRM*. It contains information about how your program will use DB2 and will be used as input in a later step of this development process.

After the precompiler is finished, the COBOL compiler compiles the modified source program into an *object module*. Then, the *linkage editor* links the object module with other required modules including DB2 interface modules. This produces a *load module*.

Before the load module can be executed, though, DB2 must *bind* the program. This bind procedure uses the DBRM that was created by the precompiler to check all the DB2 functions used in the program to make sure they are valid and that you are authorized to perform them. In addition, this procedure selects the most efficient access paths to the data in the DB2 database.

You can bind a program directly to a *plan* or, optionally, to a *package* and then to a plan. A package is a single DBRM with optimized access paths. You'll learn about the benefits of using packages in a moment.

The output of this bind procedure is an *application plan* that contains information about how DB2 will complete each database request made by all the packages in the plan. As you can see in this figure, the load module, DB2 catalog, and DB2 directory (which contains the application plan) are required when a program is executed.

The steps in program development

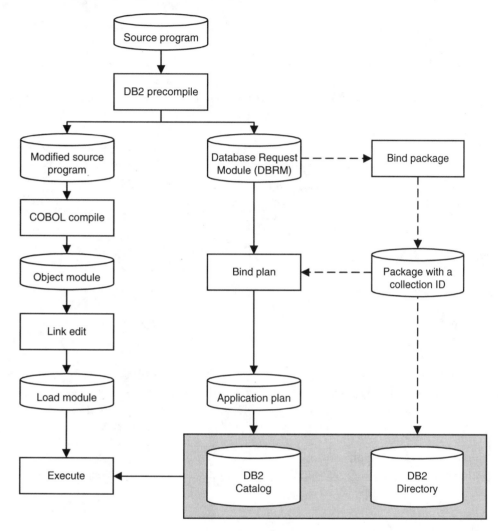

Description

- The DB2 catalog stores information about the plan and package.
- The DB2 directory stores the actual plan and package.
- The load module, DB2 catalog, and DB2 directory must be available when you execute a program.
- A package contains a location identifier, a collection identifier, and a package identifier. The location identifier specifies the site where the package was bound. The collection identifier represents a logical grouping of packages. And the package identifier is the DBRM name bound into the package.
- You can bind a program to a package or directly to a plan. However, you can't run a program that is bound to a package until that package is bound to a plan. For efficiency, a program should be bound to a package that is bound to a plan.

Figure 12-1   The steps in program development

How to set up plans, collections, and packages

Before you bind programs into packages and plans, you should develop a bind strategy that helps you manage them. This is illustrated by figure 12-2. Here, the first diagram represents a company with two divisions and two departments in each division. This diagram also shows that three or four programs have been developed for each of the departments. Then, the second diagram shows how a bind strategy can reflect the company structure. This, of course, is just one approach to developing a bind strategy.

Prior to DB2 version 2.3, you could only bind programs at the plan level. In that case, all of the programs in the personnel system would be bound into one plan and all of the programs in the manufacturing system would be bound into another plan. In this example, that's only seven programs in each plan, but I've supported systems that had over 400 programs in a single plan. Then, if any program in the plan requires a change in an SQL statement, the entire plan must be rebound.

Starting with version 2.3, though, you can bind programs into packages and group these packages into *collections*, as illustrated in this figure. Then, you can use wildcards (*) in the bind plan statements to indicate that all of the packages in the current collections and any packages added to those collections in the future should be bound into the plan. This is illustrated by the statements at the bottom of this figure.

When you use a bind strategy like this, you must bind the application plan before you bind any of the packages that will go into the plan. However, you only have to bind the plan once. Then, as each package is bound, it automatically gets added to the plan without rebinding the plan. In this chapter, you'll learn how to first bind the application plan and then bind the packages because that's the most effective binding strategy. You should realize, though, that some shops still bind programs directly into plans without using collections and packages.

The structure of a company

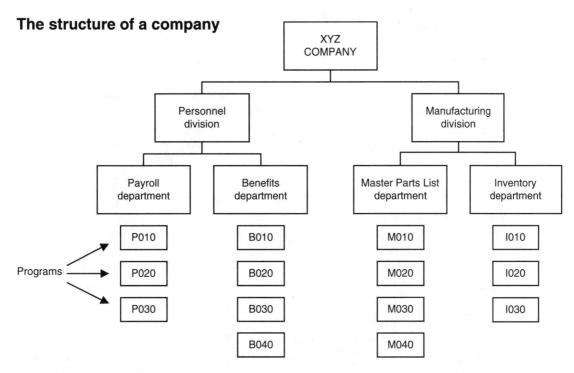

A bind strategy for the company

- Each program is bound into its own package. Packages are grouped into logical collections. The collections are bound into plans.

The plans, collections, and packages

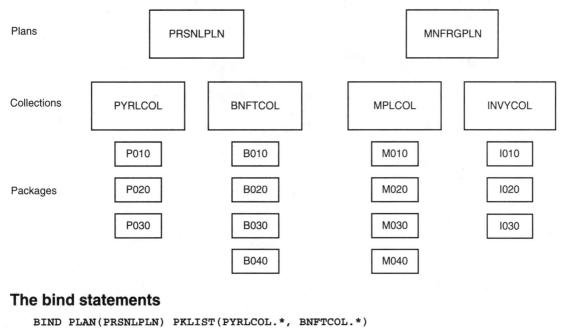

The bind statements

```
BIND PLAN(PRSNLPLN) PKLIST(PYRLCOL.*, BNFTCOL.*)
BIND PLAN(MNFRGPLN) PKLIST(MPLCOL.*, INVYCOL.*)
```

Figure 12-2   How to set up plans, collections, and packages

How to access DB2I

DB2I is usually one of the choices on ISPF's Primary Option Menu. In figure 12-3, for example, DB2I is option 8 on the ISPF menu. Although the menu used in your company may be somewhat different, DB2I will probably be there somewhere. If it isn't, check with a co-worker or your database administrator to find out how to access it.

To invoke DB2I from the ISPF Primary Option Menu in this figure, you type an 8 in the *command area*, which is the second line in the screen. Then, when you press the Enter key, the DB2I Primary Option Menu appears as shown in this figure. As a programmer, the three options you'll use the most are DCLGEN (option 2), Program Preparation (option 3), and Run (option 6). However, you should also know how to bind a plan (option 5) before you prepare a program. As you will see, the Program Preparation option includes precompiling so you usually don't need to access Precompile (option 4) separately.

SPUFI (option 1) is another useful option for programmers because SPUFI lets you execute SQL statements that query, create, and alter tables. In addition, you can use SPUFI to test all of your SQL statements before you run them in your DB2 COBOL programs. In chapter 14, you can learn how to use this valuable development tool.

Since options 7 and 8 are for facilities that database administrators use more frequently than programmers, they are presented in *Part 2* of this series. In the next figure, though, you can learn how to set the DB2I defaults (option D). The last option (X) just lets you exit from DB2I.

To choose any option in the DB2I menu, just type the option number or letter in the command area, then press the Enter key.

How to get help in DB2I

If at any time you need help when you're using DB2I, you can press the PF1 key. Often, you'll find that the help information for a panel provides just what you need to know like the valid keywords for an option or reminders about what infrequently used options do. To leave a help panel and return to your DB2I panel, press PF3.

An ISPF Primary Option Menu

```
🖳 MMA - EXTRA! for Windows 95/NT                                    _ 🗗 ✕
File  Edit  View  Tools  Session  Options  Help
------------------------- ISPF/PDF PRIMARY OPTION MENU ----------------------
OPTION  ===> 8_
                                                      USERID   - MM01
     0   ISPF PARMS   - Specify terminal and user parameters  TIME     - 14:33
     1   BROWSE       - Display source data or output listings TERMINAL - 3278
     2   EDIT         - Create or change source data           PF KEYS  - 12
     3   UTILITIES    - Perform utility functions
     4   FOREGROUND   - Invoke language processors in foreground
     5   BATCH        - Submit job for language processing
     6   COMMAND      - Enter TSO command or CLIST
     7   DIALOG TEST  - Perform dialog testing
     8   DB2          - Perform DATABASE 2 interactive functions
     9   QMF          - QMF Query Management Facility
     D   DATA-XPERT   - DATA-XPERT Interactive File Manipulation System
     E   EPIC         - EPIC/MVS Tape Management System
     J   JHS          - Job History System
     V   VPS61        - LRS Virtual Printer System V6.1
     S   SDSF         - System Display and Search Facility
     X   EXIT         - Term ISPF using log and list defaults

Enter END command to terminate ISPF.
```

The DB2I Primary Option Menu (option 8 in the menu above)

```
🖳 MMA - EXTRA! for Windows 95/NT                                    _ 🗗 ✕
File  Edit  View  Tools  Session  Options  Help
                       DB2I PRIMARY OPTION MENU          SSID: DSN
COMMAND ===> _

Select one of the following DB2 functions and press ENTER.

     1   SPUFI                (Process SQL statements)
     2   DCLGEN               (Generate SQL and source language declarations)
     3   PROGRAM PREPARATION  (Prepare a DB2 application program to run)
     4   PRECOMPILE           (Invoke DB2 precompiler)
     5   BIND/REBIND/FREE     (BIND, REBIND, or FREE plans or packages)
     6   RUN                  (RUN an SQL program)
     7   DB2 COMMANDS         (Issue DB2 commands)
     8   UTILITIES            (Invoke DB2 utilities)
     D   DB2I DEFAULTS        (Set global parameters)
     X   EXIT                 (Leave DB2I)




PRESS:                 END to exit      HELP for more information
```

Program preparation functions

Option 2   DCLGEN
Option 3   PROGRAM PREPARATION
Option 5   BIND/REBIND/FREE
Option 6   RUN

Figure 12-3   The ISPF Primary Option Menu and DB2I Primary Option Menu

How to set the DB2I and COBOL defaults

When you use DB2I for the first time, you should check its defaults to make sure they're set properly for your DB2 environment. Once you set these values, they remain in effect until you change them, so you won't return to this panel often. To display the current settings for defaults, select option D from the DB2I Primary Option Menu. Then, the DB2I Defaults panel in figure 12-4 is displayed. Here, you can see the defaults we used for preparing the programs in this book.

The first ten items in this panel are all required. Since the first two options are installation-dependent, you should check your shop's standards or ask your database administrator what values to use for these options.

In option 3, you identify the programming language you're using. This determines the compiler that will be used as well as the format of the DCLGEN output. Since our shop uses VS COBOL II, COB2 has been entered for this option, and this is also the entry you should use if your shop uses COBOL/370. If you're still using OS/VS COBOL, you enter COBOL, which is still the IBM default for this panel.

In options 4 through 10, you can usually accept the defaults. For instance, option 4 determines how many lines appear on a page of printed DB2I output like the output from SPUFI or the precompiler. Option 5 lets you specify the severity levels of the messages that should be displayed during BIND operations (from I for all the messages to S for severe messages only). Option 6 lets you specify the character you want to use as the delimiter for SQL statements. Option 7 lets you specify the character that should be used as the decimal point in numeric values. Option 9 lets you specify the number of input entry rows that should be used on the initial display of panels. And option 10 lets you change the name of the BookManager book that you'll refer to for online help.

In option 8, you can specify the lowest value of the return code from the precompile, compile, link-edit, or bind steps that will prevent later steps from running. Here, the default value of 8 causes cancellation on errors and severe errors.

Last, option 11 lets you set up a default JOB statement that's used when you run a program preparation function as a background job or when you use the EDITJCL option to submit your own program preparation job. Later in this chapter, you'll learn more about running jobs in these ways, but you can see that a JOB statement and two comments have been entered in the panel in this figure.

If you chose COBOL or COB2 as your application language on the DB2I Defaults panel, the COBOL Defaults panel in this figure is displayed when you press the Enter key. Then, you can choose the symbol that should be used to delimit a string in COBOL. You can also specify whether you want Double Byte Character String (DBCS) data defined as PIC G(n) or PIC N(n).

The DB2I Defaults panel

```
MMA - EXTRA! for Windows 95/NT                                    _ 日 ×
File  Edit  View  Tools  Session  Options  Help
                              DB2I  DEFAULTS
COMMAND ===> _

Change defaults as desired:

  1   DB2 NAME ............. ===> DSN        (Subsystem identifier)
  2   DB2 CONNECTION RETRIES ===> 0          (How many retries for DB2 connection)
  3   APPLICATION LANGUAGE   ===> COB2       (ASM,C,COBOL/COB2,FORTRAN,PLI)
  4   LINES/PAGE OF LISTING  ===> 60         (A number from 5 to 999)
  5   MESSAGE LEVEL ........ ===> I          (Information, Warning, Error, Severe)
  6   SQL STRING DELIMITER   ===> DEFAULT    (DEFAULT, ' or ")
  7   DECIMAL POINT ........ ===> .          (. or ,)
  8   STOP IF RETURN CODE >= ===> 8          (Lowest terminating return code)
  9   NUMBER OF ROWS ....... ===> 20         (For ISPF Tables)
 10   CHANGE HELP BOOK NAMES?===> NO         (YES to change HELP data set names)

 11   DB2I JOB STATEMENT:   (Optional if your site has a SUBMIT exit)
      ===> //MM01S JOB (99999),'C GARVIN',CLASS=C,MSGCLASS=X,
      ===> //       REGION=4M,NOTIFY=&SYSUID
      ===> //*
      ===> //*

PRESS:  ENTER to process     END to cancel          HELP for more information
```

The COBOL Defaults panel

```
MMA - EXTRA! for Windows 95/NT                                    _ 日 ×
File  Edit  View  Tools  Session  Options  Help
                              COBOL  DEFAULTS
COMMAND ===> _

Change defaults as desired:

  1   COBOL STRING DELIMITER ===> DEFAULT    (DEFAULT, ' or ")
  2   DBCS SYMBOL FOR DCLGEN ===> G          (G/N — Character in PIC clause)









PRESS:  ENTER to process     END to cancel          HELP for more information
```

Description

- Before you prepare any programs using DB2I, you should be sure that the DB2I defaults have been set properly. In particular, you should check the settings for DB2 name, application language, and the SQL and COBOL delimiters.

- If you have any doubt about the DB2I defaults, check with your database administrator.

Figure 12-4   The DB2I Defaults and the COBOL Defaults panels

How to prepare DCLGEN output

In most of the programs in this book, you can see the use of SQL IN-CLUDE statements that copy DCLGEN library members into the COBOL program. Although the database administrator is usually responsible for creating the DCLGEN members used for production tables, the COBOL programmer is often responsible for creating the DCLGEN members for test tables. To do that, you choose option 2 in the DB2I Primary Option menu so the DCLGEN panel in figure 12-5 is displayed.

When you include DCLGEN output in a COBOL program, you benefit in two ways. First, you don't have to code the host variables for the DB2 data that your program uses. Second, because the Declarations Generator extracts the information it needs directly from the DB2 catalog, you can be sure the host variable definitions are correct.

How to set the DCLGEN options

Figure 12-5 presents the DCLGEN panel and a summary of the entries you usually need to make when you create DCLGEN output for the tables you've created. If you're creating output for tables created by someone else, however, you may need to make entries for options 2, 3, and 5.

If you leave option 2 blank, DB2 assumes that the table qualifier is your TSO logon ID. So if the table owner is your DBA who has a logon ID of MMADBA, you need to enter MMADBA in this option. Similarly, option 3 defaults to the local location name when it is left blank. But if the table or view is located at another DB2 subsystem, you need to enter that location. In that case, you must also specify a qualified name in option 1. Then, the value of option 3 prefixes the table name on the SQL DECLARE statement as follows:

```
location_name.owner_id.table_name
```

The DCLGEN status message at the bottom of this figure shows the message that's displayed for a successful execution of the DCLGEN panel. In this case, the DCLGEN member named PAYROLL was successfully added to the data set named MM01.DB2.DCLGENS. If, however, the output can't be generated successfully, an error message is displayed.

Although none of the DCLGEN listings used in the programs in this book have generated prefixes, you will often want to use these prefixes for test and production tables. To do that, you enter a prefix name for option 9 and YES for option 11. Then, each host variable consists of a prefix name followed by a column name as shown in the next figure.

The DCLGEN panel

```
MMA - EXTRA! for Windows 95/NT                                    _ |&| X

File  Edit  View  Tools  Session  Options  Help
                        DCLGEN                    SSID: DSN
===>  _

Enter table name for which declarations are required:
  1  SOURCE TABLE NAME ===> MM01.PAYROLL                (Unqualified)
  2  TABLE OWNER ..... ===>                             (Optional)
  3  AT LOCATION ..... ===>                             (Optional)

Enter destination data set:      (Can be sequential or partitioned)
  4  DATA SET NAME ... ===> 'MM01.DB2.DCLGENS(PAYROLL)'
  5  DATA SET PASSWORD ===>        (If password protected)

Enter options as desired:
  6  ACTION .......... ===> REPLACE   (ADD new or REPLACE old declaration)
  7  COLUMN LABEL .... ===> NO        (Enter YES for column label)
  8  STRUCTURE NAME .. ===> PAYROLL-ROW                 (Optional)
  9  FIELD NAME PREFIX ===> PYRL-                       (Optional)
 10  DELIMIT DBCS .... ===> YES       (Enter YES to delimit DBCS identifiers)
 11  COLUMN SUFFIX ... ===> YES       (Enter YES to append column name)
 12  INDICATOR VARS .. ===> NO        (Enter YES for indicator variables)


PRESS: ENTER to process    END to exit      HELP for more information
```

Panel entries

Option	Entry
1	The unqualified name of the table you're creating the DCLGEN for.
4	The name of the data set in which the DCLGEN should be stored.
6	REPLACE to replace the DCLGEN if it exists or to create it if it doesn't exist, or ADD to create the DCLGEN only if it doesn't exist.
7	NO, so you don't use column labels, which add any values defined by SQL LABELS ON statements as comments to the host variable names.
8	The structure name, which becomes the 01 level name of the host structure.
9	A prefix that gets added to each field name in the host structure.
10	Applies to DBCS (Double Byte Character Set) data, which you probably won't be using.
11	YES, so the field name prefix in option 9 is combined with the column name for each column, thus creating the host variable name.
12	NO, so indicator variables aren't generated for columns that can be null because it's better to define your own indicator variables as shown in chapter 8.

The DCLGEN status message

```
MMA - EXTRA! for Windows 95/NT                                    _ |&| X

File  Edit  View  Tools  Session  Options  Help
DSNE905I EXECUTION COMPLETE, MEMBER PAYROLL ADDED
***  _
```

Figure 12-5   How to use the DCLGEN panel

DCLGEN output with prefixed host variables

Figure 12-6 presents the DCLGEN output that's generated from the panel entries of figure 12-5. Here, you can see that the host variable names consist of the prefix PYRL- followed by the column name for each column in the table. (Note that the hyphen must be included in the prefix.)

If you use a different prefix for the DCLGEN output of each table in a database, you won't have duplicate host variable names in your programs even if the same column name is used in more than one table (which is relatively common). As a result, prefixes are commonly used when DCLGEN output is generated for production tables. Note, however, that this capability wasn't available prior to DB2 version 4.

Incidentally, if you enter YES in option 12 in the DCLGEN panel, the DCLGEN output includes one indicator variable for each column in the host structure. If you've read chapter 8, you know that an indicator variable is used to determine whether or not a column contains a null value. We recommend that you avoid using this DCLGEN option, though, since it generates more indicator variables than you need. Worse, it generates them in this format:

```
01  IVARCUST.
    10  INDSTRUC   PIC S9(4) USAGE COMP OCCURS 9 TIMES.
```

Since this format makes it hard to tell which variable applies to which column, you're better off defining your own indicator variables.

The DCLGEN output for the PAYROLL table

```
**********************************************************************
* DCLGEN TABLE(MM01.PAYROLL)                                         *
*       LIBRARY(MM01.DB2.DCLGENS(PAYROLL))                           *
*       ACTION(REPLACE)                                              *
*       LANGUAGE(COBOL)                                              *
*       NAMES(PYRL-)                                                 *
*       STRUCTURE(PAYROLL-ROW)                                       *
*       QUOTE                                                        *
*       COLSUFFIX(YES)                                               *
* ... IS THE DCLGEN COMMAND THAT MADE THE FOLLOWING STATEMENTS       *
**********************************************************************
      EXEC SQL DECLARE MM01.PAYROLL TABLE
      ( EMPNO                         CHAR(6) NOT NULL,
        FNAME                         CHAR(20) NOT NULL,
        LNAME                         CHAR(30) NOT NULL,
        ADDR                          CHAR(30) NOT NULL,
        CITY                          CHAR(20) NOT NULL,
        STATE                         CHAR(2) NOT NULL,
        ZIPCODE                       CHAR(10) NOT NULL,
        SALARY                        DECIMAL(9, 2) NOT NULL,
        BONUS                         DECIMAL(5, 2) NOT NULL
      ) END-EXEC.
**********************************************************************
* COBOL DECLARATION FOR TABLE MM01.PAYROLL                          *
**********************************************************************
  01  PAYROLL-ROW.
*                         EMPNO
      10 PYRL-EMPNO            PIC X(6).
*                         FNAME
      10 PYRL-FNAME            PIC X(20).
*                         LNAME
      10 PYRL-LNAME            PIC X(30).
*                         ADDR
      10 PYRL-ADDR            PIC X(30).
*                         CITY
      10 PYRL-CITY            PIC X(20).
*                         STATE
      10 PYRL-STATE            PIC X(2).
*                         ZIPCODE
      10 PYRL-ZIPCODE            PIC X(10).
*                         SALARY
      10 PYRL-SALARY            PIC S9(7)V9(2) USAGE COMP-3.
*                         BONUS
      10 PYRL-BONUS            PIC S9(3)V9(2) USAGE COMP-3.
**********************************************************************
* THE NUMBER OF COLUMNS DESCRIBED BY THIS DECLARATION IS 9          *
**********************************************************************
```

Description

- Since the field name prefix was set as PYRL- and the column suffix option was YES, the host variables created by DCLGEN all have PYRL- as their prefix. When you use this technique for creating host variables, you avoid duplicate field names.

Figure 12-6   DCLGEN output with prefixed field names

How to bind an application plan

When you use a bind strategy like the one in figure 12-2, you bind the application plan before you bind any of the packages. To bind the application, you start by accessing the Bind Plan panel.

How to access the Bind Plan panel

To access the Bind Plan panel, you select option 5 in the DB2I Primary Option menu. Then, you select option 1 in the Bind/Rebind/Free panel that's displayed. This is illustrated by figure 12-7.

As you can see, the other options in the Bind/Rebind/Free panel let you rebind or erase an application plan. However, if you use collections and wildcards as explained in figure 12-2, you should only need to rebind a plan if you add or delete a collection. Although this panel also lets you bind or rebind a package, it's usually more efficient to do that by using the Program Preparation panel, which you'll soon learn about.

The DB2I Primary Option Menu

```
🖳 MMA - EXTRA! for Windows 95/NT                                    _ ⊡ ✕
File  Edit  View  Tools  Session  Options  Help
                            DB2I PRIMARY OPTION MENU          SSID: DSN
COMMAND ===> 5_

Select one of the following DB2 functions and press ENTER.

    1  SPUFI                 (Process SQL statements)
    2  DCLGEN                (Generate SQL and source language declarations)
    3  PROGRAM PREPARATION   (Prepare a DB2 application program to run)
    4  PRECOMPILE            (Invoke DB2 precompiler)
    5  BIND/REBIND/FREE      (BIND, REBIND, or FREE plans or packages)
    6  RUN                   (RUN an SQL program)
    7  DB2 COMMANDS          (Issue DB2 commands)
    8  UTILITIES             (Invoke DB2 utilities)
    D  DB2I DEFAULTS         (Set global parameters)
    X  EXIT                  (Leave DB2I)




PRESS:                  END to exit      HELP for more information
```

The BIND/REBIND/FREE option menu

```
🖳 MMA - EXTRA! for Windows 95/NT                                    _ ⊡ ✕
File  Edit  View  Tools  Session  Options  Help
                            BIND/REBIND/FREE              SSID: DSN
COMMAND ===> 1_

Select one of the following and press ENTER:

    1  BIND PLAN        (Add or replace an application plan)

    2  REBIND PLAN      (Rebind existing application plan or plans)

    3  FREE PLAN        (Erase application plan or plans)

    4  BIND PACKAGE     (Add or replace a package)

    5  REBIND PACKAGE   (Rebind existing package or packages)

    6  FREE PACKAGE     (Erase a package or packages)



PRESS:  ENTER to process    END to exit        HELP for more information
```

Description

- Select option 5 in the DB2I Primary Option Menu.
- Select 1 in the BIND/REBIND/FREE menu.

Figure 12-7   How to access the Bind Plan panel

How to use the Bind Plan panel

Figure 12-8 presents the Bind Plan panel that you use for creating an application plan. Here, the first option is used if you're binding a specific program to the plan. If you're using a bind strategy like the one in figure 12-2, though, you're not going to do that so you can leave this option blank.

In option 3, you enter the name of the library that will contain the DBRMs for the programs that will be bound to the plan later on. In option 5, you name the plan that the package is going to be put into. And in option 6, you should enter YES so you can double check the binding defaults for binding plans since they can have a significant effect on the locking efficiency of the programs in the plan.

In option 8, you specify whether you want to include a *package list* for this plan. In this example, the entry is YES, because you want to bind all of the packages in the collections named in the package list into the plan. You'll see how this works in a moment.

The Bind Plan panel

```
🖳 MMA - EXTRA! for Windows 95/NT                               _ 🗗 ✕
 File  Edit  View  Tools  Session  Options  Help
                           BIND PLAN                    SSID: DSN
 COMMAND ===> _

 Enter DBRM data set name(s):
  1  MEMBER ......... ===>
  2  PASSWORD ....... ===>
  3  LIBRARY ........ ===> 'MM01.DB2.DBRMLIB'
  4  ADDITIONAL DBRMS? ........ ===> NO        (YES to include more DBRMs)

 Enter options as desired:
  5  PLAN NAME ................ ===> PRSNLPLN  (Required to create a plan)
  6  CHANGE CURRENT DEFAULTS? .. ===> YES      (NO or YES)
  7  ENABLE/DISABLE CONNECTIONS? ===> NO       (NO or YES)
  8  INCLUDE PACKAGE LIST?...... ===> YES      (NO or YES)
  9  OWNER OF PLAN (AUTHID)..... ===> MM01      (Leave blank for your primaryID)
 10  QUALIFIER ................ ===> MM01      (For tables, views, and aliases)
 11  CACHESIZE ................ ===> 4096      (Blank, or value 0-4096)
 12  ACTION ON PLAN ........... ===> REPLACE   (REPLACE or ADD)
 13  RETAIN EXECUTION AUTHORITY. ===> YES      (YES to retain user list)
 14  CURRENT SERVER ........... ===>                    (Location name)


 PRESS:  ENTER to process    END to save and exit    HELP for more information
```

Panel entries

Option	Entry
1	The member name of a DBRM if a program is being bound to a plan.
2	The password if the plan is password protected.
3	The name of the partitioned data set that contains the DBRMs for the programs that will be bound to the plan.
4	NO, when you're using a bind strategy like the one in figure 12-2.
5	The name of the application plan that you're creating.
6	YES, to change the current defaults for binding plans.
7	This applies to remote connections, which is site specific.
8	YES, to include a package list for the plan.
9	The primary authorization ID of the owner of the new application plan. The owner must have the privileges required to run the SQL statements contained in the plan.
10	The implicit qualifier for unqualified tables, views, and aliases contained in the plan. The default is the owner of the plan.
11	The size (in bytes) of the authorization cache. This should be 32 bytes plus 8 bytes for each concurrent user of a plan.
12	REPLACE to replace the plan if it exists and to create it if it doesn't, or ADD to create the plan only if it doesn't exist.
13	YES, if the users with the authority to bind or run the existing plan are to keep that authority over the changed plan.
14	This is site specific for a system with multiple locations.

Figure 12-8   How to use the Bind Plan panel

How to set the defaults for binding plans

Figure 12-9 presents the Defaults For Bind Plan panel that's displayed when option 6 in the previous panel is YES. Here, the entries that we recommend for binding plans are shown in the panel. For most programs, the entries for options 1, 3, and 8 will maximize locking efficiency. If you've already read chapter 11, you may remember how the isolation level and the release and acquire parameters can affect locking efficiency. Otherwise, you can study that chapter at a later time.

The Defaults For Bind Plan panel

```
≜ MMA - EXTRA! for Windows 95/NT                                    _ ⓔ ✕
File  Edit  View  Tools  Session  Options  Help
                    DEFAULTS FOR BIND PLAN              SSID: DSN
COMMAND ===> _

Change default options as necessary:

 1   ISOLATION LEVEL .........  ===> CS        (RR, RS, CS, or UR)
 2   VALIDATION TIME .........  ===> BIND      (RUN or BIND)
 3   RESOURCE RELEASE TIME ...  ===> COMMIT    (COMMIT or DEALLOCATE)
 4   EXPLAIN PATH SELECTION ..  ===> YES       (NO or YES)
 5   DATA CURRENCY ...........  ===> NO        (NO or YES)
 6   PARALLEL DEGREE .........  ===> ANY       (1 or ANY)
 7   DYNAMIC RULES ...........  ===> RUN       (RUN or BIND)
 8   RESOURCE ACQUISITION TIME  ===> USE       (USE or ALLOCATE)
 9   DEFER PREPARE ...........  ===> NO        (NO or YES)
10   SQLRULES ................  ===> DB2       (DB2 or STD)
11   DISCONNECT ..............  ===> EXPLICIT  (EXPLICIT, AUTOMATIC,
                                                or CONDITIONAL)




PRESS:  ENTER to process    END to save and exit    HELP for more information
```

Entry recommendations

- The BIND PLAN parameters in the panel above usually produce the most efficient DB2 application plan.

Panel entries

Option	Entry
1	Sets the isolation level for the plan (see figure 11-5).
2	Specifies whether DB2 should check the authorization at run time or bind time.
3	Sets the parameter for releasing locks (see figure 11-5).
4	Lets you get EXPLAIN information about how SQL statements in the plan execute.
5	Lets you specify whether you need data currency for ambiguous cursors opened at remote locations. For more information, see "Maintaining Data Currency" in *DB2 for MVS/ESA V4 Application Programming and SQL Guide*.
6	Lets you run queries using parallel processing (ANY) or request that DB2 not execute queries in parallel (1).
7	Lets you specify whether run-time (RUN) or bind-time (BIND) rules apply to dynamic SQL statements at run time.
8	Sets the parameters for acquiring locks (see figure 11-5).
9	This is site specific for a system with multiple locations. For more information, see "Deferring Remote PREPARE for Better Performance" in chapter 4 of *DB2 for MVS/ESA V4 Application Programming and SQL Guide*.
10	This is site specific. It lets you specify whether a CONNECT statement executes according to DB2 rules (DB2) or the SQL standard rules (STD).
11	This is site specific. It lets you specify which remote connections end during a commit or rollback.

Figure 12-9   How to set the defaults for the Bind Plan function

How to use the Package List panel

Figure 12-10 presents the Package List For Bind Plan panel that's displayed next. Here, you enter the *collection IDs* for the collections that group the packages that are going to be bound into the plan. In this example, all of the packages in the PYRLCOL and BNFTCOL collections are going to be bound into the PRSNLPLN plan. By specifying an asterisk (*) in the PACKAGE-ID column, all of the packages in the collection (and all packages added to the collection in the future) are included in the plan so you only need to bind the plan once.

When you press PF3 to save the package list, DB2I creates a *DSNH CLIST* based on the entries that you've made in the binding panels. This CLIST is then executed so it creates the application plan. In the second panel in this figure, you can see the messages that are displayed when this CLIST finishes. The last line shows that the processing was successful.

The Package List for Bind Plan panel

```
MMA - EXTRA! for Windows 95/NT                                          _ 日 X
File  Edit  View  Tools  Session  Options  Help
                       PACKAGE LIST FOR BIND PLAN              SSID: DSN
COMMAND ===> _                                          SCROLL ===> PAGE

Enter names to be included in PACKAGE list for PLAN: PRSNLPLN

CMD       LOCATION         COLLECTION         PACKAGE-ID
''''''                     PYRLCOL            *
''''''                     BNFTCOL            *
''''''
''''''
''''''
''''''
''''''
''''''
''''''
```

Panel entries

- On the first empty line, enter the collection ID in the COLLECTION column and an '*' in the PACKAGE-ID column to bind all of the packages in the collection to the plan.

- If there is more than one collection in the plan, enter them in subsequent lines.

- If you aren't including all of the packages in the collection, enter the package ID in the PACKAGE-ID column for each package.

- When you're finished making entries, press PF3 to save your entries and continue. DB2I then creates and runs a DSNH CLIST, which creates the application plan. When this process is finished, completion messages are displayed as shown below.

The bind plan messages

```
MMA - EXTRA! for Windows 95/NT                                          _ 日 X
File  Edit  View  Tools  Session  Options  Help
DSNT252I - DSNTBCM1 BIND OPTIONS FOR PLAN PRSNLPLN
            ACTION          REPLACE RETAIN
            OWNER           MM01
            VALIDATE        BIND
            ISOLATION       CS
            ACQUIRE         USE
            RELEASE         COMMIT
            EXPLAIN         YES
            DYNAMICRULES    RUN
DSNT253I - DSNTBCM1 BIND OPTIONS FOR PLAN PRSNLPLN
            NODEFER         PREPARE
            CACHESIZE       4096
            QUALIFIER       MM01
            CURRENTSERVER
            CURRENTDATA     NO
            DEGREE          ANY
            SQLRULES        DB2
            DISCONNECT      EXPLICIT
DSNT200I -  BIND FOR PLAN PRSNLPLN SUCCESSFUL
***_
```

Figure 12-10   How to use the Package List For Bind Plan panel

How to use the Program Preparation functions

Figure 12-11 presents the Program Preparation panel that you can use to precompile, bind, compile, link, and run a COBOL program. In short, this panel lets you do all of the functions in the chart in figure 12-1. To display this panel, you choose option 3 in the DB2I Primary Option Menu.

How to set the Program Preparation options

Figure 12-11 also summarizes the entries that you make in the Program Preparation panel. In option 1, for example, you need to identify the data set that contains the source code for the COBOL program that you're developing, which is normally a member in a partitioned data set. In option 4, you need to identify the environment in which the program will be running. Since all the programs in this book run under TSO, TSO is entered in this example, but you use CICS if you're developing CICS programs that use DB2 data.

In option 3, you can tell DB2I how you want the program preparation functions run. If you enter FOREGROUND, the functions are run in the TSO foreground. Since this requires significant system resources, though, some shops prohibit programmers from running these functions in the foreground. In that case, you can either enter BACKGROUND to run the functions as a batch job in the background. Or, you can enter EDITJCL so DB2I creates the JCL for a batch job that you can modify and submit as shown in figure 12-16.

In options 6 through 15, you select the functions that you want to run in the "Perform function?" column. In this example, precompile, bind package, compile, and link (but not run) have been selected. These are the functions that you normally select when you prepare a program. Run hasn't been selected because you can do that after these steps have been done successfully and the load module and application plan have been created. For each of the functions you select, you can also enter Y in the "Display panel?" column if you want to adjust the options for the function.

After you set the options for each function properly, you don't need to deal with them again unless you want to change them. In fact, the values you enter are maintained from one TSO session to another. In addition, because the values you enter on the Program Preparation panel are automatically carried through the subordinate panels, you can often simply name your source program data set in this first panel and disable all of the other panel displays.

When you press the Enter key from the Program Preparation panel, DB2I displays each of the screens you requested in the "Display panel?" column. After you work through each of those, DB2I begins to execute the functions you requested in the "Perform function?" column. If one of the steps produces a return code greater than or equal to the value you specified for the STOP IF RETURN CODE option in the DB2I defaults, though, DB2I stops performing the functions. Or, to cancel the process, you can press the PA1 key.

The DB2 Program Preparation panel

```
🖳 MMA - EXTRA! for Windows 95/NT                                    _ ⊟ ×
 File  Edit  View  Tools  Session  Options  Help
                        DB2 PROGRAM PREPARATION              SSID: DSN
COMMAND ===> _

Enter the following:
 1   INPUT DATA SET NAME .... ===> 'MM01.DB2.SOURCE(P010)'
 2   DATA SET NAME QUALIFIER  ===> TEMP     (For building data set names)
 3   PREPARATION ENVIRONMENT  ===> FOREGROUND (FOREGROUND, BACKGROUND, EDITJCL)
 4   RUN TIME ENVIRONMENT ... ===> TSO      (TSO, CAF, CICS, IMS)
 5   OTHER DSNH OPTIONS ..... ===>
                                            (Optional DSNH keywords)
Select functions:           Display panel?     Perform function?
 6   CHANGE DEFAULTS ........ ===> N (Y/N)
 7   PL/I MACRO PHASE ....... ===> N (Y/N)        ===> N (Y/N)
 8   PRECOMPILE ............. ===> Y (Y/N)        ===> Y (Y/N)
 9   CICS COMMAND TRANSLATION                     ===> N (Y/N)
10   BIND PACKAGE ........... ===> Y (Y/N)        ===> Y (Y/N)
11   BIND PLAN .............. ===> N (Y/N)        ===> N (Y/N)
12   COMPILE OR ASSEMBLE .... ===> Y (Y/N)        ===> Y (Y/N)
13   PRELINK ................ ===> N (Y/N)        ===> N (Y/N)
14   LINK ................... ===> Y (Y/N)        ===> Y (Y/N)
15   RUN .................... ===> N (Y/N)        ===> N (Y/N)

PRESS:  ENTER to process    END to save and exit    HELP for more information
```

Panel entries

Option	Entry
1	The name of the data set that contains the source program.
2	The name of the qualifier for any work data sets. The default is TEMP.
3	FOREGROUND to run the selected functions in the TSO foreground, BACKGROUND to run the functions as a batch job in the background, or EDITJCL to create a batch job that you can modify and submit by yourself.
4	The environment in which the program is going to run. In the example above, TSO is used because P010 is a TSO interactive program.
5	The options for the DSNH CLIST that gets generated and run by DB2I based on the options set in the panels. Since the default DSNH options are usually acceptable, you can probably leave this blank. To learn about DSNH options, see DSNH in chapter 2 of *DB2 for MVS/ESA V4 Command Reference*.
6-15	The first set of Yes/No choices for these options lets you show the DB2I panel for a function. The second set of Yes/No choices lets you select the functions you want performed. The choices in the example above will precompile the program, bind the package, compile the program, and link the program. For each of these choices, the related DB2I panel will be displayed.

Figure 12-11   How to use the DB2 Program Preparation panel

How to precompile a DB2 COBOL program

Figure 12-12 shows the Precompile panel, which is the first panel you would see after pressing the Enter key for the Program Preparation panel in figure 12-11. The precompiler adds the code you specify in INCLUDE statements (like the SQLCA and DCLGEN output) to your program, verifies and translates SQL statements into COBOL, and builds a DBRM that the bind process uses.

The panel in this figure is the same one that you see if you select option 4 from the DB2I Primary Option Menu to access the precompiler directly. However, when you access the panel through Program Preparation, some of the items on it are automatically set to agree with the values you entered in the Program Preparation panel. In this figure, you can see typical entries for the seven options.

Later, when all the functions that you requested in the Program Preparation panel are run, the precompiler generates diagnostic messages if it finds any invalid SQL statements in your source program. These messages, which are displayed on your terminal, are usually sufficient to let you find and correct the problems. If they aren't, though, you may need to run the precompile as a batch job as shown in the next chapter so you can turn the SOURCE option on and browse through the diagnostic messages that are generated.

The Precompile panel

```
┌─────────────────────────────────────────────────────────────────────────┐
│ 🖳 MMA - EXTRA! for Windows 95/NT                                _ 🗗 ✕ │
├─────────────────────────────────────────────────────────────────────────┤
│ File  Edit  View  Tools  Session  Options  Help                           │
│                             PRECOMPILE                    SSID: DSN        │
│ COMMAND ===> _                                                            │
│                                                                           │
│ Enter precompiler data sets:                                              │
│  1   INPUT DATA SET .... ===> 'MM01.DB2.SOURCE(P010)'                     │
│  2   INCLUDE LIBRARY ... ===> 'MM01.DB2.DCLGENS'                          │
│                                                                           │
│  3   DSNAME QUALIFIER .. ===> TEMP       (For building data set names)    │
│  4   DBRM DATA SET ..... ===> 'MM01.DB2.DBRMLIB(P010)'                    │
│                                                                           │
│ Enter processing options as desired:                                      │
│  5   WHERE TO PRECOMPILE ===> FOREGROUND  (FOREGROUND, BACKGROUND, or EDITJCL) │
│  6   VERSION .......... ===>                                              │
│                                        (Blank, VERSION, or AUTO)          │
│  7   OTHER OPTIONS ..... ===>                                            │
│                                                                           │
│                                                                           │
│                                                                           │
│                                                                           │
│ PRESS:  ENTER to process    END to cancel         HELP for more information │
└─────────────────────────────────────────────────────────────────────────┘
```

Panel entries

Option	Entry
1	The name of the data set that contains the source program.
2	The name of the library that contains any members that the precompiler needs. In the example above, the name of the library that contains the DCLGEN output is entered. If you don't enclose the name in apostrophes, the user ID qualifies the name.
3	The name of the qualifier for any work data sets that are created. The default is TEMP, which is usually acceptable.
4	The name of the data set that will receive the precompiler output. Usually, the name of the program and the name of the DBRM member should be the same.
5	FOREGROUND, BACKGROUND, or EDITJCL to precompile in the TSO foreground, precompile in the background, or create a job that you can edit and submit by yourself.
6	The use of versions is site specific so find out how this is handled in your shop. For more information about versions see "Identifying a Package Version" in *DB2 for MVS/ESA V4 Application Programming and SQL Guide*.
7	Any options that the DSNH CLIST accepts, but this is usually site specific.

Figure 12-12   How to use the Precompile panel

How to bind a package

Figure 12-13 presents the Bind Package panel along with a description of the entries. In option 2 in this panel, you must enter the collection ID for the collection that the package is going to be grouped into.

In option 3, you enter DBRM to indicate that you're binding the DBRM created by the precompiler step, not a copy of an existing DBRM. Then, you enter the member name of the DBRM in option 4, the password if it is protected by one in option 5, and the data set name for the DBRM library in option 6. In this example, the DBRM is named P010 (it's a good idea to name the program and the DBRM the same), it isn't password protected, and it's in the library named MM01.DB2.DBRMLIB.

Every time you bind a package, you should enter YES for option 7 so the Defaults For Bind Package panel is displayed. That way, you can be sure that the options are set correctly. This is important because these options can have a significant effect on the locking efficiency of your program as well as the other programs that are running at the same time as explained in chapter 11.

The Bind Package panel

```
 MMA - EXTRA! for Windows 95/NT                                    _ ⊟ ✕

 File  Edit  View  Tools  Session  Options  Help
                          BIND PACKAGE                     SSID: DSN
 COMMAND ===> _

 Specify output location and collection names:
   1   LOCATION NAME ............. ===>            (Defaults to local)
   2   COLLECTION-ID ............. ===> PYRLCOL       (Required)

 Specify package source (DBRM or COPY):
   3   DBRM:       COPY:       ===> DBRM     (Specify DBRM or COPY)
   4   MEMBER    or  COLLECTION-ID ===> P010
   5   PASSWORD  or  PACKAGE-ID .. ===>
   6   LIBRARY   or  VERSION ..... ===> 'MM01.DB2.DBRMLIB'
                                           (Blank, or COPY version-id)
 Enter options as desired:
   7   CHANGE CURRENT DEFAULTS? .. ===> YES     (NO or YES)
   8   ENABLE/DISABLE CONNECTIONS? ===> NO      (NO or YES)
   9   OWNER OF PACKAGE (AUTHID).. ===> MM01    (Leave blank for primary ID)
  10   QUALIFIER ................. ===> MM01    (Leave blank for OWNER)
  11   ACTION ON PACKAGE .... .... ===> REPLACE (ADD or REPLACE)
  12   REPLACE VERSION ........... ===>
                                           (Replacement version-id)

 PRESS:  ENTER to process   END to save and exit   HELP for more information
```

Panel entries

Option	Entry
1	This applies to a system with multiple locations so it is site specific. You can usually leave this option blank to default to the local DBMS. Otherwise, you can use from 1 to 16 characters to specify a location name that must be defined in the catalog table SYSLOCATIONS.
2	The name of the collection that the package belongs to. If you're not sure, ask your database administrator. In our bind strategy, package P010 is bound to collection PYRLCOL.
3	DBRM when you're binding the DBRM created by the precompiler into a package.
4-6	The member name of the DBRM; its password if one is required; and the name of the DBRM library.
7	YES, to change the current defaults for binding packages.
8	This applies to remote connections, which is site specific.
9	The primary authorization ID of the owner of the new package. The owner must have the privileges required to run the SQL statements contained in the package.
10	The implicit qualifier for unqualified tables, views, indexes, and aliases contained in the package. The default is the owner of the package.
11	REPLACE to replace the package if it exists or to create it if it doesn't, or ADD to create the package only if it doesn't exist.
12	Leave blank to create a new package, or enter the version of the package you want to replace. Versions, however, are site specific so find out if and how they are used in your shop.

Figure 12-13   How to use the Bind Package panel

How to set the defaults for binding packages

Figure 12-14 presents the Defaults For Bind Package panel that's displayed when option 7 in the previous panel is YES. Here, the entries that we recommend for binding packages are shown in the panel. For most programs, the entries for options 1 and 3 will maximize locking efficiency. If you've already read chapter 11, you may remember how the isolation level and release parameters can affect locking efficiency. Otherwise, you can study that chapter at a later time.

When you enter YES for option 4, DB2 stores explanatory information about the access paths that are used by all the SELECT, DELETE, UPDATE, and INSERT statements that the package uses. This information is stored in a table named PLAN_TABLE. Before you can use this option, though, you need to use the CREATE TABLE statement to create a starting version of PLAN_TABLE. In chapter 14, you can learn how to use SPUFI to do that. If this table hasn't been created, you should enter NO for option 4, which is acceptable in a training environment. Otherwise, you won't be able to bind the package.

Since the first options in this panel are the same as the first seven options in the Defaults For Bind Plan panel in figure 12-9, you may wonder what happens when the entries are different. If, for example, the isolation level in the bind plan panel is set to cursor stability (CS) but the package level is set to repeatable read (RR), what happens? This illustrates one of the benefits of using packages.

By specifying different parameters for packages and plans, many combinations of isolation level and resource release times are possible. For example, you can bind the PRSNLPLN plan with the recommended entries in figure 12-9. Then, to override those settings, you can bind an interactive program like P010 into a package with an isolation level of CS and bind a batch program into a package with an isolation level of RR. Because a combination of strategies isn't possible when you bind all programs directly into a plan, we recommend that you always bind programs into packages that are automatically bound into plans through collections.

The Defaults For Bind Package panel

```
MMA - EXTRA! for Windows 95/NT                                    _ 🗗 ✕
File  Edit  View  Tools  Session  Options  Help
                    DEFAULTS FOR BIND PACKAGE              SSID: DSN
COMMAND ===> _

Change default options as necessary:

 1   ISOLATION LEVEL ......... ===> CS        (RR, RS, CS, UR, or NC)
 2   VALIDATION TIME ......... ===> BIND      (RUN or BIND)
 3   RESOURCE RELEASE TIME ... ===> COMMIT    (COMMIT or DEALLOCATE)
 4   EXPLAIN PATH SELECTION .. ===> YES       (NO or YES)
 5   DATA CURRENCY ........... ===> NO        (NO or YES)
 6   PARALLEL DEGREE ......... ===> ANY       (1 or ANY)
 7   DYNAMIC RULES ........... ===> BIND      (RUN or BIND)
 8   SQLERROR PROCESSING ..... ===> NOPACKAGE (NOPACKAGE or CONTINUE)




PRESS:  ENTER to process    END to save and exit    HELP for more information
```

Entry recommendations

- The BIND PACKAGE parameters in the panel above usually produce the most efficient DB2 package.

Panel entries

Option	Entry
1	Sets the isolation level for the package (see figure 11-5).
2	Specifies whether DB2 should check the authorization at run time or bind time.
3	Sets the parameter for releasing locks (see figure 11-5).
4	Lets you get EXPLAIN information about how SQL statements in the package execute.
5	Lets you specify whether you need data currency for ambiguous cursors opened at remote locations. For more information, see "Maintaining Data Currency" in *DB2 for MVS/ESA V4 Application Programming and SQL Guide*.
6	Lets you run queries using parallel processing (ANY) or request that DB2 not execute queries in parallel (1).
7	Lets you specify whether run-time (RUN) or bind-time (BIND) rules apply to dynamic SQL statements at run time.
8	Lets you continue to create a package after finding SQL errors (CONTINUE) or avoid creating a package after finding SQL errors (NOPACKAGE).

Figure 12-14   How to set the defaults for the Bind Package function

How to compile and link a DB2 COBOL program

Figure 12-15 presents the panel for compiling and linking a COBOL program. Here, options 1 through 3 are for the compile step. Options 4 through 9 are for the link-edit step (although option 8 applies only to C programs). And options 10 through 12 are for the run step. However, since you usually run the program as a separate DB2I function or as a batch job, you don't need to make entries for the run options.

After you've made the entries to this panel, you press Enter to run the functions that you selected in the Program Preparation panel shown in figure 12-11. On that panel, the precompile, bind package, compile, and link functions are selected, and option 3 specifies that these functions are supposed to be run in the foreground. These functions are then done in that sequence.

As each function is done, completion messages or error messages are sent back to your terminal. If a function returns an error code that's greater than or equal to the STOP IF RETURN CODE value that's used as the DB2I default, all subsequent functions are cancelled. In this case, the error messages are usually informative enough to help you fix the problem. Then, you can go back to the Program Preparation panel, turn off any display panels that you don't need, and run the functions again. When the load module is successfully prepared, you're ready to test the program.

The Compile, Prelink, Link, and Run panel

```
 MMA - EXTRA! for Windows 95/NT                                    _ ⊡ ✕
 File  Edit  View  Tools  Session  Options  Help
                  PROGRAM PREP: COMPILE, PRELINK, LINK, AND RUN     SSID: DSN
 COMMAND ===> _

 Enter compiler or assembler options:
   1  INCLUDE LIBRARY ===> 'MM01.DB2.DCLGENS'
   2  INCLUDE LIBRARY ===>
   3  OPTIONS ....... ===>

 Enter prelink and linkage editor options:
   4  INCLUDE LIBRARY ===> 'MM01.DB2.DCLGENS'
   5  INCLUDE LIBRARY ===>
   6  INCLUDE LIBRARY ===>
   7  LOAD LIBRARY .. ===> 'MM01.DB2.LOADLIB'
   8  PRELINK OPTIONS ===>
   9  LINK OPTIONS .. ===>

 Enter run options:
  10  PARAMETERS .... ===>
  11  SYSIN DATA SET  ===> TERM
  12  SYSPRINT DS ... ===> TERM


 PRESS:  ENTER to process    END to save and exit    HELP for more information
```

Panel entries

Option	Entry
1-2	One or two names of libraries that contain members for the compiler to include. The members can be output from DCLGEN.
3	Any compiler options. If, for example, you want to dynamically link your program to subprograms at run time, you can enter DYNAM here.
4-6	Up to three names of libraries that contain members for the linkage editor to link. If you want to link your program to subprograms that you've created, you can enter the name of the library they're in.
7	The name of the library that should receive the load module. The default is RUNLIB.LOAD.
8	Blank. This applies only to programs using C.
9	A list of link-edit options that are separated by commas, spaces, or both.
10	A list of parameters that you want to pass to either the host-language run-time processor or to your program.
11	The name of the SYSIN data set, but the default (TERM) is usually okay.
12	The name of the SYSPRINT data set, but the default (TERM) is usually okay.

Figure 12-15   How to use the Compile, Prelink, Link, and Run panel

How to create and submit a separate program preparation job

Figure 12-16 presents a DB2 Program Preparation panel with option 3 set to EDITJCL. In this case, the job in the second panel in this figure is created and displayed when you press the Enter key at the Compile, Prelink, Link, and Run panel shown in the previous figure.

Although the job panel shows just the first 19 lines of the job, you can scroll through it to see all of the steps and all of the parameters that were created from the DB2I panels. You can also make changes to the JCL if that's necessary. At the top of this job, you can see the JOB statement that I entered into option 11 of the DB2 Defaults panel shown in figure 12-4.

By looking at the line above the command area, you can see the data set name that's created for this job. Here, the name is MM01.TEMP.CNTL. Since this data set is allocated and cataloged, you can access it through the standard TSO panels.

To submit this job, you type SUB in the command area and press the Enter key, just as you would for any other TSO job. Then, when the job is done, you can view the results of the job using a system display utility like the System Display and Search Facility (SDSF).

If you study the job created by DB2I, you may be surprised to see that the job stream doesn't invoke programs like the precompiler, compiler, and linkage editor. Instead, a single job step invokes a program named IKJEFT01, which is the name of the TSO *Terminal Monitor Program* (*TMP*). Then, the statements after the SYSTSIN DD statement are TSO statements and parameters that are processed by TMP. Although you can change any of these parameters before submitting the job, you shouldn't need to do that if you set the options right when you were working through the DB2I panels.

The Program Preparation panel for preparing a job

```
 MMA - EXTRA! for Windows 95/NT                                      _ |ᵈ|✕|

File  Edit  View  Tools  Session  Options  Help

                         DB2 PROGRAM PREPARATION              SSID: DSN
COMMAND ===> _

Enter the following:
 1  INPUT DATA SET NAME ....  ===>  'MM01.DB2.SOURCE(P010)'
 2  DATA SET NAME QUALIFIER   ===>  TEMP      (For building data set names)
 3  PREPARATION ENVIRONMENT   ===>  EDITJCL   (FOREGROUND, BACKGROUND, EDITJCL)
 4  RUN TIME ENVIRONMENT ...  ===>  TSO       (TSO, CAF, CICS, IMS)
 5  OTHER DSNH OPTIONS .....  ===>
                                             (Optional DSNH keywords)
Select functions:             Display panel?      Perform function?
 6  CHANGE DEFAULTS ........  ===>  N (Y/N)
 7  PL/I MACRO PHASE .......  ===>  N (Y/N)        ===>  N (Y/N)
 8  PRECOMPILE ............  ===>  Y (Y/N)        ===>  Y (Y/N)
 9  CICS COMMAND TRANSLATION                       ===>  N (Y/N)
10  BIND PACKAGE ..........  ===>  Y (Y/N)        ===>  Y (Y/N)
11  BIND PLAN .............  ===>  N (Y/N)        ===>  N (Y/N)
12  COMPILE OR ASSEMBLE ....  ===>  Y (Y/N)        ===>  Y (Y/N)
13  PRELINK ...............  ===>  N (Y/N)        ===>  N (Y/N)
14  LINK ..................  ===>  Y (Y/N)        ===>  Y (Y/N)
15  RUN ...................  ===>  N (Y/N)        ===>  N (Y/N)

PRESS:  ENTER to process    END to save and exit     HELP for more information
```

The job created by the Program Preparation panel

```
 MMA - EXTRA! for Windows 95/NT                                      _ |ᵈ|✕|

File  Edit  View  Tools  Session  Options  Help

  File   Edit   Confirm  Menu   Utilities   Compilers   Test   Help
---------------------------------------------------------------------------
EDIT      MM01.TEMP.CNTL                        Columns 00001 00072
Command ===> SUB_                                    Scroll ===> CSR
***** *************************** Top of Data ****************************
000001 //MM01S  JOB (99999),'C GARVIN',CLASS=C,MSGCLASS=X,
000002 //       REGION=4M,NOTIFY=&SYSUID
000003 //*
000004 //DSNHTMP  EXEC PGM=IKJEFT01,DYNAMNBR=20,REGION=4096K
000005 //SYSTSPRT DD SYSOUT=*
000006 //SYSPRINT DD SYSOUT=*
000007 //SYSUDUMP DD SYSOUT=*
000008 //SYSTSIN DD *
000009   PROFILE PREFIX(MM01)
000010   ALLOC DA('DSN410.SDSNCLST') F(SYSPROC) SHR
000011   %DSNH +
000012   MACRO(NO) +
000013   PRECOMP(YES) +
000014   CICSXLAT(NO) +
000015   PBIND(YES) +
000016   BIND(NO) +
000017   COMPILE(YES) +
000018   PRELINK(NO) +
000019   LINK(YES) +
```

Description

- In option 3 of the Program Preparation panel, enter EDITJCL.

- When you finish working your way through the program preparation panels, DB2I creates a job for doing the functions you've requested based on the options you've set. You can then modify the JCL, if that's necessary, and submit the job.

Figure 12-16   How to create and submit a program preparation job

How to run a program under DB2I

After you successfully precompile, bind, compile, and link your COBOL program, you're ready to test it. To do that, you use the Run panel shown in figure 12-17. To access this panel, you select option 6 in the DB2I Primary Option menu. Although you can also run a program as the last function done by the Program Preparation panel, it's usually better to run the program as a separate procedure.

How to allocate data sets

If your program uses any standard data sets like VSAM files, you need to allocate them before you execute the program. To do that, you use the TSO ALLOCATE command as shown in this figure. When you issue this command, you need to specify the name your program uses to refer to the data set and the name MVS uses to refer to it.

If your program uses ACCEPT and DISPLAY statements, you also need to provide a SYSIN allocation for the ACCEPT input and a SYSOUT allocation for the DISPLAY output. Since a TSO terminal is used for this input and output, two ALLOCATE commands with an asterisk as the value for the DSNAME option must be issued. This is illustrated by the two commands in the command area of this figure.

When you enter a native TSO command in this area, you must enter TSO before it. If you want to enter more than one command in this area, you can separate them with a semicolon. Then, when you press the Enter key for this panel, the allocations are performed, but the program isn't run. Instead, the Run panel is displayed again with an empty command area so you can key in more allocations if they're necessary.

How to run a program

When there is no command in the command area and you press the Enter key, the program is run using the entries given in the Run panel. In option 1, you need to enter the data set name for the load module that is to be executed. In option 2, you need to enter a password if the program is password protected. And in option 4, you need to enter the name of the application plan.

In addition, you can use option 3 to enter any parameters that you want passed to your program at execution time. This is similar to the parameters in a PARM card for a batch job. In option 5, you can tell DB2I how you want the program to be run.

After you run a program, control returns to DB2I, where a message appears on the Run panel that reports the status code for the run. Although this message isn't particularly useful when you run an interactive program like P010, it's helpful when you run a program that doesn't do any screen input or output. In that case, this message is the only feedback you get about the execution of your program.

The TSO ALLOC command in the RUN panel

```
MMA - EXTRA! for Windows 95/NT                                    _ 日 X
File  Edit  View  Tools  Session  Options  Help
                                    RUN                    SSID: DSN
===> TSO ALLOC F(SYSIN) DA(*); TSO ALLOC F(SYSOUT) DA(*)_

Enter the name of the program you want to run:
 1  DATA SET NAME ===> 'MM01.DB2.LOADLIB(P010)'
 2  PASSWORD .... ===>            (Required if data set is password protected)

Enter the following as desired:
 3  PARAMETERS .. ===>
 4  PLAN NAME ... ===> PRSNLPLN   (Required if different from program name)
 5  WHERE TO RUN  ===> FOREGROUND (FOREGROUND, BACKGROUND, or EDITJCL)








NOTE : Information for running command processors is on the HELP panel.
PRESS: ENTER to process     END to exit      HELP for information
```

How to allocate data sets

- Enter the TSO ALLOCATE command in the command area of the Run panel to allocate the data sets used by the program to be run. In the example above, SYSIN (for ACCEPT) and SYSOUT (for DISPLAY) data sets are allocated to the terminal.

- When you press the Enter key, the command in the command area is processed and you are returned to the Run panel. If necessary, you can then enter any other ALLOCATE commands that are required.

Panel entries

Option	Entry
1	The name the data set that contains the load module you want to run.
2	The password if the data set is password protected.
3	Any run-time parameters.
4	The plan name.
5	FOREGROUND, BACKGROUND, or EDITJCL to run the program in the foreground, to run it as a batch job in the background, or to create a job that you can edit and submit by yourself.

How to run the program

- Press the Enter key after all the panel entries have been made and all ALLOCATE commands have been processed so there's no command in the command area.

Figure 12-17   How to allocate data sets and run a program from the Run panel

Perspective

Although DB2I has many excellent features, some shops won't let you use it because it uses too many system resources. In other shops, you can use DB2I to do some, but not all, of the program preparation tasks. In particular, you may be required to test your programs as batch jobs.

In the next chapter, then, you can learn how to develop and test programs by using batch jobs and CLISTs instead of DB2I. As you will see, this is also an efficient way to do these tasks. In addition, it improves the overall performance of the system.

13

How to develop programs outside of DB2I

Even though DB2I provides a convenient way to do program development work, some shops restrict its use because it requires substantial system resources and thus can degrade overall system performance. In that case, you can submit batch jobs to precompile, compile, link, bind, and run your COBOL programs. As you will see in this chapter, though, using batch jobs is also the most efficient way to do some development functions.

If you know how to use TSO and MVS JCL, you should have little difficulty adapting the job streams and CLIST presented in this chapter to your own system. If you need more information about TSO or MVS JCL, though, please refer to two of our other books: *MVS TSO, Part 2: Command and Procedures* and *MVS JCL*.

How to use batch jobs for developing programs

In the last chapter, you learned how to use the DB2I panels to bind plans and packages and to precompile, compile, and link-edit a program. Now, you can learn how to use JCL and a cataloged procedure for these functions.

How to use JCL to bind a plan

Figure 13-1 presents the JCL for a job that binds all the packages in two collections to a plan named PRSNLPLN. The only step in this job runs a program named IKJEFT01. This is the generic program name for the TSO *Terminal Monitor Program* (*TMP*), and all DB2 batch jobs must run through this program. Later in this chapter, you'll see that you can use the name IKJEFT1B when you want to run a batch application program through TMP.

To run a DB2 command under TMP, you issue the DSN command, which invokes the DSN command processor. Once this processor is running, you can issue subcommands like the RUN and BIND subcommands. To terminate the DSN command processor, you issue the END subcommand.

In the job in this figure, the first command after the SYSTSIN DD statement is the DSN command. This is followed by a RUN subcommand that runs a program named DSNTEP2, which is a program that allows dynamic SQL statements to be processed. Although this book doesn't present dynamic SQL, it's often a shop standard to run DSNTEP2 in all bind jobs. In *Part 2* of this DB2 series, you can learn how to use dynamic SQL in your programs.

The second DSN subcommand in this job is the BIND subcommand, which includes a long list of parameters. In the package list parameter (PKLIST), you can see the names of two collections followed by wildcards (PYRLCOL.*, BNFTCOL.*). This means that the plan should include all of the packages in those collections plus any packages that are added to those collections in the future. This means that this plan won't ever have to be bound again unless another collection of packages is added to the plan.

After this parameter, you can see the parameters that are the same as those entered in the DB2I panel in figure 12-9. When you bind a plan through DB2I, of course, it constructs the required control statements based on the values you entered in the Bind panel. When you use a JCL procedure, though, you must make sure that it includes the correct parameters.

JCL that binds a plan

```
//MM01P    JOB  (99999),CURTIS.GARVIN,CLASS=C,MSGCLASS=X,
//              REGION=4M,NOTIFY=&SYSUID
//*------------------------------------------------------------------*
//*    BIND DB2 PLAN                                                  *
//*------------------------------------------------------------------*
//BIND     EXEC PGM=IKJEFT01,DYNAMNBR=20,COND=(4,LT)
//DBRMLIB   DD DSN=MM01.DB2.DBRMLIB,DISP=SHR
//SYSTSPRT  DD SYSOUT=*
//SYSPRINT  DD SYSOUT=*
//SYSUDUMP  DD SYSOUT=*
//SYSOUT    DD SYSOUT=*
//REPORT    DD SYSOUT=*
//SYSIN     DD *
//SYSTSIN   DD *
 DSN SYSTEM(DSN)
 RUN  PROGRAM(DSNTEP2) PLAN(DSNTEP41) LIB('DSN410.RUNLIB.LOAD')
 END
 DSN SYSTEM(DSN)
 BIND PLAN        (PRSNLPLN)   -
   PKLIST         (PYRLCOL.*, BNFTCOL.*) -
   ISOLATION      (CS)         -
   VALIDATE       (BIND)       -
   RELEASE        (COMMIT)     -
   EXPLAIN        (YES)        -
   CURRENTDATA    (NO)         -
   DEGREE         (ANY)        -
   DYNAMICRULES   (RUN)        -
   ACQUIRE        (USE)        -
   NODEFER        (PREPARE)    -
   SQLRULES       (DB2)        -
   DISCONNECT     (EXPLICIT)   -
   ACTION         (REPLACE)    -
   RETAIN                      -
   FLAG           (I)          -
   QUALIFIER      (MM01)       -
   CACHESIZE      (4096)       -
   OWNER          (MM01)
 END
//
```

Description

- The JCL in the job above can be used to bind a plan using the bind strategy and parameters shown in figures 12-2 and 12-9 of the previous chapter.

- In the bind strategy, the bind plan named PRSNLPLN plan includes collections named PYRLCOL and BNFTCOL. Since the package list (PKLIST) for these collections uses wildcards (PYRLCOL.* and BNFTCOL.*), all packages that are bound to either collection will automatically be bound to the PRSNLPLN plan. By using this strategy, the plan will only have to be rebound if a new collection is added to it.

- In the bind step of the job, a program named IKJEFT01 is run. This is the name of the TSO *Terminal Monitor Program* (*TMP*), and all batch jobs must run through it.

- Within the bind step after the SYSTSIN DD statement, the DSN command is run twice. This invokes the command processor that executes the RUN, BIND PLAN, and END subcommands.

Figure 13-1   The JCL for binding a plan

How to use a DB2 procedure for program development

DB2 provides two cataloged procedures that you can use to precompile, compile, and link COBOL programs: DSNHCOB (for OS/VS COBOL) and DSNHCOB2 (for VS COBOL II). Since most shops today use VS COBOL II or a later compiler, figure 13-2 presents only the DSNHCOB2 procedure. If your shop is still using OS/VS COBOL, though, you can look in your system library (SYS1.PROCLIB) for DSNHCOB or ask your database administrator for its location.

As you can see in this figure, the first step in this PROC executes the precompiler program, DSNHPC. The second step executes the COBOL compiler. And the third step executes the linkage editor to create the load module. When you run this procedure, you need to issue the DD statements that give the locations of the data sets that are needed in each step.

The DSNHCOB2 procedure that precompiles, compiles, and link-edits a COBOL program

```
//*********************************************************************
//*          DSNHCOB2 - COMPILE AND LINKEDIT A COBOL PROGRAM
//*
//DSNHCOB2 PROC WSPC=500,MEM=TEMPNAME,USER=USER,
// COMPDSN='COB2.COB2COMP',
// CICSDSN='CICS410.SDFHCOB',
// DB2QUAL='DSN410',
// CICSQUAL='CICS410'
//*
//*                PRECOMPILE THE COBOL PROGRAM
//*********************************************************************
//PC       EXEC PGM=DSNHPC,PARM='HOST(COB2)',REGION=4096K
//DBRMLIB  DD   DSN=&USER..DBRMLIB.DATA(&MEM),DISP=SHR
//STEPLIB  DD   DSN=&DB2QUAL..DSNEXIT,DISP=SHR
//         DD   DSN=&DB2QUAL..DSNLOAD,DISP=SHR
//SYSCIN   DD   DSN=&&DSNHOUT,DISP=(MOD,PASS),UNIT=SYSDA,
//              SPACE=(800,(&WSPC,&WSPC))
//SYSLIB   DD   DSN=&USER..SRCLIB.DATA,DISP=SHR
//SYSPRINT DD   SYSOUT=*
//SYSTERM  DD   SYSOUT=*
//SYSUDUMP DD   SYSOUT=*
//SYSUT1   DD   SPACE=(800,(&WSPC,&WSPC),,,ROUND),UNIT=SYSDA
//SYSUT2   DD   SPACE=(800,(&WSPC,&WSPC),,,ROUND),UNIT=SYSDA
//*
//*                COMPILE THE COBOL PROGRAM IF THE PRECOMPILE
//*                RETURN CODE IS 4 OR LESS
//*
//COB      EXEC PGM=IGYCRCTL,COND=(4,LT,PC)
//SYSIN    DD   DSN=&&DSNHOUT,DISP=(OLD,DELETE)
//STEPLIB  DD   DSN=&COMPDSN,DISP=SHR
//SYSLIB   DD   DSN=&CICSDSN,DISP=SHR
//SYSLIN   DD   DSN=&&LOADSET,DISP=(MOD,PASS),UNIT=SYSDA,
//              SPACE=(800,(&WSPC,&WSPC))
//SYSPRINT DD   SYSOUT=*
//SYSUDUMP DD   SYSOUT=*
//SYSUT1   DD   SPACE=(800,(&WSPC,&WSPC),,,ROUND),UNIT=SYSDA
//SYSUT2   DD   SPACE=(800,(&WSPC,&WSPC),,,ROUND),UNIT=SYSDA
//SYSUT3   DD   SPACE=(800,(&WSPC,&WSPC),,,ROUND),UNIT=SYSDA
//SYSUT4   DD   SPACE=(800,(&WSPC,&WSPC),,,ROUND),UNIT=SYSDA
//SYSUT5   DD   SPACE=(800,(&WSPC,&WSPC),,,ROUND),UNIT=SYSDA
//SYSUT6   DD   SPACE=(800,(&WSPC,&WSPC),,,ROUND),UNIT=SYSDA  COB2 V1R3
//SYSUT7   DD   SPACE=(800,(&WSPC,&WSPC),,,ROUND),UNIT=SYSDA  COB2 V1R3
//*
//*                LINKEDIT IF THE PRECOMPILE AND COMPILE
//*                RETURN CODES ARE 4 OR LESS
//*
//LKED     EXEC PGM=IEWL,PARM='XREF',
//              COND=((4,LT,COB),(4,LT,PC))
//SYSLIB   DD   DSN=SYS1.COB2LIB,DISP=SHR
//         DD   DSN=&DB2QUAL..DSNLOAD,DISP=SHR
//         DD   DSN=&CICSQUAL..SDFHLOAD,DISP=SHR
//SYSLIN   DD   DSN=&&LOADSET,DISP=(OLD,DELETE)
//         DD   DDNAME=SYSIN
//SYSLMOD  DD   DSN=&USER..RUNLIB.LOAD(&MEM),DISP=SHR
//SYSPRINT DD   SYSOUT=*
//SYSUDUMP DD   SYSOUT=*
//SYSUT1   DD   SPACE=(1024,(50,50)),UNIT=SYSDA
//*DSNHCOB2 PEND            REMOVE * FOR USE AS INSTREAM PROCEDURE
```

Figure 13-2   The DSNHCOB2 procedure

The required DDNAMES for the DSNHCOB2 procedure

Figure 13-3 presents the DDNAMES that you need to know for the DSNHCOB2 procedure. For the precompile step (PC), you must provide DD statements for the source program, the DCLGEN output, and the DBRM that's created. For the compile step (COB), you must provide a DD statement for the COPY library if your program uses any COPY members. For the link-edit step (LKED), you must provide a DD statement for the load module and in some shops a statement for linkage-editor control statements.

The required DDNAMES for the DSNHCOB2 procedure

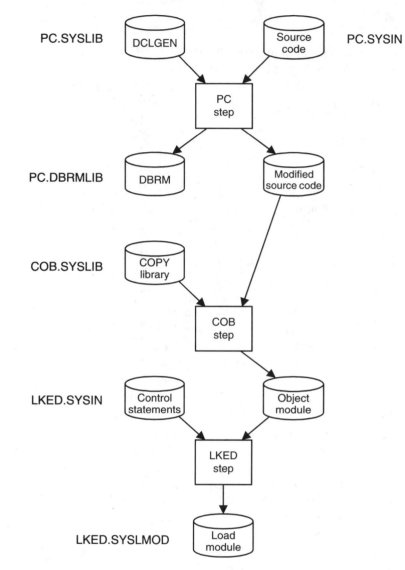

Description

- For the precompile step (PC), you must provide a DD statement for SYSIN (the COBOL source code), SYSLIB (for the members your program requests with SQL INCLUDE statements), and DBRMLIB (for the DBRM the procedure creates).

- For the compile step (COB), you must provide a DD statement for SYSLIB if your program copies any members from the COPY library.

- For the link-edit step (LKED), you must provide a DD statement for SYSLMOD (the load module that's created). However, you only need to provide a DD statement for SYSIN if you're going to provide linkage-editor control statements, which is site specific.

Figure 13-3   The required DDNAMES for the DSNHCOB2 procedure

How to use JCL to run the DSNHCOB2 procedure and bind a package

Figure 13-4 presents a two-step job that runs the DSNHCOB2 procedure. The first step runs the DSNHCOB2 procedure. Then, if this first step runs successfully, the second step binds the program to a package with a collection ID that includes the package in the plan.

The first EXEC statement in this job executes the DSNHCOB2 procedure. This is followed by the DD statements (shaded) that override or add to the DD statements in the procedure. For instance, the PC.DBRMLIB DD statement overrides the DBRMLIB DD statement in the precompile step of the DSNHCOB2 procedure. In contrast, the PC.SYSIN DD statement in this job doesn't have a matching statement in the precompile step of the DSNHCOB2 procedure so it gets added to the procedure. This statement identifies the data set that contains the source program.

The second EXEC statement in this job executes the IKJEFT01 program that invokes the Terminal Monitor Program (TMP). Then, after the DD statement for SYSTSIN, the job includes the DSN command and subcommands for binding the package. For the BIND PACKAGE subcommand, the collection ID is PYRLCOL and the member name is P010. This binds the P010 application program to the PRSNLPLN plan that's bound in figure 13-1. Note, however, that the plan must be bound before the package if this is to work correctly.

If your COBOL program uses subprograms, you can either link them to your program dynamically at run time or link them during the link-edit step of the DSNHCOB2 procedure. To link them dynamically, you just need to make sure that the DYNAM parameter is set for the COBOL compiler. To link them during the link-edit step, you need to provide statements like these:

```
//LKED.SYSLIB    DD   DSN=SYS1.COB2LIB,DISP=SHR
//               DD   DSN=&DB2QUAL..DSNLOAD,DISP=SHR
//               DD   DSN=&CICSQUAL..SDFHLOAD,DISP=SHR
//               DD   DSN=MMA.SUBLIB,DISP=SHR
```

Here, the first three statements are the same as the DD statements for SYSLIB in the link-edit step of the DSNHCOB2 procedure. Then, the fourth statement concatenates your subprogram library to the first three libraries. And all four libraries override the three libraries in the DSNHCOB2 procedure. On most systems, though, it's okay to link the subprograms dynamically.

JCL that invokes the DSNHCOB2 procedure and binds a package

```
//MM01C    JOB   (99999),CURTIS.GARVIN,CLASS=C,MSGCLASS=X,
//               REGION=4M,NOTIFY=&SYSUID
//*------------------------------------------------------------------*
//* BATCH COBOL2, DB2 AND LINK. PLAN BIND.
//*------------------------------------------------------------------*
//JOBLIB   DD   DSN=DSN410.SDSNEXIT,DISP=SHR
//         DD   DSN=DSN410.SDSNLOAD,DISP=SHR
//*------------------------------------------------------------------*
// EXEC DSNHCOB2,MEM=TEMPNAME,USER='MM01',
//    PARM.PC='HOST(COB2),APOST,APOSTSQL,SOURCE,XREF',
//    PARM.COB=('OBJECT,APOST,MAP,XREF,NONUM,OFF,FLAG(I,E),TRUNC(BIN)', X
//              'LIB,RES,DYNAM'),
//    PARM.LKED='LIST,XREF,LET,AMODE=24'
//*------------------------------------------------------------------*
//PC.DBRMLIB DD DSN=MM01.DB2.DBRMLIB(P010),DISP=SHR
//PC.SYSLIB  DD DSN=MM01.DB2.DCLGENS,DISP=SHR
//PC.SYSIN   DD DSN=MM01.DB2.SOURCE(P010),DISP=SHR
//*------------------------------------------------------------------*
//COB.SYSLIB DD DSN=MM01.DB2.COPYLIB,DISP=SHR
//*------------------------------------------------------------------*
//LKED.SYSLMOD DD DSN=MM01.DB2.LOADLIB(P010),DISP=SHR
//*------------------------------------------------------------------*
//BIND     EXEC PGM=IKJEFT01,DYNAMNBR=20,COND=(4,LT)
//DBRMLIB    DD DSN=MM01.DB2.DBRMLIB,DISP=SHR
//SYSTSPRT   DD SYSOUT=*
//SYSPRINT   DD SYSOUT=*
//SYSUDUMP   DD SYSOUT=*
//SYSOUT     DD SYSOUT=*
//REPORT     DD SYSOUT=*
//SYSTSIN    DD *
 DSN SYSTEM(DSN)
 RUN  PROGRAM(DSNTEP2) PLAN(DSNTEP41) LIB('DSN410.RUNLIB.LOAD')
 END
 DSN SYSTEM(DSN)
 BIND PACKAGE     (PYRLCOL)      MEMBER      (P010)       -
   ISOLATION      (CS)           VALIDATE    (BIND)       -
   RELEASE        (COMMIT)       EXPLAIN     (YES)        -
   CURRENTDATA    (NO)           DEGREE      (ANY)        -
   DYNAMICRULES   (BIND)         SQLERROR    (NOPACKAGE)  -
   ACTION         (REPLACE)      FLAG        (I)          -
   QUALIFIER      (MM01)         OWNER       (MM01)
 END
//
```

Description

- To adjust this JCL to your system, code the proper DD statements for the PC, COB, and LKED steps of the DSNHCOB2 procedure. These are the shaded statements above.

- When you bind a package to a collection as in this example, the package is automatically bound to the plan that contains the collection. Note, however, that the plan must be bound before the package.

- The bind parameters above are the same as the ones in the DB2I panel in figure 12-14 of the previous chapter.

Figure 13-4   The JCL for invoking the DSNHCOB2 procedure and binding a package

How to run a DB2 COBOL program

In the last chapter, you learned how to execute an interactive program using DB2I. As you may recall, it was a bit cumbersome to allocate the SYSIN and SYSOUT data sets to your TSO terminal. This gets even more cumbersome, though, when you have to allocate several data sets for a batch program. And to make this worse, you have to re-enter those ALLOCATE statements each time you run the program because they aren't saved by DB2I.

Because of these limitations, it's usually better to use a CLIST or JCL to test a program. This has the added benefit of running more efficiently than it does through DB2I.

How to use a CLIST to run a DB2 program

Figure 13-5 presents a TSO CLIST for running an interactive program. After the ALLOCATE statements for terminal input and display, this CLIST issues the DSN command and its RUN subcommand. This subcommand runs the load module for program P010, which was bound to the PRSNLPLN plan.

If the program doesn't work right when you test it, you can change the program and rerun the job in the previous figure to prepare a new load module without having to change that job. Then, you can rerun the CLIST in this figure without having to change the CLIST.

How to use JCL to run a DB2 program

Although CLISTs are okay for running interactive programs that don't use many data sets, it's usually better to use JCL for running a program when it uses several data sets. This is illustrated by the second example in figure 13-5 (even though it requires only one data set for printed output). This job runs the INVREG program, which produces a printed invoice register.

In the RUN step for this job, the program named IKJEFT1B is used to invoke the Terminal Monitor Program instead of the program named IKJEFT01 that was used in figure 13-1. That's because the IKJEFT01 program doesn't return the codes for system errors or user abends, which makes it difficult to perform error checking in subsequent JCL steps. In contrast, IKJEFT1B does pass non-zero return codes through to JES where they can be checked in the JCL job stream.

Here again, if the program doesn't work right when you test it, you can change the program and rerun the job in the previous figure to prepare a new load module without having to change that job. Then, you can rerun the job in this figure without having to change it. In other words, once you've got your jobs and CLISTs set up right, it's easier to use them for program development than it is to use DB2I.

A CLIST that runs the P010 program

```
ALLOCATE F(SYSIN) DA(*)
ALLOCATE F(SYSOUT) DA(*)
DSN SYSTEM(DSN)
  RUN PROGRAM(P010)   -
      PLAN(PRSNLPLN)  -
      LIBRARY('MM01.DB2.LOADLIB')
  END
FREE F(SYSIN)
FREE F(SYSOUT)
```

JCL that runs the INVREG program

```
//MM01R    JOB   (99999),'CURTIS GARVIN',CLASS=C,MSGCLASS=X,
//               REGION=4M,NOTIFY=&SYSUID
//*-------------------------------------------------------------*
//* BATCH JOB TO RUN A DB2 PROGRAM.
//*-------------------------------------------------------------*
//JOBLIB   DD   DISP=SHR,DSN=DSN410.SDSNEXIT
//         DD   DISP=SHR,DSN=DSN410.SDSNLOAD
//*-------------------------------------------------------------*
//DEL1     EXEC PGM=IEFBR14
//DD1         DD DSN=MM01.PRTOUT.FILE,DISP=(MOD,DELETE,DELETE),
//               UNIT=SYSDA,SPACE=(TRK,(0))
//*-------------------------------------------------------------*
//RUN      EXEC PGM=IKJEFT1B,DYNAMNBR=20
//STEPLIB  DD DSN=MM01.DB2.LOADLIB,DISP=SHR
//PRTOUT   DD DSN=MM01.PRTOUT.FILE,DISP=(NEW,CATLG,DELETE),
//               UNIT=SYSDA,VOL=SER=LIB788,SPACE=(TRK,(1,1)),
//               DCB=(RECFM=FBA,LRECL=133,BLKSIZE=133)
//SYSTSPRT DD SYSOUT=*
//SYSOUT   DD SYSOUT=*
//SYSTSIN  DD *
DSN SYSTEM(DSN)
 RUN  PROGRAM(INVREG)    -
      PLAN(MM01PLAN)     -
      LIB('MM01.DB2.LOADLIB')
 END
/*
```

Description

- You can run a program using either the TSO CLIST or the JCL shown above. For either to work properly, you must provide three options for the RUN subcommand: (1) the name of the program that you want to run; (2) the name of the application plan that contains the package (or program); and (3) the name of the library that contains the load module for the program.

- To run a DB2 application program in batch mode, you must use the TSO Terminal Monitor Program (TMP) to invoke the DSN command. Although the generic name for this program is IKJEFT01, this program doesn't return the codes for system errors and user abends. As a result, you normally use IKJEFT1B when you want these codes returned. This program passes non-zero return codes through to JES where they can be checked in the JCL job stream.

Figure 13-5   The CLIST and JCL for running a DB2 COBOL program

Perspective

Now that you've seen both ways of developing DB2 programs, I think you'll agree that there are benefits and disadvantages to both. When you use DB2I, you can easily step through the panels that you need for program development, but this requires substantial system resources. When you use JCL and CLISTs, the initial setup takes longer, but you can reuse the jobs and lists without change. No matter which method you use, though, you should always check the bind parameters for your packages and plans to make sure they maximize locking efficiency.

How to use SPUFI

In chapter 12, you learned how to use DB2I for binding, precompiling, compiling, linking, and testing your COBOL programs. In this chapter, you can learn how to use DB2's SPUFI option. This feature lets you enter SQL statements at a TSO terminal for immediate processing, and then browse the results of those statements. You can use this feature to test SQL statements before you use them in your COBOL programs and to create the tables that you need for testing your programs.

Introduction to SPUFI

SPUFI is an acronym for *SQL Processor Using File Input*. It lets you enter SQL statements at a TSO terminal for immediate processing, and then browse the results that are returned by those statements. This lets you test SQL statements at your terminal before you use them in your COBOL programs. It also lets you create the tables that you need for testing your COBOL programs.

How to use the main SPUFI panel

To access SPUFI, you select option 1 in the DB2I Primary Options menu shown in figure 12-3. The main SPUFI panel shown in figure 14-1 is then displayed.

In options 1-3 of this panel, you identify the data set used for the SQL statements that you're going to run. If you don't code the name of this data set in quotes, TSO adds your user-id to it as a qualifier. Because your SQL statements are saved in this data set, you can easily retrieve, modify, and re-run them at a later time.

In option 4, you identify the data set that will receive the results of the SQL statements. Here again, if you don't code the name of this data set in quotes, your user-id gets added to it as a qualifier. If the output data set already exists, DB2 will replace the old data with the data for the current session.

In options 5-9, you select the processing options that you want performed by setting each option to YES or NO. In this example, all five options are selected. Because you only need to set the defaults once, though, you usually don't select option 5. Similarly, you may not want to use option 8, which automatically commits the statements you run.

When you press the Enter key for this panel, SPUFI does the functions that you selected and presents any related panels as they are needed. Then, when you end your SPUFI session, the values that you used in this main SPUFI panel are retained. As a result, you can easily pick up where you left off when you start a new SPUFI session.

The main SPUFI panel

```
MMA - EXTRA! for Windows 95/NT                                   _ |□|×
File  Edit  View  Tools  Session  Options  Help
                        SPUFI                        SSID: DSN
===>  _

Enter the input data set name:       (Can be sequential or partitioned)
 1   DATA SET NAME ... ===> 'MM01.SPUFI.INPUT(DEMO1)'
 2   VOLUME SERIAL ... ===>           (Enter if not cataloged)
 3   DATA SET PASSWORD ===>           (Enter if password protected)

Enter the output data set name:      (Must be a sequential data set)
 4   DATA SET NAME ... ===> 'MM01.SPUFI.OUTPUT'

Specify processing options:
 5   CHANGE DEFAULTS   ===> YES       (Y/N - Display SPUFI defaults panel?)
 6   EDIT INPUT ...... ===> YES       (Y/N - Enter SQL statements?)
 7   EXECUTE ......... ===> YES       (Y/N - Execute SQL statements?)
 8   AUTOCOMMIT ...... ===> YES       (Y/N - Commit after successful run?)
 9   BROWSE OUTPUT ... ===> YES       (Y/N - Browse output data set?)

For remote SQL processing:
10   CONNECT LOCATION  ===>


PRESS:  ENTER to process     END to exit          HELP for more information
```

Panel entries

Option	Entry
1	The name of the data set that contains your SPUFI input. This data set can be partitioned or sequential with a logical record length (LRECL) of 79 or 80 bytes, a record format (RECFM) of F or FB, and it must already exist.
2	The volume serial number, if the data set isn't cataloged.
3	The data set password if the data set is password protected.
4	The name of the data set to receive the SPUFI output. If the data set exists, the contents are replaced; otherwise, the data set is created.
5	No, assuming you don't want to change the SPUFI defaults. The first time you use SPUFI, however, you should check the defaults to make sure they are acceptable.
6	Yes, so you can edit the SQL statements.
7	Yes, so the SQL statements are executed.
8	Yes, if you want SPUFI to automatically issue a COMMIT statement if all of the SQL statements run successfully and a ROLLBACK statement if any of the SQL statements fail. No, if you want SPUFI to display the COMMIT OR ROLLBACK panel after it runs the SQL statements (see figure 14-6).
9	Yes, so you can browse the output data set created by SPUFI.
10	Leave blank, unless the SQL statements are to run on an application server other than the default server.

Figure 14-1   How to use the main SPUFI panel

How to set the SPUFI defaults

Figure 14-2 presents the Defaults panel that's displayed for option 5 in the main SPUFI panel. In option 1, you set the isolation level for your statements, which should usually be CS. If you haven't read chapter 11 yet, you'll understand what this means after you do.

In option 2, you enter a number that limits the number of lines that are returned by the SQL statements that are processed. Here, the default is 250, which is usually more than enough to tell whether your SQL statements have worked correctly.

In options 3 through 6, you can change the attributes that SPUFI uses when it creates an output data set. Normally, though, there's no reason to change the defaults that are shown in this figure. If a row contains more characters than can fit in a record of the output data set, SPUFI truncates it, but that's not likely to happen when the record length is 4092.

In options 7 and 8, you set the defaults that determine the maximum number of output characters that are provided for numeric or character values in a column. If, for example, you change option 7 to a value of 10, all numeric values that exceed 10 characters (including a decimal point and leading plus or minus sign) are replaced by asterisks. Or, if you change option 8 to a value of 20, all character fields that are longer than 20 characters are truncated. Up to these maximums, DB2 provides the number of output characters that correspond to the data definition for each column.

In option 9, you tell SPUFI what you want in the column headings for the output. When you use NAMES for this option, SPUFI uses the column names in the database as the column headings, which is usually what you want. If you use LABELS for this option, SPUFI uses the values provided by LABELS ON statements. And if you use BOTH, both names and labels are used as the column headings.

The Current SPUFI Defaults panel

```
MMA - EXTRA! for Windows 95/NT                                    _ 8 X
File  Edit  View  Tools  Session  Options  Help
                      CURRENT SPUFI DEFAULTS              SSID: DSN
===>  _

Enter the following to control your SPUFI session:
  1  ISOLATION LEVEL   ===> CS        (RR=Repeatable Read, CS=Cursor Stability)
  2  MAX SELECT LINES  ===> 250       (Maximum number of lines to be
                                         returned from a SELECT)
Output data set characteristics:
  3  RECORD LENGTH ... ===> 4092      (LRECL=Logical record length)
  4  BLOCK SIZE ...... ===> 4096      (Size of one block)
  5  RECORD FORMAT ... ===> VB        (RECFM=F, FB, FBA, V, VB, or VBA)
  6  DEVICE TYPE ..... ===> SYSDA     (Must be DASD unit name)

Output format characteristics:
  7  MAX NUMERIC FIELD ===> 33        (Maximum width for numeric fields)
  8  MAX CHAR FIELD .. ===> 80        (Maximum width for character fields)
  9  COLUMN HEADING .. ===> NAMES     (NAMES, LABELS, ANY or BOTH)




PRESS:  ENTER to process    END to exit           HELP for more information
```

Panel entries

Option	Entry
1	You should always specify CS (Cursor Stability) as the isolation level for SPUFI. If you require RR (Repeatable Read) isolation, you should probably be accessing the data through a COBOL program, not SPUFI.
2	The maximum number of output lines that a SELECT statement can return. The default (250) is usually adequate.
3	The record length of the output data set. It must be at least 80 bytes and the default value creates a 4092-byte record.
4	The block size of the output data set. Use the normal rules for selecting a block size. For record format F, the block size is equal to the record length. For FB and FBA, choose a block size that is an even multiple of the record length. For VB and VBA, the block size must be 4 bytes larger than the block size for FB or FBA.
5	The record format of the output data set. The default (VB) is usually okay.
6	A standard MVS name for a direct-access storage device. The default (SYSDA) specifies that MVS will select an appropriate direct-access storage device.
7	The maximum width of a numeric value in the output data set.
8	The maximum width of a character value in the output data set.
9	NAMES, to use the column names in the DB2 tables as the column headings in the browse output.

Figure 14-2   How to set the SPUFI defaults

How to use the Edit panel

Figure 14-3 presents the Edit panel that's displayed for option 6 in the main SPUFI panel with three SQL statements entered into it. Since SPUFI uses the ISPF editor, you shouldn't have any trouble entering or modifying statements in this panel if you already know how to use this editor. However, you do have to follow the rules for entering SQL statements that are provided in this figure.

When you have the statements the way you want them, press the PF3 key to save the statements in the data set and continue the processing for the options that you selected in the main SPUFI panel. This returns you to that panel with an asterisk (*) in place of the YES you entered for the Edit Input function. This means that option will be bypassed when you continue processing.

To continue with the next function that you've selected, press the Enter key. If that function is to run the SQL statements, you may experience a delay before the next panel is displayed. The extent of the delay, of course, depends on the statements, the size of the tables involved, and so on. If this delay is excessive, you can press the PA1 key to cancel the processing. Then, you can review the statements to make sure you didn't make an unreasonable request.

The Edit panel

```
🖳 MMA - EXTRA! for Windows 95/NT                                    _ 🗗 ✕

File  Edit  View  Tools  Session  Options  Help
─────────────────────────────────────────────────────────────────
  File   Edit  Confirm  Menu  Utilities  Compilers  Test  Help
─────────────────────────────────────────────────────────────────
EDIT       MM01.SPUFI.INPUT(DEMO1) - 01.10          Columns 00001 00072
Command ===> _                                      Scroll ===> CSR
****** *************************** Top of Data ******************************
000100 --
000200 -- THIS SQL STATEMENT SELECTS ALL OF THE CUSTOMERS WHO LIVE
000300 -- IN VIRGINIA
000400   SELECT *
000500      FROM MM01.CUSTOMER
000600      WHERE STATE = 'VA';
000700 --
000800 -- THIS SQL STATEMENT CHANGES ALL '94114' ZIP CODES TO '94122'
000900   UPDATE MM01.CUSTOMER
001000      SET ZIPCODE = '94122'
001100      WHERE ZIPCODE = '94114';
001200 --
001300 -- THIS SQL STATEMENT ROLLS BACK THE CHANGES MADE BY ALL OF THE
001400 -- PREVIOUS SQL STATEMENTS
001500   ROLLBACK;
****** *************************** Bottom of Data ***************************
```

Description

- When this panel is displayed, its contents depend on the data set and member you specified in the main SPUFI panel. If the member exists, the contents of that member are displayed. Otherwise, an empty ISPF edit panel is displayed so you can enter the SQL statements that you want to run.

- When you finish entering or editing the SQL statements, press the PF3 key to save them in the data set that you specified. This returns you to the main SPUFI panel with an asterisk (*) in option 6 (Edit Input). This means that this option will be bypassed when you press the Enter key.

- To continue processing the options in the main SPUFI panel that are indicated by YES, press the Enter key. Or, press the PF3 key to terminate the SPUFI session without executing the SQL statements.

- If the SQL statements are taking a long time to execute, you can press the PA1 key to cancel processing.

Rules for entering SQL statements

- Don't enter more than one SQL statement on a single line. If you do, DB2 ignores all but the first statement.

- End each SQL statement with a semicolon (;), which tells SPUFI that the statement is complete.

- Use two hyphens to begin a comment. Then, DB2 treats everything to the right of the hyphens as comments.

Figure 14-3   How to use the Edit panel

How to use the Browse panel

Figure 14-4 presents the Browse panel that's displayed for option 9 in the main SPUFI panel when the processing of the SQL statements finishes. For each SQL statement, you can see the statement, the results that are returned for that statement, the run-time messages for that statement, and a completion message that gives the SQLCODE value.

In this figure, for example, you can see the SELECT statement that is the first statement in the Edit panel. Then, you can see the column headings and the one row of output that it returned, followed by one run-time message that tells the number of rows displayed and a completion message that gives the SQLCODE value. You can also see the start of the output for the second statement in the Edit panel.

In the result table that's displayed for the SELECT statement, you can see how the column names are used as column headings. You can also see that the column widths correspond to the data definitions for each column in the table with two blank characters between the columns. Since CUSTNO is defined as CHAR(6) and FNAME is defined as CHAR(18), for example, six characters are provided for the first column and 18 for the second column. Note, however, that the column widths are limited to the maximums set in the Defaults panel.

To browse the data in a data set, you use the standard ISPF function keys to scroll right, left, up, or down. Then, to end the browse process, you can press the standard key for ending a function (PF3).

The Browse panel

```
 MMA - EXTRA! for Windows 95/NT                                    _ ⊡ ✕

 File  Edit  View  Tools  Session  Options  Help

   Menu   Utilities   Compilers   Help
 ---------------------------------------------------------------------
 BROWSE    MM01.SPUFI.OUTPUT                    Line 00000000 Col 001 080
 Command ===> _                                        Scroll ===> CSR
 *************************** Top of Data ********************************
 ---------+---------+---------+---------+---------+---------+---------+
 --                                                             00010001
 -- THIS SQL STATEMENT SELECTS ALL OF THE CUSTOMERS WHO LIVE    00020011
 -- IN VIRGINIA                                                 00030011
   SELECT *                                                     00040001
     FROM MM01.CUSTOMER                                         00050009
     WHERE STATE = 'VA';                                        00060010
 ---------+---------+---------+---------+---------+---------+---------+
 CUSTNO  FNAME                LNAME                 ADDR
 ---------+---------+---------+---------+---------+---------+---------+
 400010  ENRIQUE              OTHON                 BOX 26729
 DSNE610I NUMBER OF ROWS DISPLAYED IS 1
 DSNE616I STATEMENT EXECUTION WAS SUCCESSFUL, SQLCODE IS 100
 ---------+---------+---------+---------+---------+---------+---------+
 --                                                             00070001
 -- THIS SQL STATEMENT CHANGES ALL '94114' ZIP CODES TO '94122' 00080001
   UPDATE MM01.CUSTOMER                                         00090001
     SET ZIPCODE = '94122'                                      00100001
     WHERE ZIPCODE = '94114';                                   00110001
```

Description

- If option 9 (Browse Output) is set to YES in the main SPUFI panel, SPUFI formats and displays an output data set using the ISPF Browse program. In the panel above, you can see the first 19 lines of the output data set created for the three SQL statements in the previous figure.

- Each output data set consists of (1) a copy of each SQL statement, (2) the results of that statement, (3) the run-time messages for that statement, and (4) a completion message that gives the SQLCODE value that's returned for that statement.

- To browse the data in the data set you can use the standard ISPF keys: PF11 to scroll to the right; PF10 to scroll to the left; PF8 to scroll down; and PF7 to scroll up.

- To end the browse process, press PF3.

How the data in result tables is displayed

- When the column heading default is set to NAMES, a heading row is created that contains the column names for each column of data.

- The width of each displayed column usually provides for the widest value that the column can hold including a decimal point and leading sign for numeric data. However, if this width is larger than the maximum width that's set in the Defaults panel, that default is used as the column width.

- If a character value for a row won't fit in the displayed column, the displayed data is truncated on the right. If a numeric value won't fit, it is displayed as asterisks (*). Whenever truncation occurs, the output data set also contains a warning message.

- A null value in a column is displayed as a hyphen (-).

Figure 14-4   How to use the Browse panel

How to interpret the messages

Figure 14-5 presents the last lines of the browse data including some other messages. It also summarizes the way that you interpret these messages because these messages are somewhat different than the ones returned for COBOL programs.

In figure 14-4, for example, you can see that the SQLCODE value that's returned for a successful SELECT statement is 100, instead of zero. That's true whether or not any rows are returned for the SELECT statement. So if the run-time message for the statement indicates that zero rows are displayed, it means that the statement was successful but it didn't find any rows that matched the selection condition. For all other SQL statements that you run in SPUFI, an SQLCODE of zero means that the statement ran successfully.

In figure 14-5, the two messages at the top of the panel are for the UP-DATE statement in the Edit panel. They say that one row was updated and that the statement ran successfully. These messages are followed by the output for the ROLLBACK statement in the Edit panel. As you can see, its SQLCODE is zero so it ran successfully, which means that the processing done by the previous statements including the INSERT statement was rolled back. That way, you know that the INSERT statement worked correctly, but you don't actually update the table.

The next two messages in this panel say that a commit was performed successfully. This output is present because the Autocommit option is selected in the main SPUFI panel. In other words, since all of the statements in the panel ran successfully, they are automatically committed. If one of the statements failed, however, the message would say that a rollback was performed and that would apply to all of the statements that ran before the statement failed.

In this example, though, the ROLLBACK statement in the Edit panel already rolled back the results of the UPDATE statement so there's nothing to commit. Similarly, this automatic commit message is displayed for Edit panels that contain only SELECT statements, even though they don't provide any units of work that need to be committed.

The last three messages in this panel are the summary messages for all the processing that was done. Note, however, that this data gives the number of records in the input data set and the number of records in the output data set. This has nothing to do with the number of rows processed in the DB2 tables.

The messages for the last two statements in the Edit panel

```
MMA - EXTRA! for Windows 95/NT                                    _ 8 X
File  Edit  View  Tools  Session  Options  Help
  Menu   Utilities   Compilers   Help
------------------------------------------------------------------------
BROWSE     MM01.SPUFI.OUTPUT                  Line 00000020 Col 001 080
Command ===> _                                    Scroll ===> CSR
-----------+----------+----------+----------+----------+----------+-----+
DSNE615I NUMBER OF ROWS AFFECTED IS 1
DSNE616I STATEMENT EXECUTION WAS SUCCESSFUL, SQLCODE IS 0
-----------+----------+----------+----------+----------+----------+-----+
--                                                        00120001
-- THIS SQL STATEMENT ROLLS BACK THE CHANGES MADE BY ALL OF THE   00130001
-- PREVIOUS SQL STATEMENTS                                00140001
  ROLLBACK;                                               00150001
-----------+----------+----------+----------+----------+----------+-----+
DSNE616I STATEMENT EXECUTION WAS SUCCESSFUL, SQLCODE IS 0
-----------+----------+----------+----------+----------+----------+-----+
-----------+----------+----------+----------+----------+----------+-----+
DSNE617I COMMIT PERFORMED, SQLCODE IS 0
DSNE616I STATEMENT EXECUTION WAS SUCCESSFUL, SQLCODE IS 0
-----------+----------+----------+----------+----------+----------+-----+
DSNE601I SQL STATEMENTS ASSUMED TO BE BETWEEN COLUMNS 1 AND 72
DSNE620I NUMBER OF SQL STATEMENTS PROCESSED IS 3
DSNE621I NUMBER OF INPUT RECORDS READ IS 15
DSNE622I NUMBER OF OUTPUT RECORDS WRITTEN IS 38
****************************** Bottom of Data ********************************
```

Description

- For a SELECT statement run with SPUFI, the SQLCODE for a successful execution is 100. However, if the run-time message shows that zero rows are displayed, it means that DB2 was unable to find any rows that satisfied the selection condition.

- For all other types of SQL statements run with SPUFI, the SQLCODE for a successful execution is 0.

- If the Autocommit option is on in the main SPUFI menu, an automatic commit is performed for all statements that ran successfully. In the example above, the fifth and sixth messages from the bottom are for this commit. In this case, though, the previous statement was a rollback so there's nothing to commit. Similarly, the messages for the automatic commit are displayed after SELECT statements are run, even though there's nothing to commit for those statements.

- At the end of the data set are messages that summarize the number of SQL statements processed, the number of records read from the input data set, and the number of records written to the output data set. These statistics do *not* indicate how many rows in DB2 tables were read or written.

Figure 14-5   How to interpret the messages

How to use the commit and rollback features

Figure 14-6 presents the Commit and Rollback panel that's displayed when the Autocommit option in the main SPUFI panel isn't selected. This panel is displayed when you end the browse processing. You can then decide whether you want to commit or roll back the processing that has been done. If you enter COMMIT, the results of all of the statements that ran successfully are committed. If you enter ROLLBACK, the results of all of the statements are rolled back.

Remember, though, that you can include your own COMMIT and ROLLBACK statements in the input data set. That gives you more control over the processing that's done.

The Commit Or Rollback panel

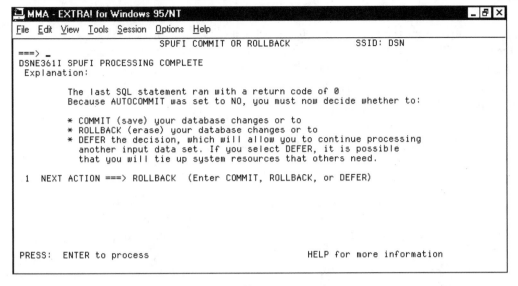

Description

- If you enter NO for option 8 (Autocommit) in the main SPUFI panel, the panel above is displayed when you end the browse processing by pressing the PF3 key.

- This panel lets you COMMIT your database changes, ROLLBACK your database changes, or DEFER the decision so you can process another input data set. Since the DEFER option can tie up system resources, however, you shouldn't use it.

- If you enter YES for the Autocommit option in the main SPUFI panel, the results of the SQL statements are automatically committed if they all run successfully. If one SQL statement fails, however, processing is cancelled and the results of all preceding statements are rolled back.

- You can also code your own COMMIT and ROLLBACK statements in the Edit panel to make sure the commits and rollbacks work the way you want them to.

Figure 14-6   How to use the commit and rollback features

Basic SPUFI uses

Perhaps the most common SPUFI use is to run SQL statements and review the results. That way, you can be sure the statements work the way you want them to before you use them in your COBOL programs. As you will see next, though, you can also use SPUFI to create the tables that you need for testing your programs.

The SQL statements that you can and cannot use in SPUFI

Figure 14-7 summarizes the statements that you can use in SPUFI. Besides the DML statements that you're already familiar with, you can use the DDL statements to create and alter the tables that you need for testing your programs.

Note, however, that this figure also summarizes the types of statements that you can't use in SPUFI. In general, you can't use any DB2 statements that are related to COBOL programs like precompiler statements, statements that process cursor-controlled result tables, statements that use host variables, and dynamic SQL statements.

The SQL statements that you can use in SPUFI

Data manipulation language (DML) statements

```
SELECT
INSERT
UPDATE
DELETE
COMMIT
ROLLBACK
```

Data definition language (DDL) statements

```
CREATE TABLESPACE
CREATE TABLE
CREATE INDEX
CREATE SYNONYM
ALTER TABLESPACE
ALTER TABLE
DROP
EXPLAIN
```

The SQL statements that you can't use in SPUFI

- Precompiler statements like the DECLARE TABLE and INCLUDE statements.

- SQL statements that are related to cursor-controlled result tables like the DE-CLARE CURSOR, OPEN, FETCH, and CLOSE statements as well as the UP-DATE and DELETE statements when they use the CURRENT OF phrase.

- SQL statements that use host variables and indicator variables.

- Dynamic SQL statements (which you can learn about in *Part 2* of this series).

Figure 14-7   The SQL statements that you can and cannot use in SPUFI

How to create test tables with unique indexes

To create test tables, you use CREATE TABLE statements like those shown in figure 14-8. These statements are included in the DCLGEN output that's presented for each table that's used by a program in this book. As a result, you should easily be able to enter the required statements into SPUFI and create the test tables that you need for running the programs in this book.

Although the IN DATABASE clause in these statements creates a simple table space for the table that's created, that's acceptable for small test tables. If you've read chapter 11, though, you know that you shouldn't use simple table spaces for production tables. For those tables, you should use a CREATE TABLESPACE statement to create a table space before you create a table that goes into the table space. Although you can learn more about that in *Part 2* of this DB2 series, you shouldn't need to do that for the test tables that you need for the programs in this book.

You should, however, use the CREATE UNIQUE INDEX statement to create a unique index for each of the tables that has a primary key. In this figure, you can see the statements used for two of the four tables; the other two tables don't require unique indexes because they don't have primary keys. To create unique indexes for your own tables, you can use the statements in this figure as guides. Before you do that, though, you need to ask your database administrator what values you should use in the STOGROUP and BUFFERPOOL clauses.

After you've created the tables and their indexes using SPUFI, you can use QMF to add rows to the tables, which you can learn how to do in the next chapter. That's the best way to develop the tables that you need for testing programs. Although you can use INSERT statements in SPUFI to add one row at a time to a table, that just isn't practical.

Customer table statements

```
CREATE TABLE MM01.CUSTOMER
   (CUSTNO    CHAR(6)       NOT NULL,
    FNAME     CHAR(20)      NOT NULL,
    LNAME     CHAR(30)      NOT NULL,
    ADDR      CHAR(30)      NOT NULL,
    CITY      CHAR(20)      NOT NULL,
    STATE     CHAR(2)       NOT NULL,
    ZIPCODE   CHAR(10)      NOT NULL,
    PRIMARY KEY (CUSTNO) )
 IN DATABASE MMADBV;




CREATE UNIQUE INDEX MM01.XCUSTOMER
   ON MM01.CUSTOMER
     (CUSTNO)
   USING STOGROUP PUBSG001
   BUFFERPOOL BP1
   CLOSE YES;
```

Payment table statements

```
CREATE TABLE MM01.PAYMENT
   (PAYINVNO  CHAR(6)       NOT NULL,
    PAYDATE   DATE          NOT NULL,
    PAYAMT    DECIMAL(9,2)  NOT NULL,
    PAYCHECK  CHAR(20),
    PAYCARD   CHAR(20),
    PAYEXP    CHAR(5),
    PAYNOTE   VARCHAR(254),
    FOREIGN KEY INVNO (PAYINVNO)
       REFERENCES MM01.INVOICE
       ON DELETE CASCADE)
 IN DATABASE MMADBV;
```

Invoice table statements

```
CREATE TABLE MM01.INVOICE
   (INVCUST   CHAR(6)       NOT NULL,
    INVNO     CHAR(6)       NOT NULL,
    INVDATE   DATE          NOT NULL,
    INVSUBT   DECIMAL(9,2)  NOT NULL,
    INVSHIP   DECIMAL(7,2)  NOT NULL,
    INVTAX    DECIMAL(7,2)  NOT NULL,
    INVTOTAL  DECIMAL(9,2)  NOT NULL,
    INVPROM   CHAR(10)      NOT NULL,
    PRIMARY KEY (INVNO)
    FOREIGN KEY CUSTNO (INVCUST)
       REFERENCES MM01.CUSTOMER
       ON DELETE CASCADE)
 IN DATABASE MMADBV;


CREATE UNIQUE INDEX MM01.XINVOICE
   ON MM01.INVOICE
     (INVNO)
   USING STOGROUP PUBSG001
   BUFFERPOOL BP1
   CLOSE YES;
```

Line item table statements

```
CREATE TABLE MM01.LINEITEM
   (LIINVNO   CHAR(6)       NOT NULL,
    LIPCODE   CHAR(10)      NOT NULL,
    LIQTY     DECIMAL(7)    NOT NULL,
    LIPRICE   DECIMAL(7,2)  NOT NULL,
    LIDISC    DECIMAL(7,2)  NOT NULL,
    FOREIGN KEY INVNO (LIINVNO)
       REFERENCES MM01.INVOICE
       ON DELETE CASCADE)
 IN DATABASE MMADBV;
```

Description

- To create a test table, you use CREATE TABLE statements. Then, to create a unique index for each table that has a primary key, you use CREATE UNIQUE INDEX statements.

- Although the IN DATABASE clause of the CREATE TABLE statement implicitly creates a simple table space (see chapter 11), this is acceptable for small test tables.

- To add data to the test tables you create, you can use QMF as explained in the next chapter.

Figure 14-8   How to create test tables with unique indexes

When and how to create a PLAN_TABLE

If you turn the EXPLAIN option on when you bind a plan or a package as recommended in chapter 12, DB2 adds explanatory information to a table named PLAN_TABLE when the bind operation is performed. In that case, the binding operation fails if the PLAN_TABLE doesn't already exist.

Since your shop is likely to have a PLAN_TABLE that should be used for all the explanatory information, you probably won't have to create one on your own. If you need to create one, though, you can run the statement in figure 14-9 through SPUFI. To save the entry time, you can download this statement from our web site (www.murach.com). Then, you can change the table name and database name so they're suitable for your shop, and run it. (In *Part 2* of this series, you can learn how to use the EXPLAIN information.)

A CREATE TABLE statement for a PLAN_TABLE

```
CREATE TABLE MM01.PLAN_TABLE
    ( QUERYNO            INTEGER        NOT NULL,
      QBLOCKNO           SMALLINT       NOT NULL,
      APPLNAME           CHAR(8)        NOT NULL,
      PROGNAME           CHAR(8)        NOT NULL,
      PLANNO             SMALLINT       NOT NULL,
      METHOD             SMALLINT       NOT NULL,
      CREATOR            CHAR(8)        NOT NULL,
      TNAME              CHAR(18)       NOT NULL,
      TABNO              SMALLINT       NOT NULL,
      ACCESSTYPE         CHAR(2)        NOT NULL,
      MATCHCOLS          SMALLINT       NOT NULL,
      ACCESSCREATOR      CHAR(8)        NOT NULL,
      ACCESSNAME         CHAR(18)       NOT NULL,
      INDEXONLY          CHAR(1)        NOT NULL,
      SORTN_UNIQ         CHAR(1)        NOT NULL,
      SORTN_JOIN         CHAR(1)        NOT NULL,
      SORTN_ORDERBY      CHAR(1)        NOT NULL,
      SORTN_GROUPBY      CHAR(1)        NOT NULL,
      SORTC_UNIQ         CHAR(1)        NOT NULL,
      SORTC_JOIN         CHAR(1)        NOT NULL,
      SORTC_ORDERBY      CHAR(1)        NOT NULL,
      SORTC_GROUPBY      CHAR(1)        NOT NULL,
      TSLOCKMODE         CHAR(3)        NOT NULL,
      TIMESTAMP          CHAR(16)       NOT NULL,
      REMARKS            VARCHAR(254)   NOT NULL,
      PREFETCH           CHAR(1)        NOT NULL WITH DEFAULT,
      COLUMN_FN_EVAL     CHAR(1)        NOT NULL WITH DEFAULT,
      MIXOPSEQ           SMALLINT       NOT NULL WITH DEFAULT,
      VERSION            VARCHAR(64)    NOT NULL WITH DEFAULT,
      COLLID             CHAR(18)       NOT NULL WITH DEFAULT,
      ACCESS_DEGREE      SMALLINT,
      ACCESS_PGROUP_ID   SMALLINT,
      JOIN_DEGREE        SMALLINT,
      JOIN_PGROUP_ID     SMALLINT,
      SORTC_PGROUP_ID    SMALLINT,
      SORTN_PGROUP_ID    SMALLINT,
      PARALLELISM_MODE   CHAR(1),
      MERGE_JOIN_COLS    SMALLINT,
      CORRELATION_NAME   CHAR(18),
      PAGE_RANGE         CHAR(1)        NOT NULL,
      JOIN_TYPE          CHAR(1)        NOT NULL,
      GROUP_MEMBER       CHAR(8)        NOT NULL,
      IBM_SERVICE_DATA   VARCHAR(254)   NOT NULL )
  IN DATABASE MMADBV;
```

Description

- If you use the EXPLAIN option when you bind a plan or package (see chapter 12), a table named userid.PLAN_TABLE must be available for the EXPLAIN output that's produced.

- Before you create your own PLAN_TABLE, though, you should talk with your database administrator to find out if your shop already has one that all programs must use.

- To create a PLAN_TABLE, you can run the statement above with SPUFI. To do that, you can either enter this code into SPUFI or download it from our web site into a SPUFI data set. Before you run it, of course, you must change the table name and database name so it works in your shop.

Figure 14-9   When and how to create a PLAN_TABLE

Perspective

You should now realize that SPUFI is a valuable tool that you can use for testing SQL statements and creating test tables. Its primary limitation is that it doesn't make it easy for you to add data to a table. However, you can learn how to use QMF to add, update, and delete data in the next chapter.

15

How to use QMF to update tables

In the last chapter, you learned how to use SPUFI to create DB2 tables. In this chapter, you can learn how to use QMF to add, update, and delete rows in those tables because there's no easy way to do that with SPUFI. By combining the use of SPUFI and QMF in this way, you can create the tables that you need for testing your DB2 programs.

An introduction to QMF

The *Query Management Facility*, or *QMF*, is an IBM product that supplements DB2. Two of its primary purposes are (1) to make it easy for you to run queries against the tables in a database and (2) to prepare reports from the data in the result tables. However, you can also use QMF to create objects like tables and indexes and to insert, update, and delete rows in the tables of a database.

In this chapter, you'll only learn how to use QMF for adding, updating, and deleting the rows in DB2 tables. In *Part 2* of this DB2 series, though, three chapters are devoted to QMF. There, you can learn the three ways QMF helps you create queries including how to use the Query By Example and prompted SQL features. You can also learn how to use QMF for extracting formatted reports from a database whenever you need to provide a quick, ad hoc report for a user. As you will see, QMF is a valuable program that every DB2 programmer should master.

The QMF main menu

Figure 15-1 presents the QMF main menu that you can usually access from the ISPF Primary Option menu. In the menu in figure 12-3, for example, you can use option 9 to access QMF. If QMF isn't on that menu, though, you can ask a co-worker or your database administrator how to access QMF.

As you can see in this figure, the QMF menu provides 12 functions that are available from the PF keys. However, you can also enter other QMF commands in the command area at the bottom of this panel.

When you are at any of QMF's panels, you can press the PF1 key to get help for that panel. You can also press the PF3 key to end the current function and return to the panel at the next level up. When you press PF3 at the main menu, you are returned to the ISPF Primary Option menu.

To add, update, or delete rows, you use the PF8 key (Edit Table). That's the key that leads to the panels that you're going to learn about in this chapter. If you review the functions of the other keys, though, they will give you some idea of what QMF can do.

Using QMF terminology, an *item* is a query, data returned by a query, a form, a procedure, or a profile. A *form* is an item that specifies how the result table returned by a query should be formatted into a report. A *procedure* is a series of QMF commands that are packaged together to do a task. And a *profile* is a description of how a user interacts with QMF. If you know these terms, the menu functions in this figure make more sense. By saving and modifying the QMF items, you can perform many database functions with relative ease.

The QMF main menu

```
MMA - EXTRA! for Windows 95/NT                                    _ 回 X
File  Edit  View  Tools  Session  Options  Help

IBM*    Licensed Materials - Property of IBM
5706-254 5706-255 (c) Copyright IBM Corp. 1982, 1990.  All rights reserved.
US Government Users Restricted Rights - Use, duplication
or disclosure restricted by GSA ADP Schedule Contract with IBM Corp.
* Trademark of International Business Machines Corp.


QMF HOME PANEL
Version 3                            ******    **    **    *********
Release 1.0                        **    **   ***   ***      **
                                   **    **  ****  ****    *******
Query                              **    **  ** ** ** **     **
Management                         **  * **   **   ****  **  **
Facility                           ******    **    **    ** **
                                      *

Type command on command line or use PF keys. For help, press PF1 or type HELP.

1=Help       2=List       3=End       4=Show       5=Chart      6=Query
7=Retrieve   8=Edit Table 9=Form      10=Proc      11=Profile   12=Report
OK, you may enter a command.
COMMAND ===> _
```

Menu options

Option	Function
PF1-Help	Get context-sensitive information about the panel you're viewing.
PF2-List	Show a list of QMF items of a specific type.
PF3-End	End the current function and return to the panel at the next level up.
PF4-Show	Present a sequence of prompts for a QMF function.
PF5-Chart	Produce a graphic representation of a query.
PF6-Query	View, change, and execute the query in temporary storage.
PF7-Retrieve	Get a copy of a QMF command you recently entered.
PF8-Edit Table	Add, change, or delete rows in a table.
PF9-Form	View and change the form in temporary storage.
PF10-Proc	View, change, and execute the procedure in temporary storage.
PF11-Profile	View and change your user profile.
PF12-Report	View the result table of the current SELECT query with it formatted as specified by the current form.

Figure 15-1   The QMF main menu

How to add, change, or delete rows

To add, change, or delete rows, you press PF8 at the QMF main menu. QMF then displays the Edit Table panel.

How to use the Edit Table panel

Figure 15-2 presents the Edit Table panel. In this panel, you identify the table you want to work with and the function that you want to perform (Add or Change). You also specify when you want the additions or changes made (immediately or at the end of the session) and whether you want confirmation prompting. Then, you press the Enter key to move to the next panel.

When you start using QMF to add data to test tables, you may want to set the Save and Confirm options to END and YES as shown in this figure. That way, you can cancel the additions, changes, and deletions that you make to a table if you decide that you didn't do them correctly. Once you're comfortable with QMF, though, you can change these settings to IMMEDIATE and NO. This will help you work more quickly because you won't be interrupted by confirmation prompts.

The Edit Table Command Prompt panel

```
┌─────────────────────────────────────────────────────────────────────┐
│ ▣ MMA - EXTRA! for Windows 95/NT                           _ ☐ ✕     │
├─────────────────────────────────────────────────────────────────────┤
│ File  Edit  View  Tools  Session  Options  Help                      │
├─────────────────────────────────────────────────────────────────────┤
│                                                                       │
│ ┌─────────────────────────────────────────────────────────────────┐ │
│ │                    EDIT TABLE Command Prompt                      │ │
│ │                                           1  to 15 of 16          │ │
│ │   EDIT type TABLE                                                 │ │
│ │                                                                   │ │
│ │   Name    ( MM01.BENEFITS_____ )              │ │
│ │           Enter the name of the table in the database you        │ │
│ │           want to edit.                                          │ │
│ │                                                                   │ │
│ │   Mode    ( ADD____ )                                            │ │
│ │           Enter ADD to add new rows, or CHANGE to update         │ │
│ │           or delete rows.                                        │ │
│ │   Save    ( END___ )                                            │ │
│ │           Enter IMMEDIATE to save database alterations as        │ │
│ │           they are made, or END to hold database alterations     │ │
│ │           until the session is completed.                        │ │
│ │   Confirm ( YES_ )                                              │ │
│ │           Enter NO to turn off confirmation prompting.           │ │
│ │                                                                   │ │
│ │   F1=Help  F3=End  F7=Backward  F8=Forward                       │ │
│ └─────────────────────────────────────────────────────────────────┘ │
│ Please identify table name.                                          │
└─────────────────────────────────────────────────────────────────────┘
```

Panel entries

Option	Entry
Name	The name of the DB2 table that you want to add rows to, change rows in, or delete rows from.
Mode	ADD to add new rows, or CHANGE to change or delete rows.
Save	END to hold the database updates until the session is complete, or IMMEDIATE to save the database updates as they are made.
Confirm	YES to turn on confirmation prompting, or NO to turn it off.

Description

- For test tables, IMMEDIATE and NO are efficient entries for the Save and Confirm options once you're comfortable with QMF. If you're updating a production table, though, you should enter END and YES for these options so you can verify the updates before they are made permanently.

Figure 15-2   The Edit Table Command Prompt panel

How to add rows

When you use ADD as the Mode in the Edit Panel and press the Enter key, the Add panel in figure 15-3 is displayed. This panel provides one line for each column in the table with the exact number of character places for each column. Since the EMPNO column is defined as CHAR(6), for example, this panel provides six places for this column. And since SALARY is defined as DECI-MAL(9,2), this panel provides eleven spaces for this column (nine for digits, one for the decimal point, and one for a leading plus or minus sign).

As you enter data, you can't exceed the number of character places that are provided for each. You must also enter data that's consistent with the character type for each column. For instance, you can't enter alphabetic characters in a numeric column like SALARY, and you must enter a decimal point and two decimal positions for this column.

When you complete the entries for a new row, you press the PF2 key to add the row. Then, if the add operation is successful, a confirmation message is displayed. Otherwise, an error message is displayed that describes the problem. After you successfully enter a row, the entries are cleared so you can enter another row.

When you're finished adding rows to the table, you can press the PF3 key to end the function and return to the QMF main menu. Or, if the Save option is END, you can press the PF12 key to cancel the additions. Then, the Cancel Confirmation panel in figure 15-6 is displayed if the Confirm option is YES.

The Add panel

```
MMA - EXTRA! for Windows 95/NT                                  _ | 8 | X
File  Edit  View  Tools  Session  Options  Help
ADD                MM01.BENEFITS                    MODIFIED

                                                    1 to 17 of 22
EMPNO . . . . . . . . . ( 400001 )
FNAME . . . . . . . . . ( TIM                 )
LNAME . . . . . . . . . ( WILLIAMS                    )
ADDR. . . . . . . . . . ( 4595 FIRST ST             )
CITY. . . . . . . . . . ( MOBILE               )
STATE . . . . . . . . . ( AL )
ZIPCODE . . . . . . . . ( 36608     )
DATE_OF_BIRTH . . . . . ( 1961-08-11 )
HIRE_DATE . . . . . . . ( 1995-11-10 )
SALARY. . . . . . . . . (     36000.00 )
COMMISION . . . . . . . (      2000.00 )
BONUS . . . . . . . . . (    -      )
HEALTH_PLN. . . . . . . ( A )
LIFE_INS_OPTN . . . . . ( B )
AD_D_OPTN . . . . . . . ( A )
DISABILITY_OPTN . . . . ( C )
RETIREMENT_PLN. . . . . ( A )
1=Help      2=Add       3=End      4=          5=Show Field   6=Previous
7=Backward  8=Forward   9=Clear    10=         11=            12=Cancel
OK, BACKWARD performed. Please proceed.
```

Menu options

Option	Function
PF1-Help	Get context-sensitive information about the panel you're viewing.
PF2-Add	Add the row to the table.
PF3-End	End the add function and return to the QMF main menu.
PF5-Show Field	Show the data definition for the column.
PF6-Previous	Get the data for the all of the columns from the previous row that you added.
PF7-Backward	Scroll backward (or upward) when the number of columns in each row doesn't fit on one panel.
PF8-Forward	Scroll forward (or downward) when the number of columns in each row doesn't fit on one panel. In the panel above, pressing PF8 shows columns 18 to 22.
PF9-Clear	Clear all of the entries.
PF12-Cancel	Cancel the additions to the database and end the editing session. However, this key is only active when the Save option is set to END.

Description

- When you press the PF2 key to add the data to the table, an error message is displayed if the insertion isn't successful.

Figure 15-3   The Add panel

How to search for rows

When you use CHANGE as the Mode in the Edit Panel and press the Enter key, the Search panel in figure 15-4 is displayed. In this panel, you enter search criteria in one or more columns. Then, when you press the PF2 key, QMF tries to find the rows in the table that match the criteria. If it finds one or more rows, the Change panel in the next figure is displayed.

The Search panel

```
MMA - EXTRA! for Windows 95/NT                              _ 🗗 ☒
File  Edit  View  Tools  Session  Options  Help
SEARCH              MM01.BENEFITS

                                            1  to 17 of 22
EMPNO . . . . . . . . ( _____ )
FNAME . . . . . . . . ( =_____ )
LNAME . . . . . . . . ( =_____ )
ADDR. . . . . . . . . ( =_____ )
CITY. . . . . . . . . ( =_____ )
STATE . . . . . . . . ( CA )
ZIPCODE . . . . . . . ( =_____ )
DATE_OF_BIRTH . . . . ( =_____ )
HIRE_DATE . . . . . . ( =_____ )
SALARY. . . . . . . . ( =_____ )
COMMISION . . . . . . ( =_____ )
BONUS . . . . . . . . ( =_____ )
HEALTH_PLN. . . . . . ( = )
LIFE_INS_OPTN . . . . ( = )
AD_D_OPTN . . . . . . ( = )
DISABILITY_OPTN . . . ( = )
RETIREMENT_PLN. . . . ( = )
1=Help      2=Search    3=End       4=Show Change   5=Show Field    6=Previous
7=Backward  8=Forward   9=Clear     10= .           11=             12=
OK, enter search criteria and press PF2 to SEARCH.
```

Menu options

Option	Function
PF1-Help	Get context-sensitive information about the panel you're viewing.
PF2-Search	Search for the row that has values that match the entries in this panel.
PF3-End	End the search function and return to the QMF main menu.
PF4-Show Change	Show the Change panel. However, this doesn't work until you've done a search and have returned to this panel. (If you haven't done a search before pressing this key, this message is displayed: "You must SEARCH for the rows you want to CHANGE.")
PF5-Show Field	Show the data definition for the column.
PF6-Previous	Get the data for all of the columns from the previous search.
PF7-Backward	Scroll backward (or upward) when the number of columns in each row doesn't fit on one panel.
PF8-Forward	Scroll forward (or downward) when the number of columns in each row doesn't fit on one panel. In the above panel, pressing PF8 shows columns 18 to 22.
PF9-Clear	Clear all of the entries.

Description

- Enter search criteria in one or more of the columns. Then, press the PF2 key to run the search.

- If the search is successful, it will return a result table that contains one or more rows. Then, the first row in the result table is displayed in the Change panel shown in the next figure.

Figure 15-4   The Search panel

How to change or delete rows

Figure 15-5 presents the Change panel that's displayed when the query in the Search panel is run and one or more rows match the criteria. Here, the data for the first row that matches the search criteria is displayed. But if you want to move to the next row that matches the criteria, you can press the PF9 key.

When you find a row that you want to change, you can change the data for any of the columns and press the PF2 key to change the row. If, however, you try to put invalid data into the database, QMF won't let you do that. For instance, QMF won't let you change the primary key for a row if that would damage the referential integrity of the database. And, of course, QMF won't let you enter alphabetic characters in a column that's been defined as numeric. Whenever the data is invalid, QMF displays an appropriate error message. Otherwise, it displays "CHANGE performed" and moves to the next row in the result table.

When you find a row that you want to delete, you just press the PF11 key. If you used IMMEDIATE for the Save option in the Edit Table panel, this function is done immediately with no intervening message. Then, "DELETE performed" is displayed if the deletion was successful. Otherwise, an appropriate error message is displayed.

After you've made one or more changes or deletions, you can cancel them by pressing the PF12 key if the Save option is END. Then, the Cancel Confirmation panel in the next figure is displayed if the Confirm option is YES.

The Change panel

```
╔═══════════════════════════════════════════════════════════════════════════╗
║ 🖳 MMA - EXTRA! for Windows 95/NT                                 _ 🗗 ☒ ║
╠═══════════════════════════════════════════════════════════════════════════╣
║ File  Edit  View  Tools  Session  Options  Help                          ║
║  CHANGE              MM01.BENEFITS                                         ║
║                                                                           ║
║                                                  1  to 17 of 22           ║
║  EMPNO . . . . . . . . ( 400003 )                                         ║
║  FNAME . . . . . . . . ( ANNE               )                             ║
║  LNAME . . . . . . . . ( JOHNSON                   )                       ║
║  ADDR. . . . . . . . . ( 2998 LINCOLN AVE          )                       ║
║  CITY. . . . . . . . . ( TURLOCK            )                             ║
║  STATE . . . . . . . . ( CA )                                             ║
║  ZIPCODE . . . . . . . ( 93726-2394 )                                     ║
║  DATE_OF_BIRTH . . . . ( 1975-08-01 )                                     ║
║  HIRE_DATE . . . . . . ( 1996-04-25 )                                     ║
║  SALARY. . . . . . . . (    42000.00 )                                    ║
║  COMMISION . . . . . . (        0.00 )                                    ║
║  BONUS . . . . . . . . ( -         )                                      ║
║  HEALTH_PLN. . . . . . ( A )                                              ║
║  LIFE_INS_OPTN . . . . ( B )                                              ║
║  AD_D_OPTN . . . . . . ( A )                                              ║
║  DISABILITY_OPTN . . . ( B )                                              ║
║  RETIREMENT_PLN. . . . ( C )                                              ║
║  1=Help      2=Change    3=End     4=Show Search  5=Show Field  6=Refresh ║
║  7=Backward  8=Forward   9=Next    10=           11=Delete    12=Cancel   ║
║  OK, SEARCH performed. Please proceed.                                    ║
╚═══════════════════════════════════════════════════════════════════════════╝
```

Menu options

Option	Function
PF1-Help	Get context-sensitive information about the panel you're viewing.
PF2-Change	Change the row.
PF3-End	End the change function and return to the QMF main menu.
PF4-Show Search	Show an empty Search panel.
PF5-Show Field	Show the data definition for the column.
PF6-Refresh	Restore the data from the row that's currently stored in the table.
PF7-Backward	Scroll backward (or upward) when the number of columns in each row doesn't fit on one panel.
PF8-Forward	Scroll forward (or downward) when the number of columns in each row doesn't fit on one panel. In the above panel, pressing PF8 shows columns 18 to 22.
PF9-Next	Go to the next row that meets the search criteria.
PF11-Delete	Delete the row.
PF12-Cancel	Cancel the updates to the database and end the editing session. However, this key is only active when the Save option is set to END.

Description

- You can't change the data in the primary key column when referential constraints prohibit that.
- When you press the PF2 key or the PF11 key to change or delete the row in the database, an error message is displayed if the change or deletion isn't successful.

Figure 15-5   The Change panel

How to cancel your updates

Figure 15-6 presents the Cancel Confirmation panel that's displayed when you press the PF12 key at either the Add or Change panel when the Save option is END and the Confirm option is YES. Then, you can cancel the database updates by entering 1 and pressing the Enter key. Or, you can return to the editing session by pressing PF12 or by entering 2 and pressing the Enter key.

The Cancel Confirmation panel

```
MMA - EXTRA! for Windows 95/NT                                   _ ☐ ✕
File  Edit  View  Tools  Session  Options  Help
 CHANGE            MM01.BENEFITS
┌──────────────────────────────────────────────────────────────┐
 EMPNO . . . . .         Table Editor CANCEL Confirmation
 FNAME . . . . .  Your CANCEL command will cancel the Table Editor and lose
 LNAME . . . . .  any data base alterations.
 ADDR. . . . . .         Changed     Deleted      Added
 CITY. . . . . .            1           0            0
 STATE . . . . .
 ZIPCODE . . . .  Do you want to lose the database alterations?
 DATE_OF_BIRTH .  1 1. YES - End the Table Editor.  The alterations to the
 HIRE_DATE . . .        data base will be lost.
 SALARY. . . . .    2. NO  - Do not end the Table Editor.  You may
 COMMISION . . .        continue editing your data.
 BONUS . . . . .
 HEALTH_PLN. . .  F1=Help  F12=Cancel
 LIFE_INS_OPTN .
└──────────────────────────────────────────────────────────────┘
 AD_D_OPTN . . . . . . ( A )
 DISABILITY_OPTN . . . ( B )
 RETIREMENT_PLN. . . . ( B )

 Please follow the directions on the confirmation prompt panel.
```

Menu options

Option	Function
1-Yes	Cancel the database updates and end the editing session.
2-No	Return to the editing session without cancelling the updates.
PF1-Help	Get context-sensitive information about the panel you're viewing.
PF12-Cancel	Return to the editing session without cancelling the updates.

Description

- This panel is displayed when the Save option is END, the Confirm option is YES, and you press the PF12 key at the Add or Change panel. Then, you can cancel all of the updates made during the editing session.

Figure 15-6   The Cancel Confirmation panel

Perspective

You should now realize how easy it is to add, update, or delete the rows in a DB2 table when you use QMF. In contrast, you have to use the INSERT, UPDATE, and DELETE statements to do these functions with SPUFI. Since that's impractical, we recommend that you use SPUFI to create your test tables and QMF to put the data in them. And you should now be able to do that.

Remember, though, that QMF is a powerful program that every DB2 programmer should master. So in *Part 2* of this series, you can learn how to use the other functions and features that QMF offers. In particular, you'll learn how easy it is to run queries with its Query By Example and prompted SQL features. You'll also learn how to prepare ad hoc reports for users who need information in a hurry.

Appendix A

Source code generated by the DB2 precompiler

This appendix presents the source code generated by the DB2 precompiler for the customer inquiry program presented in chapter 1. In the working-storage section, you can see that each SQL INCLUDE statement is converted to COBOL comments that are followed by the COBOL code that defines the fields included in the program. You can also see other fields that are added to the COBOL code by the precompiler.

In the Procedure Division, you can see the three COBOL paragraphs that the precompiler adds at the start of this division. You can also see that the SQL SELECT statement in module 120 is converted to comments that are followed by a COBOL PERFORM and a CALL statement that calls a DB2 subprogram that does the processing that the SQL statement requires. In short, the precompiler comments out all SQL statements and converts them to COBOL code that can then be compiled and executed.

```
000100 IDENTIFICATION DIVISION.
000200*
000300 PROGRAM-ID.    CUSTINQ.
000400*
000500 ENVIRONMENT DIVISION.
000600*
000700 INPUT-OUTPUT SECTION.
000800*
000900 FILE-CONTROL.
001000*
001100 DATA DIVISION.
001200*
001300 FILE SECTION.
001400*
001500 WORKING-STORAGE SECTION.
001600*
001700 01  SWITCHES.
001800*
001900     05  END-OF-INQUIRIES-SW     PIC X    VALUE 'N'.
002000         88  END-OF-INQUIRIES              VALUE 'Y'.
002100     05  CUSTOMER-FOUND-SW       PIC X.
002200         88  CUSTOMER-FOUND                VALUE 'Y'.
002300*
002400*****EXEC SQL
002500*****    INCLUDE CUSTOMER
002600*****END-EXEC.
       ****************************************************************
       * DCLGEN TABLE(MM01.CUSTOMER)                                  *
       *        LIBRARY(MM01.DB2.DCLGENS(CUSTOMER))                   *
       *        ACTION(REPLACE)                                       *
       *        LANGUAGE(COBOL)                                       *
       *        STRUCTURE(CUSTOMER-ROW)                               *
       *        QUOTE                                                 *
       * ... IS THE DCLGEN COMMAND THAT MADE THE FOLLOWING STATEMENTS *
       ****************************************************************
       *****EXEC SQL DECLARE MM01.CUSTOMER TABLE
       *****( CUSTNO                     CHAR(6) NOT NULL,
       *****  FNAME                      CHAR(20) NOT NULL,
       *****  LNAME                      CHAR(30) NOT NULL,
       *****  ADDR                       CHAR(30) NOT NULL,
       *****  CITY                       CHAR(20) NOT NULL,
       *****  STATE                      CHAR(2) NOT NULL,
       *****  ZIPCODE                    CHAR(10) NOT NULL
       *****) END-EXEC.
       ****************************************************************
       * COBOL DECLARATION FOR TABLE MM01.CUSTOMER                    *
       ****************************************************************
        01  CUSTOMER-ROW.
            10 CUSTNO           PIC X(6).
            10 FNAME            PIC X(20).
            10 LNAME            PIC X(30).
            10 ADDR             PIC X(30).
            10 CITY             PIC X(20).
            10 STATE            PIC X(2).
            10 ZIPCODE          PIC X(10).
```

```
        ****************************************************************
        * THE NUMBER OF COLUMNS DESCRIBED BY THIS DECLARATION IS 7     *
        ****************************************************************
002700*
002800*****EXEC SQL
002900*****    INCLUDE SQLCA
003000*****END-EXEC.
        01 SQLCA.
           05 SQLCAID    PIC X(8).
           05 SQLCABC    PIC S9(9) COMP-4.
           05 SQLCODE    PIC S9(9) COMP-4.
           05 SQLERRM.
              49 SQLERRML PIC S9(4) COMP-4.
              49 SQLERRMC PIC X(70).
           05 SQLERRP    PIC X(8).
           05 SQLERRD    OCCURS 6 TIMES
                         PIC S9(9) COMP-4.
           05 SQLWARN.
              10 SQLWARN0 PIC X.
              10 SQLWARN1 PIC X.
              10 SQLWARN2 PIC X.
              10 SQLWARN3 PIC X.
              10 SQLWARN4 PIC X.
              10 SQLWARN5 PIC X.
              10 SQLWARN6 PIC X.
              10 SQLWARN7 PIC X.
           05 SQLEXT.
              10 SQLWARN8 PIC X.
              10 SQLWARN9 PIC X.
              10 SQLWARNA PIC X.
              10 SQLSTATE PIC X(5).
003100*
        77 SQL-TEMP      PIC X(18).
        77 SQL-NULL      PIC S9(9) COMP-4 VALUE +0.
        77 SQL-INIT-FLAG PIC S9(4) COMP-4 VALUE +0.
           88 SQL-INIT-DONE VALUE +1.
        01 SQL-PLIST2.
           05 SQL-PLIST-CON   PIC S9(9) COMP-4 VALUE +2656256.
           05 SQL-CALLTYPE    PIC S9(4) COMP-4 VALUE +30.
           05 SQL-PROG-NAME   PIC X(8)         VALUE 'CUSTINQ '.
           05 SQL-TIMESTAMP-1 PIC S9(9) COMP-4 VALUE +370908435.
           05 SQL-TIMESTAMP-2 PIC S9(9) COMP-4 VALUE +253139128.
           05 SQL-SECTION     PIC S9(4) COMP-4 VALUE +1.
           05 SQL-CODEPTR     PIC S9(9) COMP-4.
           05 SQL-VPARMPTR    PIC S9(9) COMP-4 VALUE +0.
           05 SQL-APARMPTR    PIC S9(9) COMP-4 VALUE +0.
           05 SQL-STMT-NUM    PIC S9(4) COMP-4 VALUE +95.
           05 SQL-STMT-TYPE   PIC S9(4) COMP-4 VALUE +231.
           05 SQL-PVAR-LIST2.
              10 SQL-PVAR-SIZE  PIC S9(9) COMP-4 VALUE +16.
              10 SQL-PVAR-DESCS.
                 15 SQL-PVAR-TYPE1 PIC S9(4) COMP-4 VALUE +452.
                 15 SQL-PVAR-LEN1  PIC S9(4) COMP-4 VALUE +6.
              10 SQL-PVAR-ADDRS.
                 15 SQL-PVAR-ADDR1 PIC S9(9) COMP-4.
```

```
                    15 SQL-PVAR-IND1  PIC S9(9) COMP-4.
              05 SQL-AVAR-LIST2.
                 10 SQL-AVAR-SIZE  PIC S9(9) COMP-4 VALUE +88.
                 10 SQL-AVAR-DESCS.
                    15 SQL-AVAR-TYPE1 PIC S9(4) COMP-4 VALUE +452.
                    15 SQL-AVAR-LEN1  PIC S9(4) COMP-4 VALUE +6.
                 10 SQL-AVAR-ADDRS.
                    15 SQL-AVAR-ADDR1 PIC S9(9) COMP-4.
                    15 SQL-AVAR-IND1  PIC S9(9) COMP-4.
                    15 SQL-AVAR-TYPE2 PIC S9(4) COMP-4 VALUE +452.
                    15 SQL-AVAR-LEN2  PIC S9(4) COMP-4 VALUE +20.
                    15 SQL-AVAR-ADDR2 PIC S9(9) COMP-4.
                    15 SQL-AVAR-IND2  PIC S9(9) COMP-4.
                    15 SQL-AVAR-TYPE3 PIC S9(4) COMP-4 VALUE +452.
                    15 SQL-AVAR-LEN3  PIC S9(4) COMP-4 VALUE +30.
                    15 SQL-AVAR-ADDR3 PIC S9(9) COMP-4.
                    15 SQL-AVAR-IND3  PIC S9(9) COMP-4.
                    15 SQL-AVAR-TYPE4 PIC S9(4) COMP-4 VALUE +452.
                    15 SQL-AVAR-LEN4  PIC S9(4) COMP-4 VALUE +30.
                    15 SQL-AVAR-ADDR4 PIC S9(9) COMP-4.
                    15 SQL-AVAR-IND4  PIC S9(9) COMP-4.
                    15 SQL-AVAR-TYPE5 PIC S9(4) COMP-4 VALUE +452.
                    15 SQL-AVAR-LEN5  PIC S9(4) COMP-4 VALUE +20.
                    15 SQL-AVAR-ADDR5 PIC S9(9) COMP-4.
                    15 SQL-AVAR-IND5  PIC S9(9) COMP-4.
                    15 SQL-AVAR-TYPE6 PIC S9(4) COMP-4 VALUE +452.
                    15 SQL-AVAR-LEN6  PIC S9(4) COMP-4 VALUE +2.
                    15 SQL-AVAR-ADDR6 PIC S9(9) COMP-4.
                    15 SQL-AVAR-IND6  PIC S9(9) COMP-4.
                    15 SQL-AVAR-TYPE7 PIC S9(4) COMP-4 VALUE +452.
                    15 SQL-AVAR-LEN7  PIC S9(4) COMP-4 VALUE +10.
                    15 SQL-AVAR-ADDR7 PIC S9(9) COMP-4.
                    15 SQL-AVAR-IND7  PIC S9(9) COMP-4.

003200 PROCEDURE DIVISION.
003300*
         SQL-SKIP.
             GO TO SQL-INIT-END.
         SQL-INITIAL.
             MOVE 1 TO SQL-INIT-FLAG.
             CALL 'DSNHADDR' USING SQL-VPARMPTR OF SQL-PLIST2 SQL-PVAR-LIS
         -   T2.
             CALL 'DSNHADDR' USING SQL-PVAR-ADDRS OF SQL-PLIST2 CUSTNO OF
             CUSTOMER-ROW SQL-NULL
             CALL 'DSNHADDR' USING SQL-APARMPTR OF SQL-PLIST2 SQL-AVAR-LIS
         -   T2.
             CALL 'DSNHADDR' USING SQL-AVAR-ADDRS OF SQL-PLIST2 CUSTNO OF
             CUSTOMER-ROW SQL-NULL FNAME OF CUSTOMER-ROW SQL-NULL LNAME OF
             CUSTOMER-ROW SQL-NULL ADDR OF CUSTOMER-ROW SQL-NULL CITY OF C
         -   USTOMER-ROW SQL-NULL STATE OF CUSTOMER-ROW SQL-NULL ZIPCODE O
         -   F CUSTOMER-ROW SQL-NULL.
             CALL 'DSNHADDR' USING SQL-CODEPTR OF SQL-PLIST2 SQLCA.
         SQL-INIT-END.

003400 000-DISPLAY-CUSTOMER-ROWS.
003500*
```

```
003600        PERFORM 100-DISPLAY-CUSTOMER-ROW
003700             UNTIL END-OF-INQUIRIES.
003800        STOP RUN.
003900*
004000 100-DISPLAY-CUSTOMER-ROW.
004100*
004200        PERFORM 110-ACCEPT-CUSTOMER-NUMBER.
004300        IF NOT END-OF-INQUIRIES
004400             MOVE 'Y' TO CUSTOMER-FOUND-SW
004500             PERFORM 120-GET-CUSTOMER-ROW
004600             IF CUSTOMER-FOUND
004700                  PERFORM 130-DISPLAY-CUSTOMER-LINES
004800             ELSE
004900                  PERFORM 140-DISPLAY-ERROR-LINES.
005000*
005100 110-ACCEPT-CUSTOMER-NUMBER.
005200*
005300        DISPLAY '----------------------------------------------------'.
005400        DISPLAY 'KEY IN THE NEXT CUSTOMER NUMBER AND PRESS ENTER,'.
005500        DISPLAY 'OR KEY IN 999999 AND PRESS ENTER TO QUIT.'.
005600        ACCEPT CUSTNO.
005700        IF CUSTNO = '999999'
005800             MOVE 'Y' TO END-OF-INQUIRIES-SW.
005900*
006000 120-GET-CUSTOMER-ROW.
006100*
006200*****EXEC SQL
006300*****    SELECT CUSTNO,      FNAME,          LNAME,
006400*****           ADDR,        CITY,           STATE,
006500*****              ZIPCODE
006600*****    INTO  :CUSTNO,      :FNAME,          :LNAME,
006700*****          :ADDR,        :CITY,           :STATE,
006800*****          :ZIPCODE
006900*****    FROM   MM01.CUSTOMER
007000*****         WHERE  CUSTNO = :CUSTNO
007100*****END-EXEC.
          PERFORM SQL-INITIAL UNTIL SQL-INIT-DONE
          CALL 'DSNHLI' USING SQL-PLIST2.
007200*
007300        IF SQLCODE NOT = 0
007400             MOVE 'N' TO CUSTOMER-FOUND-SW.
007500*
007600 130-DISPLAY-CUSTOMER-LINES.
007700*
007800        DISPLAY '----------------------------------------------------'.
007900        DISPLAY '    CUSTOMER ' CUSTNO.
008000        DISPLAY '    NAME     ' FNAME ' ' LNAME.
008100        DISPLAY '    ADDRESS  ' ADDR.
008200        DISPLAY '             ' CITY ' ' STATE ' '
008210                              ZIPCODE.
008300*
008400 140-DISPLAY-ERROR-LINES.
008500*
008600        DISPLAY '----------------------------------------------------'.
008700        DISPLAY '    CUSTOMER NUMBER ' CUSTNO ' NOT FOUND.'.
008800*
```

Appendix B

SQLCODE and SQLSTATE values

This appendix lists all of the SQLCODE and SQLSTATE values for version 4.1 along with a description of each error. The SQLCODE is set by DB2 after each SQL statement is executed. DB2 conforms to the ISO/ANSI SQL standards as follows:

If SQLCODE = 0, the execution was successful.
If SQLCODE > 0, the execution was successful with a warning.
If SQLCODE < 0, the execution was not successful.

The SQLSTATE value is also set by DB2 after the execution of each SQL statement. As a result, application programs can check the execution of SQL statements by testing the SQLSTATE instead of the SQLCODE value. SQLSTATE is a 5-byte character-string variable in the SQL communication area. Often, one SQLSTATE value is equivalent to two or more SQLCODE values.

In the pages that follow, you'll first see a table of all the SQLCODE and SQLSTATE values in SQLCODE sequence. Then, you'll see a table of all the SQLSTATE values along with their SQLCODE equivalents in SQLSTATE sequence. In both tables, the descriptions are the same. Within these descriptions, an item in parentheses is an item that shows when the IBM error message for that code is displayed or printed.

Because these tables include all of the possible codes that can occur, some of the descriptions refer to terms and facilities that aren't presented in this book. Our goal, however, was to make a complete list so you shouldn't encounter a code that you can't find in this appendix. If you need more information about these codes, please refer to *DB2 for MVS/ESA V4 Messages and Codes.*

Warning SQLCODE values

SQLCODE	SQLSTATE	Description
+012	01545	The unqualified column name (column-name) was interpreted as a correlated reference.
+098	01568	A dynamic SQL statement ends with a semicolon.
+100	02000	Row not found for FETCH, UPDATE, or DELETE, or the result of a query is an empty table.
+110	01561	The SQL update to a data capture table was not signaled to the originating subsystem.
+111	01590	The subpages option is not supported for type 2 indexes.
+117	01525	The number of insert values is not the same as the number of object columns.
+162	01514	The table space (database-name.tablespace-name) has been placed in check pending mode.
+203	01552	The qualified column (column-name) was resolved using a non-unique or unexposed name.
+204	01532	(Name) is an undefined name.
+206	01533	(Column-name) is not a column of an inserted table, updated table, or any table identified in a FROM clause.
+218	01537	The SQL statement referencing a remote object can't be explained.
+219	01532	The required explanation table (table-name) doesn't exist.
+220	01546	The column (column-name) in explanation table (table-name) isn't defined properly.
+304	01515	A value with data type (data-type1) can't be assigned to a host variable because the value isn't within the range of the host variable in position (position-number) with data type (data-type2).
+331	01520	The null value has been assigned to a host variable because the string can't be translated. The reason is (reason-code), character (code-point), host variable (position-number).
+339	01569	The SQL statement has been successfully executed, but there may be some character conversion inconsistencies.
+402	01521	The location (location) is unknown.
+403	01522	The local object referenced by the CREATE ALIAS statement doesn't exist.
+535	01591	The result of the positioned update or delete may depend on the order of the rows.
+541	01543	The referential or unique constraint name has been ignored because it is a duplicate.
+551	01548	The (auth-id) doesn't have the privilege to perform operation (operation) on object (object-name).
+552	01542	The (auth-id) doesn't have the privilege to perform operation (operation).
+558	01516	The WITH GRANT option is ignored.
+561	01523	The ALTER, INDEX, and REFERENCES privileges can't be granted to public at all locations.
+562	01560	A grant of a privilege was ignored because the grantee already has the privilege from the grantor.
+610	01566	The INDEX (index-name) has been placed in recover pending mode.
+625	01518	The definition of table (table-name) has been changed to incomplete.
+626	01529	Dropping the index terminates enforcement of the uniqueness of a key that was defined when the table was created.
+645	01528	The WHERE NOT NULL is ignored because the index key can't contain null values.
+650	01538	The table being created or altered can't become a dependent table.
+653	01551	Table (table-name) in partitioned table space (tspace-name) isn't available because its partitioned index hasn't been created.
+658	01600	The SUBPAGES value is ignored for the catalog index (index-name).

+664	01540	The internal length of the limit-key fields for the partitioned index (index-name) exceeds the length imposed by the index manager.
+738	01530	The definition change of object (object-name) may require similar change on read-only systems.
+802	01519	An exception error (exception-type) has occurred during (operation-type) operation on (data-type) data, and in position (position-number).
+806	01553	The bind isolation level RR conflicts with table space LOCKSIZE PAGE or LOCKSIZE ROW and LOCKMAX 0.
+807	01554	The result of decimal multiplication may cause an overflow.
+863	01539	The connection was successful but only SBCS will be supported.
+2000	56094	TYPE 1 INDEXES with SUBPAGES greater than 1 can't become group buffer pool dependent in a data sharing environment.
+30100	01558	The operation completed successfully but a distribution protocol violation has been detected. The original SQLCODE = (original-sqlcode) and original SQLSTATE = (original-sqlstate).

Error SQLCODE values

SQLCODE	SQLSTATE	Description
-007	42601	The statement contains the illegal character (character).
-010	42603	The string constant beginning (string) is not terminated properly.
-029	42601	The INTO clause is required.
-060	42815	An invalid (type) specification: (spec) where 'type' is either LENGTH or SCALE, and "spec" is the specified length or scale. Length or scale must be specified by an unsigned integer constant and the value must be in the range allowed by the data type.
-084	42612	An unacceptable SQL statement was executed due to one of the following: (1) an attempt to PREPARE or EXECUTE IMMEDIATE an SQL statement that can't be prepared (refer to the proper SQL statement in the SQL reference manual); (2) the embedded SQL statement isn't an SQL statement supported by DB2; or (3) the statement referenced an undeclared cursor.
-101	54001	The statement is too long or too complex.
-102	54002	A literal string is too long. The string begins (string).
-103	42604	The (literal) is an invalid numeric literal.
-104	42601	Illegal symbol "token." Some symbols that might be legal are: (token-list).
-105	42604	The statement contains an invalid string.
-107	42622	The name (name) is too long. The maximum allowable size is (size).
-109	42601	The (clause) clause isn't permitted in the context in which it appears in the SQL statement. A subselect can't have an INTO clause. A CREATE VIEW statement can't have INTO, ORDER BY, or FOR UPDATE clauses. An embedded SELECT statement can't have ORDER BY or FOR UPDATE clauses. SELECT statements used in cursor declarations can't have an INTO clause.
-110	42606	The literal beginning with (string) contains one or more characters that aren't valid hexadecimal digits.
-111	42901	A column function doesn't include a column name.
-112	42607	The operand of a column function is another column function.
-113	42602	An invalid character was found in (string), reason code – nnn.
-114	42961	A 3-part SQL procedure name was provided in an SQL CALL statement. The first part of the SQL procedure name, which specifies the location where the stored procedure resides, didn't match the value of the SQL CURRENT SERVER special register.
-115	42601	A predicate is invalid because the comparison operator (operator) is followed by a parenthesized list or by ANY or ALL without a subquery.
-117	42802	The number of insert values isn't the same as the number of object columns.

-118	42902	The object table or view of the INSERT, DELETE, or UPDATE statement is also identified in a FROM clause.
-119	42803	A column identified in a HAVING clause isn't included in the GROUP BY clause.
-120	42903	A WHERE clause or SET clause includes a column function.
-121	42701	The column (name) is identified more than once in the INSERT or UPDATE statement.
-122	42803	A SELECT statement with no GROUP BY clause contains a column name and a column function in the SELECT clause or a column name is contained in the SELECT clause but not in the GROUP BY clause.
-125	42805	An integer in the ORDER BY clause doesn't identify a column of the result.
-126	42829	The SELECT statement contains both an UPDATE clause and an ORDER BY clause.
-127	42905	The keyword DISTINCT is specified more than once in a subselect.
-128	42601	Invalid use of null in a predicate.
-129	54004	The statement contains too many table names.
-130	22019	The ESCAPE clause consists of more than one character, or the string pattern contains an invalid occurrence of the ESCAPE character.
-131	42818	A statement with the LIKE predicate has incompatible data types.
-132	42824	A LIKE predicate is invalid because the second operand isn't a string.
-133	42906	A column function in a subquery of a HAVING clause is invalid because all column references in its argument aren't correlated to the GROUP BY result that the HAVING clause is applied to.
-134	42907	Improper use of a long string column (column-name) or a host variable of maximum length greater than 254.
-136	54005	The SORT can't be executed because the sort key length is greater than 4000 bytes.
-137	54006	The length of the result of a concatenation exceeds 32,764 (if character operands) or 16,382 (if graphic operands).
-138	22011	The second or third argument of the SUBSTR function is out of range.
-144	58003	Invalid section number (number).
-150	42807	The object of the INSERT, DELETE, or UPDATE statement is a view for which the requested operation isn't permitted.
-151	42808	The UPDATE statement is invalid because the catalog description of column (column-name) indicates that it can't be updated.
-152	42809	The DROP clause (clause) in the ALTER statement is invalid because (constraint-name) is a (constraint-type).
-153	42908	The CREATE VIEW statement doesn't include a required column list.
-154	42909	The CREATE VIEW failed because the view definition contains a UNION, a UNION ALL, or a remote object.
-156	42809	The statement doesn't identify a table.
-157	42810	Only a table name can be specified in a foreign key clause; (object-name) isn't the name of a table.
-158	42811	The number of columns specified for the view isn't the same as the number of columns specified by the SELECT clause.
-159	42809	The object specified in the DROP VIEW statement, DROP ALIAS statement, or COMMENT ON ALIAS statement identifies a table instead of a view or an alias.
-160	42813	The WITH CHECK OPTION doesn't apply to a view definition under either of the following circumstances: the view is read-only (for example, the view definition includes DISTINCT, GROUP BY, or JOIN) or the view definition includes a subquery.
-161	44000	The INSERT or UPDATE isn't allowed because a resulting row doesn't satisfy the view definition.
-164	42502	The authorization ID (auth-id) doesn't have the authority necessary to create views with qualifiers other than its own authorization ID. Specifically, the

		attempt to create a view with qualifier (authorization ID) is rejected.
-170	42605	An SQL statement includes the scalar function (function-name) with either too many or too few arguments.
-171	42815	Either the data type, the length, or the value of argument (nn) of scalar function (function-name) is incorrect.
-173	42801	The cursor is not a read-only cursor. WITH UR can be specified only if DB2 can determine that the cursor is read-only.
-180	22007	The string representation of a datetime value doesn't conform to the syntax for the specified or implied data type.
-181	22007	The string representation of a datetime value isn't a valid datetime value.
-182	42816	The specified arithmetic expression contains an improperly used datetime value or labeled duration.
-183	22008	The result of an arithmetic operation is a date or timestamp that isn't within the valid range of dates which are between 0001-01-01 and 9999-12-31.
-184	42610	The specified arithmetic expression contains a parameter marker improperly used with a datetime value.
-185	57008	The local format option has been used with a date or time and no local exit has been installed.
-186	22505	The logical format option has been used with a datetime value and DB2 has discovered that the datetime exit routine has been changed to produce a longer local format.
-187	22506	A reference to a CURRENT DATE/TIME special register is invalid because the MVS time-of-day (TOD) clock is bad or the PARMTZ is out of range.
-188	22503	The host variable reference in the DESCRIBE TABLE statement doesn't contain a valid string representation of a name.
-189	22522	CCSID (ccsid) is unknown or invalid for the data type or subtype.
-191	22504	A string can't be used because it is invalid mixed data.
-197	42877	A SELECT statement that specifies both the union of two or more tables and the ORDER BY clause can't use qualified column names in the ORDER BY clause.
-198	42617	The operand of the PREPARE or EXECUTE IMMEDIATE statement is blank or empty.
-199	42601	Illegal use of keyword (keyword). Token (token-list) was expected.
-203	42702	A reference to column (column-name) is ambiguous.
-204	42704	The object identified by (name) isn't defined in the DB2 subsystem.
-205	42703	No column with the specified (column-name) occurs in the table or view (table-name).
-206	42703	(Column-name) isn't a column of an inserted table, updated table, or any table identified in a FROM clause.
-208	42707	The ORDER BY clause is invalid because column (name) isn't part of the result table.
-219	42704	The required explanation table (table-name) doesn't exist.
-220	55002	The column (column-name) in an explanation table (table-name) isn't defined properly.
-221	55002	"SET OF OPTIONAL COLUMNS" in the explanation table (table-name) is incomplete. Optional column (column-name) is missing.
-250	42718	A three-part object name (table, view, or alias) can't be used until the local location name is defined.
-251	42602	Token (name) isn't valid. A location name can't contain alphabetic extenders. (The standard alphabetic extenders in the United States are #, @, $.)
-300	22024	The C string variable contained in host variable or parameter (position-number) isn't NUL-terminated.
-301	42895	The value of input host variable or parameter number (position-number) can't be used as specified because of its data type.
-302	22001	The value of an input variable or parameter number (position-number) is invalid or too large for the target column or the target value.

-303	42806	A value can't be assigned to output host variable number (position-number) because the data types aren't comparable.
-304	22003	A value with data type (data-type1) can't be assigned to a host variable because the value isn't within the range of the host variable in position (position-number) with data type (data-type2).
-305	22002	The null value can't be assigned to output host variable number (position-number) because no indicator variable is specified.
-309	22512	A predicate is invalid because a referenced host variable has the null value.
-310	22023	Decimal host variable or parameter (number) contains non-decimal data.
-311	22501	The length of input host variable number (position-number) is negative or greater than the maximum.
-312	42618	The host variable (variable-name) appears in the SQL statement, but the SQL statement is a prepared statement; the attributes of the variable are inconsistent with its usage in the static SQL statement; or the variable is not declared in the application program.
-313	07001	The number of host variables specified isn't equal to the number of parameter markers.
-314	42714	The statement contains an ambiguous host variable reference.
-330	22021	A string can't be used because it can't be translated. The reason is (reason-code), character (code-point), host variable (position-number).
-331	22021	A string can't be assigned to a host variable because it can't be translated. The reason is (reason-code), character (code-point), position (position-number).
-332	57017	The operation required the translation of a string to a different coded character set, but the particular translation isn't described in the SYSSTRINGS catalog table. The first (ccsid) identifies the coded character set of the string and the second (ccsid) identifies the coded character set to which it must be translated.
-333	56010	The subtype of a string variable isn't the same as the subtype known at bind time and the difference can't be resolved by translation.
-338	42972	An ON clause is invalid. This return code reports a violation of one of the following: (1) one expression of the predicate must only reference columns of one of the operand tables of the associated join operator, and the other expression of the predicate must only reference columns of the other operand table; (2) a VALUE or COALESCE function is allowed in the ON clause only when the join operator is a FULL OUTER JOIN or FULL JOIN; or (3) an operator other than equals (=) isn't allowed in a FULL OUTER JOIN or FULL JOIN.
-339	56082	The SQL statement can't be executed from an ASCII based DRDA application requestor to a V2R2 DB2 subsystem.
-351	56084	An unsupported SQLTYPE was encountered in position (position-number) on a PREPARE or DESCRIBE operation. Some SQL data types aren't supported by DB2 version 4. Position (position-number) is the position of the first element with an invalid data type in the SQLDA. A common reason why this error occurs is when DB2 attempts to describe large object data residing on a non-DB2 server. Some of the SQLTYPEs that can cause this error are: LOB, BLOB, CLOB, and DBLOB.
-400	54027	The catalog has the maximum number of user defined indexes (100).
-401	42818	An arithmetic operation appearing within the SQL statement has a mixture of numeric and non-numeric operands, or the operands of a comparison operation aren't compatible.
-402	42819	A non-numeric operand has been specified for the arithmetic function or operator (arith-fop).
-404	22001	An INSERT or UPDATE statement specifies a value that is longer than the maximum-length string that can be stored in column (column-name).
-405	42820	The numeric literal (literal) can't be used as specified because it is out of range.

-406	22003	A calculated or derived numeric value isn't within the range of its object column.
-407	23502	An UPDATE or INSERT value is null, but the object column (column-name) can't contain null values.
-408	42821	An UPDATE or INSERT value isn't comparable with the data type of its object column (column-name).
-409	42607	The operand of the COUNT function in the SQL statement violates SQL syntax. A common error is a column name or other expression without DISTINCT.
-410	42820	The specified floating point literal (literal) is more than 30 character in length.
-411	56040	A reference to the CURRENT SQLID special register is invalid in a statement that contains the three-part name or alias of an object that is remote to the remote server.
-412	42823	The SELECT clause of a subquery specifies multiple columns.
-414	42824	A LIKE predicate is invalid because the first operand isn't a string.
-415	42825	The corresponding columns (column-name) of the operands of a UNION or a UNION ALL don't have comparable column descriptions.
-416	42907	The UNION specified in the SQL statement couldn't be performed because one of the tables participating in the union contains a long string column (for example, a VARCHAR column with length greater than 254). The operands of a UNION can't contain long string columns.
-417	42609	A statement string to be prepared includes parameter markers as the operands of the same operation.
-418	42610	A statement string to be prepared contains an invalid use of parameter markers.
-419	42911	The decimal divide operation is invalid because the result would have a negative scale.
-420	22018	The value of a character string argument wasn't acceptable to the (function-name) function.
-421	42826	The operands of a UNION or UNION ALL don't have the same number of columns.
-426	2D528	An application using DRDA protocols has attempted to issue a dynamic COMMIT statement while connected to a location where updates aren't allowed. A dynamic COMMIT may be issued only while connected to a location where updates are allowed.
-427	2D529	An application using DRDA protocols has attempted to issue a dynamic ROLLBACK statement while connected to a location where updates aren't allowed. A dynamic ROLLBACK may be issued only while connected to a location where updates are allowed.
-440	42884	The number of parameters in the parameter list doesn't match the number of parameters expected for stored procedure (name), AUTHID (authid), LUNAME (luname). The (number) parameters were expected.
-444	42724	DB2 received an SQL CALL statement for a stored procedure and found the row in the SYSIBM.SYSPROCEDURES catalog table associated with the requested procedure name. However, the MVS load module identified in the LOADMOD column of the SYSIBM.SYSPROCEDURES row couldn't be found.
-450	39501	While returning parameters from a stored procedure to an application, DB2 detected an overlay of one of the parameters. A stored procedure overwrote storage beyond a parameter's declared length.
-469	42886	DB2 received an SQL CALL statement for a stored procedure. DB2 found the row in the SYSIBM.SYSPROCEDURES catalog table associated with the requested procedure name. However, parameter (number) was identified in the PARMLIST column of the SYSIBM.SYSPROCEDURES table as an OUT or INOUT parameter. A host variable must be supplied on the SQL CALL statement for parameters defined as OUT or INOUT.

-470	39002	DB2 received an SQL CALL statement for a stored procedure and found a null value in the incoming parameter list. The DB2 stored procedure was defined in the SYSIBM.SYSPROCEDURES catalog table with LINKAGE=, which specifies that the DB2 stored procedure doesn't accept null values.
-471	55023	The SQL CALL for stored procedure (name) failed due to reason (reason-code). See *DB2 for MVS/ESA V4 Messages and Codes* for the definition of the reason-codes.
-497	54041	An attempt was made to create an object in database (database-name), but the limit of 32767 OBIDs has been exceeded for that database.
-500	24501	The FETCH, UPDATE, DELETE, or CLOSE statement identifies a closed cursor that was defined with the WITH HOLD option. The cursor was closed when the connection where it was dependent was destroyed during a commit operation. The connection was destroyed because the application process placed it in the released state, or the application plan was bound with the DISCONNECT(AUTOMATIC) option.
-501	24501	The cursor identified in a FETCH or CLOSE statement isn't open.
-502	24502	The cursor identified in an OPEN statement is already open.
-503	42912	The application program attempted to update (using a cursor) a value in a column of the object table that wasn't identified in the FOR UPDATE clause in the cursor declaration.
-504	34000	The cursor name (cursor-name) isn't defined.
-507	24501	The cursor identified in the UPDATE or DELETE statement isn't open.
-508	24504	The cursor identified in the UPDATE or DELETE statement isn't positioned on a row.
-509	42827	The application program attempted to execute an UPDATE or DELETE WHERE CURRENT OF cursor statement where the table named in that statement didn't match the name of the table specified in the declaration for that cursor.
-510	42828	The application program attempted to execute an UPDATE or DELETE WHERE CURRENT OF cursor statement against a table or view that can't be updated or deleted. This can occur for a delete from a read-only view or for an update in which the cursor wasn't defined with the FOR UPDATE clause.
-511	42829	The result table of the SELECT statement can't be updated. This can occur if the SELECT specifies more than one table or view in the FROM clause, if the SELECT list contains a built-in function or DISTINCT, or if the statement contains an ORDER BY, GROUP BY or HAVING clause. This can also occur if a view is specified in the FROM clause and the view can't be updated.
-512	56023	The statement reference to a remote object is invalid. One of the following condition exists: (1) the statement refers to multiple locations; (2) a statement with a remote reference is being explained either by a dynamic EXPLAIN statement or the EXPLAIN(YES) option; (3) an alias is used incorrectly; or (4) a three-part name is implicitly or explicitly used in a statement that is not supported by the DB2 private protocols.
-513	42924	The alias (alias-name) must not be defined on another local or remote alias.
-514	26501	The application program has tried to use a cursor (cursor-name) that is not in a prepared state. The cursor is associated with a statement that either (1) has never been prepared, or (2) has been invalidated by a commit or rollback operation.
-516	26501	The DESCRIBE statement doesn't identify a prepared statement.
-517	07005	Cursor (cursor-name) can't be used because its statement name doesn't identify a prepared SELECT statement.
-518	07003	The EXECUTE statement doesn't identify a valid prepared statement. One of the following conditions exists: (1) the statement named in the EXECUTE statement has not been prepared; (2) the statement named in the EXECUTE statement identifies a SELECT statement; or (3) the statement named in the EXECUTE IMMEDIATE statement identifies a SELECT statement.

-519	24506	The application program has attempted to PREPARE (actually, re-PREPARE) the SELECT statement for the specified cursor when that cursor was already open.
-525	51015	The SQL statement can't be executed because it was in error at bind time for section (sectno) package (pkgname) consistency token X('contoken').
-530	23503	The INSERT or UPDATE value of foreign key (constraint-name) is invalid.
-531	23504	The primary key in a parent row can't be updated because it has one or more dependent rows in relationship (constraint-name).
-532	23504	The relationship (constraint-name) restricts the deletion of row with RID X('rid-number').
-533	21501	An INSERT operation with a subselect attempted to insert multiple rows into a self-referencing table. The subselect of the INSERT operation should return no more than one row of data.
-534	21502	An UPDATE operation attempted to update a primary key on multiple rows of the object table. An UPDATE statement updating the primary key can't be used to update more than one row of the object table.
-536	42914	The DELETE statement is invalid due to referential constraints for table (table-name).
-537	42709	The PRIMARY KEY clause, a FOREIGN KEY clause, or a UNIQUE clause identifies column (column-name) more than once.
-538	42830	The FOREIGN KEY (name) doesn't conform to the description of the primary key of table (table-name).
-539	42888	The CREATE or ALTER TABLE statement can't be executed because the indicated table (table-name) doesn't have a primary key. So, the primary key can't be dropped, or the table can't be defined as a parent in a referential constraint.
-540	57001	The definition of table (table-name) is incomplete because it lacks a primary key index or a required unique index.
-542	42831	(Column-name) can't be a column of a primary key or a unique constraint because it can contain null values.
-543	23511	A row in a parent table can't be deleted because the check constraint (check-constraint) restricts the deletion.
-544	23512	The check constraint specified in the ALTER TABLE statement can't be added because an existing row violates the check constraint.
-545	23513	The requested operation isn't allowed because a row doesn't satisfy the check constraint (check-constraint).
-546	42621	The check constraint (check-constraint) is invalid.
-548	42621	The check constraint that is defined with (column-name) is invalid.
-549	42509	The (statement) statement isn't allowed for (object_type1 object_name) because the bind option DYNAMICRULES(BIND) in the (object_type2) is in effect.
-551	42501	(Auth-id) doesn't have the privilege to perform operation (operation) on object (object-name).
-552	42502	(Auth-id) doesn't have the privilege to perform operation (operation).
-553	42503	(Auth-id) isn't one of the valid authorization IDs.
-554	42502	An authorization ID can't grant a privilege to itself.
-555	42502	An authorization ID can't revoke a privilege from itself.
-556	42504	(Authid2) can't have the (privilege) privilege (on-object) revoked by (authid1) because the revokee doesn't possess the privilege or the revoker didn't make the grant.
-557	42852	Inconsistent GRANT/REVOKE keyword (keyword). Permitted keywords are (keyword-list).
-558	56025	Invalid clause or combination of clauses on a GRANT or REVOKE statement.
-559	57002	The authorization mechanism has been disabled in the DB2 subsystem. Consequently, GRANT and REVOKE statements are ignored.

-567	42501	(Bind-type) authorization error using (auth-id) authority package = (package-name) privilege = (privilege).
-571	25000	The statement would result in a multiple site update. This SQLCODE is issued in the following situations: (1) when an application program operating in an IMS or CICS environment attempts to modify data at a remote location where multi-site update capabilities aren't supported; or (2) when an application has explicit SQL statements within a commit scope that would result in updates at multiple sites where one of the sites where data is being updated doesn't support multi-site updates.
-574	42894	The specified default value conflicts with the column definition.
-601	42710	The CREATE statement tried to create an object (name) of type (obj-type), but an object of that type with the same name is already defined in the DB2 subsystem.
-602	54008	The number of columns specified in the CREATE INDEX statement exceeds 64, the maximum permitted by DB2.
-603	23515	The index defined in the CREATE INDEX statement couldn't be created as unique because the specified table already contains rows that are duplicates with respect to the values of the identified columns.
-604	42611	A column definition in the CREATE or ALTER TABLE statement contains an invalid length, precision, or scale attribute specification.
-607	42832	The operation or option (operation) can't be performed on the catalog object specified in the SQL statement.
-611	53088	Only LOCKMAX 0 can be specified when the lock size of the table space is TABLESPACE or TABLE.
-612	42711	(Column-name) is a duplicate column name.
-613	54008	The primary key or a unique constraint is too long or has too many columns.
-614	54008	The index can't be created because the sum of the internal lengths of the identified columns is greater than the allowable maximum.
-615	55006	The operation (operation-type) can't be performed because the package is in use by the same application process. The type of bind operations are BIND, REBIND and DROP.
-616	42893	The object (obj-type1 obj-name1) can't be dropped because it is referenced by object (obj-type2 obj-name2). Some types of objects can't be dropped if there are other objects that are dependent on them. For example, a storage group can't be dropped if there are one or more existing table spaces that use that storage group.
-617	56089	All indexes defined for a table within a table space with LOCKSIZE ROW must be defined as type 2 indexes.
-618	42832	Operation (operation) isn't allowed on system databases.
-619	55011	The statements CREATE, ALTER, or DROP for a table space in the work file database can't be processed unless the work file database is stopped (using the STOP command).
-620	53001	The keyword (keyword) in (stmt-type) statement isn't permitted for a table space in the work file database.
-621	58001	A duplicate DBID (dbid) was detected and previously assigned to (database-name). An inconsistency exists between the DB2 catalog and directory.
-622	56031	FOR MIXED DATA is specified in a column description of a CREATE or ALTER TABLE statement, but the MIXED DATA install option is set to NO. FOR MIXED DATA is valid only when the MIXED DATA install option is set to YES.
-623	55012	A clustering index already exists on table (table-name). A given table can have only one cluster index.
-624	42889	Table (table-name) already has a primary key.
-625	55014	Table (table-name) doesn't have an index to enforce the uniqueness of the primary key.

-626	55015	An ALTER statement specifies a BUFFERPOOL, USING, PRIQTY, SECQTY, ERASE, or GBPCACHE clause, but the page set isn't stopped.
-627	55016	The ALTER statement is invalid because the page set has user-managed data sets.
-628	42613	Mutually exclusive clauses were specified in one or more of the following ways: (1) a CREATE TABLESPACE statement contains both the SEGSIZE and NUMPARTS clauses; (2) a (column-definition) contains both NOT NULL and DEFAULT NULL clauses; (3) a (column-definition) contains both FIELDPROC and DEFAULT clauses; (4) a SELECT statement contains both the UPDATE clause and the FOR FETCH ONLY clause; or (5) an ALTER TABLE statement contains both a DROP CONSTRAINT clause and either a DROP FOREIGN KEY clause or a DROP CHECK clause.
-629	42834	SET NULL can't be specified because FOREIGN KEY (name) can't contain null values.
-630	56089	The WHERE NOT NULL specification is invalid for type 1 indexes.
-631	54008	The FOREIGN KEY (name) is too long or has too many columns.
-632	42915	The table can't be defined as a dependent of (table-name) because of delete rule restrictions.
-633	42915	The (delete-rule) specified in a FOREIGN KEY clause of the ALTER TABLE statement is invalid. The indicated (delete-rule) is required because a self-referencing constraint must have a (delete-rule) of CASCADE or the relationship would cause the table to be delete-connected to the same table through multiple paths and such relationships must have the same (delete-rule).
-634	42915	The CASCADE delete rule specified in the FOREIGN KEY clause of an ALTER TABLE statement is invalid because the relationship would form a cycle that would cause a table to be delete-connected to itself or the relation ship would cause another table to be delete-connected to the same table through multiple paths with different delete rules or with a delete rule equal to SET NULL.
-635	42915	The delete rules can't be different or can't be SET NULL.
-636	56016	The partitioning keys aren't specified in ascending or descending order.
-637	42614	Duplicate (keyword) keyword.
-638	42601	The table (table-name) can't be created because column definition is missing.
-639	56027	A partition key of the clustering index can't be updated. Therefore, a foreign key column with a delete rule of SET NULL can't be a column of a partition key if that column is nullable. If this error occurs for an ALTER TABLE operation, the foreign key can't be created. If this error occurs for a CREATE INDEX operation, the index can't be created.
-640	56089	LOCKSIZE ROW can't be specified because a table in this table space has a type 1 index.
-642	54021	There is a limit to the total number of columns that can be used in UNIQUE constraints in a CREATE TABLE statement. The statement exceeds that limit.
-643	54024	The check constraint definition exceeds the maximum allowable limit of 3800 characters. The redundant blank spaces are excluded from this limit.
-644	42615	The value specified for the keyword (keyword) parameter in the (stmt-type) SQL statement isn't a permitted value.
-646	55017	Table (table-name) can't be created in partitioned/default table space (tspace-name) because it already contains a table. Only one table may reside in a partitioned or default table space.
-647	57003	Buffer pool (bp-name) can't be specified because it hasn't been activated.
-650	56090	The ALTER INDEX statement can't be executed, reason (reason-code).
-651	54025	The CREATE TABLE or ALTER TABLE statement causes the table descriptor (record OBD) to exceed the object descriptor size limit of 32KB.
-652	23506	The result of the SQL statement has been rejected by the installation defined edit or validation procedure (proc-name) for the object table.

-653	57004	Table (table-name) in partitioned table space (tspace-name) isn't available because its partitioned index hasn't been created.
-655	56036	The CREATE or ALTER STOGROUP is invalid because the storage group would have both specific and nonspecific volume IDs.
-660	53035	Index (index-name) can't be created on a partitioned table space (tspace-name) because key limits aren't specified.
-661	53036	Index (index-name) can't be created on a partitioned table space (tspace-name) because the number of PART specifications isn't equal to the number of partitions of the table space.
-662	53037	A partitioned index can't be created on a non-partitioned table space (tspace-name).
-663	53038	The number of key limit values is either zero or greater than the number of columns in the key of index (index-name).
-665	53039	The PART clause of an ALTER statement is omitted or invalid.
-666	57005	The (stmt-verb object) can't be executed because function (function) is in progress.
-667	42917	The DROP INDEX statement attempted to drop the cluster index for a table residing in a partitioned table space. The cluster index for such a table can't be dropped explicitly with the DROP INDEX statement.
-668	56018	The ALTER TABLE statement attempted to add a column to a table that has an edit procedure. If a table has an edit procedure, no column can be added to it.
-669	42917	A table in a partitioned table space can't be dropped by the DROP TABLE statement.
-670	54010	The record length of the table exceeds the page size limit.
-671	53040	The buffer pool attribute of the table space can't be altered as specified because it would change the page size of the table space.
-672	55035	The DROP operation failed for table (table-name) because the table being dropped has the RESTRICT ON DROP attribute, or the table space or database being dropped contains the specified table, which has the RE-STRICT ON DROP attribute.
-676	53041	A 32K page buffer pool may not be used for an index. Only 4KB buffer pools (BP0, BP1, and BP2) can be specified for indexes.
-677	57011	An attempt to either open (create) or expand a buffer pool has failed because insufficient virtual storage was available.
-678	53045	The literal (literal) specified for the index limit key must conform to the data type (data-type) of the corresponding column (column-name).
-679	57006	The object (name) can't be created because a drop is pending on the object.
-680	54011	Too many columns are specified for a table. The maximum number of columns permitted per table is 750.
-681	23507	Column (column-name) is in violation of an installation defined field procedure. RT: (return-code), RS: (reason-code), MSG: (message-token).
-682	57010	Field procedure (procedure-name) couldn't be loaded.
-683	42842	Invalid column type for fieldproc, BIT DATA, SBCS DATA, or MIXED DATA option, (column-name).
-684	54012	The length of literal list beginning (string) is too long.
-685	58002	Invalid field type, (column-name).
-686	53043	A column defined with a field procedure can't be compared with another column with a different field procedure.
-687	53044	One column can't be compared with another column that has incompatible field types.
-688	58002	Incorrect data returned from field procedure, (column-name), (msgno).
-689	54011	Too many columns defined for a dependent table. The maximum number of columns allowed for a dependent table is 749.
-690	23508	The statement is rejected by data definition control support. The reason is (reason-code).

-691	57018	The required registration table (table-name) doesn't exist.
-692	57018	The required unique index (index-name) for DDL registration table (table-name) doesn't exist.
-693	55003	The column (column-name) in DDL registration table or index (table-name) (index-name) isn't defined properly.
-694	57023	The DDL statement can't be executed because a drop is pending on the DDL registration table (table-name).
-713	42815	The value specified in the SET (special-register) statement is not a valid value of the indicated special register.
-715	56064	Program (program-name) depends on a function of DB2 that is not supported by the current active release.
-716	56065	Program (program-name) was precompiled under a release not supported by the current level of DB2, or the contents of the DBRM have been modified after the precompilation phase.
-717	56066	The (bind-type) for (object-type) (object-name) with mark (release-dependency-mark) failed because (object-type) depends on functions of the release from which fallback has occurred. The plan or package indicated depends on a function of DB2 not supported by the currently active release.
-718	56067	The REBIND for package (package-name) failed because IBMREQD of (ibmreqd) is invalid. The IBMREQD column of the SYSIBM.SYSPACKAGE catalog table for the named package contains an unrecognizable character.
-719	42710	An attempt is made to add a package that already exists. The combination of 'location.collection.package.version' must be unique in the SYSIBM.SYSPACKAGE table. In addition, the combination of 'location.collection.package.consistency-token' must be unique.
-720	42710	An attempt is made to create a version of a package that already exists. Package name = (package-name), version = (version2).
-721	42710	An attempt is made to add or replace a package with a consistency token that is not unique for that package. Package name = (pkg-id), consistency token = (contoken).
-722	42704	The indicated subcommand was issued against a package that doesn't exist. Bind type = (bind-type), authorization ID = (auth-id), package = (package-name).
-726	55030	Bind error attempting to replace package = (package-name). There are ENABLE or DISABLE entries currently associated with the package.
-730	56053	The parent of a table in a read-only shared database must also be a table in a read-only shared database.
-731	56054	User-defined data set (dsname) must be defined with SHAREOPTIONS(1,3). The VSAM SHAREOPTIONS must be (1,3) for all of the indexes and table spaces in the database.
-732	56055	The database is defined on this subsystem with the ROSHARE READ attribute, but the table space or index space hasn't been defined on the owning subsystem.
-733	56056	The description of a table space, index space, or table in a ROSHARE READ database must be consistent with its description in the owner system.
-734	56057	The ROSHARE attribute of a database can't be altered from ROSHARE READ.
-735	55004	Database (dbid) can't be accessed because it is no longer a shared database.
-736	53014	Invalid OBID (obid) specified. An invalid OBID value was given on the CREATE statement.
-737	56056	A CREATE TABLE statement was issued using an implicit table space. An implicit table space may not be used in a database that has been defined as a read-only shared database.
-741	55020	A work file database is already defined for member (member-name).
-742	53004	The WORKFILE clause can't be used on a CREATE DATABASE statement to create a work file database for a DB2 subsystem that isn't a member of a

		DB2 data sharing group. The system database, DSNDB07, is the implicit work file database.
-751	42987	A stored procedure has been placed in MUST_ROLLBACK state due to SQL operation (name).
-752	0A001	The CONNECT statement is invalid because the process isn't in the connectable state.
-802	22012/22003	Exception error (exception-type) has occurred during (operation-type) operation on (data-type) data, position (position-number). The processing of an SQL arithmetic function or arithmetic expression that was either in the SELECT list of an SQL SELECT statement, in the search condition of a SELECT, UPDATE, or DELETE statement during the evaluation of a column function, or in the SET clause of the UPDATE statement has encountered an exception error, possibly indicated by (exception-type). The SQLSTATE is 22012 if ZERO DIVIDE, and 22003 if other than ZERO DIVIDE.
-803	23505	An inserted or updated value is invalid because the index in INDEX SPACE (indexspace-name) constrains columns of the table so no two rows can contain duplicate values in those columns. RID of existing row is X(rid).
-804	07002	An error was found in the application program input parameters for the SQL statement. The reason is (reason-code). The following is a list of reason codes: (01) Open issued for non-cursor; (02) Close issued for non-cursor; (03) prepare of EXECUTE IMMEDIATE; (04) statement isn't recognized; (05) no statement string present; (06) bad SQLDA format in parameter list; (07) SQLDA length is invalid; (08) unrecognized input data type; (09) invalid length for input variable; (10) invalid data length for output variable; (11) the value of SQLDABC is not consistent with the value of SQLD; (12) invalid input data pointer; (13) invalid output data pointer; (14) SQLN has too many items for SQLDABC; (15) input RDI pointer is invalid.
-805	51002	DBRM or PACKAGE NAME (location-name.collection-id.dbrm-name.consistency) token not found in plan (plan-name). The reason is (reason-code). See *DB2 for MVS/ESA V4 Messages and Codes* for the definition of the reason-codes.
-807	23509	Access denied: Package (package-name) isn't enabled for access from (connection-type connection-name).
-808	08001	The CONNECT semantics that apply to an application process are determined by the first CONNECT statement executed (successfully or unsuccessfully) by the application process.
-811	21000	Execution of an embedded SELECT statement has resulted in a result table containing more than one row. Alternatively, a subquery contained in a basic predicate has produced more than one value.
-812	22508	The SQL statement can't be processed because a blank collection-ID was found in the current PACKAGESET special register while trying to form a qualified package name for program (program-name.consistency-token) using plan (plan-name).
-815	42920	An embedded SEELCT statement of a subquery of a basic predicate either (1) directly contains a GROUP BY or HAVING clause, or (2) specifies as its object a view having a definition that includes a GROUP BY or HAVING clause. Neither construct is permitted.
-817	25000	The SQL statement can't be executed because the statement will result in a prohibited update operation.
-818	51003	The precompiler-generated timestamp (x) in the load module is different from the bind timestamp (y) built from the DBRM (z). This problem can occur if you: (1) precompile, compile, and link, without doing a BIND of the application; (2) precompile and BIND, without doing the compile and link for the application program; or (3) BIND the application using a DBRM that resulted from a different precompile of the application program than that which produced the object module that is linked into the application module.

-819	58004	SYSIBM.SYSVTREE.VTREE is a varying-length string column that contains the parse trees of views. In processing a view, the length control field of its parse tree was found to be zero.
-820	58004	The SQL statement can't be processed because (catalog-table) contains a value that isn't valid in this release.
-822	51004	The SQLDA contains an invalid data address or indicator variable address.
-840	54004	The number of items returned in the select list or presented in an insert list exceeds the allowable maximum of 750.
-842	08002	A connection to (location-name) already exists.
-843	08003	The SET CONNECTION or RELEASE statement must specify an existing connection.
-870	58026	The number of host variables in the statement isn't equal to the number of descriptors.
-900	08003	The SQL statement can't be executed because the application process isn't connected to an application server.
-901	58004	Unsuccessful execution caused by a system error that doesn't preclude the successful execution of subsequent SQL statements.
-902	58005	The pointer to the essential control block, either the CT or the RDA, is zeroes. This precludes the successful execution of the current SQL statement, as well as any subsequent SQL statements. A rebind is required.
-904	57011	Unsuccessful execution caused by an unavailable resource. The reason is (reason-code), type of resource (resource-type), and resource name (resource-name).
-905	57014	Unsuccessful execution due to resource limit being exceeded, resource name = (resource-name) limit = (limit-amount1) CPU seconds ((limit-amount2) service units) derived from (limit-source).
-906	51005	The SQL statement can't be executed because this function is disabled due to a prior error.
-908	23510	(Bind-type) error using (auth-id) authority. The BIND, REBIND or AUTO-REBIND operation isn't allowed.
-909	57007	The application program has either (1) dropped a table and then attempted to access it, or (2) dropped an index and then tried to access its object table using that index.
-910	57007	The SQL statement can't access an object on which a DROP or ALTER is pending.
-911	40001	The current unit of work has been rolled back due to a deadlock or timeout. The reason is (reason-code), type of resource (resource-type), and resource name (resource-name).
-913	57033	Unsuccessful execution caused by a deadlock or timeout. The reason is (reason-code), type of resource (resource-type), and resource name (resource-name).
-917	42969	Bind package failed. An error has occurred that prevents the package from being created. This SQLCODE can be issued during bind or commit processing.
-918	51021	Execution of the SQL statement failed because a communication link between the local DB2 and at least one remote server no longer exists. A previous failure caused this condition.
-919	56045	A rollback operation is required.
-922	42505	Authorization failure: (error-type) error. The reason is (reason-code).
-923	57015	Connection not established: DB2 (condition), reason (reason-code), type (resource-type), name (resource-name).
-924	58006	DB2 connection internal error, (function-code), (return-code), (reason-code).
-925	2D521	COMMIT not valid in IMS/VS or CICS environment.
-926	2D521	ROLLBACK not valid in IMS/VS or CICS environment.
-927	51006	The language interface (LI) was called when the connecting environment wasn't established. The program should be invoked under the DSN command.

-929	58002	Failure in a data capture exit: (token).
-939	51021	ROLLBACK required due to unrequested ROLLBACK of a remote server.
-947	56038	The SQL statement failed because it will change a table defined with data capture changes, but the data can't be propagated.
-948	56062	The unit of work was initiated before DDF was started, and the application attempted to perform a distributed operation. The unit of work must be terminated by a rollback operation.
-950	42705	The location name specified in the CONNECT statement is invalid or not listed in the communications database.
-965	51021	Stored procedure (procname) terminated abnormally.
-2001	53089	The number of host variable parameters for a stored procedure isn't equal to the number of expected host variable parameters. Actual number (sqldanum), expected number (opnum).
-30000	58008	Execution failed due to a distribution protocol error that will not affect the successful execution of subsequent commands or SQL statements: Reason (reason-code) (sub-code).
-30020	58009	Execution failed due to a distribution protocol error that caused deallocation of the conversation: Reason (reason-code) (sub-code).
-30021	58010	Execution failed due to a distribution protocol error that will affect the successful execution of subsequent commands or SQL statements: Manager (manager) at level (level) not supported error.
-30030	58013	Commit request was unsuccessful, a distribution protocol violation has been detected, or the conversation has been deallocated. Original SQLCODE=(orginal-sqlcode) and original SQLSTATE=(original-sqlstate).
-30040	57012	Execution failed due to unavailable resources that will not affect the successful execution of subsequent commands or SQL statements. Reason (reason-code) type of resource (resource-type) resource name (resource-name) product ID (pppvvrrm) RDBNAME (rdbname).
-30041	57013	Execution failed due to unavailable resources that will affect the successful execution of subsequent commands and SQL statements. Reason (reason-code) type of resource (resource-type) resource name (resource-name) product ID (pppvvrrm) RDBNAME (rdbname).
-30050	58011	(Command-or-SQL-statement-type) command or SQL statement invalid while BIND process in progress.
-30051	58012	Bind process with specified package name and consistency token not active.
-30052	42932	Program preparation assumptions are incorrect.
-30053	42506	An authorization failure encountered for the package owner.
-30060	08004	The user isn't authorized to access an RDB.
-30061	08004	An attempt was made to access an RDB that can't be found.
-30070	58014	(Command) command not supported error.
-30071	58015	(Object-type) object not supported error.
-30072	58016	(Parameter) : (subcode) parameter not supported error.
-30073	58017	(Parameter) : (subcode) parameter value not supported error.
-30074	58018	Reply message with (codepoint) SVRCOD not supported error.
-30080	08001	Communication error (code) (subcode). A SNA communication error was detected. Appendix A in *VTAM FOR MVS/ESA Programming for LU 6.2* contains the valid 'code' and 'subcode' values that can appear in this message.
-30090	25000	An update operation or a dynamic commit or rollback was attempted at a server that was supporting an application that was in a read-only execution environment (IMS or CICS).

Warning SQLSTATE values

SQLSTATE	SQLCODE	Description
01514	+162	The table space (database-name.tablespace-name) has been placed in check pending mode.
01515	+304	A value with data type (data-type1) can't be assigned to a host variable because the value isn't within the range of the host variable in position (position-number) with data type (data-type2).
01516	+558	The WITH GRANT option is ignored.
01518	+625	The definition of table (table-name) has been changed to incomplete.
01519	+802	An exception error (exception-type) has occurred during (operation-type) operation on (data-type) data, and in position (position-number).
01520	+331	The null value has been assigned to a host variable because the string can't be translated. The reason is (reason-code), character (code-point), host variable (position-number).
01521	+402	The location (location) is unknown.
01522	+403	The local object referenced by the CREATE ALIAS statement doesn't exist.
01523	+561	The ALTER, INDEX, and REFERENCES privileges can't be granted to public at all locations.
01525	+117	The number of insert values is not the same as the number of object columns.
01528	+645	The WHERE NOT NULL is ignored because the index key can't contain null values.
01529	+626	Dropping the index terminates enforcement of the uniqueness of a key that was defined when the table was created.
01530	+738	The definition change of object (object-name) may require similar change on read-only systems.
01532	+204	(Name) is an undefined name.
	+219	The required explanation table (table-name) doesn't exist.
01533	+206	(Column-name) is not a column of an inserted table, updated table, or any table identified in a FROM clause.
01537	+218	The SQL statement referencing a remote object can't be explained.
01538	+650	The table being created or altered can't become a dependent table.
01539	+863	The connection was successful but only SBCS will be supported.
01540	+664	The internal length of the limit-key fields for the partitioned index (index-name) exceeds the length imposed by the index manager.
01542	+552	The (auth-id) doesn't have the privilege to perform operation (operation).
01543	+541	The referential or unique constraint name has been ignored because it is a duplicate.
01545	+012	The unqualified column name (column-name) was interpreted as a correlated reference.
01546	+220	The column (column-name) in explanation table (table-name) isn't defined properly.
01548	+551	The (auth-id) doesn't have the privilege to perform operation (operation) on object (object-name).
01551	+653	Table (table-name) in partitioned table space (tspace-name) isn't available because its partitioned index hasn't been created.
01552	+203	The qualified column (column-name) was resolved using a non-unique or unexposed name.
01553	+806	The bind isolation level RR conflicts with table space LOCKSIZE PAGE or LOCKSIZE ROW and LOCKMAX 0.
01554	+807	The result of decimal multiplication may cause an overflow.
01558	+30100	The operation completed successfully but a distribution protocol violation has been detected. The original SQLCODE = (original-sqlcode) and original SQLSTATE = (original-sqlstate).

01560	+562	A grant of a privilege was ignored because the grantee already has the privilege from the grantor.
01561	+110	The SQL update to a data capture table was not signaled to the originating subsystem.
01566	+610	The INDEX (index-name) has been placed in recover pending mode.
01568	+098	A dynamic SQL statement ends with a semicolon.
01569	+339	The SQL statement has been successfully executed, but there may be some character conversion inconsistencies.
01590	+111	The subpages option is not supported for type 2 indexes.
01591	+535	The result of the positioned update or delete may depend on the order of the rows.
01600	+658	The SUBPAGES value is ignored for the catalog index (index-name).
02000	+100	Row not found for FETCH, UPDATE, or DELETE, or the result of a query is an empty table.
56094	+2000	TYPE 1 INDEXES with SUBPAGES greater than 1 can't become group buffer pool dependent in a data sharing environment.

Error SQLSTATE values

SQLSTATE	SQLCODE	Description
0A001	-752	The CONNECT statement is invalid because the process isn't in the connectable state.
2D528	-426	An application using DRDA protocols has attempted to issue a dynamic COMMIT statement while connected to a location where updates aren't allowed. A dynamic COMMIT may be issued only while connected to a location where updates are allowed.
2D529	-427	An application using DRDA protocols has attempted to issue a dynamic ROLLBACK statement while connected to a location where updates aren't allowed. A dynamic ROLLBACK may be issued only while connected to a location where updates are allowed.
2D521	-925	COMMIT not valid in IMS/VS or CICS environment.
	-926	ROLLBACK not valid in IMS/VS or CICS environment.
07001	-313	The number of host variables specified isn't equal to the number of parameter markers.
07002	-804	An error was found in the application program input parameters for the SQL statement. The reason is (reason-code). The following is a list of reason codes: (01) Open issued for non-cursor; (02) Close issued for non-cursor; (03) prepare of EXECUTE IMMEDIATE; (04) statement isn't recognized; (05) no statement string present; (06) bad SQLDA format in parameter list; (07) SQLDA length is invalid; (08) unrecognized input data type; (09) invalid length for input variable; (10) invalid data length for output variable; (11) the value of SQLDABC is not consistent with the value of SQLD; (12) invalid input data pointer; (13) invalid output data pointer; (14) SQLN has too many items for SQLDABC; (15) input RDI pointer is invalid.
07003	-518	The EXECUTE statement doesn't identify a valid prepared statement. One of the following conditions exists: (1) the statement named in the EXECUTE statement has not been prepared; (2) the statement named in the EXECUTE statement identifies a SELECT statement; or (3) the statement named in the EXECUTE IMMEDIATE statement identifies a SELECT statement.
07005	-517	Cursor (cursor-name) can't be used because its statement name doesn't identify a prepared SELECT statement.
08001	-808	The CONNECT semantics that apply to an application process are determined by the first CONNECT statement executed (successfully or unsuccessfully) by the application process.

	-30080	Communication error (code) (subcode). A SNA communication error was detected. Appendix A in *VTAM FOR MVS/ESA Programming for LU 6.2* contains the valid 'code' and 'subcode' values that can appear in this message.
08002	-842	A connection to (location-name) already exists.
08003	-843	The SET CONNECTION or RELEASE statement must specify an existing connection.
	-900	The SQL statement can't be executed because the application process isn't connected to an application server.
08004	-30060	The user isn't authorized to access an RDB.
	-30061	An attempt was made to access an RDB that can't be found.
21000	-811	Execution of an embedded SELECT statement has resulted in a result table containing more than one row. Alternatively, a subquery contained in a basic predicate has produced more than one value.
21501	-533	An INSERT operation with a subselect attempted to insert multiple rows into a self-referencing table. The subselect of the INSERT operation should return no more than one row of data.
21502	-534	An UPDATE operation attempted to update a primary key on multiple rows of the object table. An UPDATE statement updating the primary key can't be used to update more than one row of the object table.
22001	-302	The value of an input variable or parameter number (position-number) is invalid or too large for the target column or the target value.
	-404	An INSERT or UPDATE statement specifies a value that is longer than the maximum-length string that can be stored in column (column-name).
22002	-305	The null value can't be assigned to output host variable number (position-number) because no indicator variable is specified.
22003	-304	A value with data type (data-type1) can't be assigned to a host variable because the value isn't within the range of the host variable in position (position-number) with data type (data-type2). (See also code 22012.)
	-406	A calculated or derived numeric value isn't within the range of its object column.
22007	-180	The string representation of a datetime value doesn't conform to the syntax for the specified or implied data type.
	-181	The string representation of a datetime value isn't a valid datetime value.
22008	-183	The result of an arithmetic operation is a date or timestamp that isn't within the valid range of dates which are between 0001-01-01 and 9999-12-31.
22011	-138	The second or third argument of the SUBSTR function is out of range.
22012/22003	-802	Exception error (exception-type) has occurred during (operation-type) operation on (data-type) data, position (position-number). The processing of an SQL arithmetic function or arithmetic expression that was either in the SELECT list of an SQL SELECT statement, in the search condition of a SELECT, UPDATE, or DELETE statement during the evaluation of a column function, or in the SET clause of the UPDATE statement has encountered an exception error, possibly indicated by (exception-type). The SQLSTATE is 22012 if ZERO DIVIDE, and 22003 if other than ZERO DIVIDE.
22018	-420	The value of a character string argument wasn't acceptable to the (function-name) function.
22019	-130	The ESCAPE clause consists of more than one character, or the string pattern contains an invalid occurrence of the ESCAPE character.
22021	-330	A string can't be used because it can't be translated. The reason is (reason-code), character (code-point), host variable (position-number).
	-331	A string can't be assigned to a host variable because it can't be translated. The reason is (reason-code), character (code-point), position (position-number).
22023	-310	Decimal host variable or parameter (number) contains non-decimal data.
22024	-300	The C string variable contained in host variable or parameter (position-number) isn't NUL-terminated.

22501	-311	The length of input host variable number (position-number) is negative or greater than the maximum.
22503	-188	The host variable reference in the DESCRIBE TABLE statement doesn't contain a valid string representation of a name.
22504	-191	A string can't be used because it is invalid mixed data.
22505	-186	The logical format option has been used with a datetime value and DB2 has discovered that the datetime exit routine has been changed to produce a longer local format.
22506	-187	A reference to a CURRENT DATE/TIME special register is invalid because the MVS time-of-day (TOD) clock is bad or the PARMTZ is out of range.
22508	-812	The SQL statement can't be processed because a blank collection-ID was found in the current PACKAGESET special register while trying to form a qualified package name for program (program-name.consistency-token) using plan (plan-name).
22512	-309	A predicate is invalid because a referenced host variable has the null value.
22522	-189	CCSID (ccsid) is unknown or invalid for the data type or subtype.
23502	-407	An UPDATE or INSERT value is null, but the object column (column-name) can't contain null values.
23503	-530	The INSERT or UPDATE value of foreign key (constraint-name) is invalid.
23504	-531	The primary key in a parent row can't be updated because it has one or more dependent rows in relationship (constraint-name).
	-532	The relationship (constraint-name) restricts the deletion of row with RID X('rid-number').
23505	-803	An inserted or updated value is invalid because the index in INDEX SPACE (indexspace-name) constrains columns of the table so no two rows can contain duplicate values in those columns. RID of existing row is X(rid).
23506	-652	The result of the SQL statement has been rejected by the installation defined edit or validation procedure (proc-name) for the object table.
23507	-681	Column (column-name) is in violation of an installation defined field procedure. RT: (return-code), RS: (reason-code), MSG: (message-token).
23508	-690	The statement is rejected by data definition control support. The reason is (reason-code).
23509	-807	Access denied: Package (package-name) isn't enabled for access from (connection-type connection-name).
23510	-908	(Bind-type) error using (auth-id) authority. The BIND, REBIND or AUTO-REBIND operation isn't allowed.
23511	-543	A row in a parent table can't be deleted because the check constraint (check-constraint) restricts the deletion.
23512	-544	The check constraint specified in the ALTER TABLE statement can't be added because an existing row violates the check constraint.
23513	-545	The requested operation isn't allowed because a row doesn't satisfy the check constraint (check-constraint).
23515	-603	The index defined in the CREATE INDEX statement couldn't be created as unique because the specified table already contains rows that are duplicates with respect to the values of the identified columns.
24501	-500	The FETCH, UPDATE, DELETE, or CLOSE statement identifies a closed cursor that was defined with the WITH HOLD option. The cursor was closed when the connection where it was dependent was destroyed during a commit operation. The connection was destroyed because the application process placed it in the released state, or the application plan was bound with the DISCONNECT(AUTOMATIC) option.
	-501	The cursor identified in a FETCH or CLOSE statement isn't open.
	-507	The cursor identified in the UPDATE or DELETE statement isn't open.
24502	-502	The cursor identified in an OPEN statement is already open.
24504	-508	The cursor identified in the UPDATE or DELETE statement isn't positioned on a row.

24506	-519	The application program has attempted to PREPARE (actually, re-PREPARE) the SELECT statement for the specified cursor when that cursor was already open.
25000	-571	The statement would result in a multiple site update. This SQLCODE is issued in the following situations: (1) when an application program operating in an IMS or CICS environment attempts to modify data at a remote location where multi-site update capabilities aren't supported; or (2) when an application has explicit SQL statements within a commit scope that would result in updates at multiple sites where one of the sites where data is being updated doesn't support multi-site updates.
	-817	The SQL statement can't be executed because the statement will result in a prohibited update operation.
	-30090	An update operation or a dynamic commit or rollback was attempted at a server that was supporting an application that was in a read-only execution environment (IMS or CICS).
26501	-514	The application program has tried to use a cursor (cursor-name) that is not in a prepared state. The cursor is associated with a statement that either (1) has never been prepared, or (2) has been invalidated by a commit or rollback operation.
	-516	The DESCRIBE statement doesn't identify a prepared statement.
34000	-504	The cursor name (cursor-name) isn't defined.
39002	-470	DB2 received an SQL CALL statement for a stored procedure and found a null value in the incoming parameter list. The DB2 stored procedure was defined in the SYSIBM.SYSPROCEDURES catalog table with LINKAGE=, which specifies that the DB2 stored procedure doesn't accept null values.
39501	-450	While returning parameters from a stored procedure to an application, DB2 detected an overlay of one of the parameters. A stored procedure overwrote storage beyond a parameter's declared length.
40001	-911	The current unit of work has been rolled back due to a deadlock or timeout. The reason is (reason-code), type of resource (resource-type), and resource name (resource-name).
42501	-551	(Auth-id) doesn't have the privilege to perform operation (operation) on object (object-name).
	-567	(Bind-type) authorization error using (auth-id) authority package = (package-name) privilege = (privilege).
42502	-164	The authorization ID (auth-id) doesn't have the authority necessary to create views with qualifiers other than its own authorization ID. Specifically, the attempt to create a view with qualifier (authorization ID) is rejected.
	-552	(Auth-id) doesn't have the privilege to perform operation (operation).
	-554	An authorization ID can't grant a privilege to itself.
	-555	An authorization ID can't revoke a privilege from itself.
42503	-553	(Auth-id) isn't one of the valid authorization IDs.
42504	-556	(Authid2) can't have the (privilege) privilege (on-object) revoked by (authid1) because the revokee doesn't possess the privilege or the revoker didn't make the grant.
42505	-922	Authorization failure: (error-type) error. The reason is (reason-code).
42506	-30053	An authorization failure encountered for the package owner.
42509	-549	The (statement) statement isn't allowed for (object_type1 object_name) because the bind option DYNAMICRULES(BIND) in the (object_type2) is in effect.
42601	-007	The statement contains the illegal character (character).
	-029	The INTO clause is required.
	-104	Illegal symbol "token." Some symbols that might be legal are: (token-list).
	-109	The (clause) clause isn't permitted in the context in which it appears in the SQL statement. A subselect can't have an INTO clause. A CREATE VIEW statement can't have INTO, ORDER BY, or FOR UPDATE clauses. An

		embedded SELECT statement can't have ORDER BY or FOR UPDATE clauses. SELECT statements used in cursor declarations can't have an INTO clause.
	-115	A predicate is invalid because the comparison operator (operator) is followed by a parenthesized list or by ANY or ALL without a subquery.
	-128	Invalid use of null in a predicate.
	-199	Illegal use of keyword (keyword). Token (token-list) was expected.
	-638	The table (table-name) can't be created because column definition is missing.
42602	-113	An invalid character was found in (string), reason code – nnn.
	-251	Token (name) isn't valid. A location name can't contain alphabetic extenders. (The standard alphabetic extenders in the United States are #, @, $.)
42603	-010	The string constant beginning (string) is not terminated properly.
42604	-103	The (literal) is an invalid numeric literal.
	-105	The statement contains an invalid string.
42605	-170	An SQL statement includes the scalar function (function-name) with either too many or too few arguments.
42606	-110	The literal beginning with (string) contains one or more characters that aren't valid hexadecimal digits.
42607	-112	The operand of a column function is another column function.
	-409	The operand of the COUNT function in the SQL statement violates SQL syntax. A common error is a column name or other expression without DISTINCT.
42609	-417	A statement string to be prepared includes parameter markers as the operands of the same operation.
42610	-184	The specified arithmetic expression contains a parameter marker improperly used with a datetime value.
	-418	A statement string to be prepared contains an invalid use of parameter markers.
42611	-604	A column definition in the CREATE or ALTER TABLE statement contains an invalid length, precision, or scale attribute specification.
42612	-084	An unacceptable SQL statement was executed due to one of the following: (1) an attempt to PREPARE or EXECUTE IMMEDIATE an SQL statement that can't be prepared (refer to the proper SQL statement in the SQL reference manual); (2) the embedded SQL statement isn't an SQL statement supported by DB2; or (3) the statement referenced an undeclared cursor.
42613	-628	Mutually exclusive clauses were specified in one or more of the following ways: (1) a CREATE TABLESPACE statement contains both the SEGSIZE and NUMPARTS clauses; (2) a (column-definition) contains both NOT NULL and DEFAULT NULL clauses; (3) a (column-definition) contains both FIELDPROC and DEFAULT clauses; (4) a SELECT statement contains both the UPDATE clause and the FOR FETCH ONLY clause; or (5) an ALTER TABLE statement contains both a DROP CONSTRAINT clause and either a DROP FOREIGN KEY clause or a DROP CHECK clause.
42614	-637	Duplicate (keyword) keyword.
42615	-644	The value specified for the keyword (keyword) parameter in the (stmt-type) SQL statement isn't a permitted value.
42617	-198	The operand of the PREPARE or EXECUTE IMMEDIATE statement is blank or empty.
42618	-312	The host variable (variable-name) appears in the SQL statement, but the SQL statement is a prepared statement; the attributes of the variable are inconsistent with its usage in the static SQL statement; or the variable is not declared in the application program.
42621	-546	The check constraint (check-constraint) is invalid.
	-548	The check constraint that is defined with (column-name) is invalid.
42622	-107	The name (name) is too long. The maximum allowable size is (size).

42701	-121	The column (name) is identified more than once in the INSERT or UPDATE statement.
42702	-203	A reference to column (column-name) is ambiguous.
42703	-205	No column with the specified (column-name) occurs in the table or view (table-name).
	-206	(Column-name) isn't a column of an inserted table, updated table, or any table identified in a FROM clause.
42704	-204	The object identified by (name) isn't defined in the DB2 subsystem.
	-219	The required explanation table (table-name) doesn't exist.
	-722	The indicated subcommand was issued against a package that doesn't exist. Bind type = (bind-type), authorization ID = (auth-id), package = (package-name).
42705	-950	The location name specified in the CONNECT statement is invalid or not listed in the communications database.
42707	-208	The ORDER BY clause is invalid because column (name) isn't part of the result table.
42709	-537	The PRIMARY KEY clause, a FOREIGN KEY clause, or a UNIQUE clause identifies column (column-name) more than once.
42710	-601	The CREATE statement tried to create an object (name) of type (obj-type), but an object of that type with the same name is already defined in the DB2 subsystem.
	-719	An attempt is made to add a package that already exists. The combination of 'location.collection.package.version' must be unique in the SYSIBM.SYSPACKAGE table. In addition, the combination of 'location.collection.package.consistency-token' must be unique.
	-720	An attempt is made to create a version of a package that already exists. Package name = (package-name), version = (version2).
	-721	An attempt is made to add or replace a package with a consistency token that is not unique for that package. Package name = (pkg-id), consistency token = (contoken).
42711	-612	(Column-name) is a duplicate column name.
42714	-314	The statement contains an ambiguous host variable reference.
42718	-250	A three-part object name (table, view, or alias) can't be used until the local location name is defined.
42724	-444	DB2 received an SQL CALL statement for a stored procedure and found the row in the SYSIBM.SYSPROCEDURES catalog table associated with the requested procedure name. However, the MVS load module identified in the LOADMOD column of the SYSIBM.SYSPROCEDURES row couldn't be found.
42801	-173	The cursor is not a read-only cursor. WITH UR can be specified only if DB2 can determine that the cursor is read-only.
42802	-117	The number of insert values isn't the same as the number of object columns.
42803	-119	A column identified in a HAVING clause isn't included in the GROUP BY clause.
	-122	A SELECT statement with no GROUP BY clause contains a column name and a column function in the SELECT clause or a column name is contained in the SELECT clause but not in the GROUP BY clause.
42805	-125	An integer in the ORDER BY clause doesn't identify a column of the result.
42806	-303	A value can't be assigned to output host variable number (position-number) because the data types aren't comparable.
42807	-150	The object of the INSERT, DELETE, or UPDATE statement is a view for which the requested operation isn't permitted.
42808	-151	The UPDATE statement is invalid because the catalog description of column (column-name) indicates that it can't be updated.
42809	-152	The DROP clause (clause) in the ALTER statement is invalid because (constraint-name) is a (constraint-type).

	-156	The statement doesn't identify a table.
	-159	The object specified in the DROP VIEW statement, DROP ALIAS statement, or COMMENT ON ALIAS statement identifies a table instead of a view or an alias.
42810	-157	Only a table name can be specified in a foreign key clause; (object-name) isn't the name of a table.
42811	-158	The number of columns specified for the view isn't the same as the number of columns specified by the SELECT clause.
42813	-160	The WITH CHECK OPTION doesn't apply to a view definition under either of the following circumstances: the view is read-only (for example, the view definition includes DISTINCT, GROUP BY, or JOIN) or the view definition includes a subquery.
42815	-060	An invalid (type) specification: (spec) where 'type' is either LENGTH or SCALE, and "spec" is the specified length or scale. Length or scale must be specified by an unsigned integer constant and the value must be in the range allowed by the data type.
	-171	Either the data type, the length, or the value of argument (nn) of scalar function (function-name) is incorrect.
	-713	The value specified in the SET (special-register) statement is not a valid value of the indicated special register.
42816	-182	The specified arithmetic expression contains an improperly used datetime value or labeled duration.
42818	-131	A statement with the LIKE predicate has incompatible data types.
	-401	An arithmetic operation appearing within the SQL statement has a mixture of numeric and non-numeric operands, or the operands of a comparison operation aren't compatible.
42819	-402	A non-numeric operand has been specified for the arithmetic function or operator (arith-fop).
42820	-405	The numeric literal (literal) can't be used as specified because it is out of range.
	-410	The specified floating point literal (literal) is more than 30 character in length.
42821	-408	An UPDATE or INSERT value isn't comparable with the data type of its object column (column-name).
42823	-412	The SELECT clause of a subquery specifies multiple columns.
42824	-132	A LIKE predicate is invalid because the second operand isn't a string.
	-414	A LIKE predicate is invalid because the first operand isn't a string.
42825	-415	The corresponding columns (column-name) of the operands of a UNION or a UNION ALL don't have comparable column descriptions.
42826	-421	The operands of a UNION or UNION ALL don't have the same number of columns.
42827	-509	The application program attempted to execute an UPDATE or DELETE WHERE CURRENT OF cursor statement where the table named in that statement didn't match the name of the table specified in the declaration for that cursor.
42828	-510	The application program attempted to execute an UPDATE or DELETE WHERE CURRENT OF cursor statement against a table or view that can't be updated or deleted. This can occur for a delete from a read-only view or for an update in which the cursor wasn't defined with the FOR UPDATE clause.
42829	-126	The SELECT statement contains both an UPDATE clause and an ORDER BY clause.
	-511	The result table of the SELECT statement can't be updated. This can occur if the SELECT specifies more than one table or view in the FROM clause, if the SELECT list contains a built-in function or DISTINCT, or if the statement contains an ORDER BY, GROUP BY or HAVING clause. This can also occur if a view is specified in the FROM clause and the view can't be updated.

42830	-538	The FOREIGN KEY (name) doesn't conform to the description of the primary key of table (table-name).
42831	-542	(Column-name) can't be a column of a primary key or a unique constraint because it can contain null values.
42832	-607	The operation or option (operation) can't be performed on the catalog object specified in the SQL statement.
	-618	Operation (operation) isn't allowed on system databases.
42834	-629	SET NULL can't be specified because FOREIGN KEY (name) can't contain null values.
42842	-683	Invalid column type for fieldproc, BIT DATA, SBCS DATA, or MIXED DATA option, (column-name).
42852	-557	Inconsistent GRANT/REVOKE keyword (keyword). Permitted keywords are (keyword-list).
42877	-197	A SELECT statement that specifies both the union of two or more tables and the ORDER BY clause can't use qualified column names in the ORDER BY clause.
42884	-440	The number of parameters in the parameter list doesn't match the number of parameters expected for stored procedure (name), AUTHID (authid), LUNAME (luname). The (number) parameters were expected.
42886	-469	DB2 received an SQL CALL statement for a stored procedure. DB2 found the row in the SYSIBM.SYSPROCEDURES catalog table associated with the requested procedure name. However, parameter (number) was identified in the PARMLIST column of the SYSIBM.SYSPROCEDURES table as an OUT or INOUT parameter. A host variable must be supplied on the SQL CALL statement for parameters defined as OUT or INOUT.
42888	-539	The CREATE or ALTER TABLE statement can't be executed because the indicated table (table-name) doesn't have a primary key. So, the primary key can't be dropped, or the table can't be defined as a parent in a referential constraint.
42889	-624	Table (table-name) already has a primary key.
42893	-616	The object (obj-type1 obj-name1) can't be dropped because it is referenced by object (obj-type2 obj-name2). Some types of objects can't be dropped if there are other objects that are dependent on them. For example, a storage group can't be dropped if there are one or more existing table spaces that use that storage group.
42894	-574	The specified default value conflicts with the column definition.
42895	-301	The value of input host variable or parameter number (position-number) can't be used as specified because of its data type.
42901	-111	A column function doesn't include a column name.
42902	-118	The object table or view of the INSERT, DELETE, or UPDATE statement is also identified in a FROM clause.
42903	-120	A WHERE clause or SET clause includes a column function.
42905	-127	The keyword DISTINCT is specified more than once in a subselect.
42906	-133	A column function in a subquery of a HAVING clause is invalid because all column references in its argument aren't correlated to the GROUP BY result that the HAVING clause is applied to.
42907	-134	Improper use of a long string column (column-name) or a host variable of maximum length greater than 254.
	-416	The UNION specified in the SQL statement couldn't be performed because one of the tables participating in the union contains a long string column (for example, a VARCHAR column with length greater than 254). The operands of a UNION can't contain long string columns.
42908	-153	The CREATE VIEW statement doesn't include a required column list.
42909	-154	The CREATE VIEW failed because the view definition contains a UNION, a UNION ALL, or a remote object.

42911	-419	The decimal divide operation is invalid because the result would have a negative scale.
42912	-503	The application program attempted to update (using a cursor) a value in a column of the object table that wasn't identified in the FOR UPDATE clause in the cursor declaration.
42914	-536	The DELETE statement is invalid due to referential constraints for table (table-name).
42915	-632	The table can't be defined as a dependent of (table-name) because of delete rule restrictions.
	-633	The (delete-rule) specified in a FOREIGN KEY clause of the ALTER TABLE statement is invalid. The indicated (delete-rule) is required because a self-referencing constraint must have a (delete-rule) of CASCADE or the relationship would cause the table to be delete-connected to the same table through multiple paths and such relationships must have the same (delete-rule).
	-634	The CASCADE delete rule specified in the FOREIGN KEY clause of an ALTER TABLE statement is invalid because the relationship would form a cycle that would cause a table to be delete-connected to itself or the relationship would cause another table to be delete-connected to the same table through multiple paths with different delete rules or with a delete rule equal to SET NULL.
	-635	The delete rules can't be different or can't be SET NULL.
42917	-667	The DROP INDEX statement attempted to drop the cluster index for a table residing in a partitioned table space. The cluster index for such a table can't be dropped explicitly with the DROP INDEX statement.
	-669	A table in a partitioned table space can't be dropped by the DROP TABLE statement.
42920	-815	An embedded SEELCT statement of a subquery of a basic predicate either (1) directly contains a GROUP BY or HAVING clause, or (2) specifies as its object a view having a definition that includes a GROUP BY or HAVING clause. Neither construct is permitted.
42924	-513	The alias (alias-name) must not be defined on another local or remote alias.
42932	-30052	Program preparation assumptions are incorrect.
42961	-114	A 3-part SQL procedure name was provided in an SQL CALL statement. The first part of the SQL procedure name, which specifies the location where the stored procedure resides, didn't match the value of the SQL CURRENT SERVER special register.
42969	-917	Bind package failed. An error has occurred that prevents the package from being created. This SQLCODE can be issued during bind or commit processing.
42972	-338	An ON clause is invalid. This return code reports a violation of one of the following: (1) one expression of the predicate must only reference columns of one of the operand tables of the associated join operator, and the other expression of the predicate must only reference columns of the other operand table; (2) a VALUE or COALESCE function is allowed in the ON clause only when the join operator is a FULL OUTER JOIN or FULL JOIN; or (3) an operator other than equals (=) isn't allowed in a FULL OUTER JOIN or FULL JOIN.
42987	-751	A stored procedure has been placed in MUST_ROLLBACK state due to SQL operation (name).
44000	-161	The INSERT or UPDATE isn't allowed because a resulting row doesn't satisfy the view definition.
51002	-805	DBRM or PACKAGE NAME (location-name.collection-id.dbrm-name.consistency) token not found in plan (plan-name). The reason is (reason-code). See *DB2 for MVS/ESA V4 Messages and Codes* for the definition of the reason-codes.

51003	-818	The precompiler-generated timestamp (x) in the load module is different from the bind timestamp (y) built from the DBRM (z). This problem can occur if you: (1) precompile, compile, and link, without doing a BIND of the application; (2) precompile and BIND, without doing the compile and link for the application program; or (3) BIND the application using a DBRM that resulted from a different precompile of the application program than that which produced the object module that is linked into the application module.
51004	-822	The SQLDA contains an invalid data address or indicator variable address.
51005	-906	The SQL statement can't be executed because this function is disabled due to a prior error.
51006	-927	The language interface (LI) was called when the connecting environment wasn't established. The program should be invoked under the DSN command.
51015	-525	The SQL statement can't be executed because it was in error at bind time for section (sectno) package (pkgname) consistency token X('contoken').
51021	-918	Execution of the SQL statement failed because a communication link between the local DB2 and at least one remote server no longer exists. A previous failure caused this condition.
	-939	ROLLBACK required due to unrequested ROLLBACK of a remote server.
	-965	Stored procedure (procname) terminated abnormally.
53001	-620	The keyword (keyword) in (stmt-type) statement isn't permitted for a table space in the work file database.
53004	-742	The WORKFILE clause can't be used on a CREATE DATABASE statement to create a work file database for a DB2 subsystem that isn't a member of a DB2 data sharing group. The system database, DSNDB07, is the implicit work file database.
53014	-736	Invalid OBID (obid) specified. An invalid OBID value was given on the CREATE statement.
53035	-660	Index (index-name) can't be created on a partitioned table space (tspace-name) because key limits aren't specified.
53036	-661	Index (index-name) can't be created on a partitioned table space (tspace-name) because the number of PART specifications isn't equal to the number of partitions of the table space.
53037	-662	A partitioned index can't be created on a non-partitioned table space (tspace-name).
53038	-663	The number of key limit values is either zero or greater than the number of columns in the key of index (index-name).
53039	-665	The PART clause of an ALTER statement is omitted or invalid.
53040	-671	The buffer pool attribute of the table space can't be altered as specified because it would change the page size of the table space.
53041	-676	A 32K page buffer pool may not be used for an index. Only 4KB buffer pools (BP0, BP1, and BP2) can be specified for indexes.
53043	-686	A column defined with a field procedure can't be compared with another column with a different field procedure.
53044	-687	One column can't be compared with another column that has incompatible field types.
53045	-678	The literal (literal) specified for the index limit key must conform to the data type (data-type) of the corresponding column (column-name).
53088	-611	Only LOCKMAX 0 can be specified when the lock size of the table space is TABLESPACE or TABLE.
53089	-2001	The number of host variable parameters for a stored procedure isn't equal to the number of expected host variable parameters. Actual number (sqldanum), expected number (opnum).
54001	-101	The statement is too long or too complex.
54002	-102	A literal string is too long. The string begins (string).
54004	-129	The statement contains too many table names.

	-840	The number of items returned in the select list or presented in an insert list exceeds the allowable maximum of 750.
54005	-136	The SORT can't be executed because the sort key length is greater than 4000 bytes.
54006	-137	The length of the result of a concatenation exceeds 32,764 (if character operands) or 16,382 (if graphic operands).
54008	-602	The number of columns specified in the CREATE INDEX statement exceeds 64, the maximum permitted by DB2.
	-613	The primary key or a unique constraint is too long or has too many columns.
	-614	The index can't be created because the sum of the internal lengths of the identified columns is greater than the allowable maximum.
	-631	The FOREIGN KEY (name) is too long or has too many columns.
54010	-670	The record length of the table exceeds the page size limit.
54011	-680	Too many columns are specified for a table. The maximum number of columns permitted per table is 750.
	-689	Too many columns defined for a dependent table. The maximum number of columns allowed for a dependent table is 749.
54012	-684	The length of literal list beginning (string) is too long.
54021	-642	There is a limit to the total number of columns that can be used in UNIQUE constraints in a CREATE TABLE statement. The statement exceeds that limit.
54024	-643	The check constraint definition exceeds the maximum allowable limit of 3800 characters. The redundant blank spaces are excluded from this limit.
54025	-651	The CREATE TABLE or ALTER TABLE statement causes the table descriptor (record OBD) to exceed the object descriptor size limit of 32KB.
54027	-400	The catalog has the maximum number of user defined indexes (100).
54041	-497	An attempt was made to create an object in database (database-name), but the limit of 32767 OBIDs has been exceeded for that database.
55002	-220	The column (column-name) in an explanation table (table-name) isn't defined properly.
	-221	"SET OF OPTIONAL COLUMNS" in the explanation table (table-name) is incomplete. Optional column (column-name) is missing.
55003	-693	The column (column-name) in DDL registration table or index (table-name) (index-name) isn't defined properly.
55004	-735	Database (dbid) can't be accessed because it is no longer a shared database.
55006	-615	The operation (operation-type) can't be performed because the package is in use by the same application process. The type of bind operations are BIND, REBIND and DROP.
55011	-619	The statements CREATE, ALTER, or DROP for a table space in the work file database can't be processed unless the work file database is stopped (using the STOP command).
55012	-623	A clustering index already exists on table (table-name). A given table can have only one cluster index.
55014	-625	Table (table-name) doesn't have an index to enforce the uniqueness of the primary key.
55015	-626	An ALTER statement specifies a BUFFERPOOL, USING, PRIQTY, SECQTY, ERASE, or GBPCACHE clause, but the page set isn't stopped.
55016	-627	The ALTER statement is invalid because the page set has user-managed data sets.
55017	-646	Table (table-name) can't be created in partitioned/default table space (tspace-name) because it already contains a table. Only one table may reside in a partitioned or default table space.
55020	-741	A work file database is already defined for member (member-name).
55023	-471	The SQL CALL for stored procedure (name) failed due to reason (reason-code). See *DB2 for MVS/ESA V4 Messages and Codes* for the definition of the reason-codes.

55030	-726	Bind error attempting to replace package = (package-name). There are ENABLE or DISABLE entries currently associated with the package.
55035	-672	The DROP operation failed for table (table-name) because the table being dropped has the RESTRICT ON DROP attribute, or the table space or database being dropped contains the specified table, which has the RE-STRICT ON DROP attribute.
56010	-333	The subtype of a string variable isn't the same as the subtype known at bind time and the difference can't be resolved by translation.
56016	-636	The partitioning keys aren't specified in ascending or descending order.
56018	-668	The ALTER TABLE statement attempted to add a column to a table that has an edit procedure. If a table has an edit procedure, no column can be added to it.
56023	-512	The statement reference to a remote object is invalid. One of the following condition exists: (1) the statement refers to multiple locations; (2) a statement with a remote reference is being explained either by a dynamic EXPLAIN statement or the EXPLAIN(YES) option; (3) an alias is used incorrectly; or (4) a three-part name is implicitly or explicitly used in a statement that is not supported by the DB2 private protocols.
56025	-558	Invalid clause or combination of clauses on a GRANT or REVOKE statement.
56027	-639	A partition key of the clustering index can't be updated. Therefore, a foreign key column with a delete rule of SET NULL can't be a column of a partition key if that column is nullable. If this error occurs for an ALTER TABLE operation, the foreign key can't be created. If this error occurs for a CREATE INDEX operation, the index can't be created.
56031	-622	FOR MIXED DATA is specified in a column description of a CREATE or ALTER TABLE statement, but the MIXED DATA install option is set to NO. FOR MIXED DATA is valid only when the MIXED DATA install option is set to YES.
56036	-655	The CREATE or ALTER STOGROUP is invalid because the storage group would have both specific and nonspecific volume IDs.
56038	-947	The SQL statement failed because it will change a table defined with data capture changes, but the data can't be propagated.
56040	-411	A reference to the CURRENT SQLID special register is invalid in a statement that contains the three-part name or alias of an object that is remote to the remote server.
56045	-919	A rollback operation is required.
56053	-730	The parent of a table in a read-only shared database must also be a table in a read-only shared database.
56054	-731	User-defined data set (dsname) must be defined with SHAREOPTIONS(1,3). The VSAM SHAREOPTIONS must be (1,3) for all of the indexes and table spaces in the database.
56055	-732	The database is defined on this subsystem with the ROSHARE READ attribute, but the table space or index space hasn't been defined on the owning subsystem.
56056	-733	The description of a table space, index space, or table in a ROSHARE READ database must be consistent with its description in the owner system.
	-737	A CREATE TABLE statement was issued using an implicit table space. An implicit table space may not be used in a database that has been defined as a read-only shared database.
56057	-734	The ROSHARE attribute of a database can't be altered from ROSHARE READ.
56062	-948	The unit of work was initiated before DDF was started, and the application attempted to perform a distributed operation. The unit of work must be terminated by a rollback operation.
56064	-715	Program (program-name) depends on a function of DB2 that is not supported by the current active release.

56065	-716	Program (program-name) was precompiled under a release not supported by the current level of DB2, or the contents of the DBRM have been modified after the precompilation phase.
56066	-717	The (bind-type) for (object-type) (object-name) with mark (release-dependency-mark) failed because (object-type) depends on functions of the release from which fallback has occurred. The plan or package indicated depends on a function of DB2 not supported by the currently active release.
56067	-718	The REBIND for package (package-name) failed because IBMREQD of (ibmreqd) is invalid. The IBMREQD column of the SYSIBM.SYSPACKAGE catalog table for the named package contains an unrecognizable character.
56082	-339	The SQL statement can't be executed from an ASCII based DRDA application requestor to a V2R2 DB2 subsystem.
56084	-351	An unsupported SQLTYPE was encountered in position (position-number) on a PREPARE or DESCRIBE operation. Some SQL data types aren't supported by DB2 version 4. Position (position-number) is the position of the first element with an invalid data type in the SQLDA. A common reason why this error occurs is when DB2 attempts to describe large object data residing on a non-DB2 server. Some of the SQLTYPEs that can cause this error are: LOB, BLOB, CLOB, and DBLOB.
56089	-617	All indexes defined for a table within a table space with LOCKSIZE ROW must be defined as type 2 indexes.
	-630	The WHERE NOT NULL specification is invalid for type 1 indexes.
	-640	LOCKSIZE ROW can't be specified because a table in this table space has a type 1 index.
56090	-650	The ALTER INDEX statement can't be executed, reason (reason-code).
57001	-540	The definition of table (table-name) is incomplete because it lacks a primary key index or a required unique index.
57002	-559	The authorization mechanism has been disabled in the DB2 subsystem. Consequently, GRANT and REVOKE statements are ignored.
57003	-647	Buffer pool (bp-name) can't be specified because it hasn't been activated.
57004	-653	Table (table-name) in partitioned table space (tspace-name) isn't available because its partitioned index hasn't been created.
57005	-666	The (stmt-verb object) can't be executed because function (function) is in progress.
57006	-679	The object (name) can't be created because a drop is pending on the object.
57007	-909	The application program has either (1) dropped a table and then attempted to access it, or (2) dropped an index and then tried to access its object table using that index.
	-910	The SQL statement can't access an object on which a DROP or ALTER is pending.
57008	-185	The local format option has been used with a date or time and no local exit has been installed.
57010	-682	Field procedure (procedure-name) couldn't be loaded.
57011	-677	An attempt to either open (create) or expand a buffer pool has failed because insufficient virtual storage was available.
	-904	Unsuccessful execution caused by an unavailable resource. The reason is (reason-code), type of resource (resource-type), and resource name (resource-name).
57012	-30040	Execution failed due to unavailable resources that will not affect the successful execution of subsequent commands or SQL statements. Reason (reason-code) type of resource (resource-type) resource name (resource-name) product ID (pppvvrrm) RDBNAME (rdbname).
57013	-30041	Execution failed due to unavailable resources that will affect the successful execution of subsequent commands and SQL statements. Reason (reason-code) type of resource (resource-type) resource name (resource-name) product ID (pppvvrrm) RDBNAME (rdbname).

57014	-905	Unsuccessful execution due to resource limit being exceeded, resource name = (resource-name) limit = (limit-amount1) CPU seconds ((limit-amount2) service units) derived from (limit-source).
57015	-923	Connection not established: DB2 (condition), reason (reason-code), type (resource-type), name (resource-name).
57017	-332	The operation required the translation of a string to a different coded character set, but the particular translation isn't described in the SYSSTRINGS catalog table. The first (ccsid) identifies the coded character set of the string and the second (ccsid) identifies the coded character set to which it must be translated.
57018	-691	The required registration table (table-name) doesn't exist.
	-692	The required unique index (index-name) for DDL registration table (table-name) doesn't exist.
57023	-694	The DDL statement can't be executed because a drop is pending on the DDL registration table (table-name).
57033	-913	Unsuccessful execution caused by a deadlock or timeout. The reason is (reason-code), type of resource (resource-type), and resource name (resource-name).
58001	-621	A duplicate DBID (dbid) was detected and previously assigned to (database-name). An inconsistency exists between the DB2 catalog and directory.
58002	-685	Invalid field type, (column-name).
	-688	Incorrect data returned from field procedure, (column-name), (msgno).
	-929	Failure in a data capture exit: (token).
58003	-144	Invalid section number (number).
58004	-819	SYSIBM.SYSVTREE.VTREE is a varying-length string column that contains the parse trees of views. In processing a view, the length control field of its parse tree was found to be zero.
	-820	The SQL statement can't be processed because (catalog-table) contains a value that isn't valid in this release.
	-901	Unsuccessful execution caused by a system error that doesn't preclude the successful execution of subsequent SQL statements.
58005	-902	The pointer to the essential control block, either the CT or the RDA, is zeroes. This precludes the successful execution of the current SQL statement, as well as any subsequent SQL statements. A rebind is required.
58006	-924	DB2 connection internal error, (function-code), (return-code), (reason-code).
58008	-30000	Execution failed due to a distribution protocol error that will not affect the successful execution of subsequent commands or SQL statements: Reason (reason-code) (sub-code).
58009	-30020	Execution failed due to a distribution protocol error that caused deallocation of the conversation: Reason (reason-code) (sub-code).
58010	-30021	Execution failed due to a distribution protocol error that will affect the successful execution of subsequent commands or SQL statements: Manager (manager) at level (level) not supported error.
58011	-30050	(Command-or-SQL-statement-type) command or SQL statement invalid while BIND process in progress.
58012	-30051	Bind process with specified package name and consistency token not active.
58013	-30030	Commit request was unsuccessful, a distribution protocol violation has been detected, or the conversation has been deallocated. Original SQLCODE=(orginal-sqlcode) and original SQLSTATE=(original-sqlstate).
58014	-30070	(Command) command not supported error.
58015	-30071	(Object-type) object not supported error.
58016	-30072	(Parameter) : (subcode) parameter not supported error.
58017	-30073	(Parameter) : (subcode) parameter value not supported error.
58018	-30074	Reply message with (codepoint) SVRCOD not supported error.
58026	-870	The number of host variables in the statement isn't equal to the number of descriptors.

Index

C

DB2 for the COBOL Programmer

Part 2 / Second Edition

Curtis Garvin and Steve Eckols

Once you've mastered the basics of DB2 programming, there's still plenty to learn. So this book teaches you all the advanced DB2 features that a senior programmer or programmer/analyst needs to know...and shows you when to use each one. You'll learn:

- how to use dynamic SQL
- how to work with distributed DB2 data
- how to execute stored procedures
- how to work with advanced locking and concurrency features
- how to use DB2 from CICS programs

- what you need to know about database administration to set up a quality assurance environment
- how to use QMF, IBM's Query Management Facility, to run SQL statements interactively and to prepare ad hoc reports whenever users need them

So don't wait to expand your DB2 skills. Get a copy of this book TODAY.

DB2, Part 2, 15 chapters, approx. 400 pages, **$45.00**
ISBN 1-890774-03-0

Scheduled for April 1999; check our web site for availability (until then, the First Edition, covering up through DB2 version 2.2, is available)

IMS for the COBOL Programmer

Part 1: DL/I Data Base Processing

Steve Eckols

This how-to book will have you writing batch DL/I programs in a minimum of time—whether you're working on a VSE or an MVS system. But it doesn't neglect the conceptual background you must have to create programs that work. So you'll gain a thorough knowledge of how DL/I data bases are structured, as

well as how to design and write COBOL programs that create, access, and update them.

7 complete COBOL programs get you started right. Use them as models for production work in your shop, and you'll save hours of development time.

IMS, Part 1, 16 chapters, 333 pages, **$36.50**
ISBN 0-911625-29-1

IMS for the COBOL Programmer

Part 2: Data Communications and Message Format Service

Steve Eckols

The second part of *IMS for the COBOL Programmer* is for MVS programmers only. It teaches how to develop online programs that access IMS data bases and run under the data communications (DC) component of IMS. So you'll learn:

- why you code message processing programs (MPPs) the way you do and what COBOL elements you use
- how to use Message Format Service (MFS), a facility for formatting complex terminal displays so you can enhance the look and operation of your DC programs

- how to develop applications that use more than one screen format or that use physical and logical paging
- how to develop batch message processing (BMP) programs to update IMS data bases in batch even while they're being used by other programs
- how to use Batch Terminal Simulator (BTS) to test DC applications
- and more!

IMS, Part 2, 16 chapters, 398 pages, **$36.50**
ISBN 0-911625-30-5

CICS for the COBOL Programmer

Second Edition   **Doug Lowe**

This 2-part course is designed to help COBOL programmers become outstanding CICS programmers.

Part 1: An Introductory Course covers the basic CICS elements you'll use in just about every program you write. So you'll learn about basic mapping support (BMS), pseudo-conversational programming, basic CICS commands, sensible program design using event-driven design techniques, testing and debugging using IBM-supplied transactions (like CEMT, CECI, and CEDF) or a transaction dump, and efficiency considerations.

Part 2: An Advanced Course covers CICS features you'll use regularly, though you won't need all of them for every program. That means you'll learn about browse commands, temporary storage, transient data, data tables (including the shared data table feature of CICS 3.3), DB2 and DL/I processing considerations, distributed processing features, interval control commands, BMS page building, and more! In addition, *Part 2* teaches you which features do similar things and when to use each one. So you won't just learn how to code new functions...you'll also learn how to choose the best CICS solution for each programming problem you face.

Both books cover all versions of CICS up through 3.3. Both cover OS/VS COBOL, VS COBOL II, and COBOL/370, so it doesn't matter which COBOL compiler you're using. And all the program examples in both books conform to CUA's Entry Model for screen design.

CICS, Part 1, 12 chapters, 409 pages, **$36.50**
ISBN 0-911625-60-7

CICS, Part 2, 12 chapters, 352 pages, **$36.50**
ISBN 0-911625-67-4

The CICS Programmer's Desk Reference

Second Edition   **Doug Lowe**

Ever feel buried by IBM manuals?

It seems like you need stacks of them, close at hand, if you want to be an effective CICS programmer. Because frankly, there's just too much you have to know to do your job well; you can't keep it all in your head.

That's why Doug Lowe decided to write *The CICS Programmer's Desk Reference*. In it, he's collected all the information you need to have at your fingertips, and organized it into 12 sections that make it easy for you to find what you're looking for. So there are sections on:

- BMS macro instructions—their formats (with an explanation of each parameter) and coding examples

- CICS commands—their syntax (with an explanation of each parameter), coding examples, and suggestions on how and when to use each one most effectively

- MVS and DOS/VSE JCL for CICS applications

- AMS commands for handling VSAM files

- details for MVS users on how to use ISPF

- complete model programs, including specs, design, and code

- a summary of CICS program design techniques that lead to simple, maintainable, and efficient programs

- guidelines for testing and debugging CICS applications

- and more!

So clear the IBM manuals off your terminal table. Let the *Desk Reference* be your everyday guide to CICS instead.

CICS Desk Reference, 12 sections, 507 pages, **$42.50**
ISBN 0-911625-68-2

MVS JCL

MVS/ESA • MVS/XA • MVS/370   **Doug Lowe**

Anyone who's worked in an MVS shop knows that JCL is tough to master. You learn enough to get by...but then you stick to that. It's just too frustrating to try to put together a job using the IBM manuals. And too time-consuming to keep asking your co-workers for help...especially since they're often limping along with the JCL they know, too.

That's why you need a copy of *MVS JCL*. It zeroes in on the JCL you need for everyday jobs...so you can learn to code significant job streams in a hurry.

You'll learn how to compile, link-edit, load, and execute programs. Process all types of data sets. Code JES2/JES3 control statements to manage job and

program execution, data set allocation, and SYSOUT processing. Create and use JCL procedures. Execute general-purpose utility programs. And much more.

But that's not all this book does. Beyond teaching you JCL, it explains the basics of how MVS works so you can apply that understanding as you code JCL. That's the kind of perspective that's missing in other books and courses about MVS, even though it's background you must have if you want to bring MVS under your control.

MVS JCL, 17 chapters, 496 pages, **$42.50**
ISBN 0-911625-85-2

MVS TSO

Part 1: Concepts and ISPF   **Doug Lowe**

Now you can quickly master ISPF with this practical book.

Chapter 1 introduces you to MVS (both MVS/XA and MVS/ESA)...good background no matter how much MVS experience you've had. It also shows you how TSO/ISPF relates to MVS, so you'll understand how to use ISPF to control the operating system functions.

The remaining 7 chapters teach you all the specifics of using ISPF for everyday programming tasks. You'll learn how to edit and browse data sets; use the ISPF utilities to manage your data sets and libraries; compile, link, and execute programs interactively; use

the VS COBOL II or OS COBOL interactive debugger; process batch jobs in a background region; manage your background jobs more easily using the Spool Display & Search Facility (SDSF) to browse JES2 queues; use member parts lists to track the use of subprograms and COPY members within program libraries; use two library management systems that support hierarchical libraries—the Library Management Facility (LMF) and the Software Configuration and Library Manager (SCLM); and more!

MVS TSO, Part 1, 8 chapters, 467 pages, **$36.50**
ISBN 0-911625-56-9

MVS TSO

Part 2: Commands and Procedures (CLIST and REXX)   **Doug Lowe**

If you're ready to expand your skills beyond ISPF and become a TSO user who can write complex CLIST and REXX procedures with ease, this is the book for you. It starts by teaching you how to use TSO commands for common programming tasks like managing data sets and libraries, running programs in foreground mode, and submitting jobs for background execution. Then, it

shows you how to combine those commands into CLIST or REXX procedures for the jobs you do most often...including procedures that you can use as edit macros under the ISPF editor and procedures that use ISPF dialog functions to display full-screen panels.

MVS TSO, Part 2, 10 chapters, 450 pages, **$36.50**
ISBN 0-911625-57-7

VS COBOL II: A Guide for Programmers and Managers

Second Edition   **Anne Prince**

This book builds on your COBOL knowledge to quickly teach you everything you need to know about VS COBOL II, the IBM 1985 COBOL compiler for MVS shops: how to code the language elements that are new in the compiler (and what language elements you can't use any more)...CICS considerations...how to use the debugger...how the compiler's features can make your programs compile and run more efficiently...plus, guidelines for converting to VS COBOL II (that includes coverage of the conversion aids IBM supplies).

So if you're in a shop that's already converted to VS COBOL II, you'll learn how to benefit from the language elements and features the compiler has to offer. If you aren't yet working in VS COBOL II, you'll learn how to write programs now that will be easy to convert later on. And if you're a manager, you'll get some practical ideas on when to convert and how to do it as painlessly as possible.

VS COBOL II, 7 chapters, 271 pages, **$27.50**
ISBN 0-911625-54-2

Structured ANS COBOL

A 2-part course in 1974 and 1985 ANS COBOL   **Mike Murach and Paul Noll**

This 2-part course teaches you how to use standard COBOL the way the top professionals do.

Part 1: A Course for Novices teaches people with no programming experience how to design and code COBOL programs that prepare reports. Because report programs often call subprograms, use COPY members, handle one-level tables, and read indexed files, it covers these subjects too. But the real emphasis in this book is on the structure and logic of report programs, because most beginning programmers have more trouble with structure and logic than they do with COBOL itself.

Part 2: An Advanced Course also emphasizes program structure and logic, focusing on edit, update,

and maintenance programs. But beyond that, it's a complete guide to the language elements that all COBOL programmers should know how to use (though many don't). So it covers: sequential, indexed, and relative file handling...alternate indexing and dynamic processing...internal sorts and merges...the COPY library...subprograms...multi-level table handling... character manipulation...and more! In fact, no matter how much COBOL experience you've had, you'll value *Part 2* as a handy reference to all the COBOL elements you'll ever want to use.

COBOL, Part 1, 13 chapters, 438 pages, **$32.50**
ISBN 0-911625-37-2

COBOL, Part 2, 12 chapters, 498 pages, **$32.50**
ISBN 0-911625-38-0

Structured COBOL Methods

Practical guidelines and model programs   **Paul Noll**

Unlike other books with "structured" in the title, this little book presents *practical* ideas on COBOL program development...ideas that are simple, cost-effective, time-tested, and yet revolutionary in many shops. It doesn't teach the COBOL language itself; instead, it teaches you how to design, code, and test your COBOL programs so they're easier to debug, document, and maintain.

Just open up to any page, take a look at the concepts or the sample design and code, and picture what a difference these methods can make in the program you're working on right now. Then, go to work and start experimenting. You'll be delighted at the results!

Structured COBOL Methods, 6 chapters + 5 model programs, 208 pages, **$25.00**
ISBN 0-911625-94-1

Client/Server Programming: Visual Basic 5

Anne Prince and Ed Koop

The learning curve just got flatter! Learn how to develop client/server applications using a Visual Basic front-end that accesses an ODBC database (like a SQL Server database) on the back-end. It's a tough subject. But this book's professional approach, packed with corporate examples, makes it more manageable than ever before.

In the first two chapters, you'll learn the concepts that apply to all client/server systems and the crucial interrelationships between the parts. In the next two chapters, you'll learn how to create simple client/server applications of your own. That means, after just 142 pages, you'll be developing your first, professional client/server application using Visual Basic.

Each chapter after that builds on your knowledge base to give you all the essential skills of a professional client/server programmer. You'll learn:

- how to develop forms that provide for all the features you need in a business application

- how to make your database processing more efficient and error-free

- how to enhance a user interface with a startup splash screen, menus, toolbars, and online help

- how to use VB's powerful debugging tools

- how to use the Data Manager to create simple databases that you can use for testing your programs

- how to use the Crystal Reports add-in

- how to move to a new level of object-oriented programming by creating your own class modules and ActiveX components (you'll learn more about ActiveX in this one chapter than you can in many full books!)

- how to distribute a finished application to all the clients

So don't wait any longer to start scaling the learning curve. Get this book today.

Visual Basic 5, 13 chapters, 457 pages, **$40.00**
ISBN 1-890774-00-6

Client/Server Programming: Access 97

Anne Prince and Joel Murach

Access is ideal for getting started in client/server. It's easier to learn because all the elements—including the database—are integrated into the development environment. And it's probably already on your system—you don't have to invest in new software.

But it's still a tough subject. To make it as manageable as possible, this book carefully explains all the pieces, shows you how they work together, and fills in the gaps that might trip you up otherwise.

And it does all this at a pace that's right for the professional programmer. In fact, at the end of the first 4 chapters (just 157 pages), you'll be writing your first true client/server application, using Access as the front-end and DAO as the data access method. The data itself can be in an Access database or in an ODBC database such as SQL Server whose tables are linked to Access tables.

Then, the remaining 10 chapters make you a more proficient programmer, as you learn how to: build sophisticated forms and do more complex database processing using DAO...improve an application's performance by accessing the data with ODBCDirect instead of DAO...enhance the user interface with a splash screen, menus, toolbars, and online help... develop reports using Access' built-in report generator...use class modules and ActiveX components (you can't create these in Access, but your applications can use them)...and test, debug, and deploy an application on the clients.

Access 97, 14 chapters, 533 pages, **$40.00**
ISBN 1-890774-01-4

Comment Form

Your opinions count

If you have any comments, criticisms, or suggestions for us, I'm eager to hear from you. Your opinions today will affect our products of tomorrow. And if you find any errors in this book, typographical or otherwise, please point them out so we can correct them in the next printing.

Thanks for your help.

Mike Murach

Book title: DB2 for the COBOL Programmer, Part 1 (Second Edition)

Dear Mike: _____

_____

_____

_____

_____

_____

_____

_____

_____

_____

_____

_____

_____

_____

_____

_____

_____

_____

Name _____

Company (if company address) _____

Address _____

City, State, Zip _____

Fold where indicated and tape closed.

No postage needed if mailed in the U.S.

BUSINESS REPLY MAIL

FIRST-CLASS MAIL   PERMIT NO. 3063   FRESNO, CA

POSTAGE WILL BE PAID BY ADDRESSEE

Mike Murach & Associates, Inc.

2560 W SHAW LN STE 101
FRESNO CA 93711-9866

NO POSTAGE
NECESSARY
IF MAILED
IN THE
UNITED STATES

Order Form

Our Unlimited Guarantee

To our customers who order directly from us: You must be satisfied. Our books must work for you, or you can send them back for a full refund...no questions asked.

Name & Title _____

Company (if company address) _____

Street address _____

City, State, Zip _____

Phone number (including area code) _____

Fax number (if you fax your order to us) _____

Qty	Product code and title	*Price
Database		
___ DB1R	DB2 for the COBOL Programmer Part 1 (Second Edition)	$45.00
___ DB2R	DB2 for the COBOL Programmer Part 2 (Second Edition) **Scheduled for April 1999**	45.00
___ IMS1	IMS for the COBOL Programmer Part 1: DL/I Data Base Processing	36.50
___ IMS2	IMS for the COBOL Programmer Part 2: Data Communications and MFS	36.50
MVS		
___ MJLR	MVS JCL (Second Edition)	$42.50
___ TSO1	MVS TSO, Part 1: Concepts and ISPF	36.50
___ TSO2	MVS TSO, Part 2: Commands and Procedures (CLIST and REXX)	36.50
___ MBAL	MVS Assembler Language	36.50
VSAM		
___ VSMX	VSAM: Access Method Services and Application Programming	$27.50
___ VSMR	VSAM for the COBOL Programmer (Second Edition)	22.50

Qty	Product code and title	*Price
CICS		
___ CC1R	CICS for the COBOL Programmer Part 1 (Second Edition)	$36.50
___ CC2R	CICS for the COBOL Programmer Part 2 (Second Edition)	36.50
___ CRFR	The CICS Programmer's Desk Reference (Second Edition)	42.50
COBOL		
___ VC2R	VS COBOL II (Second Edition)	$27.50
___ SC1R	Structured ANS COBOL, Part 1	32.50
___ SC2R	Structured ANS COBOL, Part 2	32.50
___ SCMD	Structured COBOL Methods	25.00
DOS/VSE		
___ VJLR	DOS/VSE JCL (Second Edition)	$34.50
___ ICCF	DOS/VSE ICCF	31.00
___ VBAL	DOS/VSE Assembler Language	36.50
Client/Server		
___ VB50	Client/Server Programming: Visual Basic 5	40.00
___ AC97	Client/Server Programming: Access 97	40.00

❑ Bill my company for the books plus UPS shipping and handling (and sales tax within California).
P.O.# _____

❑ I want to **SAVE 10%** by paying in advance. Charge to my
___Visa ___MasterCard ___American Express:

Card number _____

Valid thru (mo/yr) _____

Cardowner's signature _____

❑ I want to **SAVE 10% plus shipping and handling.**
Here's my check or money order for the books minus 10% ($_____). California residents, please add sales tax to your total. (Offer valid in U.S.)

*Prices are subject to change. Please call for current prices.

To order now,

Call toll-free 1-800-221-5528
(Weekdays, 8 am to 5 pm Pacific Time)

Fax: 1-209-440-0963

Web: www.murach.com

Mike Murach & Associates, Inc.
2560 West Shaw Lane, Suite 101
Fresno, California 93711-2765
(209) 440-9071